National Days/National Ways

NATIONAL DAYS/NATIONAL WAYS

Historical, Political, and Religious Celebrations around the World

Edited by
Linda K. Fuller

Westport, Connecticut
London

Library of Congress Cataloging-in-Publication Data

National days/national ways : historical, political, and religious celebrations around the
world / edited by Linda K. Fuller.
    p. cm.
    Includes bibliographical references and index.
    ISBN 0–275–97270–4 (alk. paper)
    1. Holidays.   2. Special days.   3. Anniversaries.   I. Fuller, Linda K.
    GT3930.N38   2004
    394.26—dc22   2004011894

British Library Cataloguing in Publication Data is available.

Library of Congress Catalog Card Number: 2004011894
ISBN: 0–275–97270–4

First published in 2004

Praeger Publishers, 88 Post Road West, Westport, CT 06881
An imprint of Greenwood Publishing Group, Inc.
www.praeger.com

Printed in the United States of America

The paper used in this book complies with the
Permanent Paper Standard issued by the National
Information Standards Organization (Z39.48–1984).

10   9   8   7   6   5   4   3   2   1

Contents

Acknowledgments

This book is symbolic of my incredible intellectual life. In 1989, visiting Singapore for the first time, delivering a paper for the World Communication Association, I arranged to see Lim Heng-Tow, head of public relations for the Singapore Broadcasting Corporation and a participant in my international survey on audiences for *The Cosby Show: Audiences, Impact, and Implications* (Greenwood, 1992). When he offered my husband and me tickets to the country's National Day celebration, we had no idea what a special event it would be. When I returned to Singapore in 1996 on a Fulbright to teach at Nanyang Technological University, part of my purpose was to deconstruct that event. Fruits of that effort owe a debt of thanks to the following Singaporeans and others: Michael Anderson, U.S. State Department; Quah Swee Bee, Singapore Ministry of Information and the Arts; Phyllis G. L. Chew, National University of Singapore; Anura Goonasekera and Vijay Menon at AMIC (Asian Mass Communication Research and Information Center); Mak Ying Kwan, Singapore Tourist Promotion Board; Gerard Ong, Singapore military; George Pearce, choreographer, SBC; Lock Thi Xuan, Librarian at Ngee Ann Polytechnic; Kesavan Yoo Weng, EDB Singapore and Jonathan Yuen, EDB/USA; and Marla Win, Institute of Southeast Asian Studies. My colleagues at NTU also deserve special attention: Ang Peng Hwa, Annette Aw, Serajul Bhuiyan, Alfred Choi, Chua Chong Jin, Ong Siow Heng, Duncan Holaday, Mark Hukill, Rebecca Ang Pei Hui, Chunwah R. Lee, Sharon Liu, Aran Mahizhnan, Dennis Martin, Jim Richstad, Joseph Sommerville, Michael Steele, Tan Lai Kim, Hao Xiaoming, Lee Chun Wah, and especially our chair, Eddie C. Y. Kuo.

LKF

Introduction

Linda K. Fuller

Whatever its origins, the nation has involved a complex and rarely consistent mixture of geography, language, custom, law, religion, economy, race, and collective will ... [it] has been for some time now a powerful and effective way of responding to both objective social needs and subjective feelings of collective solidarity.
—Vincent P. Pecora, *Nations and Identities*

With daily media reminders about the role of nationalism around the world, the human and political rights of communication become ever more critical. As communication scholars interested in the intersection of nation-building with media support systems of journalism and public relations, development, patriotism, rhetoric, and propaganda, global events demand our examination of how individual countries organize to celebrate their nationalism.

The literature on nationalism is wide-ranging. Some studies deal with histories (e.g., Barthel, 1996; Emerson, 1960; Greenfield, 1992; Hobsbawm, 1992; Kohn, 1962; Minahan, 1996), others with its role as a force in politics (e.g., Beiner, 2003; Gillis, 1994; Hutchinson and Smith, 1994; Kellas, 1991; Pye, 1963; Spencer, 1998), in problem areas (e.g., Brown, 2000; Keating, 1990; Wilson and Donnan, 1998), in economics (e.g., Furedi, 1994), in psychological circumstances (e.g., Kecmanovic, 1996), in philosophy and religion (e.g., Gilbert, 1998; Hastings, 1997; Marty and Appleby, 1997; O'Brien, 1988), law (Malnes, 1994), and of course in terms of ethnicity (e.g., Bentley, 1981; Diamond and Plattner, 1994; Farner, 1994; Kruger, 1993; McNeill, 1986; Shafir, 1995; Smith, 1986, 2004; Wimmer, 2002), gender (e.g., Cohen, 1995; Moghadam, 1994; Wilson and Frederiksen, 1995), rhetoric (e.g., Bhabha, 1990); ethics (e.g., Moore, 2001), and communication issues (e.g., McKim and McMahan, 1997; Schnapper, 1998; Schramm, 1964; Williams, 2002). While the writings of Karl W. Deutsch (1953/1966), Benedict Anderson (1983), and Anthony

D. Smith (1986), are considered classics in the field for analyzing nationality, Derek Heater, James G. Kellas, and Pradip N. Thomas demonstrate important areas of related research.

To date, though, the single study related to the symbolism of a country's celebration of its national day is Leslie Witz's *Apartheid's Festival* (2003), which analyzes the conflicts and debates surrounding the 300th anniversary of the landing of Jan Van Riebeck in South Africa. There is also a web site dedicated to the topic: The Nationalism Project can be accessed at http://www.nationalismproject.org. Obviously, we are on to an important trend.

Admitting the difficulty of portraying concepts of nation and nationalism, Heater (1998) makes these distinctions:

Hitler expounded a nationalism of racial *hatred*; Mazzini taught us that national self-determination is a stairway to universal *harmony*. For Bismarck, national ambitions had to be achieved by *blood and iron*; for Woodrow Wilson, national self-determination was to be arranged justly for the sake of *peace*. Verwoerd's Afrikaner nationhood required the *authoritarianism* of the apartheid police system; John Stuart Mill believed national self-determination to be an integral part of the liberal agenda of *representative government*. Bolivar sought *cohesion* for the Spanish-American colonies in their process of national liberation; Jinnah insisted on the *partition* of India at the moment of freedom. Mussolini boasted of his revival of the *historical* greatness of the Roman Empire; Sun Yat-sen's Three Principles sought the *modernisation* of China. Thus is it possible by illustrative means starkly to polarise the various manifestations of this Protean ideology. (4; emphasis in original)

"Nationalist passions are probably the strongest in the whole political spectrum, and are generally stronger today than those aroused by religion, class, individual or group interest," according to James G. Kellas (1991, 1). Consider the route nationality has gone, beginning centuries ago if only being theorized and written about since the 18th century,[2] with the movement from state to nation, sometimes reversing again and most commonly evolving postcolonialism, postindustrialism, postindependence, and postauthoritarianism. In an opening article for a special issue on "Communication and National Identity" in *Media Development*, Pradip N. Thomas (1997) suggests four trends in national identity formation:

1. Conflicts between internal expressions of privileged identities and national identity.
2. The tension between national and "supra-national" identities.
3. The break-up [*sic*] of nation-states—which has no parallel in the context of the history of modern nations.
4. The fourth trend, which in some respects is the most serious, is directly related to the globalisation of cultural identities in the light of the so-called "demise of the nation-state, cross-border flows of data and people." (3)

The underlying argument here is that unless and until nations and their citizens are aware of the role of communication in their survival, both internally and externally, ignorance can put them in peril. By examining something that might seem so simple—means of celebrating nationhood—the opportunity is open to better assess underlying ideologies. The *days*, then, bespeak the *ways* a country operates. How those holidays are experienced by the public, and how those nations are viewed by the wider world, become pivotal. National images, we learn, can help form attitudes and affect behaviors. National days encourage that image making.

Perhaps an explanation is in order relative to how this book was conceived. As a member of a number of international communication associations, I constructed a call for contributions to this volume that met with tremendous enthusiasm. While they are quite representative, nevertheless there is a notable lack of entries, despite my efforts, from critical hot spots around the world. Perhaps this first volume will convince members of missing places to consider contributing to another one.

Many of the chapters here have been subjected to extensive revision, and it has been heartening to see various participants stay the course for the wider purpose. At this point, their various reportages will appear here alphabetically. What follows are reports from Argentina, Australia, Canada, China, Ethiopia, Ghana, Japan, Kuwait, New Zealand, Nigeria, Norway, Romania, Singapore, South Africa, Spain, Turkey, the Ukraine, and the United States.

Argentina: Susana N. Vittadini Andrés describes how two Argentinean major parties celebrate their Emancipation (May 25,1810) and Independence Day (July 9, 1816) in "Argentine National Ways in Politics: Elites and Caudillism," pointing out how they relate not only to nationalist sentiments but also to anti-Spanish feeling. Employing a historical-sociological approach, she traces the roots of political leadership there to two different groups: elites and charismatic leaders called "caudillos" who drew blind followers.

Australia: Leanne White's "The Bicentenary of Australia: Celebration of a Nation" brings the surprising fact that the nation-state first decided to celebrate its existence on January 26, 1988. The federal government established the Australian Bicentennial Authority to coordinate events, which eventually turned into a classic case of commercial nationalism, replete with logo. She refers to other times in Australia's history when celebrations took place: 1838—50 years since the establishment of a penal colony at Sydney Cove at which the British flag was unfurled; 1888—a forerunner to the Tall Ships, a centenary celebration at the harbor; and 1938—a sesquicentenary celebration opposed by the Aboriginal community. While the event was great fun, White concludes that Australia still has a long way to go before resolving many of its (mainly racial) issues.

Canada: Derek Foster's "Canadian Days: Non-Canadian Ways" begins this way: "Each year the occasion of Canada Day traditionally begets many opportunities to ask what it means to be Canadian." Suggesting that the country suffers an ongoing identity crisis, he points out how the official birthday is July 1, marking the day in 1867 that the Royal Proclamation granting its independence was issued. Yet, a nationalist holiday is celebrated in the province of Quebec on June 23. He finds that the ongoing union of Canada and the union of Canadians temporarily coming together to celebrate national holidays is both tenuous and contradictory, a unity founded on diversity.

China: Xu Xiaoge's "National Image on Nation Day: The 50th National Day of the Peoples' Republic of China" reviews the history: founded in 1949, it held national day parades from 1950 to 1959, then stopped during the time of the Cultural Revolution. In 1984, there was a parade on October 1, but none had been held for 15 years. For the 1999 celebration, there was a 50-gun salute over Tian'anmen Square in honor of the country's 50th anniversary. For some 500,000 participants, there was a military parade and a civilian one, the latter representing periods led by Mao Zedong, Deng Xiaoping, and Jiang Zemin. Overall, it was a demonstration to the world of what China had achieved in the last half century: military strength, social stability, racial harmony, determination to reunify the country, and, most importantly, "face engineering."

Chen Yanru has also written about China's national day. Discussing a patriotic education campaign waged by the government to coincide with it, her chapter "From National Day to National Way: The Story of October 1 and Patriotic Education in China" points out how the state, the media, and the public all played a joint role in the production of knowledge about the nation during its celebration. An overall integrated nation is projected, with five dimensions: connectedness, togetherness, oneness, all-inclusiveness, and coherence.

Ethiopia: Tsegay Wolde-Georgis, former head of the Press and Public Affairs Department of the Embassy of Ethiopia in Washington, DC, contributes "Holiday Celebrations among the Highlanders of Ethiopia." Pointing out how Ethiopia is one of the oldest independent countries in Africa, where the three great religious traditions of Judaism, Christianity, and Islam thrive together, the emphasis there is so much on religion that it is one of the few countries in the world without a day of independence.

Ghana: Kwasi Ansu-Kyeremeh's "Globalization and Broadcasting the Ghanaian National Day" centers on how symbolism such as flags and coats of arms work to counteract divisions within the country in its celebrations. While the broadcast media would lead one to believe that March 6 is universally followed, in fact the civil/military story of the country's Incumbency Day is something else indeed. From a broader perspective, Ansu-Kyeremeh underscores the role of foreignization in broadcasting for further dividing indigenous Ghana for the more modern country.

Japan: Stephen M. Ryan's "Japan's National Foundation Day: Lack of Consensus Leads to Lack of Celebration" discusses how the ascension dating to 660 B.C. of Jimmu, the first emperor of Japan, is marked as a public holiday each year on February 11. Yet, he provides a fascinating report on how this is actually the least observed of all the country's national holidays. "For most workers outside the emergency services and the retail trade it is a holiday," he writes, "but there are neither mass public events nor private rituals or customs to mark the occasion." There are no established patterns of public gatherings, parades, processions, fiestas, or fireworks displays—an indifference reflected in the media. It is basically, he reflects, a day off in February.

Kuwait: Nibal K. Bourisly and Maher N. Al-hajji discuss how the Kuwati government considers its National Day an ideal chance to revive patriotism and promote unity among its 2 million residents. Yet, as the authors point out in "Kuwait's National Day: Four Decades of Transformed Celebrations," those orchestrated celebrations have differed widely since June 19, 1961.

New Zealand: Parehau Richards and Chris Ryan present "Waitangi Day: New Zealand's National Day." Not really a national day, since it includes a whole weekend of cultural performance, Waitangi Day commemorates the signing of the Treaty of Waitangi in 1840. The chapter accounts for the historical background of that treaty signing and the subsequent Maori experience, describes events surrounding Waitangi Day, and analyzes how the celebration reflects the country, both in its current reality and in terms of a people wanting to reaffirm their sense of identity.

Nigeria: Mohammed Musa and Ayo Oyeleye's "Nationalism, Mass Media, and the Crisis of National Identity in Nigeria" traces what has occurred in the country since attaining independence on October 1, 1960. It becomes a fascinating model for other emerging nations to consider.

Norway: Knut Mykland's "Norway's 17th of May: A Historical Date and a Day of National Celebrations" was submitted with compliments of the Royal Norwegian Consulate General. It details how the country's 1814 demarker, instituting the triumph of a constitutional government, positions itself yet today.

Romania: Sorin Matei's "The Romanian Way: From Nationalism to Privatism" points out how the new Romanian National Day, which only began in 1990, has been surrounded by a mixture of popular apathy and political infighting. He argues that the slow transformation in Romanian social and economic structures after the fall of Communism, while frequently blamed on lack of political will, is in fact based on a national ethos (e.g., sinecure), leading to new values that are centered around personal goals. While National Day is scheduled to be celebrated on December 1 each year, in fact Romanians recently have subordinated their public goals to private pursuits, and their lives evolve in very narrow social circles.

Singapore: Linda K. Fuller, who was privy to attending Singapore's 24th celebration, became so inspired from that experience that she wanted to look at the phenomenon in other countries. Ever since the country emerged as a separate, independent nation-state on August 9, 1965, the Republic of Singapore has been forging and celebrating its newfound identity. Her chapter, "Reading Singapore's National Day: A Case Study in the Rhetoric of Nationalism," briefly examines a context for Singapore's development from a discourse perspective, looking at its national symbols and songs, and then focuses on how patriotism is manifest in Singapore's National Day.

South Africa: Scott M. Schönfeldt-Aultman and Gust A. Yep's "(Re)Building a Nation: South Africa's Heritage Day as a Site of Renaming, Reimaging, and Remembering" uses as its base Benedict Anderson's notion of the nation as "an imagined political community." Arguing that the African National Congress's current program of nation-building undergirds the renaming, reimaging, and rituals of remembering, while simultaneously highlighting forgotten history and "heritage," it points out how the current celebration deals with an emphasis on the Black liberation struggle and calling for reconciliation for past wrongs. They cite Robert Thornton:

On 9 May 1994, Nelson Mandela addressed the people of South Africa on the occasion of the opening of the new Parliament. He did not speak of "the people" or "the nation." As he stood on the balcony of the Cape Town City Hall with the majestic Table Mountain as his backdrop, he pointed to the landscape on which "the beginning of the fateful convergence" of Black and White had begun.... South African identities cross-cut each other in multiple ways and in multiple contexts.... A Muslim, or a Coloured, may span many religious, political, social and cultural contexts and thus link them together into a social universe.... On the other hand, these differences are also seen as the principal source of conflict in South Africa. (1996)

Spain: Ignacio Molina A. de Cienfuegos and Jorge Martínez Bárcena's "National Days throughout the History and Geography of Spain" focuses on the country's Day of Hispanity, October 12.

Turkey: Halil Nalçaoglu includes visuals with his article "Nation and Celebration: The Iconology of the Republic of Turkey." He focuses on three particular events over a 75-year period: 1923—the Republic Holiday in honor of the ending of the Ottoman Empire; 1973's "loosing the spirit"; and the 1990s use of national icons like the Turkish flag, founder Ataturk's portrait, and the map of the country to perpetuate nationalism. The author draws this insight: "Turkey, by opening its gates to the world, and by realizing the importance and the concomitant responsibility of being a 'respectful' member of the so-called international community, has entered into a cultural mode in which the performative aspect of identity formation is becoming dominant."

Ukraine: Natalie Kostenko, Tatyana Androsenko, and Ludmila Males's "In Search of a Holiday: The Case of Ukraine" is the most recent example of a country's celebration, as it just became an independent state in 1991. Citizens there mark both traditional and former Soviet holidays and newly introduced secular and religious festivals:

- Former Soviet holidays: Great October Revolution Day, Working People Day/May Day, Women's Day (March 8)
- New Ukrainian holidays: Independence Day, Constitution Day, Ukranian Police Forces Day
- Religious holidays, not officially marked before: Orthodox Christian Christmas, Easter, Trinity, Salvation, and other confessions' holidays
- Recently emergent holidays from the West: St. Valentine's Day, Halloween

The authors have performed a survey of Ukranians' perception of and attitudes toward holidays, finding that the official national day needs to be more developed. They conclude: "One thing is clear: the search of a real holiday will be a success only when its sense of value indisputably encourages the largest proportion of Ukranian citizens."

United States: Instead of the Fourth of July, when the United States gained its independence, Teixeira Nash and Irelene P. Ricks have chosen to include "Martin Luther King Day: A Day in Remembrance of the American Architect of the Beloved Community." January 20, 2000, marked the first time in the nation's history that the clergyman/civil rights reformer's birthday was celebrated by all 50 states. It has been a journey for hundreds of people that the King holiday become a reality, and such an awesome one to describe that the authors are finding it could be a life-long commitment to document.

"Nation-preserving, nation-building, and nationalism or the preference for the real and/or imagined interests of one's own nation and its members," Karl W. Deutsch (1966, 4) reminds us, "these still remain a major and even a still growing force in politics, which statesmen of good will would ignore at their peril." We hope that this book, relying as it does on various holistic approaches, particularly discourse analyses (see Wilkins and Mody 2001) opens numerous discussions about the role(s) of National Days/National Ways.

On a personal note, I might add that observing red, white, and blue symbolism 24/7 here in the United States since 9/11, it fills me with pride to know that so many colleagues want to share their stories. Through this volume, we welcome you to travel through reportage on 18 countries. Maybe your journey will be like that of Wiley, who has "moved from a traditional view of the nation as the container of society to a critical-historical view of the nation as social construction, to a relational view of the nation as subject to neocolonial and neoimperialist forces, to a globalization perspective emphasizing the destabilizing effects of accelerating global flows, to a contextualist view of the nation as an articulated space." Enjoy these historical, political, and religious celebrations from around the world.

NOTES

1. James G. Kellas (1991) discusses the role of churches as sustainers of nationalism:

the Armenian and Georgian Christian churches; Moslems in Punjab and Pakistan and Buddhists in Sri Lanka in opposition to Hindus; Catholics in Northern Ireland in opposition to Protestants; Catholics in Poland, Czechoslovakia and Hungary in opposition to Russian Communists and Orthodox Christians. Even where churches are international, as with Islam and Roman Catholicism, they usually display national characteristics in the context of different nations. (26)

2. T. K. Oommen (1997) cites this date/demarker in his introduction to *Citizenship and National Identity: From Colonialism to Globalism*: "For three centuries, since the Treaty of Westphalia concluded in 1648, the world has been electrified by the notion of the nation-state" (35).

REFERENCES

Anderson, B. R. O'G. (1983). *Imagined communities: Reflections on the origins and spread of nationalism*. London: Verso.

Barthel, D. L. (1996). *Historic preservation: Collective memory and historical identity.* New Brunswick, NJ: Rutgers University Press.

Beiner, R. (2003). Liberalism, nationalism, citizenship: Essays on the problem of political community. Vancouver: UBC Press.

Bentley, G. C. (1981). *Ethnicity and nationality: A bibliographic guide.*Seattle, WA: University of Washington Press.

Berher, R. (2003). *Liberalism, nationalism, citizenship: Essays on the problem of political community.* Vancouver: UBC Press.

Bhabha, H. K. (Ed.). (1990). *Nation and narration.* London: Routledge.

Brown, D. (2000). *Contemporary nationalism: Civics, ethnocultural and multicultural politics.* New York: Routledge.

Cohen, P. N. (1995). Nationalism and suffrage: Gender struggle in nation-building America. *Signs: Journal of Women in Culture and Society. 21*(3): 707–727.

Deutsch, K. W. (1966). *Nationalism and social communication: An inquiry into the foundations of nationality.* Cambridge, MA: MIT Press. (Originally published in 1953)

Diamond, L., and Plattner, M. F. (Eds.). (1994). *Nationalism, ethnic conflict, and democracy.* Baltimore: Johns Hopkins University Press.

Emerson, R. (1960). *From empire to nation: The rise of self-assertion of Asian and African peoples.* Cambridge, MA: Harvard University Press.

Farner, R. F. (Ed.), (1994). *Nationalism, ethnicity and identity: Cross nationalism and comparative perspective*s. New Brunswick, NJ: Transaction.

Fuller, L. K. (2000, February). *Nationalism and national celebrations.* Paper presented at the 17th annual International Intercultural Conference, Miami, FL.

Furedi, F. (1994). *The new ideology of imperialism: Renewing the moral imperative.* London: Pluto Press.

Gilbert, P. (1998). *The philosophy of nationalism.* Boulder, CO: Westview Press.

Gillis, J. R. (Ed.). (1994). *Commemorations: The politics of national identity.* Princeton, NJ: Princeton University Press.

Greenfeld, L. (1992). *Nationalism: Five roads to modernity.* Cambridge, MA: Harvard University Press.

Hastings, A. (1997). *The construction of nationhood: Ethnicity, religion, and nationalism.* Cambridge, UK: Cambridge University Press.

Heater, D. (1998). *The theory of nationhood: A platonic symposium.* London: Macmillan Press.

Hobsbawm, E. J. (1992). *Nations and nationalism since 1780: Programme, myth, reality.* Cambridge, UK: Cambridge University Press.

Hutchinson, J., and Smith, A. (Eds.). (1994). *Nationalism.* Oxford, UK: Oxford University Press.

Keating, M. (1990). *Nations against the state: The new politics of nationalism in Quebec, Catalonia, and Scotland.* New York: St. Martin's Press.

Kecmanovic, D. (1996). *The mass psychology of ethnonationalism.* New York: Plenum Press.

Kellas, J. G. (1991). *The politics of nationalism and ethnicity.* New York: St. Martin's Press.

Kohn, H. (1962). *The age of nationalism: The first era of global history.* New York: Harper.

Kruger, P. (Ed.) *Ethnicity and nationalism: Cast studies in their intrinsic tension and political dynamics.* Marburg, Germany: Hitzeroth.

Malnes, R. (1994). *National interests, morality, and international law.* Oslo, Norway: Scandinavian Press.

Marty, M. E., and Appleby, R. S. (Eds.). (1997). *Religion, ethnicity, and self-identity: Nations in turmoil.* Hanover, NH: University Press of New England.

McKim, R., and McMahan, J. (Eds.). (1997). *The morality of nationalism*. Oxford, UK: Oxford University Press.

McNeill, W. H. (1986). *Polyethnicity and national unity in world history*. Toronto: University of Toronto Press.

Minahan, J. (1996). *Nations without states: A historical dictionary of contemporary national movements*. Westport, CT: Greenwood Press.

Moghadam, V. M. (Ed.). (1994). *Gender and national identity: Women and politics in Muslim societies*. London: Atlantic Highlands Press.

O'Brien, C. C. (1988). *God land: Reflections on religion and nationalism*. Cambridge, MA: Harvard University Press.

Oommen, T. K. (Ed.). (1997). *Citizenship and national identity: From colonialism to globalism*. New Delhi, India: Sage.

Pecora, Vincent P. (Ed.). (2001). *Nations and identities*. Oxford, UK: Blackwell.

Pye, L. W. (Ed.). (1963). *Communications and political development*. Princeton, NJ: Princeton University Press.

Schnapper, D. (1998). *Community of citizens: On the modern idea of nationality*. New Brunswick, NJ: Transaction.

Schramm, W. (1964). *Mass media and national development: The role of information in the developing countries*. Stanford, CA: Stanford University Press.

Shafir, G. (1995). *Immigrants and nationalists: Ethnic conflict and accommodation in Catalonia, the Basque Country, Latvia, and Estonia*. Albany: State University of New York Press.

Smith, A. D. (Ed.). (2004). *Nations and Nationalism*. Oxford, UK: Blackwell.

Spencer, M. (Ed.). (1998). *Separatism: Democracy and disintegration*. Lanham, MD: Rowman and Littlefield.

Spencer, P., and Wollman, H. (2002). *Nationalism: A critical introduction*. London: Sage.

Thomas, P. N. (1997). Communication and national identity: Towards an inclusive vision. *Media Development, 2,* 3–6.

Thornton, R. (1996). The potentials of boundaries in South Africa: Steps towards a theory of the social edge. In R. Webner and T. Ranger (Eds.), *Postcolonial identities in Africa* (pp. 136–61). London: Zed Books.

Wiley, S. B. C. (2004). Rethinking nationality in the context of globalization. *Communication Theory 14*(1) February 78–96.

Wilkins, K. G., and Mody, B. (2001). Reshaping development communication: Developing communication and communicating development. *Communication Theory, 11*(4) 385–96.

Williams, A. (Ed.). (2002). *Film and nationalism*. Princeton, NJ: Rutgers University Press.

Wilson, F., and Frederiksen , B. F. (Eds.). (1995). *Ethnicity, gender, and the subversion of nationalism*. London: F. Cass in association with the European Association of Development Research and Training Institutes.

Wilson, T. M., and Donnan, H. (Eds.). (1998). *Border identities: Nation and state at international frontiers*. Cambridge, UK: Cambridge University Press.

Witz, L. (2003). *Apartheid's festival: Contesting South Africa's national past*. Bloomington: Indiana University Press.

ARGENTINA

Argentine National Ways in Politics

Elites and Caudillism

Susana N. Vittadini Andrés

Nationalism is an important force in Latin America countries but it is quite difficult to analyze because of the existence of different types and the lack of a precise definition. At the same time, in each country, there is an extremely complex variety of nationalism (Atkins 1989). Each group of people or society has certain special turning points that are considered symbols of its cohesiveness, as well as accepted behaviors, customs, concepts, and ways of living; thus, each one evolved according to different orientations, local tendencies, and backgrounds. For them, loyalties, ideologies, and social values depended on their particular domestic conflicts, external interference, and, of course, particular moment in history. For example, nationalism in Mexico is closely connected with the important Spaniards' presence and also the mestizos who turned out to be the main leading group (Carrasco and Céspedes 1985) , so it could not have been compared with Brazil, where the presence of the Portuguese Crown until almost the end of the 19th century yielded different connotations of national ideals, or even with the Peruvian way of understanding love for their nation that is closely connected with Incan tradition. At the same time, national ideals or identity could be altered, transformed, or even disintegrated to let appear or grow another conception. It could also be vanished as more than once it is not closely linked to people's desires and needs, as certain classes imposed principles or decisions, totally or partially, against people's wills, or even without taking them into account.

Something similar happened with Argentina. It developed as a close society situated very far from its so-called motherland of Spain, but it copied certain of its attitudes such as imposing decisions on lower classes without taking into account their desires and feelings. From a geopolitical point of view, the territory that at present belongs to Argentina was also too far from the most important Spaniard routes to and from Latin America or Asia. Silver and gold were not available there, so in a way it was regarded as not very important for the Spanish Crown. Thus, as neither Hapsburgs nor Bourbons valued the territory and its society, which in turn evolved in quite a different way from the viceroyalty of Peru or the government of Paraguay, in fact, both Argentina and Chile were the last two territories conquered and colonized by the Spaniards, not only because of their geographic location but also because of indigenous defensive attitudes and difficulties to survive without much food (Séjourné 1989). Despite all those disadvantages, Argentina accepted the crown's rule until certain groups felt that they could not improve more unless the state was reorganized, then they gradually tended to achieve emancipation first and, later on, independence. This explains why Argentine national ideals included nationalist sentiments and a wide spectrum of feelings toward Spain that went from love to hate and from imitation to just the opposite, but, in fact, hate and imitation were the most common.

Argentina commemorates two important national days—May 25, 1810, and July 9, 1816—both of which are connected with two different moments of its special relationship with Spain. May 25 is the day that the viceroy's authority ended, and it is remembered as Emancipation Day because from then on there was a new government appointed by the members of the Cabildo,[1] even though the Spanish Crown was still considered the main source of power. July 9 commemorates Argentina's independence from Spain. The celebration of Independence Day began in 1835 (Delgado Martín, 1988) in the Province of Buenos Aires during the government of Juan Manuel de Rosas, one of the most powerful provincial governors before 1850. Manuel de Rosas, who developed a special relationship with an important part of society, could be considered an elite member and the most important Argentine caudillo. One could be born an elite member, but being a caudillo depended on one's charismatic and personal attitudes. Yet, caudillos, not always belong to elites, as the last ones included not only "criollos" (those who were born in Latin American but whose parents were born in Spain), but also Spaniard people, "mestizos," and even "mulattos" or national breeds.

Both caudillos and elites played important roles in Argentine nation-building, but at the same time, they gave a distinctive characteristic to politics that led people to refrain from their self-development. Considering all the things that the elites said and did, before and during Emancipation Day and Independence Day, it can be concluded that they have a special way of understanding patriotism and communication. So, to analyze Argentina national days, it is important to take into account elites and caudillos to have an accurate idea of their importance for the development of the country and how their "national attitudes" affected, and still affect today, Argentine history. That is why an analysis of the difference between elites and caudillos will be considered before the history of those days, which in turn will be preceded by a brief background about the indigenous people (amerindios) and different Spanish policies in order to have a better idea of the processes.

ELITES AND CAUDILLOS

Among the most important characteristics of Argentine society were urban centers, where urban bourgeoisie and the middle class had been regarded as the only ones whose ideas and orders could be considered valuable for everyone. All members of the urban bourgeoisie were Spaniards, who monopolized the most important offices. The middle class consisted mainly of Creole criollos, which is to say all those whose parents were Spaniards but who were born in Latin American territories—such as clergymen, men who occupied minor positions in the army or as public officials, and all those who studied at the university. Women, according to Spanish custom, had to remain at home, while only those who belonged to the lower class worked, if only mainly as servants. Political culture had been conformed according to Spanish patterns and also included local traditions mainly in rural areas or copied from other groups like the British after their invasions, Spanish past attitudes, or Amerindians still living according to their customs in certain parts of the territory.

Both the urban bourgeoisie and the middle class turned out to be the most important groups, although there was a weak economy. The lower class was not as highly regarded as to be included in politics but they were not badly treated so they could go on living without much interference from others.

The urban bourgeoisie's power gradually diminished while the others increased, but for the lower class life did not change much, as they were always supposed to accept others' rule. During the Emancipation period, both groups could be considered as elites with an important difference: while the criollos remained an elite group even during the time of independence, by that same time, only very few members of the first group still kept the leading positions. Thus, there were two main important political actors: the elites and the caudillos, both with different types of leadership not very easy to define, as they do not always present similar characteristics regardless of time and place.

Gaetano Mosca (1939), one of the classic elite theorists, considered the ruling class as unified and integrated. Their members usually shared common social, economic, political, and educational backgrounds, and tended to have the same or quite similar beliefs, values, and aims, although they might disagree about the methods to accomplish them. In Argentina, during the end of the 17th century and the beginning of the 18th century, elitism was induced by Spanish ideals and principles as well as other European ones, like the ones related to Liberalism (McDonough 1983; O'Donnell 1973). So, education as well as social elements, such as one's connections and importance within the family structure, could be regarded as most important, and it does not matter whether they belonged to the army or were intellectuals, because even lawyers had been appointed as members of the army just because they were considered elite members.

The Spanish language dictionary *Diccionario Etimológico de la Lengua Castellana* cites two different definitions for *caudillo*: the first one refers to one who leads and guides people during a war, and the second one refers to one who rules within a union, community, or corp (Entrena Durán 1995). But at the same time, it mentions other meanings such that it has denotations depending on place and time. In the case of Argentina at the end of the 18th century and the beginning of the 19th century, most caudillos influence was centered in the province or region or where they had their properties or lived; only after Emancipation did they try to extend their power over the whole territory. Such an event could only be accomplished in February 1820 when they defeated the national government in the Battle of Cepeda.

During that previous period, Argentine the "caudillos' world" evolved according to certain characteristics and facts:[2] (1) Central power diminished a lot and a new distribution of power was needed; (2) Neither Spaniards nor the new central government power were strong enough to be truly accepted by the provinces and, at the same time, many regional and local caudillos were suspicious of Buenos Aires' authorities who by then were invested with national power; (3) An incipient national identity was identified with local customs and ways of living. So, caudillos needed a special environment in which to develop, like territories with large properties, even though they owned nothing at all but it was important that where they lived authoritarian relationships and hierarchical patterns were socially accepted; besides, they usually had been previously appointed as policemen or in some other important position within bureaucratic or political structure, mainly connected with the army (Di Tella 1990); that is why they had adequate knowledge and influence to lead people.

The caudillo was, and still is, considered a charismatic leader whose orders were always followed for no one dared argue with them. From the beginning, dating to the European domination period, the caudillo aimed to seize power because he considered himself the people's legitimate representative, owing to his very special relation with the group, and to establish a centralized control to eliminate possible rivals. But not all of them acted in a similar way, as their authoritarian attitudes were quite different from one another, for some could be crueler than others. Although their behavior could be quite different, in any case they easily mobilized many people. Besides, no one caudillo really empowered people with long-standing powers and faculties in order to improve their lives. To keep people "attached" to their needs and desires was an important source of power for the caudillos; moreover, most people accepted such relationship without complaining.

That type of relationship could also be found in elites and caudillos during that period in Argentina, as both of them tried to exercise power. Because power means participation in the making of decisions, they usually concluded that they were the only ones legitimized to exercise such power. This particular style of politics and leadership is rooted in long-standing practices and is transformed slowly after many important social events, depending on the institutional framework, formal rules of the political game, and the social and economic environment. It is not the same to speak about caudillism in the 19th century as in present times. For example, in Argentina, Juan Manuel de Rosas was empowered with legislative, executive, and judicial power, so he could sentence a person by his own rule and desire; yet, such a thing was impossible for Argentine president Carlos Saul Menem,[3] even though he could deeply influence judicial and legislative matters.

INDIGENOUS PEOPLE AND THE CROWN OF SPAIN'S MAIN INTERESTS

Amerindians

There were not too many Amerindians' tribes in Argentina before the European arrival,[4] and none was so important and powerful as to build up an empire, like the Aztec's or the Inca's establishing a unified tribe with all different groups. So, each one evolved in a different way and more than once deepening hate and disunion conflicts broke out among them, although some of them, like the Tehuelches, were peaceful people.

Spaniard Rule over Latin American Countries

Spaniard rule over Latin American countries was not the same for every territory and society, as they had different interests. Consider these different dynasties:

1. The Catholic king and queen, Ferdinand and Isabel, wanted to look for another route to reach the Indies, which is to say Asia, in order to improve their kingdom's commercial activity. At the same time, the queen was very involved in the Catholic religion, so her acts resembled such involvement. When they realized that "new" territories were discovered, conquest and colonization began. They appointed Adelantados to go there, most of whom were adventurers who wanted to earn money at any cost, so although the queen's orders spoke about behaving as good Catholics, in fact, things turned out quite differently.

2. During 16th and 17th centuries, the Habsburgs were deeply interested in gold and silver, so they devoted all their attention to Mexican, Peruvian, and Bolivian territories where those metals could easily be found and ravished. But, as what easily comes easily goes, such huge amounts of metals were not enough to solve their problems and improve their lives forever. They continued to have debts, which, in fact, grew larger, and no industries were developed because they found it easier to buy things than to produce them (Galeano 1990).

3. The Bourbons, who governed Latin American territories until the beginning of the 19th century, were deeply interest in developing the Spanish economy, as most gold and silver taken from those territories almost

vanished not only while paying debts to northern European countries, but also because of pirates and privateers (*corsarios*) and the Family Wars, a fierce struggle for the Crown of France that lasted until the beginning of the 18th century. As their resources were exhausted to accomplish such an aim, they imposed a hard rule over Latin American territories.

As previously mentioned, Argentina had neither gold nor silver, so it could develop rather freely during the first two periods, but during the last dynasty, it suffered a lot. The Bourbons decided to put an end to all Latin American industries and manufacturers to impose a strict monopoly (Anna 1986), and they ordered destroyed anything that could mean local improvement without Spanish presence. For example, almost all olive plants in the Argentine province of Mendoza were destroyed except for one that even now exists. But they also ordered that main authorities could only be Spaniards, and gradually dismissed all criollos from the most important official appointments.

The Historic Evolution of Spanish and British Presence in Argentina

Spanish presence in Argentina did not develop according to a specific scheme but a general one that consisted in exploring the territory to try to find gold, silver, or better routes to reach the Far East; on the other hand, for the British, commerce and political influence were the main interest. So, different persons with different itineraries entered Argentina.

THE YEARS PRECEDING THE 19TH CENTURY

During the first years of the 16th century, Juan Díaz de Solis, a Spaniard with Real Orders, arrived in that territory, where he founded, for the first time, a city that later was to be known as Buenos Aires[5]; in 1516, he was killed by local inhabitants. It was not until some years later that Pedro de Mendoza, another Spaniard, refounded that same city, but he had to suffer persecutions from Amerindians (Séjourné 1989). Although things were not easy, the city gradually developed, but not at the same pace as Lima or the Mexico Federal District, where people could more easily get rich in a short period of time. On the contrary, Buenos Aires was in a rather plain territory without minerals or any other natural resources.

The rest of the territory was explored and conquered by the Spaniards who entered through three different routes:

1. Since 1537, from Spain, the ones who founded the principal cities in the present provinces of Santa Fe, Corrientes, and Buenos Aires, in the central and northeastern parts of Argentina.

2. Since 1543, from Peru, those who colonized the present provinces of Jujuy, Salta, La Rioja, Tucumán, Santiago del Estero, Córdoba, and Catamarca, in the central and northwestern parts of Argentina.
3. Since 1553, Spaniards departed from Chile to the provinces of Mendoza, San Juan, and San Luis, in the center western parts of Argentina.

Spanish Crown control over cities and villages far from Buenos Aires or other important cities, like Córdoba, was not tight, and more than once the authorities appointed there behaved in extremely abusive ways.[6]

Besides, the city of Buenos Aires was surrounded by Amerindians, and without highly developed agriculture activities, the city was unable to improve the lifestyle of its inhabitants. During the 17th century, smuggling was the main commercial activity in Buenos Aires, and up to a certain extent, such activity was permitted by the Spanish Crown as the only way to keep people from leaving (Linch 1958). In spite of all of those negative characteristics, Buenos Aires had a strategic location for the ships that passed to the south on their way to Asia.

THE EARLY YEARS OF THE 19TH CENTURY

At the beginning of the 19th century, the British attacked Buenos Aires twice, in 1806 and 1807, and on both occasions, they were repulsed by the people without any assistance from the motherland. Such triumphs helped foster the region's growing sense of independence. It did not matter that the leaders were Spaniards or criollos, as the most important thing was that they did it alone without a trained army or excellent equipment.

During the first British invasion, its chief was General Lord Beresford, the marquis of Sobremonte, who escaped to Córdoba with the crown's treasure. While in Buenos Aires, Juan Martín de Pueyrredón, a criollo, and Santiago de Liniers, a Spaniard,[7] led different groups of people and they were the most important leaders for the recovery. In 1807, the British defeated Santiago de Liniers, so Martín de Alzaga, a member of the Cabildo,[8] reorganized the forces and put an end to the British invasion. People felt very excited because of such victories, but at the same time some British customs have been adopted like 5 o'clock tea. Some British soldiers were also kidnapped and "forced" to marry local girls.

EMANCIPATION DAY—MAY 25, 1810

Some years later, the French captured the king of Spain, Charles IV, and his son Ferdinand, who later became Ferdinand VII when his father gave him his own crown. While both of them were in prison in Bayonne, the people in Buenos Aires decided to urge the viceroy, Baltasar Hidalgo Cisneros, who was highly unpopular, to give up his power or at least give them more power. But, as the viceroy wanted the people to remain loyal to the king of Spain, he authorized several important sessions within a special assembly called "Open Cabildo."[9] Locals, both criollos and Spaniards, undertook several important meetings to discuss the whole matter.

The Cabildo was the first and, for some time, the most democratic institution settled in Latin America whose functionaries were popularly elected by all the inhabitants,[10] but as time passed, each one adopted their own rules with the Spanish Crown's acceptance. In Buenos Aires, even up to the 19th century, some of those municipal appointments "could nominally be elected by the people" (Linch 1958, 203). But not all of the people could be eligible as public officials; only Spaniards who were born in Spain could hold the best positions. At last, different positions were sold and all those who fulfilled the necessary requirements could buy one of them.[11] During the Bourbon period there also were legal restrictions to working in certain governmental positions, as only the Spaniards could be appointed, so gradually criollos were dismissed from those previously available positions (Anna 1986, 39–40). Even lawyers could only submit legal cases up to a certain amount of money or importance, so, consequently, their income would not be raised even though their studies were the same or even better than the ones the Spaniards had. These were some reasons to consider that the 1810 Emancipation movement was just accomplished for the sake of a particular group of people who were lawyers and well-taught criollos whose economic and labor possibilities had been reduced due to Bourbon rules (Linch 1958, 222–25). In fact, most criollos, who attended Open Cabildo sessions during May 1810, were lawyers, and all of them belonged to certain elites, so none of them could be considered common people.

As was previously pointed out, the events that took place on May 25, 1810, were closely connected with Ferdinand VII, who by then was a French prisoner. Baltasar Cisneros, the viceroy, wanted the people to remain loyal to the king. Thus, an Open Cabildo was prepared and 450 invitations were dispatched to the "best and more sane part of the community," still, only 251 attended the meetings.[12]

When the Spanish Crown collapsed in 1808, as a result of French invasion, Latin American–born elites decided to put an end to the Spaniards administration. At the same time, in the metropolis as well as in many Latin American places, a number of local committees named "juntas" had been settled according to a legal Spanish principle that expressed that whenever the king was unable to rule, sovereignty reverted to the people (Rodríguez 1998). Such principle turned out to be the main topic for discussion as the Spaniards wanted to accept the juntas while the criollos considered that such committees could not rule over those territories because they lacked the necessary power to do so.

There were several main points regarding the relationship between Latin America and Spain, but one of the most important was connected with this territory's legal status, as they had never been Spanish colonies because the pope gave them to the Crown of Spain, not to the people. In fact, Argentina, as well as other Latin American countries, had been proprieties of the Crown of Spain and their successors. Spanish people had no right over these territories, as it was stated in several documents signed by the pope to give advice, rights, or settle disputes called "bullas": "Eximiae Devotionis" (March 4, 1493) and "Dudum siquidiem" (September 26, 1493), or the Santa Fe and Granada Capitulations signed by Ferdinand and Isabel and Cristobal Colon in 1493 (Levene 1962, 15–16). Even though the Spaniards knew that these territories belonged to the Spanish Crown, they did not want to give up their important positions there, and the criollos were too much accustomed to the Spaniards' behavior.

The Open Cabildo sessions lasted for several days and different decisions were voted on, but none of them connected with an independence to defeat the viceroy and organize another type of government. That it had to include criollos was the main issue. The king of Spain was still recognized as the supreme power,[13] but a junta including criollos and Spaniards was going to be in charge of the administration instead of the viceroy. Thus, criollos decided to oblige all the other inhabitants of the Río de la Plata Viceroyalty to obey them as they considered themselves as elders. The people did not feel that was the right thing to do, but later they accepted the new junta's decisions as an army was dispatched from Buenos Aires to oblige them to recognize new government.

After the Emancipation movement, members of the new junta of the government tried to impose their power on the provinces, but for some, it meant that a new power from the main city was going to order them what to do and how to behave. Unrest occurred. Such feelings also arose because the so-called First Government Junta also gradually lifted all commercial restrictions, allowing foreigners to trade freely, something that was against local interest. Thus, Buenos Aires as an important harbor grew and the interior became impoverished as their industries and products were no longer protected; besides, they could not compete with foreign merchandise even though its quality was not as good as local ones.

Regional caudillos felt that their own interests were in peril, but at the same time, they knew that they were too useful to be set aside by the first junta because all those Spaniards who remained loyal to the Spanish Crown revolted, so their importance grew even more. In fact, more than once the army sent from Buenos Aires was not enough to put an end to the Spaniard's rebellion; thus, they needed caudillo help and assistance.

Elites decided by themselves not to advocate for independence, during the Open Cabildo sessions, without seriously considering the right of other people to decide. They also decided to send an army to impose their rule, which also included the revoking of any limit to commercial activity. But they could not fulfill their plan without help from caudillos. As the caudillos weight grew, central authority power diminished in the provinces to the extent that those regional leaders were even more powerful, defeating the so-called national government, in 1820, after Independence Day. It is also interesting to point out that some caudillos began to increase their commercial activity without setting aside their lands.

INDEPENDENCE DAY—JULY 9, 1816

Even though Emancipation in Argentina had been assured, there were no unified opinions within elites regarding what to do, even to decide which was the best course of action, so quite soon partisan strife broke out. Some wanted Ferdinand's sister, Princess Carlotta, to come to the territories, also known as Río de la Plata, to rule instead of her brother. But they failed. Later on, Spanish triumph over the French army and Ferdinand VII's restoration were starting points for an aggressive reaction to restrain revolutionary tendencies in Latin America. An important expedition leaded by General Pablo Morillo was sent to put an end to independence or emancipation movements. The Spaniards again dominated Venezuela by 1815, and the following year, the criollos were defeated in Nueva Granada. Similar setbacks happened in Ecuador and Peru. So many victories represented an important backward movement for criollos.

While all those events were taking place, there still was partisan strife in Argentina that delayed any important decision connected with independence. Part of the elites, mainly those who belonged to the upper class, were "always hesitant to become identified too closely with the new regime" (Bethell 1989). For example, Supreme Director Carlos María de Alvear supported those who wanted to achieve reconciliation with Spain, or at least a British protectorate. Besides, there was no clear revolutionary leadership, but when the supreme director was replaced by another, the previous state of affairs seemed to change a little bit.

By 1816, the deep division between Argentina and its mother country had become quite apparent, as it was too difficult to return to those times when the Spaniards were the most important authorities. In a similar way, inside that territory there was no unified criteria as no one wanted to put aside personal interests, so elites decided to convene a congress to discuss what was the best thing to do. The so-called Congress of Tucuman turned out to be the best place to exchange ideas, while José de San Martin and Manuel Belgrano troops protected them against any possible disturbance or menace.[14]

Finally, a group of separatists, one of the most important being San Martin, who was born in 1778 and died in 1850, decided to declare the country's independence. Despite the fact that most of them were in favor of a constitutional monarchy, they all agreed that they could not accept Ferdinand VII's aggressive attitude and continue their relationship as if nothing had happened since 1810. So they declared that all of the territories that formed part of the so-called United Provinces of the Río de la Plata were going to be an independent country from then on, without adequate representation from all of the territories (Garcia Samudio 1945). Once more, elites had a particular idea of what political representation meant, as the lower class and those who did not belong to the elites were not highly considered for that final decision, even though there was an important reason: Spaniard's occupation and still important influence over certain parts of the viceroyalty.

Later, one of those patriots, José de San Martin, crossed the Andes and captured Lima. Along with Simon Bolivar, San Martin is credited with breaking the shackle of Spanish rule in South America. José de San Martin was one the most important heroes in Argentine history, and he was not a caudillo but could be considered an elite member in a broad sense as he neither had a lot of money nor great ambition to reach a high political position. To better understand his importance during the Congress of Tucuman and the independence declarations, it is worth knowing more about him. He was a soldier who wanted to fulfill a task according to his heart and feelings. He was a master of military strategy and one of the principal revolutionary fighters against royalist forces in South America. While a member of the Spanish army, he was loyal to his motherland, Spain, when he fought against Napoléon, even though he disliked the traditional absolute monarchy and its colonial system. In 1811, he decided to resign from Spanish service and follow the ideals of Logia Lautaro members, a secret society that originated in England whose aim was to fight for Latin American independence.

Upon his arrival in Buenos Aires in March 1812, San Martin began to organize an armed force to defeat the Spanish royalists in Peru, and at the same time, he became more involved in internal politics as a member of Logia Lautaro. In fact, he was given specific instructions to go ahead with that organization's aims (Ruiz Moreno 1961). But, in those territories, there were other political tendencies and ambitions that made persons and groups struggle for power. As soon as San Martin won different battles, his political position was better even though his health was rather weak. In spite of all the political, economic, and health difficulties, he prepared the so-called Army of the Andes to free other Latin American territories like Peru and Chile.

In 1816, while representatives of some Argentine provinces met at the Congress of Tucuman, San Martin advocated for a clear declaration of independence from Spain, which the congress finally released on July 9. He believed that a liberal-constitutional monarchy was the best hope for stability in the new nations of Spanish America. In January 1817, he started to cross the Andes and began his most important liberation campaign. But, by 1822, he was tired of so much political struggle and, having even more serious health problems, he decided to leave his military and political career to live in France with his daughter.

Postindependence in Argentina was marked by an often-bitter struggle between two political groups: the Unitarists and the Federalists. The Unitarists wanted a strong central government, while the Federalists wanted local control. Up to a certain extent, these two groups represented the elites (Unitarists) and the caudillos (Federalists) that found it very difficult to put aside their personal interest to follow a common way.

CONCLUSION

Argentine national days have been marked by the presence of elites and caudillos, which in turn began to struggle for more power once Spaniard authority was weakened. No other social group played an active role in either of the national days.

At the same time, in Argentina, landowners and commercial activity turned out to be the most important. Even the British celebrated these achievements; for example, while the events of May 25, 1810, were taking place, British war navies saluted nosily from the river (Galeano 1990), only two years after they had been defeated in that same place. From then on, British presence and influence in the Río de la Plata increased. They lost battles but won a new market.

The May 25 national day was not celebrated until 1835, when a caudillo wanted to stress national feelings among people and at the same time emphasize his own importance as a charismatic leader. To stress, any type of leadership was too closely connected with "national" feelings, as elites and caudillos were the only ones who took part in such moments, which in turn were also being considered as turning points for national feelings. So, the connection between such sentiments and strong caudillos leadership made military importance grow even more, and that is why national days' celebrations are being stressed during nonelected governments, that is, when army forces ruled over the whole country,[15] or populist ones, when the president is considered a caudillo.

To a certain extent, Argentine national sentiments were the result of those two groups whose interest was more involved in their own improvement than with the rest of the society's needs and desires, as those were part of the adopted Spanish customs. It is also worthwhile to point out that regarding those national days, not all of the names of the ones who took part in them were remembered, just a few. For example, the names of all of the members of the First Government Junta in 1810 are more commonly known than the names of those who declared the independence; in this last case, only very few have generally being considered, like San Martin's importance.

Once again, the acts were mentioned but not all of the people—just the leaders who made final decisions were highly considered, as if the roles of the elites and the caudillos during those events wanted to be accentuated. In a similar way, whenever national days' events are being studied, just parts of the whole are considered, and economic circumstances and decisions are almost never mentioned. Spaniards' hierarchical attitudes were deeply rooted in Argentine's past days and were forged to mold national identity. At the same time, it was one of the reasons nonelected governments and despotic ones had been so widely accepted: their behavior resembled elites and caudillos.

NOTES

Caudillos (used in the chapter title and throughout this chapter) are charismatic leaders who people followed without arguing whether their orders were good or bad. According to the *Diccionario Etimológico de la Lengua Castellana* (1992), the word *caudillo* has its origin in the Latin word *capitellum*, from *caput* that means head. See also Entrena Durán (1995).

1. The Cabildo was the most important and old Latin American institution settled by the Spaniards to govern cities, small towns, and villages. It resembled the Ayuntamiento, the

still-existing government of Spanish cities and towns, and in Argentina it has been the predecessor of present municipality.

2. This expression and leading characteristics have been analyzed by Entrena Durán (1995, 82–89) to explain the "caudillos' world" in Mexico.

3. Carlos Saul Menem was president of Argentina from 1989 to 1999, and was considered a caudillo.

4. Principal Amerindians were the Diaguitas and the Quilmes in the Northwest; the Tehuelches in Patagonia; the Matacos, the Tobas, and the Pilagá in the present provinces of Chaco and Formosa; the Guarany in the Mesopotamia provinces; and the Puelches and the Huarpes in the Cuyo region (Carrasco and Céspedes 1985, 235–52). Immigrant European population greatly affected Argentina, contributing to the demise of pre-Colombian cultures, so now there is no dominant indigenous population (Levene 1973, 143).

5. At present, Buenos Aires is Argentina's capital city.

6. For example, Tucumán's governor during the 1550s menaced and killed many people and it was very difficult for the crown to try to sentence him because of distances and lack of adequate police structure (Vittadini Andrés 1992).

7. Santiago de Liniers was appointed military chief by an "open Cabildo" that took place on August 14, 1806.

8. Juan Martín de Alzaga was Alcalde de Primer Grado (first grade mayor) in the Cabildo.

9. Open Cabildo is the name of special and extraordinary Cabildo sessions to solve or discuss important and urgent matters.

10. For long periods of time, until the end of the 16th century, women were not allowed to travel to America.

11. The most important requirements for being appointed to lower Cabildo positions were to have a job, to own a house, and to have a certain amount of money. For the most important positions, there were other requirements, such as an important income that had to exceed the salary, unless they were professionals who had no boss.

12. All those who could take part in the Cabildo activities were considered the only members and most important people in the city.

13. The supreme power decision is known as "Ferdinand VII's mask."

14. Manuel Belgrano was a criollo lawyer who was appointed as general, and one of his main orders was to oblige provinces to accept the new junta's decisions. José de San Martin was a military man who occasionally was appointed as a public functionary.

15. Nonelected or de facto authorities have been very important in Argentine history from 1862 until 1983, but even nowadays, they influence Argentina from a social and political point of view, as the most important laws were enacted during those illegal periods. Also, their behavior is deeply rooted in its society.

REFERENCES

Anna, E. T. (1986). *España y la independencia de América.* México, DF, México: Fondo de Cultura Económica.

Atkins, G. P. (1989). *Latin America in the international system.* (2nd. ed., rev. and up.). Boulder, CO: Westview Press.

Bethell, L. (Ed.). (1989). *The independence of Latin America*. Cambridge, UK: Cambridge University Press.

Carrasco, P., and Céspedes, G. (1985). *Historia de América Latina*. (Vol. 1). Buenos Aires, Argentina: Alianza Editorial.

Delgado Martín, J. (1988). *Juan de Rosas, presidente de los porteños y Señor de los Gauchos*. España: Biblioteca Iberoamericana.

Di Tella, T. (1990). *Latin American politics: A theorical framework*. Austin: University of Texas Press.

Entrena Durán, F. (1995). *Mexico: del caudillismo al populismo Estructural*. Sevilla, Spain: Publicaciones de la Escuela de Estudios Hispanoamercanos de Sevilla.

Galeano, E. (1990). *Las venas abiertas de América Latina*. (61st ed.). España: Siglo XXI de España Editores S.A.

García Samudio, N. (1945). *La independencia de Hispanoamérica 111-112*. México, DF, México: Fondo de Cultura Económica.

Halperin-Donghi, T. (1975). *Politics, economics and society in Argentina in the revolutionary period*. Cambridge, UK: Cambridge University Press.

Levene, R. (1962). *Manual de historia del derecho Argentino*. Buenos Aires: Guillermo Kraft.

Levene, R. (1973). *Las Indias no eran colonias*. Madrid, España: Espasa Calpe S.A.

Linch, J. (1958). *Spanish colonial administration, 1782–1810*. Westport, CT: Greenwood Press.

McDonough, P. (1983). Let's us make the revolution before the people do: Elite mass relations in Brazil. In M. M. Czudnowski (Ed.), *Political elites and social change*. Northern Illinois University Press.

Mosca, G. (1939). *The ruling class, (elementi di Scienzia Politica)*. [Elements for Political Science]. New York: Mc Graw-Hill.

Rodríguez O., and Jaime, E. (1998). *The independence of Spanish America*. Cambridge, MA: Harvard University Press.

Ruiz Moreno, I. (1961). *Historia de las relaciones exteriores Argentina, 1810–1955*. Buenos Aires: Ed. Abeledo Perrot.

Séjourné, L. (1989). *América Latina, I.- Antiguas colonias precolombinas*. Argentina: Siglo XXI.

Vittadini Andrés, S. N. (1992). *Juicio político al presidente de la república: Caso Martinez de Perón*. Unpublished doctoral dissertation, University of Buenos Aires.

AUSTRALIA

The Bicentenary of Australia

Celebration of a Nation

Leanne White

THE IMAGINED COMMUNITY KNOWN AS THE NATION

Few would argue that the term *the nation* has a significantly broader meaning than the geographical boundaries of a particular country. The term encompasses more far-reaching notions than territory alone. Writers on the subject have acknowledged that the nation can embrace a combination of political, social, cultural, historical, economic, linguistic, and religious factors.

When an individual is said to belong to a nation, it is generally understood that the person has his or her foundations in that country. The word *nation* originated from the Latin term *natio*, which means place/community of birth and the place of which one is native. Nation is therefore associated with words such as *nature*, *innate*, *natal*, and *renascent*.

Anthony Smith (1991) defines nation as a "named human population" with shared territory, myths, history, culture, economy, and rights and responsibilities by all members of that community (14). While Smith's notion is useful, it has been Benedict Anderson's theories on the subject that seem to have made a significant contribution to the discourse of the nation in recent years. Anderson (1983) claims that the nation is an "imagined political community." Unlike previous theories, he breaks away from the interpretation that the nation is intrinsically bound up with factors such as religion or kinship, by emphasizing the imagined status of the community by the people. Anderson states, "It is imagined because members of even the smallest nation will never know most of their fellow members, meet them, or even hear of them, yet in the minds of each lives the image of their communion" (15).

Anderson asserts that the imagined community is limited because even large communities have restricted boundaries beyond which other countries exist. His

concept of the community stems from the myth of fraternity, the perceived comradeship, rather than the actual (16). Anderson's definition of the nation presupposes
a close connection both among citizens and between citizens and their country.

NATIONAL IDENTITY AND SENTIMENT

The concept of national identity is clearly much more complex than nation.
Smith (1991) examines the nature, causes, and consequences of national identity
and explains that it is "fundamentally multidimensional." He acknowledges that
national identity and the nation are constructions formed from many interrelated
components such as the cultural, territorial, economic, and political. Members of
communities are consequently united by shared memories, myths, and traditions
(14–15).

The intensity of an individual's feelings about their national identity appears
directly related to his or her level of national sentiment. Sentiment for the nation involves a sense of personal identification and empathy with an entity far beyond that
of the individual. As a particular level of emotion is involved, national sentiment is
a highly subjective feeling and can vary enormously in different circumstances. To
illustrate the point, while it is possible that possessing Australian citizenship might
not register any emotional involvement, it is often the case that being a member of
the nation-state does carry some meaning, even if it is possibly regarded as the most
abstract of identities that the individual possesses. Additionally, national sentiment
might be more concentrated when the citizen is younger and possibly more im-
pressionable than when the citizen becomes older and increasingly aware of
manipulative forces.

Many organizations, including advertising agencies, have become highly com-
petent at promoting national symbols and images, but their efforts might not elicit
the desired resonance unless some degree of national sentiment existed within the
reader of the text. Hence, having undertaken a brief examination of the nation, national identity and national sentiment in general, an analysis of the concept of
nation in Australia will begin.

THE ROLE OF THE AUSTRALIAN NATION IN
A GLOBAL WORLD

This chapter explores the means by which the nation-state and private industry have attempted to associate their product or idea with distinct Australian
signifiers. A central reason for adopting such a technique is, of course, to obtain
profit by appealing to people's perception of themselves as part of the invented
national community.

Without entering into an examination of the abundant methods by which the
idea of nation is presented to the consumer, it is worth noting one regularly used

technique. A popular strategy employed by image makers that most Australians encounter daily is the representation of the landmass/map of their island continent in various forms. The masthead of the daily national newspaper *The Australian* includes a red map of the nation. The landmass is also shown from the perspective of a satellite with the nightly television weather forecast, and countless organizations feature a stylized version of the Australian map as their logo. Although citizens may not always consciously register that they are viewing the symbol, the point remains that these images are being generated and presented by numerous individuals and organizations.

While one acknowledges arguments that enter into the debate about the nation and the nation-state, such as the existence of states without nations and nations without states, the nation-state remains the effective political entity in terms of the way the world is organized. In a world that is operating increasingly at a global level, and political and trade associations often emphasizing regional and global alliances, there is significant reason to argue that the nation-state might be becoming somewhat redundant as these larger forms of association assume increasing importance. However, during 1988 (the period of time in which this chapter is principally concerned), the Australian nation-state was a distinct entity and even organized the celebration of its own existence with the "Celebration of a Nation" theme via its principal agent, the Australian Bicentennial Authority (ABA).

While the nation-state is an important concept for this chapter, the enormous cultural, social, and economic impact of globalization deserves some further attention. Smith (1991) contends that global culture is comprised of a number of discrete elements including efficiently promoted mass commodities, ideological discourses concerned with human rights and values, and a constantly changing cosmopolitanism. It is a culture that is universal and timeless, fluid and fundamentally artificial (157–58). Smith's conception of a global culture is inherently postmodern in its shapelessness and lack of structure. It is possible to identify current popular culture phenomena that have global, rather than national, signifiers. Numerous advertisements for global brand names such as Coca-Cola, Nike, and Sony; music video clips; youth fashion; and multinational fast-food outlets are some examples.

If global influences on culture are part of the lifestyle of the late 20th century and the early 21st century, one might then wonder if the ideology of the nation will continue to play a significant role in the future. Smith (1991) maintains that the nation displays little indication of being transcended and that nationalism does not seem to be failing in its power and meaning (170). He predicts that the nation will continue to produce for the people its "central cultural and political identities" fully into the next century (177). There appear to be two main reasons to suggest that nationalism will remain an important ideology in the 21st century. The attraction of nationalism has much to do with two key elements: the issue of immortality and the flexible nature of the ideology. Participating in the national arena, even in a seemingly insignificant way, is perceived by many to transcend the mortal and enter into the realm of the immortal. Also, the different interpretations that can be placed on nationalism provide the ideology with its popular appeal.

AUSTRALIA'S OFFICIAL AND COMMERCIAL NATIONALISM

The Australian nation-state decided to celebrate its own existence in 1988. When the federal government established the ABA in 1980 to coordinate a yearlong program of events, what was about to be produced was an official discourse on nationalism that provided the infrastructure for commercial operators to replicate.

The bicentennial promotions that began in mid-1987, and the subsequent celebrations throughout 1988, represented the most comprehensive official nationalism project that had ever been initiated by the nation-state in this country. The ABA developed a stylized logo of the Australian landmass. With an official licensing program, the ABA also encouraged commercial operators to publicly display an association with the bicentenary and promote an illusion to consumers that the commercial players were part of the bicentennial celebrations. Such an option was clearly attractive to many private organizations as a significant amount of advertising had effectively been paid for by the government. The condition might be considered as an official subsidy from the nation-state to the commercial sector, as the doctrine surrounding the bicentenary had been planted in the minds of Australians by the government. The role of the nation-state in organizing an official discourse on nationalism will be examined in further detail shortly.

After significant time and effort had been expended by the nation-state in establishing the celebration of 200 years of white settlement, numerous business organizations decided to jump on the bandwagon and promote their product by incorporating bicentennial and Australian signifiers into their advertising.

Commercial nationalism, the adoption of national signifiers in order to generate profit, is a continuation and extension of the overall theme, style, and symbols of the official nationalism. Commercial nationalism and official nationalism are directly related. Both contribute to the total discourse on nationalism. The official and commercial strands of nationalism are not binary oppositions, there is a significant degree of overlap between the areas, as will be further examined throughout this chapter. Commercial nationalism operates like a paradigm, it continues the pattern that has been firmly established by the official body. It is not in the interest of the private company to create conflict between these two types of nationalism; they are merely used for different purposes. And while the commercial sector manipulates national symbols, it should be emphasized that the state does not own or control these symbols in a monopolistic way.

Commercial nationalism might be regarded as a contradiction in terms: two potentially conflicting notions competing for the same space—the broader concept of nationalism, which deals with ideas and beliefs, combining with the world of commerce, which competes for the consumer dollar. Commercial nationalism was, of course, not a new phenomenon; it had existed for many years. The methods by which advertisers have appropriated images of the Australian nation have also been examined by a number of theorists.

CELEBRATIONS OF SELECTED NATIONAL DAYS: 1838, 1888, AND 1938

This section briefly explores the methods by which an official nationalism of Australia was presented by the nation-state in the previous anniversaries of European settlement in order to examine the way various themes and representations of history have been modified over time. The anniversaries of 1838, 1888, and 1938 are worthy subjects for analysis. In examining the ways in which the act of European settlement had been marked in the past, it appears that specific events such as fireworks, regattas, and reenactments of the landing were part of the ritual that organizers thought appropriate for the national birthday to be celebrated. Some of the themes and events from earlier celebrations also become represented as national icons by advertising agencies keen to include celebratory signifiers in the advertisements they produced.

January 26, 1838, marked the passing of 50 years since the establishment of a penal colony at Sydney Cove at which the British flag was unfurled. The 1838 celebration was known as Anniversary Day and loyalty was directed toward England. A public holiday was declared and events such as a 50-gun salute, regatta, jubilee waltz, and fireworks display took place. The national newspaper, *The Australian*, proudly reported that "instead of savages and beasts of the field, human beings now populate the land" (Horne1989, 16). Various reports of Australian Aboriginal maltreatment by white settlers had reached England and a report tabled in the House of Commons made recommendations for their protection. Regrettably, what became known as the "Myall Creek Massacre" clearly indicated that it would take more than directives from England to change the attitudes of some early settlers toward the Australian Aboriginal community.

The centenary celebrations of 1888 had many similarities with the bicentennial celebrations that would be held 100 years later. The centennial festivities were mainly centered in and around Sydney. The harbor regatta of 1888 was a forerunner to the Tall Ships and First Fleet parades of sail that were held in 1988. In 1888, an area known as the Lachlan Swamps was renamed Centennial Park and dedicated to the people of Sydney, while a site of 100 hectares in the geographical center of metropolitan Sydney was named Bicentennial Park 100 years later. During the centenary celebrations, a foundation stone for the New South Wales (NSW) Parliament Building was uncovered, while in 1988 Australia's first permanent Parliament House in Canberra was declared officially opened. Finally, the Centennial International Exhibition held at Melbourne's Exhibition Buildings was basically a 19th-century equivalent of the World Expo that was held on the banks of the Brisbane River for the bicentenary. However, the centenary was not without its detractors. The widely read national journal, *The Bulletin*, described the celebrations as "childish, frothy and boastful." Similar sentiments emerged 100 years later.

Australia's sesquicentenary celebrations in 1938 had two main features in common with the bicentenary: organizers focused on the nation, and the Aboriginal community expressed their opposition. Australia had changed significantly in the past 50 years, and two key dates that contributed to this change were January 1, 1901, and April 25, 1915. On the first day of the 20th century, the Commonwealth of Australia came into being and the proclamation of the Federal Constitution was celebrated at Sydney's Centennial Park. In May of that year, Australia's first Federal Parliament began and four months later the flag, a crucial symbol for a new nation, was hoisted. While the political genesis of Australia can be traced to the events of 1901, some historians have argued that it was the Anzac landing at Gallipoli on April 25, 1915 that marked the emergence of Australia as a nation.

The theme of the 1938 celebrations was "Australia's March to Nationhood" and a procession of 120 floats was watched by 1 million people as it passed through Sydney. An emphasis on Australia rather than Britain was reflected in some of the floats that included Bondi lifesavers, wildflowers, writer Henry Lawson, and opera singer Dame Nellie Melba. Fifty years later, Sorbent was to advertise its brand of toilet paper by using Bondi lifesavers. A symbolic acknowledgment of the traditional owners of the land was made by the parade organizers as the event was led by an Aboriginal float followed by one commemorating Captain Cook (Horne 1989, 23).

The Australian Aboriginal community declared January 26, 1938, a "Day of Mourning and Protest" and held a conference that attracted about 100 Aborigines. However, unlike the bicentenary when Australian Aboriginal issues were given a reasonable amount of media coverage, this event was almost entirely ignored by the media. But it was the white Australians on the Sesquicentenary Celebrations Council based in NSW, whose interpretation of Australian history was expounded in the public domain. One particular style of national symbolism, a human map of Australia, would continue to be replicated frequently in both the domains of official nationalism and commercial nationalism until the bicentenary and beyond. The year also saw Australian athletes triumph at the Empire Games in Sydney as Australia won 24 of the 70 events.

THE AUSTRALIAN BICENTENNIAL AUTHORITY INITIATES NATIONALISM

The ABA was established in 1980 to plan and coordinate a yearlong program of national events for Australia's bicentenary in 1988. The authority was formed by the federal government, headed by the prime minister of the day, Malcolm Fraser, as an incorporated company responsible to commonwealth, state, and territory governments.

An important dilemma that confronted the ABA was the promotion of the anniversary of European settlement as a national celebration. If Australia officially became a nation in 1901, one might then assume that a bicentenary in 1988 could not possibly be the "Celebration of a Nation" as the ABA slogan would have us believe. Such an event would occur in 2101. While this sort of logic might be interpreted as pedantic, it does appear to have been a concern for some, particularly those who resided in places other than New South Wales where the act of settlement being marked for celebration took place. Some perceived the bicentennial celebrations as a mainly NSW event, and the location of the ABA's head office in Sydney might have suggested that the bicentenary was owned by NSW politicians and bureaucrats. However, with the assistance over the 1970s and 1980s of nationalist pronouncements by Australian prime ministers Gough Whitlam, Malcolm Fraser, and Bob Hawke, along with patriotic rhetoric in many sections of popular culture such as cinema and advertising, part of the discourse of the public culture was that Australia was one nation.

Since its early days, the ABA was afflicted with controversy and a number of the concerns centered around what many perceived as an extravagant waste of taxpayers' money. The first general manager, David Armstrong, was dismissed in August 1985, and the chairman, Jim Reid, resigned not long after. In November 1985, Jim Kirk was appointed chairman and chief executive of the authority. From the time of Kirk's appointment, it seemed that the authority was going to adopt a rather conservative stance in its role as organizer of bicentennial activities and events. In an interview conducted toward the end of the bicentenary, Kirk stated, "I took a decision early on that I wasn't going to have controversy." He explained how groups approached the ABA to promote or oppose matters such as a new flag, a republic and "the Aboriginal problem." Kirk claimed that when these arguments are entered into "you have got emotionalism, not intellectualism" (qtd. in O'Neill 1988, 3).

The authority's five planning principles were to strengthen national pride; involve all Australians; provide lasting and useful mementos for future generations as well as exciting events; offer stimulating educational and cultural programs on Australia: past, present, and future; and achieve international participation (Australia Post 1984, 11). In response to public criticism about the authority's handling of its budget of just over $200 million, Kirk emphasized the financial benefits to the country stating that bicentennial spending was a "national investment" and that it was estimated that for every $1 spent, $3 would be put back into the economy (see Cowell 1987, 5). State governments were responsible for capital works, and almost all of the planning of local events was left to the Bicentennial Community Committees (BCC) in Australia's 839 local government areas, which were described by Kirk as "the essence of the whole Bicentenary" (qtd. in Cowell 1987, 5). The ABA's head office allocated $330,000 for Bicentennial Community kits, and once the kits were distributed, the state and territory ABA offices assisted the BCCs (O'Brien 1991, 263). Financial support was not provided to the BCCs as they were expected to organize their own funds. Communities created bicentennial legacies such as new parks, statues, walking trails, and even restoration of a church and graveyard. An 11-minute promotional video was sent to the BCCs to promote the Bicentenary at the "grassroots" level. Titled *Join the Celebration!* the video contained significant visual and acoustic references to Australian nationalism and patriotism, and concluded with a female voice-over stating, "The spirit of the Bicentenary is springing from the heart of the Australian community" (ABA 1985).

The BCCs cost the ABA comparatively little to establish and enabled thousands of volunteers to be involved with the bicentenary. The idea of forming the committees was based on a similar scheme adopted for the U.S. bicentenary in 1976 (O'Brien 1991 263). Apart from decentralizing many of the 40,000 bicentennial activities that took place in 1988, the BCCs were also an effective merchandising arm of the ABA. The public was able to purchase a limited number of bicentennial souvenirs through their local BCC and receive information about retailers who sold a wide range of bicentennial products from flags to bricks.

Merchandise endorsed by the ABA carried the official logo—a ribbon broadly representing the shape of the Australian continental landmass—designed by Bruce Radke. An earlier version of the logo featured a flat base, which effectively meant that the states of Victoria and Tasmania were excluded.

In addition to controversial changes within the ranks of ABA senior management, and the evolving ABA logo, there were also differences of opinion on the bicentennial theme. The original theme conceived for the bicentenary by writer and advertising man Phillip Adams was "Living Together." It was an attempt to reflect the "co-operative effort of all Australians of all backgrounds and cultures" (Australia Post 1984, 11). However, in December 1981, Prime Minister Fraser changed the theme to "The Australian Achievement," much to the surprise and annoyance of the ABA. Fraser claimed that his theme was broader and encompassed "the widest possible range of life and experience" (qtd. in O'Brien, 1991, 49). When the Hawke government took office in 1983, the theme was reverted to the original.

However, in 1986, when the advertising agencies Mojo Australia and Monahan Dayman Adams (MDA) combined to manage the ABA's $10.5 million account, the agency recommended that "Living Together" be abandoned as it was "vacuous and uninspiring" and did not embody a "call to action" (see O'Brien 1991, 122). The decision seemed somewhat ironic as Adams, the originator of the theme, was a senior partner with MDA. The agency suggested the theme "Celebration of a Nation" and the idea was met with enthusiasm by senior ABA executives. Once the slogan was adopted and the advertising campaign launched, it was clear that Australia's bicentenary would place emphasis on celebrating and encouraging Australians to have a good time. The party message was evident in the "Celebration" bumper stickers and posters that included balloons, streamers, and ribbons in the design.

ADVERTISING AND PUBLIC RELATIONS BUILD ENTHUSIASM FOR THE BICENTENARY

In March 1986, the ABA announced that the Sydney-based advertising agency Mojo Australia and the Melbourne-based MDA would combine their distinctly Australian styles of advertising to handle the ABA's lucrative account. The advertising partnership was planned for this campaign alone, but led to a merger of the companies soon after and it became the largest Australian-owned advertising agency in the late 1980s. The agency suggested that the ABA's theme "Living To-gether," which was adopted to acknowledge Australia's Aboriginal people and significant multicultural community, be abandoned and "Celebration of a Nation" adopted. The new theme was well suited to an advertising jingle, and words were soon penned by Fran Allan and Tim Phillip; the music was composed by Les Gock (O'Brien 1991, 123).

In November 1986, 60 Australian celebrities gathered in central Australia for a two-day shoot with the famous monolith Uluru/Ayers Rock in the background. All volunteered their services for the exhaustive 30 takes, but were somewhat com-pensated by having been flown to Alice Springs and accommodated at the Yulara Resort near one of Australia's most recognized landmarks. The group of famous Australians comprised television personalities, actors, singers, sports people, writ-ers, artists, and fashion designers.

The television advertising for Australia's bicentenary was launched in July 1987. To supplement the television commercial, similar Mojo MDA promotions were de-veloped for the print media, radio, cinema, billboards, and the sides of public transport. Market research conducted later that year revealed that 99.3 percent of the population had an awareness of the forthcoming bicentenary (O'Brien 1991, 125).

The television commercial featured famous and some not-so-famous Australians singing, waving arms, and generally preparing both themselves and Australians for the celebration of a nation. In the advertisement, Rick Price and a female singer led a group of Australian personalities including Delvene Delaney, Jenny Kee, Bert Newton, Thomas Keneally, Ken Done, Prue Acton, Cliff Young, and Jeff St. John.

The technical details of the Celebration of a Nation advertisement are worthy of analysis. The 90-second commercial comprises 62 shots, averaging a duration of 1.45 seconds per shot. The visual narrative begins and ends with two significant symbols: the Australian flag and the bicentennial flag displaying the green and gold ABA logo on a white background. In the opening shot, an Australian flag waving in the breeze is superimposed on a moving outback landscape. As the flag occupies a greater proportion of space in the frame, the powerful symbol of Uluru is sighted in the distance. In the penultimate shot of the commercial, the group is shown with Uluru as the backdrop. As the group of people raise their arms in the air, there is a quick fade to the final shot: the ABA flag waving in the breeze.

Many of the people in the advertisement are wearing combinations of red, white, or blue, while some are dressed in the green and gold bicentennial T-shirt. Delvene Delaney, the first celebrity to be shown in the advertisement, with the ex-ception of the lead singers, is dressed in orange and black with a straw hat that consequently blends in with the red ochre surroundings at this location.

The location of Uluru may have been chosen to help the ABA extend a sign of respect to Australia's indigenous people, but some members of the Aboriginal com-munity might have interpreted the choice as another action of European dominance and obvious disregard for a sacred Aboriginal site. The Mutitjulu community, to whom the area was officially handed back in October 1985, was consulted before permission was granted for the filming. The community's response was that it "neither supports nor opposes" the application to film and believes that "the Bicentennial celebrations are a matter of European celebration" (O'Brien 1991, 123).

There was an obvious attempt by Mojo MDA to present a gathering that was sensitive to issues of ethnicity, age, gender, and class; however, it appears that any well-meaning attempt was not entirely successful when one closely analyzes the advertisement. Only one Australian Aborigine can be identified in the advertisement. Standing directly behind the two singers, an Australian Aboriginal man wearing a light blue T-shirt and white sun hat is shown. An indigenous presence is heard with a didgeridoo after the words "Have you noticed there's a feeling of something in the air?" Other minority groups are also included in the gathering. The disabled community is represented by singer Jeff St. John; representing older Australians is potato farmer and long-distance runner Cliff Young; while the ethnic communities appear to have only one representative: the Asian Australian fashion designer Jenny Kee, who is located toward the front of the gathering. The others in the group are a farmer wearing an Akubra hat, adorable children, and bicentennial T-shirt-clad women. The obvious attempt either by the ABA, Mojo MDA, or both to not leave anyone out of the national portrait seems to have failed.

The identifiable consumer to which this advertisement is addressed is all Australians. However the choice of words "give us a hand to celebrate" clearly places the supposed typical Australians at Uluru in a position of power. Although the group in the advertisement are the "us" for the life of the commercial, the "us" who have orchestrated the yearlong celebrations are the ABA, headed by chairman Jim Kirk.

This advertisement played an important role in building an awareness of the forthcoming bicentenary and helped generate an expected $100 million in retail sales of ABA-endorsed products over the following 18 months.

THE BICENTENARY BEGINS WITH
AUSTRALIA LIVE TELECAST

In the lead-up to January 1, 1988, a four-hour television program, *Australia Live—Celebration of a Nation*, was promoted as the most ambitious live program in television history (Martin 1987, 4). It was an important mode of communication by which the message of official nationalism was able to exploit technology to gain saturation coverage for its social marketing on the first day of the bicentennial year.

Project director Wilf Barker was given a brief by the ABA to devise a televised opening to 1988 that would both "unite and excite" the nation. The program was simultaneously broadcast on the Nine Network, the Australian Broadcasting Corporation, the Special Broadcasting Service, and regional stations on January 1 at 7:30 P.M. eastern standard time. The ABA contributed almost $4 million to the event, while major telecommunications providers volunteered technical services worth more than $2 million. Director Peter Faiman was given total creative and editorial control to produce the "slice-of-life" program. Although the event was principally designed for an audience of up to 16 million Australians, the program was also shown in the United States, Canada, New Zealand, Papua New Guinea, and parts of Europe and Asia. Much of the publicity surrounding the event emphasized the technical complexity of the operation. Television audiences were told that no one had attempted to stage a live production on such a scale. High-tech equipment such as satellites, mobile earth stations, microwave links, fiber optics, and receiver dishes would be called on to stage the ambitious technological adventure into the unknown.

When *Australia Live* officially opened Australia's bicentennial year, viewers were greeted by the quintessential Australian male, Paul Hogan. As "arm-chair critic" Hogan predicted that Australians would be "so sick" of the bicentenary within months they would be contemplating "givin'" this land back to the Abos." His comment about commercial nationalism, "everyone that's got a bad product to flog is gonna be sort of pushin' the Bicentenary down our necks," turned out to be closer to the truth than one might have expected.

The three studio hosts—journalists Jana Wendt, Ray Martin, and Clive James—were then introduced. For the next four hours, an audience of millions was delivered a visual montage of travelogue, documentary, and current affairs. The live-crosses began with a bicentennial party at the prime minister's residence, followed by Phillip Adams at Uluru, high-profile lawyer Geoffrey Robertson at Portsmouth in England, and Australian Aboriginal actor Ernie Dingo at Botany Bay. While the optimists hoped for some serious analysis of nationalism, before too long it was obvious that the television audience was to be subjected to an exhaustive array of tourist destinations such as Kakadu National Park, the Barossa Valley, and Hamilton Island.

Australia Live—Celebration of a Nation was described by media writers and academics as superficial and boring. Meaghan Morris described the special as "not riveting television." She also claimed that the show allowed one version of history to be repeatedly pronounced dead, "Australia as a space of isolation, slow development and eccentricity" (qtd. in Foss 1988, 165).

WHITE AUSTRALIA HAS A BLACK HISTORY

An important and somewhat ironic outcome of the bicentenary was that the very act of celebrating 200 years of white settlement also put an end to the supposedly official version of Australia's origins. For the European Australians who had ignored or suppressed earlier calls for Aboriginal issues to be given serious consideration on the national agenda, it became increasingly obvious, in 1988, that concerns such as land rights and a treaty needed to be addressed. The European Australians who controlled the flow of information and ideas could no longer continue to present rhetoric and images that privileged Anglo-Australians and excluded marginal groups such as Australian Aborigines, women, and those of non-Anglo background.

While the organizers of the bicentenary might not have fully realized it at the time, they were faced with an integral dilemma from the moment they were formed in 1980. The very reason for the existence of the ABA, organizing the celebration of the invasion of another people's land, was a contentious issue and the debate surrounding ownership of land would continue into the following decade and beyond. Although much public criticism was directed toward the ABA about the very philosophy behind the national anniversary, it seems that a positive outcome of 1988 was a maturing public conscience that challenged some of the previously held fundamental beliefs about Australian history. Australians emerged from 1988 with a clearer realization that it was no longer appropriate for white Australians to disregard the traditional owners of the land.

Some sections of the Australian community saw Australia's bicentenary as a time of hope for reconciliation on key Aboriginal issues such as sovereignty and land rights, sacred sites, black deaths while in custody, housing, unemployment, health, and even a possible treaty. Others believed that the beginning of a black/white negotiation process might be a more realistic expectation of the year (Stevens 1988, 13). Many views about Australian Aboriginal issues were publicly voiced and could vary enormously depending on whether one was reading or listening to the words of H. C. (Herbert Cole) Coombs, Manning Clark, Henry Reynolds, Kevin Gilbert, Michael Dodson, Marcia Langton, or numerous others.

Thousands of Aborigines and their supporters voiced established beliefs that had been inadequately dealt with or ignored by government authorities in previous anniversaries and commemorative events such as the 1938 sesquicentenary and the 1982 Commonwealth Games in Brisbane. At demonstrations and public meetings, and via television current affairs shows and radio talk-back programs, it seemed that some serious dialogue was beginning to take place in 1988. With the assistance of slogans such as "White Australia Has a Black History" and "40,000 Years Don't Make a Bicentenary," many non-Aboriginals were being confronted with an interpretation of history that seriously challenged prior concepts of history and that was morally negligent to continue to avoid confronting.

Aboriginal supporters protested throughout the year and many boycotted any participation in the public arena. Writer Patrick White claimed that the Australian people "should do more for the Aborigines" (qtd. in Schumpeter 1988, 1). He described the bicentennial celebrations as a "circus" and requested that none of his works be published or performed in the year. Australia Day was declared "Invasion Day" by Aboriginal groups and their supporters and a day of mourning rather than celebration was advocated. Many politicians ensured that their words were carefully scripted by "speech-writers in an effort to cause minimal offence to the nation's indigenous people. Prime Minister Hawke spoke of Australia's debt to the Aboriginal people in his Australia Day message with the words, 'Australians should remember the past and what we owed to the Aborigines who had lived on this continent for about 40,000 years'"(Garran 1988, 3).

An important objective of the protest agenda was to focus international attention on the plight of Australia's indigenous people. One particular media event showed Aboriginal elder Burnum Burnum reclaiming Britain on behalf of his people by displaying the Aboriginal flag on a beach at Dover. Australia House in London was another target at which Aboriginal concerns were directed as the windows were graffitied with messages about "fascist murderers" and groups protested outside the building for various international media organizations. Canadian television news focused on the Aboriginal protests of Australia Day, French newspapers reported that "Aborigines Play No Part" in Australia, and leading newspapers in Japan also noted the protests (Benesh 1988).

BICENTENNIAL LEGACIES AND ASSESSMENTS

The ABA spent $151 million on the bicentenary. However, the combined amount disbursed by federal and state governments was more than $4.5 billion on various bicentennial projects and activities (Jopson 1988, 12). Consequently, when the party was over, some were left wondering what had been left behind, apart from the memories. The tangible bicentennial legacies and their cost to the nation were well documented. The list included Australia's new Parliament House ($1 billion), the bicentennial roads program ($2.5 billion), the redevelopment of Sydney's Darling Harbour ($500 million), the Stockman's Hall of Fame at Longreach ($6 million), and the Australian Ballet Centre ($5.2 million). Other projects to emerge in 1988 were the Imparja television station in central Australia, the converting of Ningaloo Reef to a national marine park, and the Bicentennial Park in the Sydney suburb of Homebush.

On the final day of 1988, an editorial in *The Age* commented, "As a nation, we shall wake up tomorrow a little older and perhaps a little wiser" ("Goodbye" 1988, 13). The contemplative piece suggested that the celebrations were not a waste of money as Australians had emerged more united than divided on issues such as multiculturalism, national identity, and Aboriginal inequality. As would be expected, the ABA's Jim Kirk claimed that the celebrations were not in vain, and $3 was actually generated for every $1 spent (an estimate he had given before the year commenced). The two legacies he perceived as most important were the establishment of the multicultural foundation and the youth foundation. However, not all Australians saw much merit in the bicentenary. While historian Manning Clark acknowledged that the debate on Aboriginal issues had intensified, he claimed that Australia still had "a long way to go" before resolving black/white relations (qtd. in McNamara 1988, 5).

AUSTRALIA DAY IN THE NEW MILLENNIUM

An editorial in *The Australian* on January 26, 2000, stated, "We have to celebrate this Australia Day. At the dawn of a new century, Australia is among the most fortunate countries in the world: few nations can look forward with as much confidence." The editorial acknowledged that reconciliation between black and white

Australia was a significant hurdle yet to be overcome, as "Australians generally fail to make efforts to understand why Aborigines are so alienated by our prosperous society" (Qantas Airways Limited 2000, 12).

On Australia Day 2000, a quietly confident and relaxed form of patriotism seemed to be emerging. In Sydney, the day was celebrated by people choosing to wave flags, wear green and gold, and sing the national anthem. The theme of the celebrations was "Australia G'Day," a campaign designed to encourage strangers to greet each other (Overington 2000, 4). In Melbourne, the festivities were reported as "more of a people's day than a whiz-bang celebration, but that seems to be the Australian way" (Farouque 2000, 4).

In the style of true commercial nationalism, the Australian airline Qantas took out a two-page advertisement in the national broadsheet *The Australian* (January 26, 2000) announcing, "When it comes to the art of relaxation, Australians are recognised as truly world class. Perhaps that's why the people at Qantas are so naturally good at making you feel at home, wherever in the world you happen to fly" (44–45). The image accompanying these words was that of a wet bronzed Aussie lying facedown on the beach. The slogan to the left of the image was Qantas" well-known "The Spirit of Australia."

REFERENCES

Anderson, B. R. O'G. (1983). *Imagined communities: Reflections on the origin and spread of nationalism*. London: Verso.

Australia Post. (1984). *The first Australians: Our heritage in stamps*. Scoresby, Victoria: Cambec Press.

Australian Bicentennial Authority. (1985). *Join the celebration!* (ABA video for Bicentennial Community Committees). Sydney: Hamilton.

Benesh, P. (1988, January 28). Quirks and quarks from around the world. *The Age*.

Cowell, A. (Ed). (1987). *The bicentenary: The official magazine*. Sydney: Australian Consolidated Press.

Farouque, F. (2000, January 27). Celebrating our day the people's way, with just a dash of pomp. *The Age*, 4.

Foss, P. (Ed.). (1988). *Island in the stream: Myths of place in Australian culture*. Leichhardt, New South Wales: Pluto Press.

Garran, R. (1988, January 26). Remember our debt to blacks, says PM. *The Age*, 3.

Goodbye to the bicentenary. (1988, December 31). *The Age*, 13.

Horne, D. (1989). *Ideas for a nation*. Sydney: Pan Books.

Jopson, D. (1988). Enduring legacies of "88." *Bicentenary 88, 88*(4) 12.

Martin, G. (1987). Magic carpet ride is unique. *Bicentenary 88, 7*(4), 4.

McNamara, M. (1988, December 24). Parliament House one of few highlights, says Clark. *The Age*, 5.

O'Brien, D. (1991). *The bicentennial affair: The inside story of Australia's birthday bash*. Crows Nest: Australian Broadcasting Corporation.

O'Neill, J. (1988, May 28). The Barbie bicentenary. *The Sydney Morning Herald*, 3.

Overington, C. (2000, January 27). Sydney's way, well it's just not cricket. *The Age*, 4.

Qantas Airways Limited. (2000, January 26). Confronting the challenge of our future. *The Australian*, 12.

Schumpeter, P. (1988, January 25). Festivities will benefit greedy con men, says Patrick White. *The Age*, 1.

Smith, A. (1991). *National identity*. London: Penguin Books.

Stevens, J. (1988, January 1). Progress likely on black treaty but no end in sight. *The Age*, 13.

CANADA

Canadian Days

Non-Canadian Ways

Derek Foster

THE CELEBRATION OF CANADA'S NATIONAL DAYS

Each year the occasion of Canada Day on July 1 traditionally begets many opportunities to ask what it means to be Canadian. It is argued here that Canada, as a country, suffers from an ongoing identity crisis, due in no small part to the expectation that it can manage multiple nations within the confines of its state. This chapter will not undertake a lengthy explanation of what it means to be a nation. Nor will it attempt to explain the constitutional crisis within Canada over the issues of nationality. Library shelves are already filled with volumes dedicated to the subject. Rather, the underscrutinized issue of Canada Day is highlighted in order to question the nature of Canadian identity.

The fashion in which Canadians commemorate their national days certainly reflects on their national ways. While it is difficult to summarize what constitutes the national ways of any country, this is even more problematic when one realizes that Canadians observe three distinct national days. Contrary to the mythic nature of the United States as a melting pot of different ethnicities and nationalities, Canada is often celebrated as more of a patchwork quilt, integrating rather than assimilating different peoples. Officially, Canada celebrates its birthday on July 1. This marks the day in 1867 when a Royal Proclamation granting its independence from Britain was issued. However, in addition to this national day, some attention must be paid to the nationalist holiday that is celebrated in the province of Quebec on June 24. Also, in addition to these two holidays honoring the cultures of Canada's two major original settler groups of the English and the French, Canada's federal government has redressed a long-standing historical blind spot by recently recognizing a third national day (June 21) in honor of Canada's aboriginal population, its first nations' people.

Canada is indeed a nation of nations. One would be remiss then, if, in any discussion of Canadian nationality, the means by which different Canadians express their differences and celebrate their uniquely Canadian nature were not addressed. Consequently, the focus here is on recent commemorations of Canada Day in the nation's capital of Ottawa, and in Montreal, which is the largest city in the province of Quebec. These events are contrasted with Montreal's observance of Quebec's Fête Nationale, which is held a week earlier for reasons that will be explained later. And even though there are three national days within 10 days of each other, very few Canadians celebrate each occasion. Yet, for those who do partake in any of the celebrations, these days represent a passionate—albeit temporary—investment in one's fellow Canadians. To demonstrate this, a brief description of the particular condition of Canadian nationality is undertaken. Following this, the holidays themselves and Canadian behavior on these days will be examined and related to Canadian ways for the rest of the year.

NATIONALISM AND ITS EXPRESSION IN CANADA

What is Canada and what does it mean to its citizens? A superficial answer is that Canada is comprised of a definable geographic area that gave itself a central government in 1867. Canada is the world's second-largest country after Russia and stretches across extremes of climate and geography that span over 10 million square kilometers and six different time zones. It shares with the United States the largest undefended border in the world. Canada is home to 30 million people of increasingly diverse origins and yet it is held together by tolerance and respect for democratic values. The distinct nationalisms that are found thriving in Canada certainly speak to this condition and to the conflict that lies under the surface of this diversity.

Canadians traditionally have been seen as a rather taciturn people, not much given to nationalistic emoting or flag-waving to express their true patriot love. Canadians typically wave the flag on Canada Day and at international sports events, but let that suffice. In Quebec, the Canadian flag is often taken as a symbol of federalism, and therefore seen as an affront to some of those who celebrate the nationalist aspirations of the Quebecois peoples. In this environment, conflict over flying the flag is more heated. The following sentiments relate to a senior citizen war veteran who insists on flying the Maple Leaf, as opposed to the provincial fleur-de-lis:

"I have told him not to fly the flag, I have discouraged him as much as I can," says landlord Mike Tzinevrakis. "It is not a good idea to do this. Maybe on holidays you fly the flag, but not all the time. Someone could hurt him." Huguette Martin, the tenant who lives directly above Mr. Rynd, says she has considered leaving the building because of the flags. "It is just provocation," says Ms. Martin. "He has four or five flags flying on Canada Day. That's fine. It's a holiday. But you should take the flags down the next day. Don't abuse it." (Corbett 1998, A3)

This is, however, a special case of the power of Canadian national symbolism. In the recent past, the Canadian government has intervened in an attempt to bolster feelings of national pride; for example, it established a toll-free number that any Canadian can call to obtain a free flag. Yet, even then, to many Canadians there is still something oddly forced about Canada Day and its overt attempt to pump nationalism into a nation that has been traditionally nonnationalistic. For instance, in 1998, just after Canada Day, the World Cup soccer semifinals saw far more fervent flag-waving by "hyphenated Canadians" expressing their variegated identity and their allegiance to the nations of Brazil, France, Croatia, and the Netherlands.

Before progressing any further, an important semantic observation must be made. Nation, nationality, and nationalism have all proved notoriously difficult to define, and this is certainly no less the case with Canada. Smith (1998), for instance, defines nation in something other than reductive, narrowing terms that reek of fascism; instead, he sees it as "a community of persons of all origins sharing one culture and one language of communication, who have the political and social institutions necessary for their survival" (141). Yet, with its two official languages of French and English, and its nondogmatic approach to establishing any uniform culture, Canada immediately problematizes Smith's definition with its official policies of bilingualism and multiculturalism. On the other hand, Anderson (1991) suggests that the nation can be seen as an imagined political community: "It is imagined because the members of even the smallest nation will never know most of their fellow-members, meet them, or even hear of them, yet in the minds of each lives the image of their communion." He continues, "Communities are to be distinguished not by their falsity or genuineness, but by the style in which they are imagined" (6).

This realization is a crucial one to bear in mind throughout this discussion of Canadian national days; Canadians' imagined sense of nationhood is far different from the real nature of communion that takes place when members of the Canadian nation actually gather—not in their living rooms but in the streets—and meet to create the spectacle of national celebrations. Unable to physically join the celebration, most Canadian citizens simultaneously consume the event in the privacy of their own living rooms. Sharing a collective vision, the fiction of nationalism can be made real. Watching or reading about Canada Day ceremonies individually, "each communicant is well aware that the ceremony he performs is being replicated simultaneously by thousands or millions of others of whose existence he is confident, yet of whose identity he has not the slightest notion" (Anderson 1991, 35). This ambiguity of identity, especially that of the particular Canadian sense of nationality, will be a recurring theme.

To understand the case of Canada, it is first important to identify two principal modern meanings of nation. Referring to Eric Hobsbawm, Verdery (1996) identifies "a relation known as citizenship, in which the nation consists of collective sovereignty based in common political participation, and a relation known as ethnicity, in which the nation comprises all those of supposedly common language, history, or broader cultural identity" (227). Ethnic nationalism maintains itself through bloodlines, language, and religion. In turn, civic nationalism is expressed through common institutions, symbols, and values. Arguably, if the former can be said to be felt Canada-wide, it is in only a fractured sense. And the latter does not carry the same sense of importance as could once be taken for granted.

Furthermore, Conlogue (1996) suggests that these meanings are irreconcilable in the Canadian landscape: "Quebeckers [sic] consider themselves to be a 'people,' an idea which comes from a tradition usually called romantic or 'cultural' nationalism. English [-speaking] Canada, on the other hand, believes itself to be an instance of 'civic' nationalism" (20).

Of course, this overstates the idea that Canadians as a whole do not see themselves as a unified people. True, insisting upon unity through diversity makes this seem less intuitive, or at least difficult to realize. But surely there must be something more holding English Canada together than a sense of civic nationalism that maintains that "the nation should be composed of all those—regardless of race, colour, creed, gender, language, or ethnicity—who subscribe to the nation's political creed" (Ignatieff 1993, 6). Yet, when relying on anything more than their territorially defined identity, Canadians experience notorious difficulty expressing what makes them unique as a people. Rather than defining it positively by suggesting certain special qualities, Canadians often resort to intimating that Canadians have qualities that others do not. Ethnic nationalism that is based on "a social boundary among groups within a territory" (Keating 1996, 6) is ambiguously asserted by Canadians, as evidenced by the fact that almost 20 percent of the population listed its ethnic origin as Canadian in answer to a new question in the 1996 national census.

This ambiguity of nationhood is central not only to its realization in Canada, but also as a theoretical concept. To these ends, Bhabha (1990) refers to Michael Oakeshott and reiterates that the national space is "constituted from competing dispositions of human association as societas (the acknowledgement of moral rules and conventions of conduct) and universitas (the acknowledgement of common purpose and substantive end)" (2). Refusing to merge into a unified discourse, these competing claims underscore the ongoing ambiguity of nation. Obviously, then, there is a great ambiguity over the term *nation*, not to mention the nation of Canada itself, a nation that is in constant search of itself and timid in its exhortations of this spirit. National days of celebration are very visible—and singular—opportunities that Canadians can use to reconcile this ambiguity over their own sense of nationhood.

This ambiguity can sometimes be troubling. For instance, polls are being constantly produced to help Canadians take some measure of their own identity. In a 1994 poll for the Canadian magazine *Maclean's*, 90 percent of Quebecers and 95 percent of other Canadians said Canada is the best country in the world (Chambers 1994, B3). In 1997, a UN study ranked Canada as the nation with the highest quality of life for the fourth year in a row. Still, part of what it means to be Canadian is the difficulty encountered in trying to define what makes it so. The contradictory nature of Canadian identity is also revealed in the same poll results suggesting that 40 percent of Quebecers wished to separate from Canada.

Another poll for *Maclean's* in 1995 reported 89 percent of its respondents saying that seeing the Canadian flag or hearing the national anthem made them feel proud. Similarly, the same poll showed 74 percent of respondents believing that Canadians have a distinct character (Henderson 1995, B5). However, the most recognized traits of nonviolence and tolerance of people with different backgrounds do not easily lend themselves to boasting about the country. It is these qualities that Canadians celebrate on their national days: the political liberties, material comforts, and social security enjoyed by most of the citizenry. Recognizing these qualities is enough of an excuse for a party, even in the wake of sometimes divisive national debates.

Notably, the observance of the birth of the Canadian nation can always be counted on for an annual recurrence of surveys questioning Canadian identity. The following is a prime example: "A survey released this week showed that Canadians' national pride is the third highest in the world. Also released this week was the latest Dominion Institute survey of Canadians' civic and historical knowledge" (Gardner 1998, A9).

It seems as though anxiety over Canadian's knowledge of Canada is also a part of what it means to be Canadian. But knowing the names of previous prime ministers indicates nothing about what Canadians know about the cleavages within and between their different nations. Neither is it a prerequisite for having pride in one's national identity. It is less important to have memorized the letter of the law and recite it for a survey, than to live it daily in spirit. Or, barring daily expression, this spirit of nationalist pride and identity can be seen at least once a year on national holidays.

DEFINING THE CHARACTER OF CANADIAN NATIONAL CELEBRATIONS

National celebrations such as Canada Day certainly do not hold Canada together nor define it as much as a national broadcaster, health-care, and pension system. But all of these civic institutions that grant a uniquely Canadian character to the nation find their existence and universal accessibility increasingly threatened. And, certainly, it is not uncommon to hear purely economic arguments that contemporary Canadians are less prepared than in the past to serve as their brother's keeper. Still, national celebrations can be, at the very least, a temporary solvent to the divisiveness that lies among the diversity of Canada. Whether this potential is realized in any significant or long-standing fashion is an entirely different matter though.

The history of these celebrations is an interesting one. Canadians commemorate the formation of their state by observing an official holiday on July 1 each year, which is the date of confederation. Every year, however, the province of Quebec kick-starts its summer with two successive holiday weekends: the first marked by St. Jean Baptiste Day (known as the Fête Nationale) and the second by Canada Day (known as the Fête du Canada). Montreal's St. Jean Baptiste parade, organized by the society of the same name, has often been viewed by some people as an annual pro-independence rally. But for the majority of Quebecers, the holiday is simply that: a holiday, a chance to get together with friends and family and attend community events, as well as a chance to show pride in being a Quebecer. Since 1977, June 24 has been Quebec's official Fête Nationale, a day when nationalists parade the streets in blue and white, waving Quebec flags and trumpeting their cultural pride. Buchanan (1996, A6) characterizes the history of Quebec's nationalist holiday as one of reverie that was politicized in 1834 with the search for a patron saint for French-Canadians. The lineage of this holiday, however, can be tracked to a custom of lighting bonfires in 1636. Viewed this way, Fête Nationale engenders the same styled activity as Canada Day is expected to encourage.

This party atmosphere cannot be emphasized too strongly. There are two modes of expression paramount to the vitality of Canadian national days: first, there are the official addresses from leaders such as the prime minister, provincial premiers, or even the Queen that are meant to instill pride in Canadians. A sampling of recent annual statements by Canada's prime minister demonstrate both the assumed nature of Canadian-ness, and the quest to break free of this yoke, at least on Canada Day. In 1994, for instance, Prime Minister Jean Chretien's Canada Day opinion was that Canadians do not need psychologists to know who they are. "They're Canadians, period," Chretien told the crowd on Parliament Hill (Chambers 1994, B3). "Let's not analyse Canada," said Jean Chretien on July 1. "Let's celebrate it." Gordon (1994, A13), however, believes that it is the act of analyzing Canada that makes Canadians Canadians. To him, it is the quintessential Canadian act. Deprived of it, Canadians would cease to be uniquely themselves. Given an opportunity to simply enjoy the day's proceedings on Parliament Hill, Gordon believes that Canadians are just as likely to count the number of songs sung in French and compare them with the number of songs sung in English. Yes, it is easy to say that Gordon goes too far in his characterization of "Canadian human nature." But just as every caricature is based in reality at some point, there is some element of truth to this notion of an undemonstrative and analytical Canadian-ness.

Indeed, official calls to cast off this inhibited nature and to celebrate continue to gain prominence. In 1995, Prime Minister Chretien acknowledged the anomalous nature of these celebrations: "It's the one day of the year we let our patriotism show. For the rest of the year we are more quiet about our patriotism. We are modest. We are reserved. We are low-key. We are Canadian" ("Canada Day" 1995, A3). Finally, in 1998, Chretien once again exhorted Canadians to cast off the shackles of their restraint: "On this day every year we do what some people think is downright un-Canadian. We celebrate with one voice strong and free the greatest success story in the world: Canada" (qtd. in Dube 1998, A1). This celebration is key to the continued vitality of Canada—to stress the joy that can be found in simply being together rather than stressing the divisive elements that are present in any diverse group of people if one looks diligently enough.

The second mode of expression, also crucial to the festive atmosphere, is the nonofficial or "underground" forms of what it means to be Canadian. These are found not in ambiguous, ephemeral expressions of nationality or starkly political versions thereof, which typify too much of Canadians' everyday existence already; rather, these underground expressions are found in spontaneous forms of being-together, forms of communing and celebrating together. They can be seen in the parade, the festival, the crowds milling downtown taking in fireworks displays, cavorting just for the sake of it—just to be together and to celebrate this union. Canada Day, then, is a testament to the inherent energy and vital force of Canadians. One could go so far as to suggest that the crowds of people congregating together to celebrate the state of the nation are not posited on any precise logic of identity. Without any exact goals, they are "networks which have no other goal than of congregating, with no fixed purpose, and which more and more cut across the everyday lives of all collectivities" (Maffesoli 1996, 23). This statement may appear to be cynical. However, given the preceding characterization of Canadian-ness, and the atypical outpouring of emotion that Canada Day elicits, this description may be entirely appropriate.

The fact is that this ongoing union of Canada and the union of Canadians temporarily coming together to celebrate national holidays is both tenuous and contradictory. It is a unity founded on diversity, with diverse elements that do not always fit easily together. Most of the rest of the year, this quest for unity through diversity is troubling. This is not a problem, however, on this day of celebration. National holidays provide Canadians with the foundation for the spectacle of community. A nation of nations expresses itself with Dionysian fervor as people of all shapes, sizes, colors, and creeds commingle with the desire to revel taking precedence over a concern with differences. "The nature of spectacle is to accentuate, either directly or by euphemism, the sensational, tactile dimension of social existence" (Maffesoli 1996, 77).

This atypical aspect of being Canadian is only really seen on its national days, which represent a moment of the carnivalesque, a rupture in the usual state of being. July 1 is a red-letter date, when staid old Ottawa makes a point of shedding its conservative cloak. Downtown streets are blocked off and fill with tens of thousands of people. This is the exact opposite of the usually sedate condition of both Canada and its nation's capital. "In Canada you are reminded of the government every day. It parades itself before you. It is not content to be the servant, but will be the master" (Henry David Thoreau, qtd. in Berton 1982, 11). Canadian national days serve as a reminder of this ever-present condition of sobriety, but also grant the people the opportunity, through the occasion of a giant party, to at least temporarily break free, to express the irrational and the fun, the playful and the emotional.

Indeed, the true spirit of Canada Day on July 1 in Ottawa is not adequately summed up in all of the official events and festivities that are planned for that special day. Their importance recedes when compared to the simple joy of being part of the country's biggest party. As one downtown celebrant noted, "What makes this day is the company you keep and the bar you're at, not the Queen [who was in Ottawa this year]" (Mercer 1997, A1).

It is in the crowd that exists only for the moment, whose vitality is derived from its comminglers, indifferent to difference, that all can come together, celebrate the present, and live for the future. Yet, "the community is characterized less by a project oriented towards the future than by the execution of the 'being-together.' In everyday language, the communal ethic has the simplest of foundations: warmth, companionship—physical contact with one another" (Maffesoli 1996, 16). National days of celebration offer Canadians the chance to be the masters of their own nationality, if only in the moment.

Canada throughout the year is a place for all citizens to exist and express their individuality. But in the effervescent partying of its national days, there is an opportunity to come together in a collective sensibility. Admittedly, this ambience may not be universally felt, but a vision of what it means to be Canadian involves this negotiation of both neutrality and self-expression with collective enthusiasm. It is notable that Canadians, as a whole, only permit themselves such outbursts once a year, and even then are unsure of how strongly such emotions should be expressed. Arguably, then, Canadian national celebrations do not tend toward jingoistic displays of nationalism; rather, the potentially fascistic us-versus-them mentality is accompanied, and possibly overwhelmed, by a love for one's nation and one's fellow citizens.

TOWARD A FURTHER UNDERSTANDING OF CONTESTED, CANADIAN-STYLE CELEBRATION

What is really being discussed is a concept perhaps best labeled "sociality." According to Bauman (1993), "Sociality has no objective, is an instrument of nothing but itself; this is, perhaps, why sociality lives only in fits and starts, in spasms and explosions; it reaches its end the moment it erupts" (129). This mentality is akin to a description of Canada Day celebrations, and in some fashion, to Canadian identity itself. Often understood in opposition to an overly rationalized "social," sociality is not built on a precise identity but "is founded on the fundamental ambiguity of symbolic structuring" (Maffesoli 1996, 95). The ambiguous nature of Canadian nationality and the relative dearth of strong symbols around which all Canadians can gather have already been described here. In truth, most Canadians are not socialized to exhibit strong patriotism. This is true of the 59 percent of Canadians whose mother tongue is English, and true, though perhaps to a lesser extent, to newer citizens and immigrants. The 23 percent of the population whose first language is French and the approximately 3 percent of Canadians who belong to one or more of the three officially recognized aboriginal groups (of this group, 69 percent are North American Indian, 26 percent

Métis, and 5 percent Inuit) are, however, often mobilized in a more overtly patriotic fashion.

Canada's national days of celebration emphasize this contradictory nature of celebration. Though they are three isolated days, they may underscore the following belief of Maffesoli (1996): "Briefly, and taking the terms in their most accepted sense, we can say that we are witnessing the tendency for a rationalized 'social' to be replaced by an empathetic 'sociality', which is expressed by a succession of ambiences, feelings and emotions" (11). For instance, rational attempts to establish national identity, so long ridden by conflict and lack of amenable common vision, take a welcome backseat to the passion that is allowable and freely expressed in national celebrations. In the last twenty years, the notion of Canada as a "community of communities" has been popularized by ex-Prime Minister Joe Clark. In a manner of speaking, this is never more obvious than in Canada Day celebrations. Certainly, "the paroxysm of the carnival, its exacerbated theatricality and tactileness . . . the ground-swell [sic] of the crowd . . . the spectacle . . . the function of communion" (Maffesoli 1996, 77) sums up the reveling of the masses on Parliament Hill on Canada Day, gathered to celebrate anything but the goings-on of Parliament.

Through the gathering together in a crowd, Maffesoli (1996) suggests that "tactile relationships, through successive sedimentations, create a special ambience—what I have called a diffuse union" (73). This union is infused with affections and a spirit of joviality on Canada Day that gives power to the expression "unity through diversity." This is made more than rhetoric, at least on this one day, when a carnival atmosphere takes over the streets of Canada's national capital.

In this communal atmosphere, commingling and carefree merrymaking definitely represent an outbreak of irrationality. Yet, on national holidays, there need be no real rationale for these actions. Nor should one expect a rational explanation for an expression of devotion for one's country or for one's fellow citizens. Dube (1998) notes that even on Canada Day, this enthusiasm is particularly Canadian: Unlike other countries where the national anthem is second nature, Canadian endorsement of national sentiment, even on this national day, is conditional: "The noon celebration concluded with the traditional stumble through 'O Canada'; people's hearts clearly in it but many too shy or too unsure of the words to join in with hearty confidence" (A1).

The significance of this sense of togetherness, then, is not about words. It is not even about history, current events, or hopes for the future. National days are about celebrating people, something Canadians believe in but too rarely have the opportunity to express. Notably, the sociality that is expressed in contemporary celebrations was also evident upon the birth of the Canadian confederation in 1867. For instance, Donald Creighton (1998, A10) describes the commemoration of Canada's first-ever national day, noting that there were banners seen in the eastern region of the country that welcomed the new regime: "Bienvenue a la nouvelle puissance." "The term 'puissance' in French conveys the idea of the inherent energy and vital force of the people, as opposed to the institutions of 'power' ('pouvoir')"

(Maffesoli 1996, 1). So, the banners seen in 1867 did not celebrate a new form of government as much as they celebrated a new community, a new vitality to be found in the aggregation of many different peoples. This vitality—or sociality—is transmitted through the sharing of experience and has an autonomous existence from the state.

In Canada, however, even in the midst of the nation's birthday celebrations, collective ecstasy is a rare commodity with Canadians generally exhibiting a diffident disdain for the showier trappings of patriotism. Canadians arguably define themselves with some amount of pride as quiet and unassuming. That spirit comes through even on days when rowdy behavior is assumed to be triumphant. As proof of this, consider the incident in Vancouver on Canada Day 1998 where a teenager was ticketed for waving a flag and honking his horn. This is just one striking case of how Canadian collective civility trumps individual passions and expressions of national pride. In reducing the fine to a suspended sentence, the judge in the case said that despite the teenager's obvious love for Canada, there is nothing in the city bylaw that allows honking of horns to express patriotism. After reporting on the case, one letter to the editor of *The National Post* reinforced this contradictory message: "There is no need to make noise when expressing pride in Canada. The youngster's patriotism is no acceptable excuse for their wanton behaviour" (Schmid 1999, A21).

Canadians, then, generally exhibit an unforced patriotism, generally accustomed to celebrating the country in an understated fashion, with minimal flag-waving and chest-pounding sentiment. Canadians, overall, exhibit little zeal over being Canadian. Ecstasy is tempered with a widely acknowledged sense of Canadian decorum. Yet, this is not to say that there is no collective joy to be found in celebrating Canadian-ness. One selected letter to the editor of *The Ottawa Citizen* expresses what is assumed to be a typical Canadian attitude, signifying the latent potential for a "we-feeling/puissance" of the masses: "I find patriotic demonstrations mildly embarrassing but I go to Parliament Hill each year on the anniversary of Confederation, not to listen to the bands or the politicians' speeches, but just to mingle for an hour or so with other Canadians" (Marjoribanks 1996, A14). This attitude is not ends oriented, except insofar as one might feel pleasure and simply enjoy being Canadian and celebrating it with fellow Canadians.

THE POLITICS OF NATIONALISM IN
CANADIAN CELEBRATIONS

As indicated, Canadians demonstrate a general reluctance to engage in the pleasure of such wide-scale enthusiastic communing, even on national holidays. This need to curtail collective passions might have something to do with the origins of these anniversaries. Take the nationalist holiday commemorated in Quebec: June 24 was initially the birthday of St. John the Baptist, a prophet chosen as patron saint of the French-Canadian Catholics. Later, the Quebec government declared the St. Jean Baptiste holiday to be the Fête Nationale. A change in outlook was supposed to come with the change of name in which, apart from a celebration of French-Canadian culture, every ethnic group would be welcomed. However, no great event, no popular hero, no founding myth, no unifying principle has been able to get everybody to vibrate as one people. Coincidentally, this is the same sort of identity crisis from which Canada Day suffers. Since 1867, July 1 was always referred to as Dominion Day. This regal sounding title did not refer to Canada's being under the Dominion of Britain but to the new Canadian nation's dominion of the land from one ocean to the next. But even this amount of significance was stripped when, in 1982, it became Canada Day as the prime minister, Pierre Trudeau, without debate and with only 13 members present in the 282-member House of Commons, pushed a bill through Parliament changing the name.

Still, any degree of sentimentalizing over Canada is somewhat suspect. As Robertson Davies (1991) a celebrated Canadian novelist declared, "You don't love Canada; you are a part of Canada and that's that" (302). But Canada Day offers Canadians the once-a-year opportunity to express a love for one's nation. Sometimes, this might even be marred by hostility for other nations that make up the country as a whole. This is to be expected. "It is rare to find a nationalist who can recognize a nationalist of another and hostile nation" (D. W. Brogan, qtd. in Conlogue 1996, 19). Just as these various nations are a part of Canada, these passions are part of what it means to be Canadian. But, of course, this passion also implies conflict. As Maffesoli (1996) reminds us, "The sociality which is being defined integrates a good portion of passionate communication, pleasure in the present and incoherence—all things that are characterized by both acceptance and rejection" (106).

This sociality is not always harmonious. Even on Canada Day, the ever-present nature of conflict can be seen across the country; in 1998, for example, fishermen in the province of Newfoundland flew Canadian flags at half-mast and upside down to protest federal government policies. This is, of course, in addition to the usual scuffles that break out in any large congregation of people celebrating in public. Even in the nation's capital, not to mention more politically fueled ceremonies in the province of Quebec where annual skirmishes are not out of the ordinary, "the 'side-by-side' experience, the living-together and the 'all for one and one for all' can go hand in hand with a 'one against the other'" (Maffesoli 1996, 113). An article in *The Ottawa Citizen* reminds us of this: "Vandals caused about $10,000 in damage to buses, which isn't out of the ordinary for Canada Day. . . . Civility is inversely proportionate to the amount of beer consumed. When you have so many people waiting for buses downtown it can be a zoo" ("Canada Day" 1996, C1).

In the end, "sociality is counter-structural. It is disinterested as opposed to the purposefulness of socialization. Its only mode is the momentary synchronization of sentiments. It is also fragile. Sociality is inherently divisive" (Bauman 1993, 143). So, when the day is over, and all the garbage is picked up, and people go back to their usual daily regimen, these national days should not be seen as providing any real solution to the ongoing problem of nationality in Canada. There may be some repercussions, some latent feelings of neighborliness and goodwill to one's fellow Canadians, just as some conflicts may rear their ugly head and demand to be dealt with. But these days are anomalies. They bundle sentiments in exaggerated, somewhat caricatured form, and project them with enough power for all to see. In essence, Canada's national days are not the truest expressions of Canada's national ways. Without them, however, any vision of what it really means to be Canadian would be hopelessly truncated.

Still, "at the same time as the aspiration, the future and the ideal no longer serve as a glue to hold society together, the ritual, by reinforcing the feeling of belonging, can play this role and thus allow groups to exist" (Maffesoli 1996, 140). But which ritual does one choose to commemorate, if one celebrates nationality within Canada at all? If one lives in Quebec, one has a choice to make: Canada Day, St. Jean Baptiste Day, both, or neither. Whatever choice is made, somebody is going to be unhappy. How communities make this choice is indicative of the sometimes precarious, sometimes confusing ambiguity that marks the occasions. For instance, years ago, Dollard des Ormeaux, a Quebec town, opted—for financial reasons—to celebrate only one of the holidays. For about seven or eight years, the town alternated between celebrating Canada Day one year, St. Jean Baptiste the next. But it was popularly thought that the town was taking sides. So, since 1994, the town has celebrated both holidays on the Saturday between their official dates (Seidman 1998, G4). To some extent, this utilitarian dispensation of a holiday undermines the special quality of both days. In accounting for the underlying importance of pure celebration, though, this continues to express the play-form of sociality. It serves no purpose but to exist for itself and to encourage people to have fun simply for the sake of it.

CONFLICTING CELEBRATIONS: RECOGNIZING AND COMMEMORATING MULTIPLE NATIONALISMS

Unfortunately, vestiges of politics continue to permeate both Canada's national and Quebec's nationalist holidays. But before focusing on the Quebec issue, some mention must be made of a third national day. McRoberts (1997) suggests that Canada is truly a multinational construct that is composed of Quebecois, English Canadians, and First Peoples, all nations within a nation. It is, therefore, perhaps understandable that a separate occasion other than Canada Day or Fête Nationale should be commemorated to recognize this. And indeed, Canada's national celebrations now recognize this tripartite nature. Throughout far too much of Canada's history, its aboriginal peoples have been ignored. However, a proclamation on June 13, 1996, that declared June 21 of every year to be National Aboriginal Day is one step toward redressing this situation. This marks an official government acknowledgment that "the aboriginal people who gave us the keys to Canada found the door closed to them at Confederation." June 21 is also the summer solstice, the longest day of the year, a day with inherent historical meaning for aboriginal culture and heritage. It is, however, not a national holiday in the popularly understood sense of the term, as no one gets a day off from work to commemorate it. Interestingly, the official slogan of National Aboriginal Day is "Share in the Celebration." While this is somewhat consistent with sociality, as it has already been described, it is not, as has been argued, very Canadian, given the Canadian people's presumed reticence to celebrate.

Indeed, the calls for the observance of National Aboriginal Day are wrapped in the auspices of government conciliation, which carry with them laudable centripetal tendencies. But for many, the debate over aboriginal rights is just as explosive an issue as that of language rights. This also means that there is no easy reconciliation of these issues, even though July 21 initiates a special "10-day week" commemorating the rich heritage of Canada's different nations. Simple entreaties to celebrate cannot smother the politics of nationalism within Canada: "Canada Day is a day of mourning, like Oct. 12," says Brian McLeod, senior editor of the magazine *Aboriginal Voices*, referring to Christopher Columbus's landing in North America. "Our traditional governments are in domestic exile and our people are refugees in their own land" (qtd. in White 1997, C1).

Canadians need to recognize each other and engage in discussion with one another if they hope to find new ways of living together as equal nations. And, certainly, one of the means of representing these different ways is through the celebration of various national days. However, the politics of civic nationality too often intrude on the quest to achieve a diverse sense of cultural nationality. Like McRoberts, Saul (1997) suggests that Canada is built on a triangular foundation consisting of three national groups: First Peoples, French, and English. Quebec and the rest of Canada are like Siamese twins, attached but uncomfortable with this nature. Separating them is risky. Still, Canada must accept its unusual collective nature and live with its unique myth.

The difficulty of turning this complexity into strength is evident in the debates over Fête Nationale celebrations. Originally commemorating St. Jean Baptiste, the day is known as a holiday for Francophones, but it is not meant to be just for Francophones anymore. It is meant as a day for all cultures in Quebec to celebrate. Officially, it is a day to put aside the fact that some may be federalists (celebrating the unified nation of Canada) and others may be separatists (seeking an independent nation of Quebec), and to simply celebrate the pride that people have in their nation. Whether this is successful is another question. As some argue, "You can come to the Canada Day parade with any kind of flag and participate, whereas it's taboo to carry a Maple Leaf at a St. Jean Baptiste Day parade" (William Johnson, qtd. in Cherry and Lampert 1998, A1).

William Johnson, in fact, is the leader of an English-rights group within Quebec who feels that Anglophone Quebecers are excluded by Quebec's Fête Nationale. In 1998, his insistence on joining the parade suggested to many of the day's revelers that he was against the very existence of a Francophone people. A recent survey by the Centre for Research and Information on Canada underscores this mentality. It found that a majority of Quebecers think other Canadians see them as inferior. In fact, according to the same survey, the reverse tends to be true (see Hebert 1998, A13). This is, unfortunately, the very opposite of what commentators such as Saul recommend. Of course, the achievement of reveling in each other's strength is easier said than done. In this capacity, the complexity, the cultured diversity of Canada is both a strength and a weakness.

William Johnson did participate in the parade, succeeding in injecting his own brand of diversity into the Fête Nationale celebrations. And, in a suitably Canadian protest, three cream pies were crushed in his face and police eventually escorted him away from the festivities for his own protection. As one protester stated, "It's as if I went to the Canada Day parade and spat on the Canadian flag" (qtd. in Contenta 1998, A1). Obviously, then, the tactile relationships that settle in nationalist crowds are not always passionately inclusive. Even still, this lack of tolerance, and sometimes lack of civility, speak to an enthusiasm and sheer pleasure in communing. As Brownstein (1998) noted, "Funny, but before the [William Johnson] brouhaha, there was nary a hint of politics in the air. Sure, it was too damned hot. But people came to party" (A3). This mix of politics and party (the nonpolitical kind) prompted Lysiane Gagnon to question whether Quebec's national holiday truly is one:

St. Jean must be one or the other, a celebration of the French-Canadian identity, as it is in other provinces, or something else. The French-Canadians of Quebec, being at one and the same time a minority (in Canada) and a majority (in Quebec), oscillate between the two, and the Societe St. Jean Baptiste plays both ends against the middle. Thus, the deep ambiguity of today's celebrations, which is stamped national but feels ethno-cultural. (qtd. in Chambers 1998, B3)

Unity through diversity is an idea that has varying levels of appeal throughout the country. As both an ideal and a practice, it has had repercussions. This ensures that the same criticism levied on the Fête Nationale can be applied to the Canada Day parade. In Montreal, for instance, the 1998 Canada Day parade became the subject of controversy when the city's Canada Day Committee, uncomfortable with the parade's emphasis on unity, granted the parade only $7,500 from its $2.5 million budget. "The parade featured entries from a variety of ethnic groups, from Scots to Pakistanis. But as one spectator wondered: 'It's nice to have all these groups representing countries from all over the world but where is the Francophone Quebecois culture?'" (Carmichael 1998, A7). Reporting on the 1997 Canada Day, the French-language paper Le Devoir noted that the festivities "on the whole made little room for linguistic duality." The headline read "Canada Day . . . English-style."

This, and statements such as the following by the parade organizer, reveal why the 1998 Canada Day parade in Montreal had its funding cut by more than half. "This parade is not only a celebration of this nation's greatness but it also underlies the truth about Canada: that this nation is indivisible, by virtue of constitution, history and practicality" (qtd. in Vu 1998, A3). In most other countries, one might expect this kind of enthusiasm, especially on a day of national celebration. But in the politically charged environment of Quebec, such statements are part of the reason why even the federal government denies financial support for these celebrations. "Quebec's chapter of the Committee for Canada Day sees these comments by the parade's organizer as part of a political agenda which runs contrary to their belief that Canada Day is an apolitical event. It shouldn't be associated with a political movement or party or leader" (Vu 1998, A3). Celebration and politics bleed too easily into each other. This demonstrates why nationalist sentiments, both the cultural and civic varieties, often fit together in an uncomfortable fashion in Canada's national days.

Of course, in the midst of the negotiation of these passions, ambivalence exists alongside celebration, even on Canada's national days. This is indicated by the easily observable phenomenon of more people in Montreal moving from one apartment to another on July 1 than attending any Canada Day parade. July 1 is the day most leases expire in Quebec and has for years been the official Moving Day for the province since 1973. A separatist provincial government seeking to hijack Canada Day festivities did not initiate this move. It was moved from May 1 by an English-friendly Liberal government in order to limit disruption for young students, who were forced to switch schools at the end of the year. Still, "for more than 100,000 Montrealers, as tradition has it, July 1 is Moving Day. It is estimated that 60 per cent [sic] of moves in the city happen on this date, and it can safely be said that they will be going [on] late in[to] the night, long after Ottawa has enjoyed its fireworks" (Leblanc 1998, D3).

CONCLUSION: THE SOMETIMES CONTRADICTORY CELEBRATION OF CANADIAN NATIONHOOD

A certain amount of enthusiasm can be expected of those who make the effort to come together to celebrate Canada's national days. But the fact that many choose to not engage in such behavior should not be a cause for reproach. Part of being a proud Canadian is not shoving this realization down others' throats. One aspect of this is the country's deference for national symbols. Some people choose to fly the Canadian flag, some choose to join in a carnivalesque celebration, and some do not, just as some do not put out Christmas lights in December. Even the fact that crowds swell and streets get congested as people simply mill about on Canada Day hides the ambivalence of the occasion. Prentice (1998) underscores this with the observation that "about 850,000 of the [Ottawa] region's approximately one million residents preferred to stay home, go to the cottage, attend neighbourhood Canada Day celebrations, or find something else to do" (A2).

Interestingly, there is some suggestion that the strength of sentiments and commingling is constant no matter what activity one undertakes on the occasion of a national holiday. However, the anti-means-to-an-end nature of sociality can be seen even in the etymological origins of the day's activities: "In the early 1900s the social event of the year was the community picnic on the First of July. . . . The word picnic comes from the French pique-nique, meaning 'nothing much.' A lot of us will be doing just that on Canada Day and enjoying it immensely" (J. Creighton 1998, F6).

Hopefully, through this discussion of Canada's national days, an (admittedly partial) image of some aspect of what might be said to be "Canadian ways" has been constructed. From this, no giant leap is required to realize that Canadian nationalism is an imagined construct, continually in the process of reconstituting itself. As Anderson (1991) has stated, "It is imagined as a community, because, regardless of the actual inequality and exploitation that may prevail in each, the nation is always conceived as a deep, horizontal comradeship" (7). Yet, the quality of this fraternity, especially in Canada, continues to leave something to be desired. This comradeship is an unfinished project, one that is perhaps destined to remain unfinalized, yet one to which national celebrations certainly contribute.

Canada, then, is a perfect case study in what Bhabha (1990) calls "the impossible unity of the nation as a symbolic force" (1). The nation's symbolism gains force in its representation as a unity. This unity, however, is ultimately impossible precisely because it can only be represented through a suppression, symbolic or otherwise, of difference. Canada, with its celebration of bilingualism and multiculturalism, is an ongoing testament to this conflict. Canada's national (and nationalist) celebrations, struggle, in turn, with this coexistence of multiple cultures.

Canada's national(ist) days act as zones in which citizens can negotiate their Canadian-ness which is not imagined as something fixed and historically given but as something that is in the process of becoming. Combining both separatist and assimilationist tendencies, common identities and differences are melded in the space of the national into an ambience that Canadians reluctantly acknowledge as patriotism. Gellner (1983) argues that "it is nationalism which engenders nations, and not the other way round" (55). If this is the case, the expressions of nationalism evidenced in Canada's national and nationalist days augur a contradictory future for the Canadian nation, a mixture of ambivalence and militant particularisms.

In any event, Canada's national days are causes for celebration. Speaking of 1998's inclement Canada Day weather, Prime Minister Chretien said, "We have to celebrate. The sunshine isn't at the rendezvous, but it's in the hearts of all Canadians" ("Thousands" 1998, A5). However, as with any expression of sociality, there will be conflict. Sunshine will not be present in all of the diverse hearts that might be said to comprise the Canadian nation. But, Canada Day is ostensibly a time to forget the country's mind-numbing constitutional bickering and focus on the values that its citizens have in common. Freedom, civility, social fairness, tolerance, and the love of peace are values that draw us together. They are, however, also points of contention whose distribution is called into question on nationalist celebrations such as the Fête Nationale in Quebec. For instance, a dispute over language rights can call into question the fair treatment and tolerance of minorities as incivility can raise its ugly head even in the midst of celebratory airs. Diversity, part of the social cement that constitutes Canada's nation of nations, also serves to demonstrate how Canada's citizens can be borne apart. The social values that Canadians celebrate, if indifferently, throughout the year come together in its national day(s). These expressions of nationality are, however, anomalies. As such, the vital expression of these values on these days alone cannot be expected to ensure a continued federation of Canadians. Nor can they be said to be the best representation of what it means to be Canadian. However, to discount these national days in any account of Canada's national ways is to ignore a vital aspect of the privileged, contradictory, somewhat ambivalent, but celebrated—and celebratory—nature of Canadian identity.

REFERENCES

Anderson, B. R. O'G. (1991). *Imagined Communities: Reflections on the origin and spread of mationalism.* London: Verso.

Bauman, Z. (1993). *Postmodern ethics.* Oxford, UK: Blackwell.

Berton, P. (1982). *Why we act like Canadians: A personal explanation of our national character.* Toronto: McClelland.

Bhabha, H. K. (1990). *Introduction: Narrating the nation.* In H. Bhabha (Ed.), *Nation and narration,* 1–7. London: Routledge.

Brownstein, B. (1998, June 25). With Pit bill, who needs fireworks? *The Montreal Gazette,* A3.

Buchanan, C. (1996, June 23). Nationalism shows fun side on St-Jean-Baptiste. The Ottawa Citizen, A6.

Canada Day 1995, What a party! (1995, July 2). *The Ottawa Citizen,* A3.

Canada Day: Revellers make buses "a zoo" after fireworks (1995, July 3). *The Ottawa Citizen,* C1.

Carmichael, K. (1998, July 2). A day to celebrate nationhood from Ottawa to Vancouver to Prince Edward Island, come rain or come shine, Canadians love a good party. *The Toronto Star,* A7.

Chambers, G. (1994, July 8). Common traits: The hedging of bets is as Quebecois as it is Canadian. *The Montreal Gazette,* B3.

Chambers, G. (1998, July 3). French press on the march. The Montreal Gazette, B3.

Cherry, P., and Lampert, A. (1998, July 2). Canada's day, rain or shine: Gray skies fail to dampen festivities. *The Montreal Gazette,* A1.

Conlogue, R. (1996). Impossible nation: The longing for homeland in Canada and Quebec. Stratford, ON: Mercury Press.

Contenta, S. (1998, June 25). Top anglo "Pit bill" attacked at march. The Toronto Star, A1.

Corbett, R. (1998, October 14). The fight to fly a Canadian flag: Veteran has been vandalized and now faces possible eviction. *The Ottawa Citizen,* A3.

Creighton, D. (1998, July 1). The first Dominion Day: Historian Donald Creighton describes the first "Canada Day" on July 1, 1867, when the British North American colonies claimed a place among the world's nations. *The Ottawa Citizen,* A10.

Creighton, J. (1998, June 24). Canada Day is picnic day. *The Toronto Star,* F6.

Davies, R. (1991). Murther and walking spirits. Toronto: McClelland.

Dube, F. (1998, July 2). Celebrating with one voice: "Rain or not this is the place to be; It's Canada Day." *The Ottawa Citizen,* A1.

Gardner, D. (1998, July 3). Ignorance wrapped in a flag on Canada Day. *The Ottawa Citizen,* A9.

Gellner, E. (1983). Nations and nationalism. Oxford, UK: Blackwell.

Gordon, C. (1994, July 6). Canadians enjoying without analyzing? How unCanadian. *The Ottawa Citizen,* A13.

Hebert, C. (1998, June 30). So, are Quebecers inferior or superior? *The Ottawa Citizen,* A13.

Henderson, G. (1995, June 30). On guard for thee; Canadians don't wave flags much. But we still love this country. *The Montreal Gazette*, B5.

Ignatieff, M. (1993). Blood and belonging. Toronto: Penguin Books.

Keating, M. (1996). Nations against the state. Houndmills, UK: Macmillan.

Leblanc, D. (1998, July 1). Moving Day in Montreal: Along with the Jazz Festival and Just for Laughs, to Montrealers, moving is an annual rite of summer. *The Ottawa Citizen*, D3.

Maffesoli, M. (1996). *The time of the Tribes: The decline of individualism in mass society*. London: Sage.

Marjoribanks, R. (1996, July 3). Happy day. *The Ottawa Citizen*, A14.

McRoberts, K. (1997). *Misconceiving Canada*. Toronto: Oxford University Press.

Mercer, J. (1997, July 2). Canada's great big party: Muggy weather doesn't slow celebration down. *The Ottawa Citizen*, A1.

Prentice, M. (1998, July 1). Playing the numbers game: Crowd of 200,000 expected to celebrate Canada's birthday. *The Ottawa Citizen*, A2.

Saul, J. R. (1997). *Reflections of a Siamese twin*. Toronto: Viking.

Schmid, H. (1999, February 27). Letters: Flag fracas. *The National Post*, A21.

Seidman, K. (1998, July 2). What flag do you fly at this time of year?: There's simply no winning when it comes to our national and nationalist holidays. *The Montreal Gazette*, G4.

Smith, D. (1998). *Beyond two solitudes*. Halifax, NS: Fernwood.

Thousands gather at Parliament Hill; But Nfld. fishermen take to sea in protest. (1998, July 2). *The Montreal Gazette*, A5.

Verdery, K. (1996). "Whither "nation" and "nationalism"? In G. Balakrishman (Ed.), *Mapping the nation*, 226–34. London: Verso.

Vu, U. (1998, June 26). Fund cuts won't rain on July 1 parade. *The Montreal Gazette*, A3.

White, N. J. (1997, July 1). First Canadians, what does Canada Day mean? For aboriginals it can be a complicated, even painful question. *The Toronto Star*, C1.

CHINA

From National Day to National Way

The Story of October 1

Chen Yanru

On October 1, 1949, China's then paramount leader Mao Zedong mounted the Tian'anmen Building in Beijing and declared to the world the founding of the People's Republic: "The Chinese people have now stood up!" And, thus, October 1 became China's national day.

It was a day that marked the beginning of a new epoch. Ever since its inception, the day has come to be associated with the new identity of the People's Republic of China, and it is celebrated every year. Over time, national day celebrations took on new meaning, starting to reflect on the political and economic condition of the Chinese nation. For example, the first major celebration, which took place in 1959, marking the 10th anniversary of the republic, featured in its Tian'anmen Square procession the agricultural harvest team. In 1961, when the whole nation had been plunged into poverty and deprivation after Mao's inappropriate policy of the Great Leap Forward in economic modernization, the agricultural sector disappeared from the limelight of national day celebrations. During the Cultural Revolution (1966–76), Tian'anmen Square witnessed the Red Guards brandishing "little red books" (quotations from Mao Zedong) and marching through.

With the passing of the residual impact of the Cultural Revolution, China gradually entered a new phase of national development. National day celebrations, which used to serve ideological purposes and were filled with propaganda bombardment at the masses, subtly shifted its focus to promoting the major themes of national development and nation-building. Sure enough, China is an old-enough nation whose people may not need to be told what they are in order for them to function, that is, national identity is not a crisis or an issue. But scholars (Link 1994; Su 1994) have identified major crises in the public's belief in Marxism, their faith in socialism, and their trust in the government. In short, a "point of purchase," which people could hold on to, was deemed lacking in China. As China delved into the market economy, impetuous market forces, newly unleashed, have been tearing at the social fabric of the nation. Repetitive and emphatic calls came from the central government for the forging of a stronger "cohesive force" binding the people together and uniting them for a national goal (Li, 1993, 1994, 1995). It was under such circumstances that a nationwide patriotic education campaign started in early 1993 (Chen 1999). At that time the national *Guideline for Patriotic Education* was still on the drawing board and being deliberated on by the delegates to the National People's Congress (the Chinese equivalent of the U. S. Senate).

Finally, 15 years after the national government shifted its focus from class struggles to the building of a modern nation, in September 1994, the national *Guideline for Patriotic Education* was issued by the Propaganda Department of the Central Committee of the Communist Party. Among other things, it stipulated that important days and festivals such as the national day should be institutionalized occasions for the propagation of patriotism among the population. Ceremonies such as flag raising and the playing of the national anthem were also included in the *Guideline* as instruments of patriotic education. By now the celebration of the national day had become part of the national way—a way in which the party and the government could control the expression and dissemination of patriotic sentiments, a way in which national identity could be mobilized, if we consider Kim and Dittmer's (1993) observation that national identity mobilization is situation specific.

The *Guideline* also specified the main contents/tasks for patriotic education, the main targets (the youth and youngsters), and the building of sites and bases for such education, as well as the creating and fomenting of a social atmosphere conducive to patriotic education. In sum, it was an unprecedented document guiding the implementation of patriotic education at grassroots levels. What impact might it have on national day celebrations?

Most remarkable is that the *Guideline* stipulated that the development policy of the party and the social achievements in national development, especially those during the open and reform era (1978–present), constituted the most important content for patriotic education. National solidarity among different nationalities was another key theme to be promoted in patriotic education. Peaceful reunification between mainland and Taiwan under the one country, two systems scheme was yet another major promotional theme.

NATIONAL DAY CELEBRATIONS AND PATRIOTIC EDUCATION

Celebrative social occasions were the largest unit of analysis in Goffman's (1983) interaction order. Simply defined, they are "gatherings of individuals in honor of some jointly appreciated circumstance where participants arrive and leave in a coordinated way" (8). National day celebrations fit into this category. And as Goffman points out, they can be engineered to extend over a number of days.

Referring back to Dittmer and Kim's (1993) claim that national identity mobilization tends to be situation specific, it follows to observe that national day is such a situation in which national identity tends to be "mobilized"—the masses have a collective chance to "feel" or experience their nation as one. During non-celebrative, mundane days of national life, the prosaic flow of events tend to be taken for granted and not acutely experienced or overtly manifest. Business transactions of various kinds constitute the ordinary national processes in mundane days, but on October 1, the population will be purposely reminded of their membership in the Chinese nation, that China is truly experienced as "China" during the celebration. In the process, the media have no small role to play. The same can be said of the state government. What remains to be found is whether the public also plays a significant and notable role in the celebration, in the joint construction and experience of a "China" that is the product of the celebration.

Approaching the topic at hand from a structural-functionalist perspective, it is apparent that China's national day, an "extra" event added to the mundane national process, has come to be integrated into the larger national process of development. It provides an occasion upon which to observe whether and to what extent the functional components of the nation, that is, the party, the state, the military, and the people, are integrated with each other. Of course, it is most likely that what we observe is the media's projection of such an integrated picture.

Following Doob's (1964) conception of a nation as encompassing land, people, and culture, a nation may be conceptualized as an aggregate of material resources, human resources, and symbolic resources. National identity mobilization is essentially invoking symbolic resources, such as the nation's historical legacy and cultural heritage, to mobilize human resources and in turn maximize the constructive use and exploitation of material resources for the purpose of national development. Here it should be noted that heroes, though part of human resources, once hallowed by the people and endorsed by the state government for their achievements and sacrifices, may well become part of the nation's symbolic resources.

METHODOLOGICAL NOTES

First, a justification is needed for my choice of China's 45th national day celebration for analysis. The national day celebration of 1994 was the first major celebration since 1984 when Deng Xiaoping was at the prime of his political career and reviewed the army, as well as the first national day celebration after the *Guideline for Patriotic Education* went into effect. Marking the 45th anniversary of the People's Republic, it surpassed the celebration of the 40th anniversary in 1989 in terms of grandness, because the latter had come right after the June 4 Incident and was simply glossed over.

Relevant news items broadcast by China Central Television Station (CCTV) during the festive period are used as the main source of information to build the analysis. This selection is justified on the grounds of the impact of CCTV news. Primetime CCTV news is watched by more than 80 percent of the Chinese population, the program commanding the largest audience in China. Moreover, it is under the control of the state government and represents the official voices in China, which is exactly what this study will examine; specifically, I will address the following question: How do the state government and the media act hand in hand to enhance the way in which an originally ritualistic national day celebration serves the purpose of patriotic education for national development?

The analysis of the 1994 national day celebration will incorporate insights from the themes of patriotic education that I discussed earlier. It combines two parts: the first dealing with the activities preceding the national day celebration and the second analyzing the celebration.

THE ANALYSIS

National day celebrations in China are more than one-day fairs. They are a holiday season, before the arrival of which a national atmosphere is fomented through the media and other promotional activities to surround the nation with a festive air. During such preparatory stages, the key themes of celebration usually emerge from the activities. For example, "in September 1994, an ad hoc committee was formed under the central government to coordinate the celebration. The main tone of the occasion was set to be 'solemn, passionate, and simple'" (CCTV news, September 22, 1994).

A day later, the Propaganda Department of the Party's Central Committee hosted a reception as part of the national day celebration, which congregated the top echelon of party and state leaders for a talk by the party's general secretary Jiang Zemin on the guiding policy for propaganda workers. He elaborated on the following four principles of propaganda work: equip people with scientific theories, guide people with correct opinions, mold people with lofty spirits, and encourage people with quality works. This celebrative occasion was turned into an occasion serving the party's propaganda purposes. Even the artistic performances featured the patriotic theme. The occasion concluded with a familiar song calling for national unity, "Solidarity Is Power." (CCTV news, September 23, 1994)

In addition to national identity mobilization, the national day celebration of 1994 was also an occasion on which to display evidence of national strength. Shortly before October 1, a grand exhibition featuring achievements in China's social development was organized in Beijing. National leaders visited the show with their endorsement of the accomplishments of economic construction and nation-building, and one of the vice premiers of the State Council observed that "people's lives have undergone profound changes" (CCTV news, September 24, 1994). The exhibition brought together the effort of the National Planning Committee, 24 ministries and commissions, and the 30 provinces on the Chinese mainland (CCTV news, September 26, 1994). It will not be an overstatement to say that such a scheme of events contributed positively to national integration and constituted one major way of the production of knowledge about the nation—part of patriotic education. In this knowledge production process, the government, the media (exhibits), and the public jointly produced a picture of national pride and national confidence. The leaders and the public, by viewing and reacting to the exhibitions, actually formed new knowledge about how people felt toward their nation.

The news media joined the rank of propagandists to highlight national strength. As part of the celebration, CCTV news (September 27, 1994) reported that before the national day celebration, both supply and demand in various markets were prosperous all over the country. This item of news, though quite routine, confirms the observation that national day celebrations reflect on the economic conditions of the nation: "Heroes and role models as representatives of the nation's population were not to be forgotten for the occasion. Some 150 heroes from the People's Liberation Army gathered in Beijing for the national day celebration" (CCTV news, September 28, 1994). Their stories of personal sacrifice for the greater goal constituted part of the nation's symbolic resources to be invoked to mobilize the nation's human resources to best utilize the nation's material resources for national development.

Like other national holidays, the 1994 celebration exuded a sense of all-inclusiveness in its preparation and celebration. The *Guideline for Patriotic Education* emphasized the importance of forging a stronger link and establishing a better understanding between various nationalities. In September 1994, the State Council's Second Meeting on National Solidarity and Progress was convened in Beijing. Members representing all minority nationalities were in attendance. The top national leaders were also present. Following the playing of the national anthem, Jiang Zemin gave a speech saluting the nationalities for their achievements in and contributions to nation-building. He said that the grand gathering symbolized solidarity, and the revival of the Chinese nation was the shared task of all nationalities in China. Premier Li Peng followed up in his speech by further integrating the minority nationalities into the big national "family." With a review of the major achievements in the preceding 45 years, he stated that the People's Republic was the joint product of all the Chinese peoples, and that the economic development of the minority regions was part of the national development. National solidarity and unity was hailed as the supreme interest of the Chinese nation and people. Patriotism was again upheld as the banner over all nationalities in a united China (CCTV news, September 29, 1994).

The National People's Political Consultative Conference (CPPCC) and the Central United Front Department, both of which were in charge of noncommunist parties in China, were also brought to the forefront of the occasion. They jointly hosted a national day reception, which featured the presence of the CPPCC chairman Li Ruihuan. The keynote speech by Vice Chairman of the CPPCC Ye Xuanping emphasized that the unity and prosperity of China was the common wish of the Chinese peoples, who now shared a common destiny and mission (CCTV news, September 29, 1994). Likewise, the National People's Congress, together with the CPPCC and the Overseas Chinese Affairs Office, hosted another reception for the overseas Chinese (CCTV news, September 29, 1994). This was another piece of evidence of the all-inclusiveness of the national "family" the Chinese government and the media attempted to project upon the occasion.

Upon the arrival of this national holiday, the national atmosphere was being fomented through media features and mass activities that a sense of peace and festivity permeated the air. The grand reception in celebration of the national day, organized by the state government, was held on September 30, 1994. Premier Li Peng greeted all the guests and extended his thanks to China's international friends who had been supportive of China's nation-building efforts. Not surprisingly, these remarks were followed by a brief review of the achievements during the preceding 45 years under the leadership of the Communist Party. New progress was promised, and Taiwan being an integral part of the Chinese nation was again brought up as a key issue on which the government's firm stance for reunion was not to be shaken. Li continued to say that regardless of all setbacks, China will resume sovereignty over Hong Kong in due time (CCTV news, September 30, 1994).

Meanwhile, news reports in the national media further fomented the atmosphere by featuring that the capital of China, Beijing, had become an ocean of flowers, fountains, and flags, all ushering in the national festival (CCTV news, September 29 and 30, 1994).

The national day celebration itself turned out to feature the following dimensions of an integrated national family. First, a sense of *connectedness* across the nation emerged from media reports. Upon the arrival of the national day, "when dawn descended upon the sleeping earth, red flags were raised" (CCTV news, October 1, 1994). And CCTV news reports of the day featured flag-raising ceremonies in different parts of and cities all over China. Youngsters were shown lining up to salute the flag and listen to the national anthem. Guangdong Province, Hainan Province, Fujian Province, Guangxi Province . . . one after another regions of the nation, which were otherwise not related in news reports in mundane days, now shared in the celebration of the national day with their similar activities such as flag raising and anthem playing. Thus, the nation became "connected" for the celebrative occasion. A sense of concerted action surfaced from the ocean of facts about celebration. It was a collective experience of the nation.

Next, a strong sense of *togetherness* was also present in the national celebration. At dawn on October 1, in Tian'anmen Square, 400,000 members of the masses joined the heroic soldiers representing the army and model workers representing laborers, as well as foreign friends, for celebrative activities (CCTV news, October 1, 1994). It must be noted that the number of participants had been preplanned by the ad hoc organizing committee.

The evening of October 1 witnessed another celebrative occasion that illustrated the togetherness of the nation. An organized fun fare in Tian'anmen Square gathered more than 100,000 participants. The square became a grand stage on which a festive evening unfolded. People were dressed in festive costumes, and an atmosphere of "peace and prosperity" hovered above the square. The colorful fireworks were unprecedented in scale and duration since the founding of the People's Republic. The square was divided into eight parts gathering workers, farmers, soldiers, students, cadres, and others. There were 1,800 actors and actresses who participated in artistic performances in the open air. Even representatives from Hong Kong, Macao, and Tibet were included. Members of the Politburo, the top echelon of China's national leaders, met with the participants. Those from Tibet presented the white *hada* (silk band) as a salutation to the party's general secretary Jiang Zemin (CCTV news, October 2, 1994).

The celebrative season also assembled artistic performances together. Stage dramas and other artistic performances, which would otherwise only be staged locally, were now congregated in their presentation on the stage in Beijing. More than 50 dramas were presented, including those from the past revolutionary base areas that had once cradled the revolution leading to the founding of the People's Republic. The General Politics Department of the People's Liberation Army hosted a song and dance party entitled "Our Nation in My Heart," and the military leaders attended the show (CCTV news, October 2, 1994). All the performances featured the patriotic theme, albeit from different angles.

Oneness of the nation between the leaders and the led, as well as that between different parts of the nation, was another sense evident in the data. During mundane days, such oneness may not be as manifest, for the structural components of the nation may not be as engaged in such highly visible, intensive, and concentrated activities. At the national day fun fare in the Working People's Cultural Palace in Beijing, national leaders joined visitors to view the exhibitions entitled "Towards the New Century," which reflected social and economic development in various parts of the nation. During his tour of the Beihai Park gala party, Vice Premier Zhu Rongji stopped before the model of the Three Gorge Dam project and inquired after the resettlement of the immigrants who had to move away from their original homes to make room for the project. At Tiantan Park, the theme featured for celebration was "Culture of the Yellow River." The achievements in economic development in the provinces along the Yellow River were highlighted. Politburo members Liu Huaqing and Hu Jintao arrived at the site just in time to see the grand dragons displayed in the giant hall of exhibition. The dragons were said to symbolize the accomplishments of the open and reform policy, which had led to the economic takeoff of the nation (CCTV news, October 1, 1994). An overall picture projected of the nation was that the leaders shared in the joy of the occasion.

All-inclusiveness of the celebration should refer to the inclusion of Hong Kong and Macao compatriots and other Chinese nationals overseas. On the eve of October 1, the Hong Kong branch of Xinhua News Agency (China's national news agency) hosted a reception attended by representatives from the compatriots, including leading businessmen. The mainland director of the agency announced that the resuming of sovereignty over Hong Kong would be a great event, and that the

Hong Kong compatriots were enthusiastic about the prospect of reunification with the mainland. Likewise, a cocktail party given by the head of the Macao branch of Xinhua News Agency was attended by more than 1,000 people from Macao, and the director expressed strong faith in the one country, two systems policy for the future of Macao (CCTV news, October 1, 1994).

Apart from the officially organized activities, the Chinese people in Hong Kong and Macao had celebrations of their own. At the Hong Kong Stadium, 1,000 singers presented a chorus "Ode to the Motherland." Mainland artists also joined the performance. In Macao, after a display of fireworks, leading businessman Ma Wanqi addressed an assembly of Chinese: "We breathe with our motherland and share in her destiny. Everywhere we experience the care and support of our nation." As evening drew nigh, celebration escalated (CCTV news, October 2, 1994).

Even the Chinese athletes in Japan who were participating in the Asian Games held there were not left out. In the Asian Games Village, at dawn, 100 choice athletes took part in the flag-raising ceremony in celebration of the national day. The head of the delegation spoke on their behalf: "We shoulder a grand commission from our home country, and we shall strive for her glory" (CCTV news, October 1, 1994).

Coherence in media presentation and interpretation of the national day celebration was another dimension in the integrated picture of the nation as a family. It refers to the media's effort in interpreting all the relevant events in the light of the key theme of celebration. It was at this point that the significance of the celebrative activities converged with patriotic education. On October 1, 1994, pupils attending the flag-raising ceremony in Tian'anmen Square for the national day celebration were quoted as saying that watching the ceremony deepened their patriotic sentiment and was a very significant event rich in meaning. A participant in the ceremony who had spent more than eight years abroad said, "I am excited to see the great change that has taken place in China." An old man born during the Qing Dynasty who had witnessed China's older days when only foreign flags were featured in public places expressed his excitement to see the five-star red flag now fluttering in China's sky (CCTV news, October 1, 1994). In such quotes the patriotic keynote was struck, which was the essence of the occasion.

When interviewed by a television reporter, a textile worker said, "We are happy and proud of our nation." Farmers lauded the party and the state government for the improvement in the quality of their life. A student of the Yi minority nationality wished for greater solidarity and prosperity of the nation. In a summary, the CCTV news reports thus provided coherence to the interpretation of the aforementioned public responses to the celebration:

This is an unforgettable night, a historic night. We no longer suffer from the wandering of the past, nor do we feel perplexed about our future. We are full of faith and hope and strength that equal heaven and earth combined. The great PRC [People's Republic of China] spends her holiday in songs of praise. (CCTV news, October 2, 1994)

Patriotic education features many themes, one of which is the fostering of a sense of national pride. In view of the century of humiliation in foreign hands (1840–1949), the achievements of the People's Republic (1949–present) were to be widely promoted among the population to arouse a sense of pride in their own nation.

Echoing this call, CCTV primetime newscasts presented a series of reports on "Strides of the Republic," highlighting the major achievements in various trades and professions. The series began on September 19, 1994, and continued into October. To the government officials, patriotic education was regarded as a propeller for people's participation in the construction of the new nation, and it must stimulate the faith of the people in the future of the nation (CCTV news, September 19, 1994). Grasping this essence, the serial reports formed its unique format. A comparison of facts and figures from the pre-Republic days with those of the present constituted the main part of the news features. From the days when there were no roads linking the mountainous regions and the outside world, no electricity in the villages, and no telephone communication, to the present prosperous condition of well-equipped and well-connected villages, thus was the great change in people's lives, and the giant stride of the Republic.

Improvement in space technology (CCTV news, September 23, 1994), modernization of the military (CCTV news, September 24, 1994), transprovincial roads (CCTV news, September 25, 1994), economic development in the outlying regions (CCTV news, September 27, 1994), emancipated farmers who have now prospered in rural township enterprises (CCTV news, September 30, 1994), the development in television industry (CCTV news, October 1, 1994), the rising electronics industry (CCTV news, October 2, 1994), through interpretation by the national media, these miraculous achievements were ascribed to the ruling party and the state government's effective policies, and one of the main themes of patriotic education—love for the socialist nation, thus emerged from the reports. Perhaps one example from the reports—"Strides of the Republic" for the Power Industry—can provide a more concrete illustration of the point:

On September 5, 1994, the last county in Shandong Province was linked up to supply of electricity. An 85-year-old man said, "The nation is good. Now I have no regrets even if I die, for I have seen the light." What their generation did not dare to dream of has now become reality. . . . Shi Dazhen, minister of the Power Industry, says that by the year 2000[,] 95 percent of the villages in China will be linked up to electricity. (CCTV news, October 3, 1994)

DISCUSSION AND CONCLUSIONS

Based on the analysis presented, it is fair to observe that the picture of an effective government and a satisfied public was projected through the media on the occasion. Although the Chinese media are enjoying increasing autonomy in a market economy (Hao and Huang 1996), on important occasions and crucial matters such as national day celebrations and patriotic education, the media still acted closely in line with the state. Moreover, the frequent presence of the state leaders in all of the celebratory activities formed a standard diet of news in the media. Overall, the government played a larger role in the shaping of the contour of an integrated China of which the public was supposed to be proud. The public's role in the activities was mostly an organized role, that is, what they did more or less fell under the organizing work of the celebration committee.

Following the *Guideline for Patriotic Education*, national day celebrations became institutionalized as an instrument of patriotic education. In fact, they were invoked as part of the nation's symbolic resources to mobilize the human resources. The proud, confident statements about the Chinese nation made by the people interviewed by the media in Tian'anmen Square on October 1, 1994, should be taken in part as evidence of the mobilizing effect. It was a moment when a sense of personal membership in the nation was acutely experienced by every participant in the activities, and through the media's reporting and interpretation, such a sense was shared across the entire nation.

Definitions of patriotism may vary from scholar to scholar, yet, fundamentally, a workable definition is universal: patriotism is love for one's home country. It should be distinguished from nationalism in that the latter has a "we versus they" mentality and often involves conflict and adverse emotions toward foreign countries. The *Guideline* made this useful and careful distinction, drawing the line between the two. The principle underlying the mechanism of the fostering of patriotism is this: people must have more knowledge about their nation first, and then they will know better how to love their nation and take pride in their nation, and with an increased national self-confidence, the people can be better builders of the nation. Following this logic, the national day celebration of 1994 involved the joint efforts of the media and the government in disseminating information about the swift development of the nation during the reform decades. Serial reports by CCTV news on "Strides of the Republic" are such an example. In other words, the national day in current China is no longer merely a day of celebration, it has become part of the national way of patriotic education. This point has been noted in this chapter but it needs to be emphasized again.

Of course, the widely perceived need to forge a stronger cohesive force binding the nation together was not to be met with national day celebration alone. The entire campaign/program of patriotic education was meant to be carried out on a long-term basis, all the way into the next century. However, the national day celebration of 1994 made its due contribution to the integration of the nation, in the following senses.

The celebration occasioned the state leaders' emphatic call for national unity and solidarity between different nationalities. And the occasion did congregate delegates from the different nationalities all over China, fomenting an atmosphere of national unity. The inclusion of compatriots from Hong Kong and Macao in the celebrative activities was another effort to project a picture of unity.

The many large-scale exhibitions of the achievements in China's socioeconomic development may be taken as, in part, an echo to the *Guideline*'s call for educating the public with the progress of the nation under the direction of the party and the state government. Ultimately, patriotism in the current Chinese context encompasses mainly love for the nation, that is, the state government and the people. So, a sense of identification with the state's interest in building socialism with Chinese characteristics under the guidance of Deng Xiaoping's theory is a must. It is sensible, though, to remind ourselves that the people in the market economy context have become more pragmatic (Chen 1999) and may be far more concerned about the balance in their bank accounts than about the macro issues of theory and ideology. To an average adult in the Chinese city today, the abundance in the supply of goods during national day seasons may be more indicative of national prosperity than the national symbols.

Here, we come to the topic of national economic prosperity. It was indeed one of the key themes featured at the 1994 celebration. But prosperity is not the whole story. The spiritual integration of the nation, as indicated, in a strong cohesive force holding all the people together seemed to be the overall image projected by the government through the national media all the time during the celebration. The analysis in this chapter cogently conceptualized such integration into five dimensions: connectedness, togetherness, oneness, all-inclusiveness, and coherence.

In sum, national day celebrations in China, once combined with patriotic education, became a joint process of conscious production of knowledge about the nation in which the state government, the media, and the public all played a part. Continuous interaction between the state, the media, and the public under the key theme of patriotic education continuously generated new knowledge as to the collective construction of "nation" that was collectively experienced during the celebration.

As this chapter was nearing completion, news has just been released regarding the upcoming celebration of China's 50th national day. The organizing committee announced that it would be solemn and warm, of appropriate scale, with an emphasis on the actual effect. It is set to display the profound social changes since the founding of the People's Republic, especially the changes that have taken place since the beginning of the reform era. Moreover, it will display the stable political situation around the nation, swift economic development, national solidarity, social progress, and improved international status of the nation, as well as the collective striving of the people toward the new century. The celebration will further revitalize the national spirit and stimulate the party, the state, the military, and the people to embark on the endeavor of building socialism with Chinese characteristics (*Guangming Daily*, April 13, 1999).

The celebration of national day in 1994, though smaller in scale compared with the one currently planned and announced, is nonetheless an epitome of such an all-around celebration with a clear purpose for nation-building.

REFERENCES

Chen, Y. (1999). *Reviving the national soul: Communications and national integration in China's market economy era*. Unpublished doctoral dissertation, Nanyang Technological University, Singapore.

Dittmer, L., and Kim, S. S. (1993). In search of a theory of national identity. In L. Dittmer and S. S. Kim (Eds.), China's quest for national identity, 1–31. Ithaca, NY: Cornell University Press.

Doob, L. W. (1964). *Patriotism and nationalism: Their psychological foundations.* New Haven, CT: Yale University Press.

Goffman, E. (1983). The interaction order. *American Sociological Review, 48*(1), 1–17.

Hao, X. M., and Huang, Y. (1996, June 1–3). *Commercialization of China's broadcast media.* Paper presented to the Asia Media Information and Communication Center (AMIC) Silver Jubilee Conference, Singapore.

Kim, S. S., and Dittmer, L. (1993). Whither China's quest for national identity? In L. Dittmer and S. S. Kim (Eds.), *China's quest for national identity.* 237–289. Ithaca, NY: Cornell University Press.

Li, P. (1993). Report on government work. Beijing: People's Publishing House.

Li, P. (1994). Report on government work. Beijing: People's Publishing House.

Li, P. (1995). Report on government work. Beijing: People's Publishing House.

Link, P. (1994). China's "core" problem. In W. M. Tu (Ed.), China in *transformation*, 189–205. Cambridge, MA: Harvard University Press.

Propaganda Department, Chinese Communist Party Central Committee. (1994). *Guideline for Patriotic Education.* Beijing: Author.

Su, S. Z. (1994). Chinese communist ideology and media control. In C. C. Lee (Ed.), *China's media, media's China*, 75–88. Boulder, CO: Westview Press.

CHINA

National Image on National Day and Patriotic Education in China

The 50th National Day of the People's Republic of China

Xu Xiaoge

National day celebrations are often designed for patriotic education and nation-building. The national image presented on that day plays an important role because a national image can form attitudes, affect decisions, influence policies and move a whole society (Boulding 1956).

As previous studies show (Dennis, Gerbner, and Zassoursky, 1991; Farmer, 1990; Hart, 1966; Hopple, 1982; Lent, 1977; McNelly, 1979; Perry, 1987; Potter, 1987; Semmel, 1977), a national image can be displayed or shaped by various media, such as newspapers, magazines, radio, and television. Nevertheless, a national day parade and national day speeches—image makers, by default—can play a large role in displaying or shaping a national image. Few studies, however, have been conducted to explore a national image presented on the national day.

By analyzing the celebration of the 50th anniversary of the founding of the People's Republic of China (PRC) on October 1, 1999, this chapter explores some China's ways of presenting a national image through its national day parade and speeches.

BACKGROUND

The People's Republic of China was founded on October 1, 1949. Between 1950 and 1959, China held an annual national day parade. In September 1960, however, the Chinese government decided to hold a small-scale national day celebration without a parade in the 5th year of each decade and a large-scale national day celebration with a parade in the 10th year of each decade. Yet, China did not hold any national day parade for 24 years, because of the Cultural Revolution (1966–76, a decade of internal turmoil).[1] Afterward, following the recovery period (1976–84), it had the 12th national day parade on its 35th national day, in 1984. Since then, no military or civilian parade had been held in China's national day celebration until the 50th national day in 1999 (Xinhua News Agency 1999).

National day in China is more than a celebration. It is designed to reflect the cohesion of the nation, to show the ability of the government to mobilize its people, and to indicate the nation's strength to the outside world. It has been institutionalized as an outlet not only for patriotic education but also for a grand display of the national image to the Chinese people both at home and abroad as well as to the rest of the world.

Therefore, it is important to understand the national image of China in order to understand its policies, decisions, and social movements. It is also important to understand the Chinese ways of presenting a national image, since such an understanding will contribute to knowledge of the image-making process in the Chinese context.

NATIONAL IMAGE ON NATIONAL DAY, 1999

Around 10 o'clock on the morning of October 1, 1999, a 50-gun salute echoed over Tian'anmen Square, launching the grand celebration of the 50th anniversary of the founding of the People's Republic of China. Accompanying that, 200 flag guards in olive-green suits marched across a 260-meter red carpet stretching north of the platform of the Monument to the Memory of the People's Heroes through the square. As the Chinese national anthem played, China's red flag, adorned with its five stars, rose up the 30-meter flagpole, surrounded by 500,000 participants for the celebration.[2]

The flag-hoisting ceremony was followed by a parade, the grandest among all the previous celebrations. The grandness of this 13th national day parade was manifested by 100 square formations accompanied by 90 colorful floats illustrating China's achievements over the past five decades, and huge portraits of the late Chinese leaders Mao Zedong and Deng Xiaoping and the present Chinese top leader Jiang Zemin. The parade was held against a background setting formed by 100,000 primary and middle school students, each holding a colored poster that formed the giant Chinese characters "Guo Qing" (National Day Celebration) in the square, facing the Tian'anmen Rostrum.

The 13th national day parade consisted of two parts: a military parade and a civilian parade. It started with the military parade in 42 formations, composed of the People's Liberation Army three services: armed police, army reserves, and militia. The military parade involved 11,000 military personnel, in 17 ground phalanxes and 25 vehicle formations, and 10 echelons consisting of 132 warplanes. It is claimed that the military parade displayed the latest and the most advanced weaponry of the country, including long-range, ground-to-ground missiles and aerial tankers (Xinhua News Agency 1999). The military parade also displayed special armed forces not seen in the previous parades: the Chinese People's Liberation Army reserves, a type of backup force founded in 1983, which can be quickly turned into an army when a war breaks out. They also include the special and quick-response police, generally off-limits to the public, who counter hijacking and terrorism, curb violent crimes, and safeguard national security and social stability. Their debut was also joined by the marine corps, which was founded in 1980 and is composed of infantry, artillery force, armored units, engineering corps, antichemical corps, a signal force, an antitank missile unit, and an amphibious scouts unit. With its multiple fighting techniques, the marine corps is known as "tiger on the land, dragon in the sea, hawk in the air" (Xinhua News Agency 1999).

While the military parade displayed the military strength of the nation, the civilian parade demonstrated the achievements of the industries of transportation, steel and iron, space, information, energy, and machinery over the past five decades. The civilian parade was divided into 38 square formations of colorful floats and people from all walks of life, marching past the Tian'anmen Rostrum. They were divided into three sections, representing the periods led by Mao Zedong (1893–1976), Deng Xiaoping (1905–96) and Jiang Zemin (1926–).

The first section focused on the efforts of the Chinese people under Mao Zedong in fighting for a new China: the creation of the PRC, the rejoicing of the Chinese people after the founding of the PRC, and their efforts in building a new China. The first section proceeded to the strains of the song "There Would Be No New China without the Communist Party," praising the immortal contributions of the first generation of central leadership with Mao Zedong at the core.

The floats displayed how the Chinese Communist Party led the Chinese people in fighting to win national independence and the people's liberation, including the well-known Long March in the 1930s, the War of Resistance Against Japan in 1937–45, and the war against the Kuomintang troops between 1945 and 1949. The floats also showed that since the founding of the PRC, under the leadership of the first generation of party leaders, China provided ample food for the world's largest population, conducted nuclear tests, launched man-made satellites, and built big oil fields. The first section of the civilian parade ended with traditional lion and dragon dances, symbolizing that China—the "Oriental Lion"—had awakened and that the Chinese nation had started striding forward (Xinhua News Agency 1999).

The second section displayed achievements during the 18-year reform and open period (1978–96) under the leadership of Deng Xiaoping. It was led by a float with a huge portrait of the late Chinese leader, who is considered the architect of the reform and opening up that began in 1979. The floats displayed achievements in different industries, ranging from energy to electronics with some huge models and sculptures, including nuclear power stations; the Three Gorges Dam; satellites, highways, and modern residential quarters—all showing that the people's quality of life has improved and that China is catching up with or surpassing developed countries in many areas. Slogans were chanted during the parade that called for holding high the great banner of Deng Xiaoping's theory and pushing forward the building of socialism with Chinese characteristics into the 21st century. The parade also exhibited the country's progress in the reunification of the motherland, with three floats representing the Hong Kong Special Administrative Region, Macao, and Taiwan (Xinhua News Agency 1999).

The third section expressed the confidence of the Chinese people toward the next millennium under the leadership of Jiang Zemin. It also showed the mission of the country in unifying all ethnic groups and reunifying the motherland as well as the objectives and tasks in the new century.

That confidence was also displayed by some 4,400 representatives from state-owned enterprises, who marched past Tian'anmen Square to the music "We Workers Have Great Power." It was taken to be an indication of the recovering might of the struggling state sector as well as an indication of China's efforts to re-structure its state-owned enterprises so as to revitalize this pillar of China's economy (Xinhua News Agency 1999).

What is worth noting is that China has attached great importance to science, technology, and education, as shown by the float displaying the words "Revitaliz-ing China through Science, Technology and Education" and "Science and Technology are the Primary Productive Force." Some slogans such as "Value knowl-edge, respect talented people, be bold in making innovations and revitalize the nation through science, technology and education!" were chanted by the students along the parade route (Xinhua News Agency 1999).

Dressed in colorful ethnic costumes, some 1,000 paraders representing China's 55 minority nationalities also participated in the civilian parade, presenting an image of ethnic representation and racial harmony. The parade ended with a model of a manned spacecraft gliding past the square in a float, indicating that China has entered a countdown for the take-off of the 21st century. After the spacecraft glided through the square, 50,000 homing pigeons were released into the sky along with tens of thousands of balloons. Shouting for joy and waving their hands, 10,000 cheering children on the square surged toward the Golden Water Bridge right below the Tian'anmen Rostrum, pushing the national day parade to its climax.

The celebration of the 50th anniversary of the People's Republic of China was not only grand but also important, offering a chance for the Chinese government to show the rest of the world what is has achieved in the past 50 years and where it will lead China in the next 50 years. This importance brought more than 1,800 do-mestic and foreign journalists to the square to cover the grand celebration. Among them, some 850 were mainland journalists; 221 were from the Hong Kong Special Administrative Region, Macao, and Taiwan; and the rest, more than 730, were for-eign journalists.

The national image displayed by the parade has its footnotes in the speeches delivered by Premier Zhu Rongji and President Jiang Zeming at the national day eve reception and the national day rally, respectively. On the eve of the 50th national day, Premier Zhu spoke at a reception attended by some 5,000 people at the Great Hall of the People, the Chinese parliament. He attributed the enormous achieve-ments that the Chinese people have scored in the 50 years since the founding of new

China to "the great, glorious and correct Communist Party of China, to the hard-working, brave and talented people of China and to the superior socialist system" (Xinhua News Agency 1999).

The premier depicted his country as "a great country which is thriving and growing with each passing day," standing "rock firm in the east of the world," and enjoying "an ever rising international standing," and with "friends all over the world." This national image is shaped after "hav[ing] never wavered in pursuing an independent foreign policy of peace and safeguarding state sovereignty, territorial integrity and national dignity and ha[ving] stood the severe tests of changes in the international situation" (Xinhua News Agency 1999).

Zhu reiterated the importance of stability in China when he told the reception that nothing could be achieved without stability and that the hard-won situation of unity and stability should be highly valued. He also urged that the interaction among reform, development, and stability should be properly managed (Xinhua News Agency 1999). As far as the Taiwan issue is concerned, Zhu told the reception that the Chinese government is engaged in a campaign against Lee Teng-hui's "two states theory" and for state sovereignty and territorial integrity in full accord with the fundamental interests of the Chinese nation. He reiterated his government's basic policy of "peaceful reunification, and one country, two systems" and President Jiang Zemin's eight-point proposal on the development of the cross-straits relations and the advancement of the process of peaceful reunification of the motherland (Xinhua News Agency 1999).

In his speech to the celebration rally on the national day, Chinese President Jiang Zemin stated, "Socialism is the only way to save and develop China," and "building socialism with Chinese characteristics is a broad road to economic prosperity and all-round social progress in China" (Xinhua News Agency 1999). For more than 5,000 years, "the Chinese nation has, with its own wisdom, ingenuity and outstanding creativeness, made indelible contribution[s] to world civilization. In the new millennium, it will contribute even more to world civilization with splendid new achievements," Jiang told the rally (Xinhua News Agency 1999).

Jiang reiterated that his party's basic theory, basic line, and basic program should be adhered to in order to achieve fresh successes in building socialism with Chinese characteristics in the coming new century by virtue of the strength of the people of all ethnic groups in China.

The national image presented by the national day parade and the national day speeches can be summarized as follows. The People's Republic of China has become increasingly powerful in terms of military strength. It can defend itself in times of war and can protect its national sovereignty and integrity. In addition to its military strength, China has also become increasingly stronger after many great achievements over the past 50 years. It has maintained its social stability and solidarity of all ethnic groups. Furthermore, China is determined to reunify the country. As displayed by the end of the national day parade, China is confident in the next 50 years, in the new millennium, that it is moving on the right track.

NATIONAL IMAGE PRESENTATION: THE CHINESE WAY

A national image has always been an important agenda for the Chinese and its government, especially on national day, which has been institutionalized in China as an important outlet to display its national image. For every small-scale national day celebration in the 5th year of a decade, or a grand one in the 10th, an ad hoc committee is set up under the central government. It is designed to organize or co-ordinate the celebration activities to make sure that everything stays in line with what the central government expects.

For the 50th national day celebration, preparations lasted more than 17 months. That preparation could be divided into three periods. During the first period, from May through August 1998, an organizing committee was formed with eight departments in charge of organizing and coordinating security, propaganda, reporting, arts and culture, exhibitions, foreign affairs, and logistics. While the committee designed the overall plan for the 50th national day celebration during this period, the general plan was approved by the central government before it was implemented in the second period, from August 1998 through March 1999. During the third period, from March through August 1999, basic training was conducted among the 140,000 paraders, 100,000 gala participants, and 100,000 participants who formed 22 kinds of gigantic backgrounds in the Tian'anmen Square with 23 props.

In a nationwide circular, the committee announced that the celebration should be solemn and warm, of appropriate scale, and cost-effective, and with an emphasis on good results. In line with this directive, all the planned celebration activities were scrutinized and approved before they were held throughout the country. To display its national image, China took full advantage of the national day parade to demonstrate its military strength, great achievements, social stability, economic growth, and determination to reunify the country.

The military parade is a centuries-old ceremony in China. The first military parade in China can be traced as far back as more than 4,000 years ago, when Yu, chief of a Chinese tribe in northern China, hosted a gathering in central China of tribes from southern China. During the gathering, soldiers danced to music and songs to welcome the guests. The military parade has since become a popular event to honor major festivals (Xinhua News Agency).

As shown in Table 1, China has held 13 national day parades in Tian'anmen Square in the Chinese capital since 1949. Eleven of them were carried out annually, from 1949 to 1959, the 12th was conducted in 1984 for the 35th anniversary of the founding of the PRC, and the 13th was held in 1999 for the PRC's 50th birthday. Table 1 offers a brief chronological account of the 13 national day parades.

In terms of weaponry display, in the previous five military parades from 1949 to 1953, all weapons displayed were made in other countries, and in the 1954 parade, the sixth, the soldiers were mostly equipped with Soviet-made weapons. The 12th parade (1984), however, displayed all home-made weapons and military equipment, mostly new at the time. The 13th parade displayed the latest home-made weaponry (Xinhua News Agency 1999). The 13th military parade carried

Table 1. National Day Military Parades (1949–99)

October 1, 1949 A long procession of field troops, composed of infantry, artillery, and cavalry soldiers, and a formation of sailors from the navy and cadets from a navy school. A small fleet of warplanes including fighter planes, bombers, and trainers.

October 1, 1950 The military paraders, totaling 24,200, included troops and cadets from the infantry, navy, and air force units as well as a division of the public security army. Exhibited weapons included 88 guns of various kinds, 80 self-propelled guns, 178 vehicles, 2,899 horses, and 28 aircraft.

October 1, 1951 The military parade was formed by 13,348 troops including soldiers and cadets from the infantry, navy, and air force, as well as the militia. Displayed in the parade were 128 guns of various kinds, 80 tanks and self-propelled guns, 192 automobiles, 1,104 horses, and 148 aircraft.

October 1, 1952 In the procession were 57 square formations of soldiers and cadets from the field, navy, and air force units, totalling 11,300, together with nine flying squads, including 153 aircraft. Also displayed were 112 guns, 99 tanks and self- propelled guns, 16 armored vehicles, 156 automobiles, 160 tricycles, and 1,104 horses. The parachute troops made their debut in this national day rally.

October 1, 1953 The military paraders included 10,038 soldiers and cadets from the infantry, navy, and air force, accompanied by 144 guns, 67 tanks and self-propelled guns, 168 vehicles, 165 tricycles, 770 horses, and 96 warplanes.

October 1, 1954 The land procession included 38 formations of soldiers and cadets, totaling 10,384, from the field, navy, and air force, as well as the public security troops, accompanied by a number of tanks, guns, and 111 warplanes, in four squads.

October 1, 1955 Soldiers and cadets marched past the Tian'anmen Rostrum in 38 square formations, wearing shoulder-marks for the first time as China began to adopt a ranking system for the army that year. Jet bombers and jet fighter planes also made their first showing. A total of 10,344 soldiers and officers joined in the military review.

October 1, 1956 Soldiers and cadets, numbering 11,929, took part in the parade. To a considerable extent, they were armed with Chinese-made weapons, marking a new progress in the country's defense industry.

October 1, 1957 Participating in the parade were 7,065 soldiers and cadets, as well 266 tanks, 112 guns, and 81 warplanes.

October 1, 1958 The military parade consisted of seven formations of cadets, six formations of infantry soldiers, and four formations of soldiers from other kinds of troops, as well as eight formations of guns, four formations of tanks, and 93 warplanes.

October 1, 1959 Fifteen formations of soldiers and cadets, 14 formations of vehicles of various kinds, and six squads of warplanes appeared in the national day show. A total of 11,018 soldiers and cadets, 144 guns, 99 tanks and self-propelled guns, 240 automobiles,

(*continued*)

Table 1. National Day Military Parades (1949–99) (*continued*)

---

and 165 warplanes participated in the parade. Many new types of arms made their first appearance.

October 1, 1984 The parading troops, soldiers, and cadets as well as guns, vehicles, and missiles of various kinds, in 46 formations and echelons, were accompanied by 117 warplanes. Missiles and strategic missiles were shown to the public for the first time. All the weapons and military equipment on display were home-made, mostly new at the time.

October 1, 1999 Participating in this parade were 42 formations composed of the People's Liberation Army's three services, the armed police, the army reserves, and the militia. The military parade involved 11,000 military personnel in 17 ground phalanxes, and 25 vehicle formations, and 10 echelons consisting of 132 warplanes.

Source: Based on the national day news stories released by Xinhua News Agency (1999).

special significance after the U.S.-led North Atlantic Treaty Organization bombed the Chinese embassy in Belgrade in early May 1999 and after Lee Deng-hui put forward his "two states theory" in June 1999 in dealing with the straits relations in an attempt to separate Taiwan from the mainland.

The military parade is designed to show to the rest of the world that China is no longer a country that can be intimidated by any power, and that it can defend itself in time of war. It also indicates that it can protect its national sovereignty and territorial integrity in the face of foreign invasion or any separation attempts.

To display its achievements during the past 50 years, China not only used floats during the parade but also held six major exhibitions in Beijing and many other places throughout the country. It also held two galas and broadcast 21 television programs in the capital city. In addition, it launched a special Web site (http://www.prc50.government.ch) to publish the news coverage of the preparation for the national day celebration, broadcast live online the grand national day parade and the night gala, and exhibit online the achievements of the country during its past 50 years.

Before the national day parade, China spent no less than US$13 billion on the cleanup and on some 67 major projects in Beijing, including a new control tower and terminal at the capital airport, a new subway line, and widening the loop roads. Furthermore, cypress trees were planted along the capital's main street, Chang'an Avenue, with new bike lanes and millions of freshly planted flower pots. About 25 factories in the capital, which produce heavy pollution, were asked to reduce or even stop production.

In the 800-meter (from north to south) by 500-meter (from east to west) Tian'anmen Square, more than 340,000 square meters of ground area were renovated with quality granite from east China's Shandong Province. The sound system and lighting installations in Tian'anmen Square were upgraded, 15 hectares of grass strips were added to the square, and many sculptures and fountains were lined up along Chang'an Avenue. In addition, the Great Hall of the People and other buildings were also renovated for the 50th national day. This is another example of how much importance the Chinese attach to "face," both individual and institutional.

As the Internet reaches into China so rapidly and radically, the Chinese government launched a national day Web site one month before the national day, providing the latest reports of the national day celebration preparation, the celebration activities, and the postcelebration activities. It also provided backgrounders, such as a chronicle of the major events since the founding of the People's Republic of China, the national day celebration slogans, the national celebration songs, major achievements during the past 50 years, live coverage and replay of the national day celebration, and online exhibitions of the nation's strengths and achievements.

In combination with radio, television, and newspaper reporting, the national day celebration Web site has far extended the reach of the national image presented by the national day parade and national day speeches. This is shown by the fact that the Web site was visited by 1.11 million people on the national day, putting the accumulated hits up to 13 million during the month of September 1999. It received 28,000 national day online greeting cards and 7,800 online greetings during the same month.

As shown by the floats and the slogans, the demonstration was very much politicized by chanting slogans that called for holding the great banner of Deng Xiaoping's theory and pushing forward the building of socialism with Chinese characteristics into the 21st century. The paraders even chanted the slogan "Long Live the Great Chinese Communist Party!" This is just one slogan, among the list of 50 slogans, that was officially approved by the government.

DISCUSSIONS AND CONCLUSIONS

The case of the 50th national day celebration illustrates that China has its own unique way of presenting its national image. Those features include the central planning and coordinating of the national day celebration activities by the central government and the politicization of the national day celebration activities.

The central planning practice is a legacy of the Soviet political system, which was copied by Mao Zedong. Since the implementation of the reform and open policies under Deng Xiaoping, the central planning practice has increasingly given way to market regulation, especially at the microlevel, in the field of economic construction and development in China. However, in noneconomic matters, the central planning practice remains alive, especially when it comes to matters like nation-building, patriotic education, and national image making.

Closely related to the central planning practice is the politicization of the national day celebration activities. As a developing nation, China is still facing the potential separation of Taiwan, Tibet, and Xinjiang from the country. One decade after the 1989 protests and tanks in Tian'anmen Square, another major threat to the authority of the government has arisen through the sit-in protests by the Falun Gong cult at Zhongnanhai, the headquarters of the Chinese government, which requested its lawful right as an organization.[3] The Chinese government was shocked by the fact that Falun Gong claimed to have more than 200 million practitioners in China alone, exceeding the number of members in the Chinese Communist Party. In addition, the increasing number of people who have lost their jobs has precipated a potential hotbed for riots or other forms of social instabilities.

These potential threats have reminded the Chinese government of the necessity of patriotic education and nation-building. One of the important ways of patriotic education and nation-building is the reinforcement of the national image among the public. Undoubtedly, the national day celebration demonstrated a great chance to reinforce the national image of being powerful, influential, and achieving prosperity in order to regain eroding faith and support from its people.

As part of the efforts to improve its national image, China has also conducted what may be called "face engineering," or taking measures to improve or enhance the national image. One example is that they have renovated, among other things, Tian'anmen Square, the symbol of China, which is as much as a face to a person. It has long been a Chinese tradition to attach much importance and care to a face, either individual or institutional.

In addition to this traditional strategy, China also fully used the Internet to publicize and promote its national image to the Chinese people both at home and abroad as well as to the rest of the world. It shows that the Chinese government has endorsed the Internet as an extended public channel to govern the country as well as to make its voice heard and influence felt.

In sum, the Chinese government has presented to its own people and the world a national image of China, consisting of military strength, great achievements, social stability, racial harmony, determination to reunify the country and to stop any attempts to separate the country, and confidence of the nation in the next millennium.

NOTES

1. The Cultural Revolution of 1966–76 was a mass mobilization of urban Chinese youth inaugurated by Mao Zedong. The purpose was to attempt to prevent the development of a bureaucratized Soviet style of Communism. Mao closed schools and encouraged students to join Red Guard units, which persecuted Chinese teachers and intellectuals and enforced Mao's cult of personality. The movement for criticism of party officials, intellectuals, and "bourgeois values" turned violent, and the Red Guard split into factions. Many people died in the ensuing purges. The Cultural Revolution also caused economic disruption; industrial production dropped by 12 percent from 1966 to 1968. In 1967, Mao ordered the army to stem Red Guard factionalism but promote the guard's radical goals. When the military itself threatened to factionalize, Mao dispersed the Red Guards, and began to rebuild the party. The Ninth Party Congress (1969), which named Marshal Lin Biao as Mao's

successor, led to a struggle between the military and Premier Zhou Enlai. After Lin's mysterious death (1971), Mao expressed regrets for the excesses of the Cultural Revolution. However, the Gang of Four, led by Jiang Qing, continued to restrict the arts and enforce ideology, even purging Deng Xiaoping a second time only months before Mao's death (September 1976). The Gang of Four was imprisoned in October 1976, bringing the movement to a close. (From http://www.infoplease.com/ce5/CE013502.html.)

2. The words for the national anthem were written by Tian Han, and the music was composed by Nie Er in 1935. Originally known as the "March of the Volunteers," it was the theme song of *The Sons and Daughters in Times of Turmoil*, a film that depicted how Chinese intellectuals marched bravely to the front in the War of Resistance Against Japan during World War II. Sonorous, militant, and inspiring, the song describes the wrath of the Chinese people against imperialist aggression and their determination to protect their motherland against foreign invaders. During World War II, it was also sung by people of other countries who sympathized with the Chinese people in their anti-Japanese struggle. In 1949, it was appropriately chosen to be the national anthem of the People's Republic of China. The lyrics of the national anthem are as follows:

> Arise, ye who refuse to be slaves;
> With our very flesh and blood
> Let us build our new Great Wall!
> The Peoples of China are in the most critical time,
> Everybody must roar his defiance.
> Arise! Arise! Arise!
> Millions of hearts with one mind,
> Brave the enemy's gunfire,
> March on!
> Brave the enemy's gunfire,
> March on! March on! March on, on!

(From http://www.chinatoday.com/general/a01.htm.)

3. Falun Gong, introduced by Li Hongzhi, claims to be an advanced system of spiritual cultivation and practice. It was banned in mainland China after its members gathered for a sit-in protest against the government's refusal to recognize it as a lawful organization.

REFERENCES

Boulding, K. E. (1956). *The image: Knowledge in life and society*. Ann Arbor: University of Michigan Press.

Dennis, E. E., Gerbner, G., and Zassoursky, Y. N. (Eds.). (1991). *Beyond the cold war: Soviet and American media images*. Newbury Park, CA: Sage.

Farmer, E. L. (1990). Shifting truth from the facts: The reporter as interpreter of China. In C. C. Lee (Ed.), *Voices of China: The interplay of politics and journalism*. New York: Guilford Press.

Hart, J. (1966). "Foreign news in U.S. and English daily newspapers: A comparison. *Journalism Quarterly, 40*, 443–49.

Hopple, G. (1982). International news coverage in two elite newspapers. *Journal of Communication, 32*, 61–73.

Lent, J. (1977). Foreign news in the American media. *Journal of Communication, 27.*

Liu, L. Q. (1991). The image of the United States in present-day China. In E. E. Dennis, G., Gerbner, and Y. N. Zassoursky (Eds). *Beyond the cold war: Soviet and American media images.* Newbury Park, CA: Sage.

McNelly, J. T. (1979). International news for Latin America. *Journal of Communication,* 156–63.

Perry, D. (1987). The image gap: How international news affects perception of nations. *Journalism Quarterly, 64,* 416–21, 433.

Potter, W. J. (1987). News from three worlds in prestigious U.S. newspapers. *Journalism Quarterly, 64,* 73–79, 276.

Semmel, A. (1977). Foreign news in four U.S. elite dailies: Some comparisons. *Journalism Quarterly, 53,* 732–36.

Xinhua News Agency. (1999, September 30 and October 1). News stories and backgrounders. Available: http://www.prc50.government.cn

ETHIOPIA

Holiday Celebrations among the Highlanders of Ethiopia

Tsegay Wolde-Georgis

Ethiopia has developed its own unique culture because it is one of the few African countries that escaped the impact of European colonialism in the 19th century. During the scramble for Africa, foreign powers such as the Ottoman Turks, the Egyptians, and the Italians attempted to make Ethiopia their colony; however, these groups failed after military defeat. The final challenge was Italy's failed invasion in 1896. In the battle of Adwa, the Ethiopian forces were victorious, and Europeans were ultimately forced to recognize Ethiopia as an independent country.

Ethiopia can trace this unique national culture to various factors: political independence, a strong centralized church, and isolation for many centuries from the West. The belief systems and the existence of an identifiable psychological makeup led to the safeguard of political independence by the people. The country's various national holidays and the ways they are celebrated have always given the population an Ethiopian self-consciousness. Such national identity and self-consciousness have strengthened the resolve of Ethiopians to resist foreign political or cultural domination. The society has also developed important national symbols that are celebrated by the culture. In addition to art and the military, religion and culture have played important roles in Ethiopian history.

Ethiopia's national holidays have both religious and political dimensions. The nonreligious holidays of Ethiopia reflect the political history of the country. For example, Ethiopia does not have a specific day of independence because of its origins in antiquity. Nonreligious national days reflect the history of the state for survival and independence as well as social change that occurred as one government replaced another. The most important occasions are wars with foreign invaders, the coronation of kings. In the last three decades, the most important national symbols, such as emblems and songs have changed along with the governments.

Ethiopia's national holidays are heavily dominated by religion. From ancient times, Ethiopia has followed Christianity, Islam, and Judaism. Christianity became a state religion in the 4th century A.D. Islam was introduced to the country during the time of the Prophet Mohammed, who ordered his followers to take refuge in Ethiopia following their persecution in Arabia. Before the revolution of 1974 that overthrew the monarchy, Islamic holidays were not celebrated nationally in Ethiopia. Ethiopia was a theocratic state where the king was head of the Ethiopian Orthodox Church. During the revolution, about 200,000 Muslims and their Christian supporters demonstrated for religious equality, demanding that all the important Islamic holidays be given equal status with the Christian ones. The military government responded positively.

Muslims celebrate their festivals following a period of fasting, abstaining from food during the day and eating after sunset and before sunrise. During Muslim festivals, there is not an abundance of overt nonreligious singing and dancing other than prayers. All Muslim holidays are strictly religious. The most important holidays are Id Alfater (Ramadan), Id Al Adha (Arefa), and the birth of the Prophet Mohammed. Attending prayer in the mosque and gathering for the evening dinner are two of the most important characteristics of these holidays. In addition, the Koran bounds Muslims to share their goods with those who are less fortunate. They raise money or share their food with the needy.

Muslims in Ethiopia perform pilgrimage to various domestic religious shrines in Ethiopia. This is in addition to their pilgrimage to Mecca, as every Muslim is encouraged to visit Mecca at least once in his lifetime.

One of the most important Islamic shrines outside Arabia is the tomb of Ahmad Negash in the Tigray region of Ethiopia. It is believed that this site was the first place where Muslims were converted outside the birthplace of Islam. When opponents in Arabia confronted the Prophet Mohammed, he told his followers to cross the Red Sea and seek shelter in the Christian Kingdom of Axum, where refugees were sheltered and protected. According to tradition, Ahmed Negash was one of the chiefs who were converted to Islam. Muslims believe, however, that it was the king or the Negasi (king) himself who was converted to Islam. The prophet then told his followers not to declare jihad, or holy war, against the Ethiopians. Many Muslims also consider the Mosque of Negash the second Mecca and conduct annual pilgrimages to this site. There are also other Islamic sites that are visited annually by Muslims, such as the shrine of Sheik Hussein in southeastern Ethiopia.

Most Ethiopian cultural holidays, then, have religious origins but with the passage of time they are losing their religious significance. Table 1 shows the distribution of national holidays in Ethiopia for 1998/99.

This chapter focuses on selected holidays practiced by most highland Ethiopians that are recognized by the state as national holidays reflecting the cultural uniqueness of Ethiopia due to its limited contact with the outside world until recently. Since most highlanders of Ethiopia are followers of the Orthodox Church, this chapter reflects that demographic and historical particularity.

Table 1 Ethiopian National Holidays, 1998–99

Meskerem 1 (September 11)	New Year
Meskerem 17 (September 27)	Meskal Day (Finding of the True Cross)
Tahsas 29 (January 7)	Lidet (Ethiopian Christmas)
Tir 11 (January 19)	Timkat (Epiphany)
Tir 9 (January 17) (date varies)	Id Alfater/Ramadan
Yekatit 23 (March 2)	Battle of Adwa
Megabit 18 (March 27)	Id Al Adha (Arefa)
Miazia 1 (April 9) (date varies)	Siklet (Ethiopian Good Friday)
Miazia 3 (April 11) (date varies)	Fasika (Ethiopian Easter)
Miazia 23 (May 1)	Labor Day
Miazia 27 (May 5)	Ethiopian Patriots Day
Ginbot 20 (May 28)	National Holiday, downfall of Dergue
Sene 18 (June 25) (date varies)	Birth of the Prophet Mohammed

Source: 1992 Ethiopian Calendar

In the description of the holidays, an attempt is made to show the various activities of the population as part of the celebration. As stated earlier, local villages and regions have developed their own unique form of celebration. The essence of the festivities, however, is the same.

Table 1 shows only those holidays recognized by the state as national holidays. Ethiopia is a very diverse society with many local and regional traditions, and there are many local religious and nonreligious holidays that are not recognized by the state as national holidays.

POPULAR TRADITIONAL HOLIDAYS

Popular holidays are those that have been celebrated nationally for a long period of time by the majority of Ethiopians, many of which originated hundreds of years back. Some of them are related to religion but have transformed themselves into secular events. Some are also associated with the change of the season and the seasonal agricultural cycle. The government recognizes most of these national holidays. During these holidays, people dress in their best attire and host feasts for themselves, family members, and friends. There are also many symbolic activities, prayers, songs, dances, and rituals unique to the particular occasion.

The cycle of seasonal activities define the calendar of the Ethiopian rural people, symbolizing the type of work practiced by farmers. As the rural Ethiopian saying goes, "There is time to work and time to dance and be merry." The land is prepared for planting at the end of the dry season and it is sowed in June when the rains begin. This is the case for most of the Ethiopian highlands, but local climate and location can also create unique local conditions. At the end of the agricultural year, farmers take a break from the drudgery of their work and engage in many social activities. Table 2 provides a listing of seasonal farming activity.

The Ethiopian year begins with the end of the rainy season. It comes when the *kremt* (rainy season) ends and the *meher* (harvest season) is in the vicinity. During kremt, the land is green and lush with new plants. This season is a period of hunger for many farmers in Ethiopia because they have finished their food. With the beginning of the new year in September, people know whether the next harvest season will be good or bad depending on the nature of rainfall in the kremt season. This period is like a thermometer that tells farmers whether the coming year will be full of marriages and celebrations (a good harvest) or a time of misery or migrations (crop failures).

The Ethiopian calendar is marked by monthly and annual dates of important events, such as angels and saints remembrance dates and celebrations. Fasting usually precedes these events. The peasants who do not read or write depend on the wisdom of the parish priest to follow the commencement and the end of the fast.

In his book, first published in 1853, the noted English traveler Parkyns said of the Ethiopians' religious fast, "Their fasts are more numerous perhaps than those of any other Christian people, more than two thirds of the year being assigned to abstinence" (1853/1966). He also added, "If the Abyssinians fast two thirds of the year, they make up for it in some degree by the number of feasts which they celebrate" (Ibid.).

The rest of this chapter briefly examines the various holidays and their respective celebrations. As stated earlier, the holidays might have local variations that have developed throughout the hundreds of years of their practice.

Table 2 Seasonal Activities in Ethiopia

Seasons	Months	Activities	Remarks	Nonpolitical holidays
Meher	September–November	Harvest	Dry	New Year, Meskal
Bega	December–February	House repair, wedding, relaxing	Very dry	X-Mass, Timkat, Ramadan
Belg	March–May	Land preparation, small planting	Small rains	*Arefa*, Easter
Kremt	June–August	Cultivation, weeding	Heavy rainfall	Birth of the Prophet Mohammed

THE NEW YEAR (KUDDUS YOHANNES, INQUTATASH)

Ethiopia's solar calendar is seven or eight years behind the Western calendar. Ethiopia just celebrated its 1992 New Year on September 12, 1999.[1] The Ethiopian year begins in September (Meskerem) and ends in August, or Pagumen, the 13th month with only five days (or six during leap years).[2] The Ethiopian Tourist Commission has a slogan that says "Visit Ethiopia, thirteen months of sunshine." Table 3 provides a comparison between the Ethiopian and the Western calendars.

The Ethiopian calendar follows the old Julian calendar. It is part of the Eastern Orthodox Church and is still used in Ethiopia. All Ethiopian Christian holidays fall on different days, divergent from the Western holidays. The same is true of the Ethiopian New Year.

Ethiopia celebrates its New Year on the 11th or 12th of September. The New Year, also known as Kuddus Yohannes, is a secular holiday that is celebrated universally in the country. The Ethiopian New Year manifests a transition from a year that ends in a rainy season to a new year that begins with a dry harvest season. During the Ethiopian New Year, many wildflowers blossom. Family and friends present each other a bunch of wildflowers and wish each other a happy New Year. At the

Table 3 Comparison of the Ethiopian and the Western Calendars

Ethiopian Calendar		Western Calendar		
Month of the Year	Name of Month in Sequence	Month of the Year	Name of Month	Date Begins
1st	Meskerem	9th	September	11
2nd	Tikimt	10th	October	11
3rd	Hidar	11th	November	10
4th	Tahsas	12th	December	10
5th	Ter	1st	January	9
6th	Yekatit	2nd	February	8
7th	Megabit	3rd	March	10
8th	Miazia	4th	April	9
9th	Ginbot	5th	May	9
10th	Sene	6th	June	8
11th	Hamle	7th	July	8
12th	Nehasse	8th	August	5 or 6
13th	Pagumien			

same time they say to each other, "inqutatash" (happy New Year) adding, "Let this 'inqutatash' make many returns."

In traditional Ethiopia, any person who comes with good news is rewarded with gifts or promises of a gift. The usual way of saying this in Amharic is "Yemisratch." Thus, uttering the word *inqutatash* is one of the best pieces of news of the morning (thought an obvious one) during the New Year. These days, children give flowers, best-wishes cards, or home-made flower drawings as a way of passing on their best wishes to their loved ones for the coming new year. Referring to the way the New Year was celebrated in Ethiopia in the 19th century, Parkyns (1953/1966) wrote:

Among equals, every one [*sic*] strives to rise earliest in the morning and be the first to offer his bouquet to his friend, who then has to give him a present according to his means. Inferiors also give flowers to their superiors; and in a great man's house there is a good deal of rivalry among the servants as to who shall be the first to wish him many happy returns of the day, for only the two or three earliest comers are usually rewarded. Ladies generally prepare a new pair of breeches for their husbands, spun with their own hands, which they offer when he presents his nosegay. While he in return gives them a new dress. So the master with his inexpressionbles, the mistress with her calico shirts presents, and the servants with their presents are all joyous: in fact, all the house is happy; and with a few exceptions, such as where there is sickness, much innocent pleasure and gaiety are[,] I believe[,] enjoyed by all classes in this country on the anniversary of Kiddos [*sic*] Yohannes. (281)

An important mark of the Ethiopian New Year is the general positive attitude of the population to the coming year. People usually compare the New Year with light, often thanking God for His help in the transition from the old year to the new year. The negation of the old year being replaced by the new year is conducted through a ritual of cleansing. People take a ritual bath on the morning of the New Year in a nearby cold spring. They also wash all their old clothes in preparation for the new year. On the day of New Year, people dress in their best attire, which usually is the white traditional dress of the men and the women. The two important elements of the celebration of Kuddus Yohannes are water and fire, which are used to clean the individuals and their households. Dancing is also an important part of the celebration. Walker (1993) stated, "On the fifth (or sixth) day of Qwagmiei [*sic*] a man will arise before the birds taste the water, and go to a stream to wash himself, and for one who cannot walk they will bring water to him" (88).

The end of the harvest season gives rural people an opportunity to rest from the drudgery of the agricultural cycle, which demands hard work. During this season, called *bega*, farmers engage in many celebrations, such as weddings, saints' days, and remembrance of a dead family member.

On the eve of the New Year, all households light their *chibo*, or torches made out of dried twigs (*shig* in Tigrigna), tied together in bundles. Unlike the countryside, where people make their own chibo, the townspeople mostly buy theirs.

According to one observer, "Some people make quite a bit of money every year by selling torches." (Lord 1970, 59). The role of torch making and lighting is reserved for the young male. Every male member of the household gets a chibo and lights it in the main house. He then takes it outside the gate. The implementation of this process varies from place to place. In some parts of northern Ethiopia, people with the torch march in a procession to their churches, giving a spectacular light that pierces the night mountain darkness. The light symbolizes the end of suffering for the people and the arrival of hope. Everything bad, both emotionally and materially, is now to be left as part of the old year. People wish and ask God to make the coming new year better than the previous one.

In their neighborhoods, people drop the torch on the ground and cleanse themselves by crossing the fire or jumping over it. Everyone—male, female, and even strangers—are offered their chance to cross the torch, wishing good things for the coming year. In the urban areas, young boys provide people with the opportunity to jump the lighted torch and then demand money. This is likely a new development that evolved with the evolution of the economy in the urban areas. Girls who go from house to house dancing in some parts of northern Ethiopia demand money as a gift for their best wishes and seasonal entertainment. They collect the money and share it at the end of the celebration.

After the procession on New Year's eve, some people return to their homes while others proceed to a prearranged place for a party. It is customary for someone in the village to provide everyone with a beer or *tejj* (honey wine) party for the New Year. After the party, the old people either go to their homes or sleep overnight, while the young people, both male and female, proceed to the valley to dance the whole night.

The New Year is part of the party season that begins in the middle of Nehase (August) and finishes in the middle of Meskerem (September). The September dance plays an important social function because it is a meeting place for future husbands and wives. According to one informer for this research, when a young man looks at a potential mate, he goes home and asks his parents if it is possible for them to pursue an arranged marriage. The ultimate decision is for the parents and elders who know whether the two families can arrange the marriage. For example, if the two families are related by blood, it will not be pursued. In the old days, there were also other obstacles, such as class and cast, that might have discouraged young people from getting married as they wished.

On the morning of the New Year, before the birds whisper, everyone in the village travels to the nearest spring to conduct a ritual bath in memory of John the Baptist. It is a way of cleansing oneself and preparing for the coming new year. People believe that there is no need for the priest to bless the water at that time. People believe that God blesses the water every New Year morning. The origin of this practice is unknown, but some believe that it is a continuation of the practices of the Old Testament that came to Ethiopia as part of its pre-Christian culture. Thus, in addition to fire, water also plays an important symbolic cleansing role in the transition from the old year to the new year.

MESKAL (THE FINDING OF THE TRUE CROSS)

Meskal (September 27), one of the most popular holidays in Ethiopia, is a time when family and friends gather in a form of thanksgiving. It is both a secular and a religious celebration at the beginning of the Ethiopian harvest season. During the rainy kremt season, there is very little socialization in the countryside because of food shortages and the activity of farmers to take care of their crops in the form of weeding and drainage. Some people from the village leave their homes for seasonal employment and return to their homes at the end of the rainy season during Meskal. According to an informer from the Gurage ethnic group, who are famous for the migration to work in the city of Addis Ababa, almost all of them (rich and poor) return to the Gurage country during Meskal for a month of celebration.

Meskal was characterized in a recent Internet report as,

A day of solemn religious services and of joyous secular celebrations; a day of parties and dance; a day of beautiful flowers and of brilliant bonfires. Meskal is all of these things and yet it is none of them. For Meskal alone and above all else, is one thing only. Meskal is the finding of the True Cross. (Walta Information Center)

Ethiopians believe that Meskal has its origins in the finding of the True Cross (where Jesus was crucified) by St. Helena (Lord 1970). It is also believed that a piece of that cross was sent to Ethiopia and deposited in the church of Mariam Geshen in the Wollo region of northern Ethiopia. Ethiopian religious leaders say that Meskal is a reminder that people should rededicate their beliefs in the symbolism of the cross (i.e., sacrifices). During Meskal, the believers chant, "The cross has saved us from sin and the cross is our power; the light of the cross is revealed; the new year has dawned." In remembrance of Christ when He was crucified, people bundle a special thorny weed in the form of a crown and put it on their heads reminding themselves of those who mocked Jesus Christ as the king of the world.

And then, at dusk the huge Maskal [*sic*] pole with the surrounding reeds is set on fire making a splendid blaze symbolizing the search for and the success in finding the original Cross on which Jesus Christ was crucified. Every village or hamlet will have its own Maskal [*sic*] fire that night and from any high place one may see many flickering points of light scattered far and near across the darkened landscape. The following morning, on Maskal [*sic*] day men and women take the charcoal of the burnt wood, bear it home and breaking it up, rub it on their palms and, with a finger of the right hand, anointing their foreheads with the sign of the Cross. For this is the Feast of the Cross—and, the Charcoal is its mark. (Walta Information Center)

The cross and fire are two important symbols of this national holiday. A lot of dried wood is put around a standing pole that resembles a tall slender cone called *damera*. The seasonal yellow Meskal flowers decorate the damera. Before the damera is set on fire, priests come to the area, circle around it, and pray. The head priest, using a chibo, sets the damera on fire. In the capital city of Addis Ababa, the patriarch of the Ethiopian Orthodox Church lights the damera, but in other towns, it is usually the local official who is invited to initiate the fire. The gathered people explode in joy and admiration. The focus of everyone at this time is to see the direction of the falling central pole. People believe that if the direction of the falling pole is to the east, the direction of the coming year will offer peace and abundance.

There are also ceremonies that take place around the homes. The fire from the chibo is used by the people to cleanse their homes. They put the torch light into the bedrooms and the storage room, and then everyone jumps over the fire. Like the celebration of the Kuddus Yohannes, or New Year, a few weeks earlier, people repeat their thanks that the rainy season is over and the harvest season has arrived. During the fire-cleansing ritual, the insects that are associated with the rainy season are told to leave the house, while those associated with the harvest season are invited. People also chant "Spinach out and porridge in." People also greet each other by saying "Thanks God we have seen the light of Meskal." It is believed that a fragment of the original True Cross where Christ was crucified lies in remote, inaccessible mountains in the Monastery of Gishen Mariam in northern Ethiopia. Meskal is a commemoration of the success of Queen Helena in finding the Holy Cross upon which Christ was crucified. It is said that in 326 A.D., through the divine guidance, the True Cross was unearthed from the spot where it was buried in Golgota. Meskal has been observed in Ethiopia as a religious and secular festival ever since. However, the event received even greater Christian sanction and significance at the end of the 14th century when a miraculous chain of events brought a fragment of the original cross to Ethiopia. This caused much rejoicing throughout the ancient Christian realm (Walta Information Center).

LIDET OR GENA (CHRISTMAS)

The word *Lidet* in Geez, the ancient language of Ethiopia, means "to be born." It is a Christian holiday celebrated on January 7 with a focus on children that is preceded by a two-week fasting by devoted adult Christians. When Ethiopian Orthodox Christians fast, they abstain from all animal products, such as meat, milk, cheese, and eggs. Some might eat fish, though that is rarely found in this mountainous country less endowed with lakes outside the Rift Valley. There are also priests who do not accept that fish is a fasting food. When Ethiopians fast, they eat food in the afternoon except for Saturdays and Sundays. Priests, nuns, monks, and the most religious usually abstain until 3:00 P.M. Fasting is terminated with an animal food such as chicken or mutton depending on one's wealth.

With the end of the harvest season in December, it is time to begin the fun and entertainment for the children, especially in the rural areas of Ethiopia. The Lidet holiday can be considered as the beginning of a vacation time for those who work on the land. There is less agricultural activity during the calendar year between January and April.

The fun begins, at least in the Tigray region of Ethiopia, before the arrival of Lidet. Young boys prepare their special stick prepared for the season, called *wurreita*. In the days when the problem of deforestation was not acute, the children cut a straight evergreen branch. They cut the bark into circles, skinning one circle, leaving another circle unpeeled, one after another until a pattern is formed. A pile of hay is lit on fire and the sticks are thrown into the flames. After a few minutes, the stick is taken off the fire. When the unpeeled bark is peeled, a black and white circular pattern is created because the circles that were peeled before the fire are now dark. The wurreita is a special item for a special day, made by the children for themselves.

The fun part for the children starts on Christmas eve. The boys in the village come together and start going to the various houses to wish people a merry Christmas. While the chibo is the symbol of the new year and Meskal, the wurreita is the symbol of Christmas in Ethiopia. When the boys go to the various houses, they make noises on the door by hitting their sticks with each other on the door or ground. They sing and chant, saying "Let Mary give you a boy that will play with us next Christmas." Everyone in the village wants his or her home to be visited by the children. As a matter of goodwill, they visit all the houses even if it takes the whole night. With a mountainous terrain and a dispersed population, it is tiring for the young children to do this. The children are offered bread or *injera* when they return on Timkat (Epiphany). A pregnant woman or a new mother has to give a big round Ethiopian bread called *Hambasha* or *dabo*. In the central highlands and around Addis Ababa, the tradition of giving dabo to children occurs in Nehasse (August) for a holiday called Buhe (Akalou 1970, 56–59).

When the children finish their Christmas wish, they usually stay outside their homes in the hay or at someone's house. When they fail to finish the good wish visit in time, they split into two groups. No household is left out of their visit. In fact, the houses that are very remote usually promise good gifts so that the children do not miss them. The next day, the children go to their respective homes to celebrate Christmas with their parents. Their gifts are collected, and on Epiphany day they will eat and celebrate the whole night with the rest of the people.

As stated earlier, this is the beginning of the rural vacation. Being the fifth month of the year, it is at the center of the two rainy seasons. The time between October and February is called the bega or dry season. After finishing the harvest activities in December, farmers are free to pursue their nonfarm activities, which include play, socialization, marriage, or sports. For example, January is the most popular month for weddings. In fact, households in one village usually synchronize their weddings into one week, making the month full of fun and happiness.

Another activity that starts with Lidet, or Gena, is the game of *gena* (hockey), a very popular game in many parts of Ethiopia. In some areas, the hockey game could be considered air hockey. The team members throw a ball into the air and hit it with a stick into their respective directions. The game is between villages, and there is no defined boundary for the game. Every able-bodied person from the village has to help stop the ball from going into the rival village. This game is called *qarsa* in Tigray. The game of qarsa continues until the Easter month. Newlyweds and their best men are tested for their strength and masculinity, joining their in-laws' teams when they visit their new spouses.

TIMKAT (EPIPHANY)

Timkat is equivalent to Epiphany and usually falls on January 19. On the eve of Timkat, the priests of a parish or group of parishes carry the *tabot* on their heads and rest it in the bank of a river close to a pool. The tabot is a copy of the Ark of the Covenant given to Moses by God. It is the most important relic and symbol of the Ethiopian Orthodox Church. It is put in the Holy of Holies of the church and is not touched by a layman. In the procession, the tabot is decorated and dressed in rich cloth. A tent is erected to rest the tabot and the priests continue their prayer and chanting in preparation for the next Timkat day. This is the annual rebaptism ritual of the community.

During the eve, everyone fasts from dusk to dawn. People collect food and drink for the priests and the elders who accompany the tabot. The priests who stay with the tabot pray, dance, and sing in praise of God. According to Parkyns (1853/1966), "The songs and dance are both of a religious kind: the latter, probably taken from the religious dancing of the Israelites, [is] frequently mentioned in the bible" (208). Young people dance until the morning. When the priests start conducting the prayer to bless the pool, all nonreligious songs are stopped.

Early in the morning of Timkat, the priests bless the water. A floating candle is put on the pool during the ceremony. When the priests show a sign that they have finished the blessing, the head priest sprinkles water in all directions at the people who are standing around the water. At the conclusion, the people jump into the water to be baptized with the holy water. People also fill bottles with the holy water for the old and sick who could not make it to the baptism ceremony and the water is then taken home and sprinkled on them. The remaining water is put on the gate of the compound to scare off the devil. The most important sites to witness the Timkat procession in Ethiopia are Axum, Lalibela, and Gondar (Amin and Willetts 1996, 36, 46).

When the tabot, or copy of the Ark of the Covenant,[3] is returned to its permanent residence in the church by procession, the young people accompany it with dances. The women also make loud and sharp *illulation* (noises) in celebration of the return of the tabot to the Holy of Holies. In some areas, guns are fired and some horsemen play *goux* on horseback. In the game of goux (pronounced guks), "the horsemen divide themselves on some broad meadow, each having in his hand three wands to hurl at the fleeing foe . . . [f]or he seeks to hit him on the head or the back" (Walker 1933, 84).

Timkat is also the time when the children collect their Christmas gifts in return for their house-to-house best wishes from two weeks earlier. There is no special ceremony when they go to the various houses to collect the food. It does not take a long time to collect the gifts because the children split into many small groups in order to cover different parts of the village. They select one house as their headquarters where they meet and stay the Timkat evening, partying before they join the older people who are gathered at the Timkat pool with the tabot.

Women who are pregnant or those with an unbaptized infant pass out the traditional Hambasha. Problems might arise between the children and a lady with an early pregnancy, one who refuses to give a Hambasha. The children have their own test to prove that the lady might be in early pregnancy. They ask the lady to cross over their special wurreita because, as traditionally, any woman who refuses to cross over the wurreita is pregnant and it is believed that it is not good for the pregnancy if she decides to cross the Christmas stick. Therefore, if she insists on neither crossing the stick nor giving the Hambasha, a consequence follows from the children. Everyone who refuses to give the children their gifts creates a conflict with the children.

If the conflict is not resolved in favor of the children, they may take the law into their own hands by defaming the family and embarrassing them in front of the community. The usual action is to improvise a mock funeral by pretending that the woman/man who refused to give them a gift has died. They follow the traditional technique of burial announcements and invite the community to participate in the funeral. If the woman was originally from another remote village, it is fun for the children to go to her village the next morning and announce her death. It is possible for some people to be cheated by the children's announcement and come to the village to attend the fraudulent funeral. When this rare act of revenge by the children is done, the name of the person is defamed for many years. There is no recourse for legal action in the village courts against these children because the person has violated an important Christmas tradition. Moreover, in traditional Ethiopian law, a shepherd or a young boy cannot be punished for any speech even when he insults the king.

FASIKA (EASTER)

Easter week, beginning April 11, is one of the biggest Christian holidays of the country. The longest fasting, or *Abiy Tsom*, season precedes the Ethiopian Easter holiday.[4]

The holidays of Lidet (Christmas), Timkat (Epiphany), Arbi Siklet (Good Friday), and Fasika (Easter) symbolize the birth, baptism, crucifixtion, and resurrection of Jesus Christ. They all occur during bega, the dry season when agricultural activities are low. There are many social activities such as weddings during this season, many occurring after the Easter holiday until the beginning of the planting period.

The last week of the Easter fast, Himamat, is a very important spiritual period for devout Orthodox Christians. The Sunday before Easter is called Hosanna, representing the coming of Jesus to Jerusalem, when the priests give all members of the congregation palm leaves in memory of the event. Everyone weaves the *siye* (palm leaves) to make finger rings, some even making palm rings for all of their fingers. The favorite food during this Sunday is bean sprout. The historical or religious reasons for this tradition are still not known.

Most people in the countryside fast until sunset during the last week of Easter. They go to church the whole day and make *sigdet* (prayer bows) and they sing *mihlela* (prayer songs). It is a very interesting sight when the young and the old count the number of sigdets they have accomplished. In some ways, the ceremony resembles that of the Muslim prayer except for its lack of organization. This tradition must have been acquired from ancient practices because it has not been observed in any other Christian tradition outside of Ethiopia. The Thursday of the last week of Easter (Good Friday eve) is also an important part of Easter. People cook an abundance of vegetarian food and eat until they are full, in preparation for the last three days of fasting between Good Friday and Easter Sunday. Beans and barley are boiled and given to people. This is a special food for that special day. Good Friday is a time of deep meditation and fasting. Many people do not eat any food or drink until Saturday morning while others fast from Friday until Easter morning. Those three days are spent praying around the church.

On the Saturday morning before Easter (*qedam seur*), priests and deacons go from house to house and distribute pieces of reed, called *qetema* in Amharic and *Setti* in Tigrigna, to be put around the head. The reed is split into two pieces and worn over the head. Everybody, including children, goes to church on Easter eve to pray and see priests pray all night and chant about the crucifixion and resurrection of Jesus Christ. After midnight, a signal is given by the priests, declaring, "Jesus has arisen from the dead." Everyone whispers to the person next to him or her, "Christ rose from the dead to free the son of Adam, and then there was peace!"[5] The excitement is heightened especially for children, when the priests distribute the *tuaf* (lighted candle) traditionally made of wax. Then the whole church is brightened. Accompanied by the big church drums, the priests change their tempo from sadness and meditation to jubilation and dancing in honor of Christ's resurrection from the dead. Thus, Easter has arrived.

The church service is dispersed around 3:00 A.M. and people break their fasting when they arrive home. People eat a small quantity of food so that they do not get hurt due to the long fasting. They usually break the fast with injera, with flaxseed sauce, which is believed to have medicinal value and adds some needed oil to the empty stomach. People also eat a small amount of chicken Doro Wat. The most important feast starts on Easter day (Sunday).

On the morning of Easter, almost everyone has to sacrifice an animal. The smallest animal is the hen. Those who can afford it usually slaughter a goat or sheep. Some wealthy people might kill an ox. It is also possible for a group of neighbors to raise money to buy a cow or an ox and share the meat. The idea is to feast with some sort of animal meat after the long fasting period.

The whole week following Easter Sunday is called Tinsae, or Easter week. The next Sunday after Easter is called Dagmai Tinsae or the second Easter and the week between the two Sundays is a time of celebration and eating. People party and invite each other over for food. Priests are invited to the different homes for their services. Young men who got married in January visit their new wives and in-laws with their best men. The visiting grooms participate in traditional games and introduce themselves to the villages of their wives. Some weddings are also conducted at this time. After Easter, the church allows people to eat meat even on Wednesdays and Fridays, until the next fasting in June.

HAWARYA AND BUHE

After the end of the big fast in Easter, Ethiopian Christians are allowed to eat animal products even on Wednesdays and Fridays until the fast of the Apostles in June. This fast is completed when the Holiday of Hawariya (Apostle) arrives at the end of June (Hamle 5, Ethiopian Calendar). In the Amhara central highlands, people celebrate the Buhe instead of the Hawariya. These two holidays are celebrated at different times by different localities during the rainy season. These holidays might have a religious origin but they are mainly associated with the rainy season in the highlands of Ethiopia. The use of *giraf* (a whiplike tool made of knotted fiber, *chugraff* in Tigray) and the baking of dabo or hambasha characterize them. The dates are either in July in Tigray or at the end of August in the Amphora areas of Ethiopia. The active members of society who celebrate this holiday are the young shepherds, who take bread from their homes and host a party for friends in the forests and mountains. They compete among themselves as to who makes the loudest sound using the giraf (*chugraf* in Tigrigna). They also share their hambasha and make merry.

In many places, the young boys will communicate among themselves not only by the use of the giraf sound but also using the cow horn. They whistle using the horn and make diverse musical sounds. It must have been inherited from ancient practices because the ancients have been utilizing the horn to communicate during times of happiness or war. In some areas, farmers also make war among themselves using the giraf. Village boys come together and whip each other with the giraf.

POLITICAL HOLIDAYS

In addition to the popular holidays, Ethiopians also celebrate many political holidays, including the Battle of Adwa, Martyrs Day, Patriots Day, and the downfall of the military government (Dergue; 1974–91).

The Battle of Adwa is one of the prime holidays in Ethiopia. It was during the Battle of Adwa, in 1896, that the Ethiopians were able to defeat Italian colonial ambitions over Ethiopia. Because of the Battle of Adwa, Ethiopia survived as the only independent country during the scramble for Africa in the 19th century. Ethiopia's independence was respected by the European powers. With the approval of Great Britain, Italian adventure in the Red Sea coast of the Horn of Africa began in the 1880s. After capturing the coastal areas, the Italians fought many battles that led to their defeat and they were unable to ascend to the highlands until the end of the 1880s. In 1889, the Ethiopian emperor Yohannes IV was killed in a fight against the Sudanese Mahdists (Islamic revivalists) who invaded Ethiopia, and Menelik II of Showa succeeded him. In the process of transition, the Italians were able to consolidate themselves in the highlands and created their colony of Eritrea in 1890. All the highlands of Eritrea were part of Ethiopia under Emperor Yohannes IV.

Fighting continued with the Italians who advanced inland. But with the consolidation of the Ethiopian forces, the final battle was fought at Adwa on March 2, 1896 (Yohannes 1996, 54). The Italians were totally defeated, the first defeat of a modern European power by a non-European country. Its international significance was immediately felt. Many Italian prisoners were taken to Addis Ababa for forced labor. Native collaborators were severely punished. The Italian government fell, and the new government recognized Ethiopian independence in the 1986 Peace Treaty of Addis Ababa. Following this, all the European powers recognized Ethiopia as a sovereign and independent country. Ethiopians have been celebrating this date since then.

The Italians again invaded Ethiopia in 1936, 40 years after their defeat at the Battle of Adwa in 1896. This time, they were armed with sophisticated weapons including airplanes and mustard gas. The invasion was faced with stiff resistance in all parts of the country. The worst Ethiopian reaction came when two Ethiopians threw hand grenades at General Graziani, the Italian fascist viceroy in Ethiopia. The Italians and their *askaris* (native soldiers hired by the invading Italian army) were given a free hand to kill all educated Ethiopians and burn houses. Many Ethiopian homes in Addis Ababa were burning and innocent Ethiopians were massacred by the Italians. That day has since been remembered as Martyrs Day. The Italian fascist occupation ended in 1941 when the patriots defeated the occupying forces.

The 1941 Patriots Day is a reminder of the struggle of the Ethiopian people during the struggle against fascism between 1936 and 1941. Ethiopians had been fighting against the Italian invaders until their liberation in 1941. Both the Battle of Adwa and Patriots Day are related with important aspects of the country's sovereignty.

The downfall of the Dergue is the youngest national holiday, celebrated on May 28 because the military dictatorship in Ethiopia was defeated on May 28, 1991. This date led to the establishment of a representative government in Ethiopia. Ethiopians celebrate this and other political holidays through parades and speeches by officials. Schools and government offices are closed and many people show up at the central square to see military and civilian parades. Songs and other entertainment are also included in the celebration.

CONCLUSION

Ethiopia is a large and diverse country inhabited by about 60 million people. Though interrelated, the diverse people have their unique traditions and customs. The predominant highlanders in Ethiopia are the Orthodox Christians. The existence of different climatic zones because of the highland–lowland difference has also led to the existence of different traditions. The emergence of urban areas at the beginning of the 20th century has also modified the traditional festivals.

As shown in this chapter, Ethiopians celebrate their holidays in different ways, through diverse symbols. Food is a common denominator of all of the holidays. People have to cook and eat different types of food and special food types are also prepared for specific holidays. Other important symbols are water and fire, which Ethiopians consider cleansing elements. Moreover, plants such as flowers, the reed, and special sticks are important as well.

The practices mentioned here are only a small representation. It is limited in scope only to practices of the Christian highlanders because of time and space constraints. National holidays are a reflection of the accumulation of the experiences from the preceding generations. The practices are altered from time to time to reflect changes.

The study of Ethiopian ceremonies is very important. This is a time of change in the country. Some of the practices are in the process of disappearing, and there is no tendency to record them yet. With modernization, the number of young or old people practicing these customs is getting smaller in number. For example, I was in the village of Atebes during the Fasika celebration of 2000. As this was my first participation in this celebration in the village since 1972, I was shocked to see that some of the ceremonies are coming to an end. With the nationalization of church land in 1974, there is no incentive for young people to serve the church. For example, during the Fasika week of the year 2000, I heard that the priests and deacons had almost refused to distribute the siye on the Saturday before Easter Sunday. I heard that it is because of the few number of priests, their age, and the lack of compensation from the community. This example shows that the old cultures are being changed and modified because of political, environmental, and social changes at the local and national level. It is hoped that the existing practices of all people of Ethiopia will be recorded adequately so that the next generation can understand what was practiced in the past.

GLOSSARY

Abiy Tsom/Arba Tsom: The two-month fast before Easter.
bega: The dry season (October–January) that follows kiremt.
Buhe: A pre-new year celebration in the central highlands of Ethiopia by young people.
chibo: A bundle of dry straws tied together that is set on fire to create a torch for the New Year and Meskal celebrations.

damera: The burning of fire during Meskal in a central public place to celebrate the finding of the True Cross.

Geez: The ancient language of Ethiopia, which is now spoken only for church services.

Gena/Qarsa: Hockey.

Goux: A war game played on horseback.

hambasha/dabo: A round-cake-type flat Ethiopian bread made of mildly fermented wheat flour.

Inqutatash: The Ethiopian New Year on Meskerem 1st or September 11 or 12 (during a leap year)

Kiremt: The rainy season (June–September) that precedes bega.

Lidet/Gena: Ethiopian Christmas (January 7).

meher: The agricultural season during kiremt.

Meskerem: The first month of the year that falls between September 11 and October 10.

mihlela: Prayer songs, usually about war, drought, and other calamities.

Pagumen: The 13th month of the Ethiopian solar calendar consisting of five days (six days during a leap year).

Ramadan: This Muslim holiday is also known as Id Alfater. In 1999, it was on January 17, but the date varies depending on the arrival of the new moon.

Sigdet: Pre-Easter ritual prayer, usually on the compound of the church by the faithful. The prayer is accompanied by frequent bows toward the church. The ritual is commonly practiced by the Muslim believers as well.

Tabot: A copy of the biblical Ark of the Covenant, found in all of the churches of Ethiopia.

Timkat: Epiphany. This holiday occurs two weeks after Christmas to celebrate Christ's baptism.

tuaf: Candle made of honey wax.

NOTES

1. The Ethiopian New Year is typically on September 11, but it changes to September 12 every four years during the leap year.

2. On Leap year, the month of Pagumen is six days.

3. The tabot is a copy of the Ark of the Covenant found in the Holy of Holies of all churches. The Ten Commandments are written on it. A church without a tabot is an empty house. The Ethiopian Orthodox Church believes that the original Ark of the Covenant now rests in the St. Mary of Zion Church in Axum.

4. The fast is termed as *Abiy.Tsom* (the big fast) or *Arba Tsom* (the 40-day fast). Easter's actual days of fasting are 55. Ethiopian Christmas fast for a total of 250 days a year. These are all Wednesdays and Fridays, 1 day on Timkat eve, 3 days of Jonah, 55 days of Lent, 40 days of the fast of the Apostles, and 16 days for the fast of the Virgin Mary.

5. In Geez, "Christos Tensae muwtan, agazo le-Adam, kone fesseha we-Selam."

REFERENCES

Akalou W. M., Buhe. (1970). In E. Ford (Ed.), *Cultural patterns of Ethiopia: Queen of Sheba's Heirs*. Washington, DC: Acropolis Books.

Amin, M., and Willetts, D. (1996). *Ethiopia: A tourist paradise*. Addis Ababa: Ethiopian Tourist Commission.

Ethiopian Embassy. (n.d.) *Ethiopia: A brief overview.* Washington, DC: Author.

Ethiopian Tourism Commission. (1987). *Discovering Ethiopia.* Addis Ababa: Author.

Lord, E. (Ed.). (1970). *Cultural patterns of Ethiopia: Queen of Sheba's Heirs.* Washington, DC: Acropolis Books.

Parkyns, M. (1966). *Life in Abyssinia.* London: Cass. (Originally published in 1853)

Walker, C. H. (1933). *The Abyssinian at home.* London: Sheldon Press.

Walta Information Center. (1993). Meskal: Its celebration in Ethiopia. Available: http://www.telecom.net.et/~walta/profile/articles/article93.html

Wonders of Africa. (1999). Public Television documentary.

Yohannes, M. (1996). *Itiopia: astedader'na poletikawi hidet.* Los Angeles: Asatami. (In Amharic)

GHANA

Globalization and Broadcasting the Ghanian National Day

Kwasi Ansu-Kyeremeh

B y several indications, Ghana's national day is March 6, for the nation gained her independence from the British on March 6, 1957. Nationhood as represented in Ghanian broadcasting against the backdrop of globalization is explored here. A brief historical background of a combination of civilian and military regimes precedes an analysis of the contribution of broadcasting to the promotion of the symbols of nationhood as characterized by a sociocultural and political dualism. In addition to an obfuscation with the notion of national day arising out of historical distortions, broadcasting seems to have succumbed to globalization, which is better interpreted as "foreignization." There is evidence that foreign (read: Western) values supersede indigenous Ghanian values in the portrayal of both sets through broadcast symbolism.

By examining the nature, content, and operation of electronic media systems in Ghana as an extension of external communication systems, this chapter portrays an intensification of the superimposition of foreign values on the Ghanian sociocultural system. Its main finding is that programs, programming, broadcast formats, and the language of broadcast indicate foreign domination deepening. This type of broadcasting both threatens erosion of Ghanian symbolism of nationhood and disenables national efforts at contributing to mainstrteam world culture. For inclusive globalization that encourages Ghanian/African input into the mainstream global communication and information flow system, certain approaches aimed at converting dominance into contribution to a world culture are proposed.

A BRIEF HISTORY OF GHANA'S
NATIONAL DAY CELEBRATIONS

For many years named "Gold Coast" by the British, "modern" Ghana assumed nationhood at midnight of March 6, 1957, when the Ghanian flag was first hoisted to replace the Union Jack. The British Empire Day had then been celebrated as the Gold Coast national day. However, following conventional practices of independent nationhood, March 6 ought to have assumed an unchallenged status of Ghana's national day, for it was the day the national flag of red, gold (with the black star in the center), and green symbols of the new nation was first hoisted. And, indeed, it was, and somehow continues to be. But other events have tended to complicate the determination of a single national day. One such event was the assumption of a republican status on July 1, 1960. Another was the declaration of a one-party state in 1962, which led to a change in the gold color in the national flag to white, in sync with the white color of the ruling Convention People's Party (CPP). This particular development seems to have signaled an intrusion of partisan party symbolism into the realm of all-embracing national symbols.

On February 24, 1966, a military coup toppled the CPP administration and reverted the white in the national flag to its original gold color. March 6 and July 1, both celebrated as national days prior to the coup, were now both superseded by the celebration of February 24 as Liberation Day. If CPP party colors intruded into national symbolism, the act of the National Liberation Council, the first of the many military juntas that have ruled Ghana, marked the beginnings of the institutionalization of an incumbency day in competition with the national day. Often, the incumbency day has been celebrated with greater pomp and pageantry than either March 6 or July 1.

October 1 joined the increasing number of incumbency days that assume national status when, in 1969, it marked the return to civilian government after the first military coup. The day was accordingly celebrated in the next two years that the Progress Party government lasted. That regime was actually replaced on January 13, 1972, with another military junta: the National Redemption Council. For the next 7 years, even when the council transformed itself into the Supreme Military Council (SMC I and II), January 13 replaced October 1 as the incumbency day known as "Redemption Day." By this time, the institutionalization of the latter, whereby the date of a government's inauguration is celebrated often in greater style than the known national day, was complete.

An Armed Forces Revolutionary Council overthrew SMC II on June 4, 1979, but it lasted just about three months; from then, it actualized June 4 as its day for national celebration. On September 21, 1979, the council was replaced by the People's National Party.

June 4, however, had its day on the return of Flight Lieutenant Jerry John Rawlings,[1] who had staged the 1979 coup with another military junta: the Provisional National Defence Council (PNDC), on December 31, 1981. On January 7, 1993, the PNDC metamorphosed into a National Democratic Congress (NDC) constitutional government. Ever since, Jerry Rawlings has ensured each May 15 (when he organized a failed putsch in 1979), June 4, December 31, and January 7 to be celebrated as a day of his PNDC/NDC incumbency with a national holiday even when the Supreme Court ruled December 31 could not be marked as such.[2] June 4, in particular, is celebrated as Revolution Day.

To these chaotic dates of a nation caught in its own subjugated and dominated past may be compared national symbolism in the period of indigenous precolonial nationhood.

INDIGENOUS NATIONHOOD AND SYMBOLISM

Indigenous Ghanian statehood's manisfestation in the current "traditional area" and the communication patterns within it, as articulated in Akan governance by Ansu-Kyeremeh (1998a), is the other sphere of the sociocultural and political dualism that characterizes postcolonial African societies. The above reviewed confused state of nationhood contrasts with stable indigenous political systems in which the symbolism of nationhood found expression in periods of annual festivals that incorporated the Durbar Day. The most famous of the Durbar Days, and also the closest to the contemporary national day in celeberation, is held during the Akwasidae Festival of the Asante. As described and explained by Opoku (1970), these were days when citizens gathered together to celebrate their ancestors through myriad ceremonies and actvities.

Precolonial kingdoms such as Asante and other Akan states had well-articulated and organized festivals during which nationhood was given expression in several ways (Opoku 1970). Days for celebrating nationhood, such as Asante Akwasidae, Berekum Kwafie, Anlo Hogbetsotso Za, or Dagbon Damba, were fixed according to the indigenous calendar (Adjaye 1987). Activities were organized to give expression to patriotism.

The notion of the national day is, therefore, not completely alien to Ghanian polity. Its indigenous celebration was, however, without the controversy that surrounds today's national day to the extent that the very act of setting a day aside or designating dates attracts so much disagreement. In marking indigenous "national" festivals, all means for publicity such as different drums and drumming, state owned or otherwise, were utilized to celebrate a common cause devoid of partisan activities. In contemporary times, however, the NDC has repeatedly been attacked for decorating state functions with party colors while relegating national colors into obscurity on occasions such as the state opening of Parliament and celebrations at Independence Square. (NDC party colors are so strategically placed that television cameras are compelled to capture them in the telecast of those events).

In fact, the cultural policy of Ghana (Ghana Ministry of Education and Culture 1975) recognized these indigenous festivals as means of communication because they facilitated gatherings of local residents, strangers, and well-wishers, as well as indigenous citizens returning from their places of work to participate in the festivities. Ansu-Kyeremeh (1992, 1997) categorizes *afahye* (festivals) among what he describes as "event-oriented," indigenous communication systems. The application of contemporary technologically mediated communication systems is, however, a far cry from the indigenous systems.

BROADCASTING THE NATIONAL DAY

Broadcasting, until recently a state-owned monopoly, has been involved in the thick and thin of national day observances. Ghana Television (GTV), right from its inauguration on July 31, 1965, has been at the center of the observation of the national days as determined by the incumbent government. Until October 1, 1998, when TV3 had its maiden broadcast, GTV was the only television station that governments used and abused in the name of Ghanian nationhood. The story was the same with Radio Ghana, which also monopolized radio broadcasting until the mid-1990s. Anniversary activities, including (military) parades, were broadcast live for hours. Programming often included items such as "patriotic songs" and recordings of speeches of past leaders.

It is this chaotic manifestation of the national day concept that confronts the Ghanian broadcasting establishment. The treatment of the national day by TV3 is symptomatic of this. TV3 is a Malaysian-owned and -operated station. It was born out of the sale of the Ghana Film Industry Corporation to the Malaysians by the Rawlings administration. The corporation had been charged with promoting Ghanian culture through film and thus was a national symbol in its own right. On each of the "Rawlings incumbency days"—all the days (May 15, June 4, and December 31) celebrated by the Rawlings administration as national days—TV3 broadcasts a feature film of the 1957 independence celebrations when the film used to be broadcast only on March 6 and July 1 by the state-owned Ghana Broadcasting Corporation (GBC) station, Ghana Television. As explained earlier, in the background of these broadcasts, NDC colors conspicuously dominate the national colors.

In fact, whatever excuses Ghanian broadcasting stations would want to attribute to unclear political agenda in the determination of national days is repudiated by the industry's cavalier attitude toward the promotion of Ghanian cultural symbolism and values. This is particularly true in their unbridled and slavish preferences for what is foreign, helping to create the impression that Ghana is not experiencing globalization but rather foreignization.

GLOBALIZATION OR FOREIGNIZATION?

While globalization may incorporate aspects of foreignization, foreignization per se cannot be globalization. This sounds like Pye's (1966) equation of Eurocentric modernization to Westernization that prompted non-Western scholar

Inayatullah's (1967) demand for infusion of non-Western culture into mainstream world culture to achieve universalism.

Today, globalization may similarly be distinguished from foreignization in Ghanian broadcasting. Foreignization seems to articulate the domination of broadcasting practice by Western foreign values in content and structure through an open-airwaves policy in which freedom of choice supersedes selective acculturation to achieve congruency. The pervasive nature of foreignness was found in the actions and contention of Professor Kwame Arhin, who also bore the additional responsibility of custodian of culture by virtue of his position as a chief or nifahene of Barekese in the Asante (Ashanti) Region where he is known by his Stool name Nana Arhin Brempong. In a radio interview conducted on the Twi (local language) Radio UNIVERS program *Obiara Nka Bi* (Let Everyone Speak) hosted by the author on Wednesday, April 8, 1998, he used English a lot. During that program, the professor asserted that Ghana's new democratic dispensation allows the cultivation of all kinds of values. The Ghana News Agency had earlier iterated the need to promote the need and use of Ghanian languages ("Teach" 1968). Professor Arhin's lack of proficiency in his mother tongue seemed to have contradicted this position.

Such incidents and attitudes exemplify an "autonomous" domestic culture yielding to "external globalized" culture, or globalism in which the substance of change is subsumed under the dynamics and symbolism of change. It is like the kind observed by Canadian Culture Minister Sheila Copps, who, speaking at a World Conference of Ministers of Culture in Ottawa in July 1998 to discuss American cultural invasion of the rest of the world (exports of film to Europe alone equals 10 times that of European export to America), stated, "Globalization must not mean a monoculture" (VOA news, July 17, 1998).

Foreignization is technology intensive and is driven by the McLuhanite dictum that the "Medium is the message." Whoever controls information technology controls the medium content, its flow, and any resultant cultural impact.

In an earlier Ghanian microstudy, Ansu-Kyeremeh (1992) identified cultural incongruencies associated with the application of Western-oriented technologically mediated communication systems to project implementation, without regard for the local "culturally friendly" indigenous communication systems, within some rural communities. Structural incongruencies identified in the study included centrifugal organization within a centripetal context; superimposition of linear communication on 2-way communication patterns; inappropriate programming, program types, and scheduling; language of broadcast; and sophistication of ownership technology designed for individualistic social situations but made to operate in communalistic communities of low technology.These and Mbachu's (1988) characterizations of Nigerian radio stations' bias for foreign music, are some of the problems of "free flow" of information that New World Information and Communication Order (NWICO) I sought to address through a "free and balanced flow" principle (Hedebro 1982, 63). However, after nearly two and a half decades of its adoption, substantial traits of the incongruencies are still observable even at the national macrolevel as evidence of foreignization.

Indeed, it now seems NWICO I was a mirage and that the reality is the 1990s NWICO II, the empirical foundation that repudiates the former's expectations, exhortations, and platitudes. In its conceptualization, NWICO I was officially articulated in its nature and implementation by UNESCO to secure international news flow balance in a globalizing world. NWICO II, on the other hand, unofficial and without an established conceptual framework or formulation, incorporates both globalization and foreignization dimensions.

If reciprocal program exchange rebroadcasting agreements are designed to achieve a 2-way flow in globalization, foreignization can induce 1-way Western broadcaster-supplied hardware (satellites) and software (programs) for a developing broadcaster to "disseminate" ("Cross-Frontier" 1992; Korem 1998). Thus, communication infrastructure may be constructed to facilitate global flow of information. But, sooner than later, the structure ends up ferreting content unidirectionally, with the venture effectively assuming the character of foreignization; in that format, the medium becomes a vehicle for propagating Western values among non-Westerners. In this mode, NWICO II is an all-new structural arrangement that perpetuates an old communication flow pattern or format or dependency deepening.

Ghanaian thinking aptly separates globalization with "autonomous domestic cultures" or "cultural autonomy," as espoused by Featherstone (1992), from "foreignized culture" in the statement, "I want the culture of all lands to be blown about my house as freely as possible, but I refuse to be blown off my feet by any one of them" (Hamelink 1983, 26). This clearly distinguishes between globalization or sharing a diversity of worldwide cultural values and foreignization or imposing Western cultural values on non-Western societies. The former is exclusive in the formulation of a "world" culture paradigm, the latter is inclusive in any such process.

ORIGINS OF GHANAIAN BROADCASTING

The cultural promotion or erosion implications of Ghanaian broadcasting may lie in its British beginnings. Broadcasting began in Ghana (then the Gold Coast) on July 1, 1935. It was a transplanted Western prototype with a total superimposition of foreign concept, technology, skills, professional behavior, time use, and value-embedded content—"merely relay stations for BBC transmissions" and a postcolonial conduit for perpetuating a world information flow imbalance by playing so much foreign music (Mbachu 1988, 2135).

CONSTRUCTION OF THE LOCAL INFRASTRUCTURE

Perhaps the most prominent indicator of foreign influence on the construction of communication infrastructure is FM radio, which began in 1988. The first

FM station in Accra, GBC FM (now Radio GAR) was actually installed with the help of Germany , with the transmitter and studio equipment donated by the Federal Republic of Germany. The national radio studios were also renovated with Japanese grants. In fact, the initiative for converting from short-wave transmission to FM broadcasting came from a conference organized by the German Friedrich Ebert Stiftung. A former director-general of the GBC claimed that many countries were being *advised* to change to FM.

A free-speech-enabling constitution, backed by public demonstration over the seizure of equipment of a pirate station, Radio EYE, compelled the NDC government to issue frequencies for FM stations in 1995, moving the nation into a new era of broadcast pluralism (Ayitevie 1996). In the last 5 years, the 1-station broadcasting monoculture of Accra has been transformed into a multiple of 13 FM stations. But these are also "foreignized" FM broadcasting with extensive direct foreign-originating content.

THE NATURE OF FOREIGNIZATION

An indicator as simple as the name of a radio or television station speaks volumes about the foreignness of broadcasting in Ghana. Names of Accra's radio and television stations illustrate this: Atlantis, CHOICE FM, GROOVE FM, JOY FM, Radio GAR, Radio GOLD, Radio UNIVERS, VIBE FM, GTV, METRO TV, and TV3.

More importantly, it has been observed that "the purpose of all external broadcasters is, at root, the same: to influence opinion in the interests—political, cultural or religious—of whoever is paying their bills" ("Cross-Frontier" 1992, 21). As indicated earlier, foreignization can exist in various forms; however, only two of its features are described and analyzed here. Official Ghanian attitude toward it says a lot, though. It is interesting to note that CNN and other foreign stations were allocated frequencies for television broadcasting in Ghana long before any Ghanian station was allocated one.

Regarding the mechanics of foreignization, an *Economist* article about Western broadcasting influence in eastern Europe is instructive, identifying two approaches to program delivery "on better wavebands [, that is,] medium wave or FM" ("Cross-Frontier" 1992, 22). One approach involves source Western broadcasters renting or buying transmitters that they install inside the countries receiving the broadcast, "and to broadcast in competition with local radio stations" (22). In the second instance, the Western broadcaster delivers

programmes, usually by satellite, to local stations, which retransmit them as part of their own output. Typically, the western broadcaster provides the re-broadcaster with satellite-receiving dish and tuner, pays for the satellite feed and provides the programmes free. The westerners may also provide scripts for translation into the local language. This is a growing trend. The buzz word is programme "placement." The BBC has made deals with state-owned and independent stations in ten East European countries to re-broadcast its programmes, and is looking for partners elsewhere. It claims that rebroadcasting has helped stem its loss of listeners in much of Eastern Europe, and has increased audiences in Poland. VOA, RFE and RL are following the same path, as are DW, RFI and others. (22)

In Africa, events are assuming the form of a new wave of media imperialism, taking advantage of liberalized airwaves. In March 1998, the BBC inaugurated rebroadcasting FM stations in Nairobi (93.7), Kampala, and Kigali. This sounds more like recolonization than neocolonialism. As if not to be outdone, then U.S. president Bill Clinton announced on March 30, 1998, in Botswana (while the BBC was inaugurating its Kigali FM station) that the United States would set up a broadcasting service in Africa to promote democracy (Corey 1998). These initiatives may be described as "domestication" of foreign media or "cultural legitimation."

Ansu-Kyeremeh (1998b) estimated total broadcast hours per week for some stations as follows: JOY FM 168, Radio UNIVERS 133, and GTV 140. Stations were then devoting the following percentages of their broadcast time to foreign content: JOY FM, 7.7; Radio UNIVERS, 6.4; and GTV, 28.5. This excludes several hours of foreign recorded programs broadcast by GTV. According to its program manager, Mark Nkrumah (in a telephone conversation on July 20, 1998), the Malaysian-owned TV3 was devoting 30 percent of its telecast time to local programs and 70 percent to foreign programs.

Both Ghanaian FM and television broadcasting are in the thick of rebroadcasting arrangements (Ansu-Kyeremeh 1998b). Perhaps unaware of culture as a commodity (at least in the materialist neo-Marxist interpretation of Pierre Bourdieu) and industry, these arrangements do not require the authorization of the frequency allocation organs of state. Canada, for example, is so concerned about the cultural ramifications of direct broadcasting that its legislation (Statutes of Canada 1991, Chap. 11, 45) prohibits rebroadcast of foreign-originating programs without authorization. A Ghanaian filmmaker/educator, Kow Ansah, criticizes the fact that Ghanaian media "features foreign artistes and films most of which are shown on pay channels which are not affordable to the majority of ordinary Ghanians" (Owusu-Afram 1998, 10). The criticism reported by Owusu-Afram (1998) further quotes Ansah: "These foreign artistes have made it to the top through the support of the western media. What do we stand to achieve by re-echoing their glory here in poor Ghana?" (10).

Live Broadcasts

Live broadcast of foreign programs originating directly from their external sources became one of the earliest manifestations of foreignization in Ghana's emerging broadcast pluralism. The first frequency allocation for a private television station went to CNN. To date, at least JOY FM, Radio GOLD, and Radio UNIVERS (all FM stations) broadcast live BBC, VOA, and Deutsche Welle (DW) programs, respectively. GTV also rebroadcasts live CNN and WorldNet from the

United States, and Deutsche Welle from Germany. They are received via terrestrial antennae constructed for that sole purpose in each case. The local stations have to adjust their programming schedules to accommodate the scheduling of the foreign stations. Both BBC and Radio France Internationale currently operate local FM stations that relay their international broadcasts 24 hours a day.

Programs aired are usually of the news and magazine types. These programs are presented from the perspectives of the nations of program origin. At other times, it is actually the culture of the nation of origin that is portrayed in the contents of these programs. Examples of such culture-specific programs are the DW early morning transmission on GTV, the WorldNet retransmission by GTV between 9:00 A.M. and 4:00 P.M. on weekdays, and many of TV3's programs, including its Australian and telenovella series.

Foreign content in programming is further deepened by locally initiated programs. For instance, a critic cites aspects of VIBE FM's productions (especially "Young Vibes") as "'*abrofosem*' (imitating western/white culture) . . . with its cinderella cum pussy-in-boots stories." He adds:

For the small pocket of expatriate children with a touch of nostalgia, this was feasible but we are moving into the millennium and I believe if Vibe is truly the station that is shaping the nation, pussy-in-boots and little miss Muffet are not for our Ghanian children who need to be in tune with our local fables, rhymes and stories. (qtd. in Ramatu 1998:10)

JOY FM, perhaps the most English of all Accra radio stations, is currently promoting, under the sponsorship of Junior Barclays Save Account and British Airways, the sale of "Disney theme books—*Pocahontas, Aladdin, Lion King, Beauty and the Beast, Hunchback of Notre Dame* and *Hercules*" (Anokye 1998, 8). The winning parent gets "an all-expense-paid-one-week trip to Disneyland in Paris, France, for a family of four as the grand prize" (Anokye 1998, 8). It is also important to note the cultural implications of the objective of the promotion, which "seeks to encourage parents to get involved in their children's education (especially in their formative years) by reading to or with them" (Anokye 1998, 8).

The Language of Broadcast

The JOY FM experience hardly promotes the use of local languages for broadcasting. A 1992 study of the languages spoken by the people of Accra by Dakubu (1997, 55) noted a high rate of "polyglotism." The same study found that 89.4 percent of respondents claimed competence in the local Ga language, 24.2 percent in Akan, 5 percent in Hausa, and 10 percent in English. In line with the language use policy of JOY FM, for example, these foreign programs are broadcast in foreign languages. Only one DW news program carried by Radio UNIVERS is broadcast in Hausa, which, although spoken by a number of Ghanians (5 percent competency in Accra), is by itself not an indigenous Ghanaian language.

The type of language used to broadcast has always been a thorny issue, as is found in Ansah's (1986) discussion of broadcasting and multilingualism. Minority groups in the upper-east region, for example, complained to the director-general of the GBC to include their languages for broadcasting. A major characteristic of Accra radio stations is the use of English, in which only 10 percent claim competence, as their main medium of communication—a kind of Stevensonian (1994, 89) idea of "linguistic colonialism." JOY FM, often regarded as the leading commercial station, broadcasts only in English. To the station then, English is more of "everyone's first language" and not Stevenson's (1994, 88) claim of "everyone's second language." This is against the speculation that local language programs such as *Afisem* (newspaper review) and *Obiara Nka Bi* (discussion) on Radio UNIVERS, *Odifo* (VIBE FM), *Opanin Kwaku Kyere* (Radio GOLD), and *Maame Dokono* (CHOICE FM) would be among the most highly rated programs. There is no properly established rating service yet.

A reader's letter pleaded the killing of the South African series *Egoli* shown by the state-owned GTV because it was "purely a white society series with black people coming in here and there in their apartheid role as servants at the homes of whites" (Ramatu 1998, 10). A magazine columnist also wrote that "GTV programming is strange! Why so many white faces?" adding, "Faces and accents are so 'un-Ghanian'" (Kaakyire 1996, 22).

Another indicator of foreignization is the aggressive promotion of the symbolism and associated values of Western cultural events, the most notable being Valentine's Day and Mother's Day, which were hardly events of any consequence before the liberalization of the airwaves. Although local festivals still do not enjoy the patronage of the media, as was the case in the 1980s (Ansu-Kyeremeh 1992), these Western cultural practices are highlighted and given a lot of publicity. Similar attention is paid to broadcast content sourced from imported religious holidays such as Christmas, New Year's Day, and Muslim festivals (Id-el-Fitr and Id-el-Kabir) that do not promote Ghanian cultural symbolism. TV3 *Gold Blast* game-show's designer was emphatic about how they work hard to adapt their set design to Christmas, New Year's Day, and Muslim holiday seasons in an interview on TV3 News (April 11, 1998). It is also revealing that when Americans go abroad "it is comforting to turn to CNN because it's our language, we know the people, and they do a good job" (an American qtd. in Tuchs 1999, 7). One wonders how Ghanians overseas, who visit JOY FM's and Radio GAR's Web sites, would feel.

CONSEQUENCES OF FOREIGNIZATION

The promotion of foreign culture, with language at the core, may be associated with certain sociocultural changes. Broadcasting organizations such as the VIBE FM and TV3 have recruiting preferences for Ghanian announcers and news readers who have developed foreign English accents from their stays in Britain. In the case of VIBE FM, a listener thought it was a British-sounding station. Other DJs, announcers, and news readers who have never set foot on any foreign soil mimic these accents in what has been locally described as "LAFA" (locally acquired foreign accents) (Arthur 1997, 2). Ramatu (1998), in a column article titled "These Presenters," stated: "There is enough LAFA (locally acquired foreign language) round to make one cringe with embarassment." She added that "Kwabena Kissi of VIBE FM sports on Saturdays fame has a local accent so prominent, so rough and raw. But it's made him a cult figure and made his show that different" (10).

Besides fostering Western consumerism by promoting the sale of Western-manufactured greeting cards and other related commodities, the raising of the profile of Western cultural practices is beginning to diminish the importance of local festivals and cultural practices. With Valentine's Day and Mother's Day, special programs encouraging the exchange of greetings through musical request programs dubbed "dedications," competitions, and prize awards on radio and television, a social transformation with ramifications for the local culture may be propagated by these media.

More importantly, foreign news sources seem to be stifling attempts to present such news from the Ghanaian perspective. Ghanaians tend to see the world through the eyes of foreign broadcasters. Because broadcasting stations pick their foreign news from the live-link facilities, Ghanaian foreign correspondents are almost non-existent. JOY FM's 6:00 A.M. news is so much of BBC news as the foreign component of GTV news is a replica of CNN.

Middle-class Ghanaians tend to rely on foreign direct broadcasting for important news. For example, the news of an altercation between President Rawlings and his vice president at a cabinet meeting was first broken to a stunned nation in a live interview of the vice-president on the BBC program *Focus on Africa* (1996). Three studies (two nationwide) by the faculty of the School of Communication Studies, University of Ghana–Legon, all indicated the interest of Ghanaians in Western-originating broadcasting.[3]

Seth K. Akuffo, a reader, wrote in the *Ghanian Chronicle*, "I love my BBC news," adding, "but occasionally, I try to listen to Radio Ghana at 6 a.m." Asking whether the latter was "Ghana news or Rawlings news," the writer indicated his preference for BBC news over "the propaganda and subtle indoctrination" of GBC news by stating, "In the first eight minutes of the news the name 'President Rawlings' was mentioned nineteen times!" ("Sychophantic GBC News" 1997, 4). This Ghanaian patronage of foreign news contrasts the observation by Hoge (1997) that "coverage of such international news in American media has steadily declined since the late seventies [and that] foreign news is even scarcer on radio" (48–49).

Not every television program, it seems, impacts negatively on the local culture. The screening of European football, German football, and other overseas football matches, including live broadcasts, must have influenced the remarkable improvement in the skills of young Ghanaians at the game. This is grounded in the fact that the small country of Ghana has won the world under-17 championship twice, in 1991 and 1995; still the affected players left for playing careers in Europe, opting not to stay in their homeland to contribute to the development of local football.

WHY FOREIGNIZATION?

It is emerging that broadcast pluralism does not necessarily equate to pluralism of voices. "Wherever local media were scarce or dissent was muzzled, listening to foreign radio stations [and one must add watching foreign programs on local television stations] became a local pastime" ("Cross-Frontier" 1992, 21). For example, for as long the GBC remained the only radio and television station, privately owned newspapers were left out in its reviews. Without contrast, the new commercial radio stations scarcely present positive images of opposition people and events (Amoakohene 1996).

Again, the Malaysian-owned private television station, TV3, supposedly dismissed a producer for airing an interview with the same opposition figure ("TV3" 1998, 1). A program on the state-owned GTV was also killed allegedly because, according to the presenter, "the President did not want to see my face on television." It all seems as if the statement, "evidence from East and Southern Africa suggests that the legalisation of commercial broadcasting is not sufficient to guarantee a plurality of voices on the airwaves" is being played out in Ghana.

SOUTH–NORTH INPUT OR BRAIN DRAIN?

Just as program content could be aiding the information imbalance, the inclusion of Africans in the decision-making strategies of foreign stations could be deepening foreignization. For example, Africans, including Edward Boateng (Ghanian regional director of the Turner Broadcasting System for Ghana and Africa), Rizu Hamid (Tanzanian program producer), and Onyekatchi Wambu (Nigerian TV programmer) recently participated in a radio debate on the influence and future of television in Africa ("BBC debates" 1997). The BBC describes its Sunday English-language instructional program *Radio English Direct* as "created by Africans."

Involvement of Ghanaians in the production and presentation of foreign-originating programs may be taken for input from the consumer into the product. Indeed, such Ghanaian participation can be found in the operations of the BBC, the VOA, and the DW. Even the worldwide broadcast cartoon series *The Planeteers* has a Ghanaian character, Kwame. Some may argue, though, that such token representation is with little cultural consequence in terms of the influence on program philosophy and orientation. It sounds more like co-optation than inclusion or reciprocity.

CULTURAL REASSERTION

Cultural autonomy or social isolation is impossible in today's wired world. The Ghanaian minister of information might have rightly stated, "By re-broadcasting news and information from all corners of the globe, *Radio Gold* is fulfilling the role of a window open unto the world" (Quakyi 1997). But he was wrong to assume that such program exchanges provide an opportunity to bring in all that is best in the different cultures of the world. This is because his assumption that the process would be two-way did not materialize. In fact, the Radio GOLD–VOA deal was not based on an exchange principle. More realistic approaches to the re-assertion of the national day with local cultural values is the promotion of local production and programming, South–South cooperation through program exchanges, and an aggressive input into Internet content.

Combating the cultural erosion that arises out of excessive foreignization could begin with greater attention to the development of improved local programs. Programs could constitute the bedrock for the strategies of reciprocity, cooperation, and finding space on the Internet or information superhighway.

It seems, though, that Ghanian electronic media audiences distinguish between foreign news and foreign programs when it comes to patronage. The *Media Monitor* observed that there appeared to be a strong patronage for locally produced programs, except for heavily politicized ones, and that people would watch local drama and film irrespective of the channel. A National Television and Film Training Institute instructor also lamented the high interest viewers show in what, in his opinion, are poorly made Ghanian films on television.[4] The interest goes for both local Akan and English films. Furthermore, discussion, and especially interactive listener phone-in programs on radio that usually focus on local issues, are very popular.

An attempt at South–South cooperation to give meaning to globalization while stemming Westernization is currently being implemented between Ghana's state-owned GTV and South Africa's public television station, operated by the South African Broadcasting Corporation. One needs to add, though, that the UNESCO-initiated and supported Union of Radio and Television Networks in Africa project is yet to move beyond exchanging music, drumming, and dancing films.

The Internet seems to have a potential for being a kind of an information flow equalizer. Irrespective of geographical location, messages can be channeled through it. Indeed, both the private station JOY FM and the state-owned Radio GAR have Web sites. Equalization, however, depends largely on the availability to a communicator of technological (including manufacturing capacity and know-how) and financial resources, the lack of which has been responsible for the original flow imbalance.

In addition, the challenge of the Internet to local culture and values has, indeed, already been felt. In April 1998, Ghanians were rudely awakened to a nightmare of nude pictures of fellow citizens that were published by a local newspaper, which attributed its source to an Internet Web site. Newspaper editorials and pronouncements by politicians and callers to radio phone-in shows were unanimous in their condemnation of the publication of the pictures. Nevertheless, no one was left in doubt about the potential of the Internet to affect local cultural values.

SUMMARY

Globalization, interpreted as a simultaneous and geographically ubiquitous reach of broadcasting, may be a worldwide system to which Ghana is wired. Much of its aspects, however, indicate foreignization interpreted as the construction of technological infrastructure inside non-Western countries for the purpose of receiving direct-broadcast messages from Western sources. In that mode, globalization assumes the form of refined subjugation, perhaps with a serendipitous or fortuitous agenda of world monoculture explained by the false assumption that non-Western cultures need to subscribe to what is purely a Western dominant paradigm as a universal value. The fallacy of the assumption is characterized in the repeated nonrecognition of *hegemonics* (social situation or condition in which power dictates values) or the reality of a minority imposing values on the majority and representing the product as national beliefs or cultures. Resulting corrosive cultural ramifications of foreignization are numerous. This has contributed greatly to an obfuscation of the notion of national day in Ghana.

There is the need, therefore, for Ghanian broadcasting and the mechanics of cultural transformation to insist upon reciprocity as both input into the global system and projecting their own culture. That way, true meaning could be given to globalization as a universal phenomenon. Finally, policy that seeks reciprocity in Ghanian input into the mainstream content of globalization needs to be constantly guided by a "We are being swallowed up by globalization" attitude and not just "We need to be part of globalization." Otherwise a "true" national day that objectifies, encapsulates, and symbolizes all that is best in Ghana would continue to elude the nation.

NOTES

1. His name is as foreign as the dismantling of Ghanian national institutions and much of the symbolism that characterized his administrations.

2. See Supreme Court ruling in *New Patriotic Party v. Attorney-General* (December 31 Case), Supreme Court, December 29, 1993, and March 8, 1994 (unreported).

3. They include Karikari and Ansu-Kyeremeh (1996a, 1996b) and Ansu-Kyeremeh (1996).

4. The comment was made at a focus group discussion by lecturers at the Institutte's Film Theatre on Wednesday, March 25, 1998.

REFERENCES

Adjaye, J. K. (1987) Time, the calendar, and history among the Akan of Ghana. *Journal of Ethnic Studies, 14*(3), 71–100.

Akuffo, S. K. (1997, September 22). Sycophantic GBC News. *Ghanian Chronicle*, 4.

Amoakohene, M. I. (1996, July–September). Kufuor heard loud but not clear. *Media Monitor, 4,* 9–10.

Anokye, F. (1998, July 10 and 12). JOY FM Disneyland family get-away. *Ghanian Chronicle*, 8.

Ansah, P. A. V. (1979). Problems of localising radio in Ghana. *Gazette, 25*(1), 1–16.

Ansah, P. A. V. (1986). Broadcasting and multilingualism. In E. G. Wedell (Ed.), *Making broadcasting useful, the African experience: The development of radio and television in Africa in the 1980s*, 47–65. Manchester, UK: Manchester University Press. 47–65.

Ansu-Kyeremeh, K. (1992). Cultural aspects of constraints on village education by radio. *Media, Culture and Society, 14*, 111–28.

Ansu-Kyeremeh. (1996, August 24–27). *The truth can only come from outside: Is foreign radio more credible?* Paper prepared for the 8th Macbride Rand Table on Communication (organized by the Korean Broadcasting Academic Society), Hoam Convention Centre, Seoul National University, Seoul, Korea.

Ansu-Kyeremeh, K. (1997). *Communication, education and development.* Accra: Ghana Universities Press.

Ansu-Kyeremeh, K. (1998a). Communication in an Akan political system. In K. Ansu-Kyeremeh (Ed.), *Perspectives on indigenous communication in Africa.* Vol. 2, *Dynamics and future directions*, 175–92. Legon: School of Communication Studies, University of Ghana.

Ansu-Kyeremeh, K. (1998b, July 26–30) *Globalization by "foreignization": A study of the foreign element in local broadcasting.* Paper prepared for the International Association of Media and Communication Research 21st General Assembly and Scientific Conference, University of Srathclyde, Glasgow, Scotland.

Arthur, R. (1997, January 8). Of presidents and LAFA. *Weekend Chronicle*, 2.

Ayitevie, A. O. (1996, April–June). Revisiting Radio Eye: Breaking into controlled territories. *Media Monitor*, 9–10.

Corey, C. W. (1998, March 30). *Africa needs more Botswanas, Clinton says; Announces radio democracy for Africa.* [Mimeo]

Cross-frontier broadcasting: And nation shall speak guff unto nation. (1992, May 2). *Economist*, 21–24.

Dakubu, M. E. K. (1997). *Korle meets the sea: A sociolinguistic history of Accra.* Oxford, UK: Oxford University Press.

Featherstone, M. (1992). Cultural production, consumption and the development of cultural sphere. In R. Munch and N. J. Smelser (Eds.), *Theory of culture*, 265–89. Berkeley: University of California Press.

Ghana. (1989). *Religious Bodies (Registration) Law*, PNDCL 221.

Ghana Ministry of Education and Culture, Culture Division. (1975). *Cultural policy in Ghana.* Paris: UNESCO.

Hamelink, C. J. (1983). *Cultural autonomy in global communications: Planning national information policy.* New York: Longman.

Hedebro, G. (1982). *Communication and social change in developing nations: A critical view.* Ames: Iowa State University Press.

Hoge, J. F. (1997, November/December). Foreign news: Who gives a damn? *Columbia Journalism Review*, 48–52.

Inayatullah. (1967). Toward a non-western model of development. In D. Lerner and W. Schramm (Eds.), *Communication and change in the developing countries*, 98–102. Honolulu, HI: East-West Center Press.

Kaakyire, K. (1996). Ordinary talk. *Media Monitor, 2*, 22.

Karikari, K., and Ansu-Kyeremeh, K. (1996, April). *Who reads the Graphic: Profile of readers of the Daily Grapic.* Legon: School of Communication Studies, University of Ghana.

Karikari, K., and Ansu-Kyermeh, K. (1996, February). *Who reads the newspapers, why and for what? A Ghanian readership survey.* A study conducted for the European Union Con-

tinuing Education for Media Practioners Project. Legon: School of Communication Studies, University of Ghana.

Korem, A. (1998, April 18). Religious intolerance. *Weekly Spectator*, 8–9.

Mbachu, D. (1988, November 14–20). The power of radio. *West Africa, 3718*, 2135.

Opoku, A. A. (1970). *Festivals of Ghana*. Accra: Ghana Publishing.

Owusu-Afram, E. (1998, July 10–16) Film director raps media. *Weekend Statesman,* 10.

Pye, L. W. (1966). *Aspects of political development*. Boston: Little, Brown.

Quakyi, K. T. (1997, April 4) Speech by the minister of information, Hon. Kofi Totobi
Quakyi, at the launching of Radio GOLD Programme Exchange Agreement with
Voice of America (VOA) at Radio GOLD premises.

Ramatu. (1998, July 17–23). These presenters. *Weekend Statesman,* 10.

Sidel, M. K. (1984, Autumn). New world information order in action in Guyana. *Journalism Quarterly,* 493–508.

Stevenson, R. L. (1994). *Global communication in the twenty-first century*. London: Longman.

Teach Twi in the School. (1968, July 1). *Daily Graphic*, 6.

Tuchs, H. (1999). *USIA: Communication with the world in the 1990s*. Washington, DC: U.S.
Information Agency.

TV3 staff sacked for interviewing Kufuor. (1998, April 7 and 16). *Independent*, 1.

JAPAN

Japan's National Foundation Day

Lack of Consensus Leads to Lack of Celebration

Stephen M. Ryan

On the first day of the first lunar month of 660 B.C., according to the *Nihon Shoki* (the eighth-century A.D. *Chronicle of Japan*), Jimmu ascended the throne and became the first emperor of Japan (Ueda 1983). The anniversary of his ascension is still marked as a public holiday in Japan: National Foundation Day, on February 11.

Far from being marked by popular outpourings of national pride or respect for the imperial family, which traces its descent directly from the Emperor Jimmu, the holiday instead is the least observed of all Japan's national holidays. For most workers outside the emergency services and the retail trade, it is a holiday, but there are neither mass public events nor private rituals or customs to mark the occasion.

The current situation stands in strong contrast to the way in which the day was marked during the period of militaristic nationalism that preceded and included the Pacific War. Indeed, the lack of pomp and custom associated with the modern National Foundation Day can be seen as a direct consequence of the pomp and razzamatazz with which Kigensetsu ([National] Origin Festival), as it was known until the end of World War II, was celebrated. The war, and the nationalism associated with it, are the subject of deep divisions within Japanese society and, as is usual with matters on which no consensus has been formed, are largely ignored.

Thus, National Foundation Day is marked each year, as will be outlined here, by the ritual of rival public meetings and rallies held, on the one hand, by those who would like to rekindle nationalism and love of Japan and, on the other hand, by those who see danger even in the granting of a public holiday to mark the mythical foundation of the country. However, such meetings attract very few people and the rest of the country appears hardly to notice.

THE FOUNDATION MYTH

Scholars are divided as to whether such a person as the Emperor Jimmu ever really existed.[1] If he did, he certainly was not known by that name, which was attributed to him posthumously in the late eighth century, or some 1,500 years after he was said to have reigned. The posthumous naming of emperors is still customary, although the process has been somewhat speeded up; for example, Emperor Hirohito has, since his death in 1989, been referred to as the Emperor Showa. The ancient chronicles of Japan, *Kojiki* (712) and *Nihon Shoki* (720), refer to the first emperor as Kamu Yamato Iware Hiko no Mikoto as well as other names. According to the chronicles, he was the great-great-grandson of Amaterasu Omikami, the sun goddess who is the main female Shinto deity. Amaterasu reportedly sent her grandson, Ninigi no Mikoto, armed with the sacred mirror, sword, and jewel, which are now the imperial regalia, to pacify the Japanese islands. Jimmu's father was a direct descendant of Ninigi no Mikoto and his mother was the daughter of the God of the Sea. The chronicles give conflicting accounts of the route by which Jimmu came to the throne but agree that he grew up in Hyuga (thought to be a part of modern Kyushu), from where he set forth to conquer the Yamato region, to the east of Nara. After several setbacks, he was victorious, thanks to the help of a golden bird, and was enthroned in the Kashihara Palace in modern-day Nara Prefecture, in the heart of the Yamato region.

Yamato is considered to have been the origin of the Japanese state and the imperial family claims direct descent from Jimmu, with the current emperor, Akihito, the 125th in the line. Clearly, the accounts of Jimmu's ancestry and his rise to the throne are heavily laced with mythical elements that serve to support the claims to legitimacy of the power elite at the time the chronicles were written. Many of the noble families of that time also claimed to be descendants of members of Amaterau Omikami's entourage. Some scholars see Jimmu as a composite figure, combining the exploits of several leaders, while others see the account of his progress from Kyushu to Nara as an allegory of the spread of Yayoi culture, which included the cultivation of rice and the working of metal. Still other scholars read the myth as an account of conquest by horse riders from continental Asia who founded the imperial line. Nevertheless, the Jimmu story was taught as history in schools and universities throughout the prewar period.

As was mentioned earlier, the year of Jimmu's ascension to the throne is given in *Nihon Shoki* as 660 B.C., but this date is considered to have been determined arbitrarily, based on the ancient Chinese belief that 660 B.C. would have been an auspicious year for revolutionary change. Certainly, it is much earlier than any of the credible claims for the existence of an emperor in Japan, which would date the imperial line to the fourth or fifth centuries A.D.

Holding the ascension ceremony on the first day of the first month would presumably be equally auspicious for the beginning of a new era. The modern commemoration of this day finds its way to the second week of February via the calendar reforms that followed the Meiji Restoration in 1868. During this period, enormous changes occurred in every facet of life in Japan as attempts were made to modernize the country and its institutions in order to "catch up with the West." When New Year was moved to January 1 in line with the Western calendar, some traditions that had previously been associated with the lunar (Chinese) New Year in February moved with it, while others became attached to specific dates in February (Chamberlain 1904/1971).

CURRENT OBSERVATION OF
NATIONAL FOUNDATION DAY

February 11 is marked in red on all Japanese calendars, just like the other 14 national holidays in the year.[2] National Foundation Day is described in a book designed to explain Japan to English-speaking foreigners as a "day for commemorating the founding of the nation and for fostering patriotic feeling" (Nippon Steel Human Resources Development 1984, 357). Unlike the other public holidays, though, it does not merit a separate entry in the otherwise comprehensive *Kodansha Encyclopedia of Japan* (1983).

In 1999, I conducted a survey about National Foundation Day among 61 third-year university students in western Japan two weeks before February 11. Responses revealed that 28 (45.9 percent) of them knew the name of the holiday, 32 did not, and 3 respondents thought they knew but mistakenly thought it was Constitution Memorial Day, which is another national holiday on May 3, regarding the granting of the postwar constitution. Asked further to describe the purpose of the day, 14 students (23.0 percent) referred to the foundation, building, or making of the nation. Six students suggested it was a day to "celebrate" or "think about" the national day, and one student said it was a time to take pride in being Japanese. Others suggested it was the day the old constitution was granted, the day Japan was named, or the day it became independent from the United States, and 27 (44.3 percent) said they did not know. Obviously, some of the students were able to glean from the name of the day that it is connected with the origins of Japan as a state, but none of them could specify what the connection is and a good number of them seemed never to have thought before about the meaning of the day.

As on other national holidays, schools, banks, public offices, and most large companies are closed on February 11, so for many people it is a day off. However, unlike many other national holidays, tradition does not prescribe specific activities for the day. There is no mass attendance at temples and shrines, as happens around New Year's Day; no visiting of the graves of immediate ancestors, as on the two equinoxes; no flying of plastic replicas of carp to wish children well, as on Children's Day; no organized sports or cultural activities, as on Sports Day or Culture Day; and no presentation of gifts to senior citizens, as on Respect for the Aged Day.

In contrast with the national days of many other countries described in this volume, on Japan's National Foundation Day there are no public gatherings, parades, processions, fiestas, or firework displays. There is no established habit of consuming special foods or beverages. People are no more likely to wear traditional, or even new, clothes on this day than any other.

Few of the students surveyed reported any particular plan for the day; rather, they would indulge in ordinary student activities, such as relaxing, spending time with friends, working at their part-time jobs, and studying (the holiday coincides with end-of-year exams in most universities). Slightly unusual plans such as going fishing or going to the theater were in no way associated with the theme of the day. If the survey had been taken in a year when February 11 fell on a Monday or a Friday, presumably there would have been more plans for three-day-weekend ski trips but, again, there is no reason to think there would have been any more activities connected with the foundation of the nation.

This indifference to the holiday is reflected in the mass media. There are no National Foundation Day special supplements in national or local newspapers, no special television broadcasts to mark the occasion, and no gala charity concerts organized by NHK, Japan's public broadcasting channel.

This lack of attention is in marked contrast to the festivals occurring immediately before and after National Foundation Day. February 3 is Setsubun, the bean-throwing ceremony, which was part of New Year's celebrations until New Year's Day was moved to January 1. The festival somewhat resembles the Anglo-American Hallowe'en in that it is concerned with driving away evil spirits for the year and welcoming benign spirits in their place. With cries of "Fuku wa uchi; oni wa soto" (In with the good spirits; out with demons), dry soybeans are scattered in each room of the house and thrown out through the main entranceway. Similar scenes are enacted at Shinto shrines, where crowds gather to watch. The television news carries reports from rural areas where strong Setsubun traditions have been preserved, showing villagers in loincloths and demon masks running through the streets carrying clubs, frightening the children, and warming the hearts of television producers in search of local color. Supermarkets sell special packs of soybeans with free demon masks. Once, on this day, flying with JAL (the national airline), I was handed a small packet of beans as I boarded and was encouraged to scatter them around the cabin. Recently, sushi shops have associated themselves with the Setsubun festival, encouraging customers to buy long cones of sushi, which, while being eaten, are to be pointed toward an auspicious compass direction (the direction varies from year to year).

March 3 is Hina-matsuri, the Dolls' Festival, a less public but no less colorful affair. Each family with daughters will display in their home a set of *hina* dolls, representing a stylized emperor, empress, and around 20 of their courtiers. Exquisitely dressed in the costumes of ancient times, the dolls are arranged on a set of steplike display shelves, carpeted in varying shades of red, along with a wealth of accessories, such as drums, brooms, a palanquin, flowers, rice cakes, and candies. A full set of dolls can fill one-third of a standard-sized room, so miniaturized and abbreviated sets are available for apartment dwellers. The dolls are a traditional gift from proud grandparents to their first granddaughter. They are on display in homes for about two weeks before March 3 (i.e., from just after the largely ignored National

Foundation Day). On the day itself, if there is a young girl in residence, she will host a little tea party of her favorite snack foods and brightly colored rice crackers that are strongly associated with this day and they will sing the Hina-matsuri song. Her parents will drink *shirozake*, a sweet drink made from rice gruel and fermented rice. Shops selling doll sets, rice crackers, and alcoholic drinks all have colorful displays at this time of year, but the festival itself is largely domestic, occurring inside each home.

Neither Setsubun nor Hina-matsuri is a national holiday. The fact that the National Foundation Day is, and they are not, clearly has more to do with politics than with the fervor with which they are celebrated.

These festivals have been described at some length to illustrate that there is no aversion to celebration in Japan—only, it would seem, to celebrating National Foundation Day. Even Valentine's Day, a recent import from the West, which is only three days after National Foundation Day, causes more of a stir than the foundation day itself.

MEMORIES OF A GRANDER OCCASION

There was not always such indifference. Those who remember the days before Japan's defeat in World War II speak of the (National) Origin Festival as a happy occasion (Yamazaki, personal communication, February 10, 1999) when, as children, they were given, celebratory red and white rice cakes with sweet-bean fillings. Schools held ceremonies where the Rising Sun flag was raised and saluted, respect was paid to the emperor, and the Origin Festival song was sung.

This was the intention of the constitutional reformers who, having restored the emperor to a (symbolic) central position in the government of Japan in 1872, declared the festival to be a national holiday ("Kigensetsu Controversy" 1983). They hoped to cement the legitimacy of the imperial line by drawing attention to the foundation myth and to increase the affection felt by all Japanese citizens for the empire. The Origin Festival thus became one of the major symbolic supports of the nationalist rhetoric that predominated before and during World War II. Seen as such by the occupation forces, who abolished the holiday along with other "nationalist" holidays in 1948 ("Kigensetsu Controversy" 1983), it was only in 1966 that the holiday, under its new name, was reinstated.

THE OBSERVANT FEW

Still, it would be an exaggeration to say that no one now celebrates National Foundation Day. Each February 12, newspapers carry (on inside pages) reports of National Foundation Day rallies and meetings, which sound just as ritualistic as the throwing of beans or the unwrapping and careful placing of dolls.

For example, the Osaka edition of the national newspaper *Asahi Shimbun* carried its report on page 14 in 1999, under the headline "National Foundation Day,

For and Against, Meetings Held in Each Region" ("Kenkoku Kinen" 1999). The article begins by explaining that the day used to be called the (National) Origin Festival and was strongly associated with the "Emperor System." Now, it says, people are divided into two camps: those who wish to celebrate the foundation of the nation and those who want to prevent the return of the nationalism symbolized by the Emperor System. Both sides had held meetings on the previous day. The article then describes two political meetings in some detail: one held in Osaka by the Teachers' Labour Union and the History Study Group under the title "Disapproving of National Foundation Day, Let's Think about Peace and Harmony," which was addressed by a professor from Nagoya University and attended by 200 people; the second was held in Kobe on a similar theme, attended by 80 "religious leaders and teachers" and addressed by the leader of the Hyogo Association to Ban Nuclear Weapons. There was a much briefer report to the effect that a meeting was also held at Meiji (Shinto) Shrine in Tokyo to celebrate the day.

It has to be said that the *Asahi Shimbun* is notoriously the most left-leaning of the national newspapers, and that other newspapers gave more attention to the "pro" meetings and less to the "anti" in their reports. Some of the terminology also needs explanation: the Emperor System is standard left-wing shorthand for the ideology of the nationalist regime in power before and during World War II that placed respect for the emperor above all other things. The banning of atomic weapons has been the rallying call of the Left since the bombing of Hiroshima and Nagasaki in 1945.

Another national newspaper, the *Daily Yomiuri*, gave more details of the main celebratory gathering in its February 12 edition ("Prime Minister" 1999, 2). It described an address made by Prime Minister Keizo Obuchi to "about 1,500 people" gathered to attend a National Foundation Day ceremony in Tokyo.

Thus, we have small groups of labor activist and left-wing intellectuals (professors, teachers) gathering in "public" meetings up and down the country to oppose the very idea of a National Foundation Day and slightly larger groups of right-wingers also attending meetings throughout the nation to celebrate the anniversary of Emperor Jimmu's ascension to the chrysanthemum throne as the symbolic beginning of the nation.

These two opposing groups are familiar from other struggles (van Wolferen 1989). The same left-wingers can be found celebrating May Day in the streets on May 1, while the right-wingers hold rallies on Northern Territories Day to demand the return of four islands occupied by Soviet forces in the closing days of World War II and now part of the Russian Federation. The two groups disagree on whether the Rising Sun should be recognized as Japan's national flag and "Kimigayou" as the national anthem, or whether they are too tainted by associations with World War II militarism to be used as national symbols. They disagree about Japan's defense treaty with the United States; reportedly, both of the speakers at the left-wing meetings described by the *Asahi Shimbun* made reference to the need to oppose revisions of the guidelines under which the treaty could be invoked, an issue under debate in the National Diet at that time, whereas Prime

Minister Obuchi spoke in support of the revisions at the nationalist gathering. They disagree about the honoring of Japan's war dead and the extent to which Japanese atrocities during the war should be described in school textbooks. Basically, the argument is about the legacy of World War II, with the Left arguing for the need to reject all forms of nationalism and militarism and the Right unrepentant over the war and insistent about the need for patriotism and moral fiber in the country.

In the past, these issues have mobilized the public and brought them onto the streets. There were violent street demonstrations in the immediate postwar period about labor affairs and again in the late 1960s about the renewal of the Japan–U.S. Security Treaty. Gradually, though, public interest has waned and to many the protagonists appear to be caught in a time warp, arguing incessantly about issues that have lost their relevance. The meetings held by both sides on National Foundation Day are ignored by all but the reporters sent to cover them.

Add to this a distinct tendency among Japanese people to shy away from any kind of controversy (Krauss, Rohlen, and Steinhoff 1984) and the causes of the general indifference to National Foundation Day become clear. Japanese public life is notoriously dominated by consensus: it is generally true that without a consensus on a given issue, nothing is done. The long-running dispute involving Narita, Tokyo's main international airport, is a classic illustration. A group of people opposed to the construction of the airport purchased land lots in the path of a proposed second runway and has been refusing to let the runway be built for the past 25 years. The government has the power to remove them by force but prefers to negotiate. The runway, which is badly needed, seems unlikely to be built until a consensus is reached. So, this dispute, like the Right/Left disagreement about the role of nationalism in public life, lingers on and on, ignored by most people, and coming to public attention only when one opinion or the other is expressed strongly through ritualized public protest.

If there is a lack of interest in National Foundation Day, then it is, at least for some, a studied lack of interest: better to do nothing than to risk becoming involved in an area of controversy.

WHY HAVE A HOLIDAY IF MOST PEOPLE IGNORE IT?

Although lack of consensus can freeze an issue almost completely, under the surface things do move, gradually, in the direction of the more powerful combatant. Japan has been governed from the Right for almost all of the last 50 years. The Rising Sun flag is flown at more and more public occasions, "Kimigayou" is played when one expects to hear a national anthem, and class-A war criminals have been enshrined in the national shrine for the war dead and are regularly visited by government ministers. Also, the word *attack* has been replaced by *advance* in textbooks describing Japan's behavior in China during the war, the revisions to the defense guidelines seem likely to be approved by the Diet, and after a

15-year debate, National Foundation Day became a national holiday once more in 1966 ("Kigensetsu Controversy" 1983).

Yet, in a classic illustration of the dictum that you can lead a horse to water but cannot force it to drink, the majority of people are grateful for National Foundation Day as a day off but prefer to do their celebrating on days that are less beset by controversy. Like schoolchildren hearing the "Kimigayou" played at school graduation ceremonies by government order, they can hear the music but are not obliged to sing. Japan's National Foundation Day seems set to remain a quiet day off in February for the foreseeable future.

NOTES

1. The following account has been compiled from Ueda (1983) and Grapard (1983).

2. Japan's national holidays are January 1 (New Year's Day), the second Monday in January (Coming of Age Day), February 11 (National Foundation Day), March 20 (Vernal Equinox), April 29 (Greenery Day), May 3 (Constitution Memorial Day), May 4 (Citizens' Rest Day), May 5 (Children's Day), July 20 (Sea Day), September 15 (Respect for the Aged Day), September 23 Autumnal Equinox), the second Monday in October (Sports Day), November 3 (Culture Day), November 23 (Thanksgiving for Labour Day), and December 23 (Emperor's Birthday).

REFERENCES

Chamberlain, B. H. (1971). *Japanese things: Being notes on various subjects connected with Japan.* Tokyo: Tuttle. (Originally published 1904)

Grapard, A. G. (1983). Amaterasu Omikami. In *Kodansha encyclopedia of Japan* (vol. 1, 51). Tokyo: Kodansha.

Kenkoku kinen hi: Sansei, hantai: Kakuchi de shuukai [National Foundation Day: For and against: Meetings in each region]. (1999, February 12). *Asahi Shimbun,* 14.

Kigensetsu controversy. (1983). In *Kodansha encyclopedia of Japan* (vol. 4, 204). Tokyo: Kodansha.

Kodansha encyclopedia of Japan. (1983). Tokyo: Kodansha.

Krauss, E. S., Rohlen, T. P., and Steinhoff, P. G. (Eds.). (1984). *Conflict in Japan.* Honolulu: University of Hawaii Press.

Nippon Steel Human Resources Development. (1984). *Nippon: The land and its people.* Tokyo: Gakuseisha.

Prime minister stresses need for reforms. (1999, February 12). *Daily Yomiuri,* 2.

Ueda, M. (1983). Jimmu, Emperor. In *Kodansha encyclopedia of Japan* (vol. 4, 57). Tokyo: Kodansha.

van Wolferen, K. (1989). *The enigma of Japanese power.* London: Macmillan.

KUWAIT

Kuwait's National Day

Four Decades of Transformed Celebrations

Nibal K. Bourisly and Maher N. Al-hajji

O n June 19, 1961, the Kuwait sheikdom gained its full independence from Great Britain, shortly after raising its new flag. Unlike other countries that had suffered under harsh and forceful colonization, relations between Kuwait and Great Britain had been more of an alliance based on an 1899 protection agreement between the two. During the protection period, Kuwait had complete autonomy over deciding its internal affairs, but to a lesser degree its external affairs. For example, even though Kuwait did not have embassies from other nations, heads of Arab states visited the amir and met with him to discuss various topics about the region (Y. Al-Gunaim, personal communication, January 21, 2001). Despite the friendly relationship between Kuwait and Great Britain, the British insisted on having the upper hand over Kuwait's oil industry during the protection period, a situation that continued until December 1975. This control played a large role in slowing down the country's development at various levels (Al-Sagaf 1986). If Kuwait had had full control over its oil revenues, it might have started its development in 1946, when Kuwaiti oil was first sold. After gaining full control over its oil, however, the country was quickly able to make up for lost time and managed to establish itself as one of the most developed Arab countries. Many Kuwaitis view the independence of 1961 as a *completion* of independence (R. Al-Feeli); and Y. Al-Gunaim, personal communication, January 9, 2001, and January 21, 2001, respectively). Even the occasion itself is referred to as a national day rather than an independence day.

Kuwait enjoyed its freedom even before its official independence. It often celebrated the day the amir in charge took hold of office in a national day called Eid Al-nsher, which literally means "the flag's feast," because flags were hung throughout the country on this day (Y. Al-Gunaim, personal communication, January 21, 2001). In May 1964, following independence, the formal decision was made to celebrate Kuwait's national day on February 25, in honor of the amir, Sheikh Abd Allah Al-Salim Al-Sabah (1895–1965), whose rule had began on this date in 1950. February was also chosen for practical reasons, as June is a very hot summer month in Kuwait and a large number of Kuwaitis travel to escape the heat from June to August, which could drastically cut down on celebration attendance (Al-Saedan 1993).

The year 2001 marked the 40th anniversary of Kuwait's National Day. Four hundred thousand Kuwaiti dinar, approximately US$1,250,000, was allocated by the government for the celebration, which included local parades, exhibitions highlighting various aspects of the Kuwaiti culture, and competitions revolving around local cultural themes of varying types ("Arbaa maet *alf* Dinar," 2000). Similar to the goals set by most countries, the national day is considered by the Kuwaiti government as an opportunity to bring to the forefront the history of the land and local cultures to revive patriotism and promote unity among its two million residents. Even though the intention to take advantage of this national holiday has always been there, the government's orchestration of such celebrations and its enthusiasm for such events have changed remarkably over the past four decades to accommodate the political, economic, and social changes occurring internally and externally. What makes Kuwait's national day unique is that it not only celebrates the national day, but also persists to confirm and reaffirm the nation's autonomous status even after 40 years of independence. Yet, as we will argue, despite 40 years of autonomy, Kuwait still finds itself needing to validate its independence and sovereignty. Its relatively small size, strategic geographic location, and natural resources give it a commercial importance that has appealed to other countries over the past three centuries. Many countries have sought opportunities to dominate the land either by force through occupation or peacefully by signing joint treaties with Kuwait's rulers. Because of such continual acquisitiveness, Kuwait's national day is one means through which the country attempts to authenticate its identity as a sovereign nation and to build unity among its people.

In the past four decades, Kuwait has witnessed numerous political, economic, and social changes. In the 1960s, the country went through political reforms as its constitution was approved and promulgated, giving the people more say in their country's affairs. The National Assembly became part of the democratic scene in Kuwait—a hallmark that was then unique to the entire Arabian Gulf region. Furthermore, the economy of the country changed dramatically with the discovery of oil, in turn causing changes in other aspects of the Kuwaiti life and culture. Ghabra (1997) puts it this way, "By means of its oil wealth, Kuwait developed from a tribal entity into a state, moving from subsistence to state-sponsored welfare, and from a nation of little importance to one of significant power in regional and international affairs" (359). As more oil revenues started flowing into the country, the wealth of the nation could be seen in the paving of the roads, construction of new schools and hospitals, the growth of new neighborhoods and districts, the establishment of modern entertainment places, and the expansion of ministerial services. The nation's wealth was reflected in people's personal lives as well. Kuwaitis' lifestyles changed rapidly and dramatically from dependence on fishing, sea trade, pearl diving, and boat building—all of which brought in little money despite the hardship—to working fixed hours as government employees for increased steady salaries.

Currently, Kuwait's wealth and strategic planning still focuses primarily on fulfilling the needs and wants of its citizens, and very little direct governmental attention is allocated to building patriotic citizens. In other words, Kuwait's nation-building strategy has been based on improving people's material status rather than on building a strong national ideology, which encourages the achievement of national aims. The government seems to believe that by providing a luxurious lifestyle for its citizens, it would automatically win fidelity and gratitude with a resulting strong sense of national coherence among its people. Such a strategy might have succeeded in the 1960s and 1970s, but from the 1980s onward, a new national strategy should have been implemented, especially as the country entered a new stage in its history as a nation confronting, as we will see, various challenges ranging from external political threats to internal political pressures.

National days are opportunities for governments to renew people's loyalty to the nation and the ruling authority. What strategies the country employs might depend largely on how it views the present status quo and the future of the nation. The following sections will highlight how Kuwait has celebrated this day over the past four decades, and in what ways the celebrations were altered to suit the challenges that occurred during specific decades. In particular, we will focus on four major challenges: modernization, tribalism, religious fundamentalism, and the Iraqi invasion, all of which, to various degrees, have shaped the country's national day celebrations and have delayed the formation of a strong sense of Kuwaiti nationhood based on coherence and social unity. The call today is for Kuwait to rethink its national day by conceptualizing it in a new way directed toward establishing a stronger "Kuwaitiness."

To go about this study, we found a large number of journal articles and political and historical books that analyzed the history of Kuwait and its independence from Great Britain. These studies, however, did not examine Kuwait's national day. Most of the studies mentioned briefly Kuwait's national day as a historical day that needs to be commemorated, but did not describe or discuss the actual celebrations. Therefore, we depended largely on original sources. In-depth interviews were conducted with people who had a leading role in planning and organizing national days in Kuwait during the 1960s, 1970s, 1980s, or 1990s. In addition, we used archival material from both the daily newspaper *Al-Qabas* and the Kuwait News Agency to obtain a comprehensive picture of the type of celebrations and specific events that occurred in the examined period. Furthermore, the Kuwait Television archive was used to obtain videotapes of programs that were relevant to the study, such as the musical concerts that were performed specifically for the national day.

MODERNIZATION AND THE ROAD TO NATIONHOOD (1960s AND 1970s)

It is important here to present an overview of Kuwait's establishment. Al-Rasheed (n.d.) provides us with a look at the discrepancies over the time of the exact establishment of Kuwait. He reveals that some have declared that the country existed when Al-Sabah family migrated to it in 1367. On the other hand, a letter from Sheikh Mubarak, Kuwait's amir from 1896 to 1915, stated that the country was established in 1610. Yet, still others argue that it was established in 1688. Al-Rasheed does not attempt to offer a concrete answer, but provides 1723 as a year in which he is sure that Kuwait was already in existence. He supports this statement with a document recording that a famous religious man, Sheikh Mohammed Ben Fairooz, passed away in Kuwait—meaning that the country existed in that year. Similarly, other historians tend to provide dates that fall in the mid-18th century (see, e.g., Abu-Hakima 1983; Al-Tamimi 1998).

Kuwait is a small area overlooking the Arabian Gulf, which witnessed the migration of a number of tribes.[2] The main tribes were Bani Khaled and Anza, the origin of the current ruling family Al-Sabah, which rose to power in 1756 (Al-Tamimi 1998). Sabah, the first ruler of Kuwait, was elected by the local tribes to administer justice and to look after the interests of the thriving town (Abu-Hakima 1983); under his rule, and with the will of the people, the country was able to establish itself as a nation that had its own identity separate from the countries surrounding it. The democracy of its ruling system and its people's liberal way of life,[3] compared to that of the other gulf countries, are two hallmarks of Kuwait's identity today. This identity has been shaped by four major forces: first, its historical attachment to the Arabian Gulf as the main source of livelihood; second, its long and friendly relationship with various countries, both Western and Eastern; third, the discovery of oil that added a new facet to the Kuwaiti identity, portrayed in what can be described as a "modern twist"; and, finally, and most importantly, the religion of the land, Islam,[4] which plays a role in the extent of Kuwaitis' acceptance of and adaptation to the influence of other cultures.

Even though the country has been modernizing since the 1940s, such moves accelerated in the 1960s, when the government began to provide its people with housing loans, various free public services, telecommunications services, and free university education. The country's small size,[5] small population, and the flow of oil revenues all helped the modernization process outpace that of other Arab countries. The striving to be a modern nation encouraged the opening of Kuwait's geographic borders to those wanting to make a living and to participate in building the country. As the first census in 1957 shows, the country's population was 206,000; by 1965, the population reached 467,339, with native Kuwaitis making up only 36 percent (168,793). Today, the Kuwaiti citizens are still a minority. In 1995, the year of the last census, Kuwaitis were about 42 percent of the population (Kuwait Ministry of Information 1999). The rest of the population is made up of expatriates, who came to Kuwait (with or without their families) on working permits. Most of those workers come from Arab countries, others come from Iran and East Asia, and fewer come from Africa and Western countries. The small number of Kuwaitis was a factor in encouraging the government to be generous in providing relatively high salaries to its citizens, eliminating the formation of a large lower class citizen, as the majority came to be considered middle class. As Sheikh Abd Allah al-Salim Al-Sabah once said, "The resources that God has blessed this country with should always be put to use in the service of the people to achieve a comfortable and a stable life and to achieve their goals in life" (Kuwait Television, n.d.). If we take the improvement of Kuwaitis' socioeconomic status as a sign of modernization, we can say that modernization was felt directly by the Kuwaitis as the socioeconomic status drastically changed during the 1950s and 1960s.

The need to reassure the people about the continuation of the "good life" was reflected in building a strong army (i.e., to protect the land and its resources) and in being responsible for educating the youth (i.e., the future generations). Such strategies came to life for the whole country during the national day celebrations of the 1960s. Hundreds of army men and policemen marched, demonstrating their special talent before the amir, representatives from various nations, and local officials. Soldiers drove their motorcycles through flamed rings, and groups of eight policemen balanced themselves on one motorcycle. School students, all boys, also participated in these shows, performing well-organized exercise routines that showed off their healthy well-being through coordinated and synchronized movements. This exhibition of the army and the future generation was displayed to confirm the country's independence and to show that it was capable of taking care of itself. At the same time, it helped establish the nation as an identifiable entity in the Arab region.

In his speech during the first national day celebration in 1962, Kuwait's amir affirmed that Kuwait would always seek consolidation with Arab countries while remaining free and independent (Kuwait Television, n.d.). The underlying message from this first anniversary of the national day was to coin a political message targeted at Abdul Kareem Gasim, who was the Iraqi president at that time, against his continual claims that Kuwait is a part of Iraq. Through the military parade, which was organized for the occasion, Kuwait wanted to demonstrate to him and his followers that it was united and was not going to give in to his threats, and, most importantly, to show him the world's support of Kuwait (Al-Gunaim, personal communication, January 21, 2001) as a number of high Arab and Western officials attended the celebration.

Kuwait's independence came at a time when the Arab world was calling for the creation of pan-Arabism based on an Arab nationalism. This political move was led by Egypt's charismatic president Gamal Abdul-Nasser, who spoke enthusiastically about the formation of an Arab nationalism that would stand in the face of any form of colonization. As a result, many Arabs, especially the youth, believed in and sought such unification by putting loyalty to their country's government to the side. The famous voice of the Egyptian radio political commentator, Ahmad Saeed, increased the fire of these youth as he encouraged them to face their authorities and seek reforms in these "backward" governments (Al-Atigi 2001). Although Kuwait had gained its independence and was going through an intense modernization phase, as a newly independent state, there were still fears regarding its sovereignty and stability. Most threats, however, came from across its northern border. To the present, Kuwait still finds itself needing to prove its sovereignty to Iraq under its current president, Saddam Hussein, who continues to threaten and claim Kuwait for his nation.

The ending of the protection agreement came at short notice to those working in Kuwait's local media; they had no national songs to air on the radio to celebrate the event (R. Al-Feeli, personal communication, January 9, 2001).[6] The first national song, "Ya Homat Al-Ariin" (The Protectors of the Land) was composed within a very short time and performed by the police band.[7] From the early days of independence, the Ministry of Information was granted responsibility to plan and organize for the national day. In 1964, when Sheikh Jaber Al-Ali became the minister of information, he realized that feelings of patriotism and nationalism can be conveyed more passionately through songs than political speeches (R. Al-Feeli, personal communication, January 9, 2001), so more efforts were put forth to develop national songs. Al-Ali wanted as many people as possible from around the world to hear about Kuwait; therefore, his strategy was to get famous Arab composers and singers to sing about the new nation. He asked famous Egyptian singers such as Mohammed Abdulwahab, Fareed Elatrush, Abdulhaleem Hafiz, and Um Kalthoum,[8] who sang her famous song about Kuwait, "Ya Darna Ya Dar" (Oh, Our Homeland) (R. Al-Feeli, personal communication, January 9, 2001). Associating Kuwait with Um Kalthoum is associating the country with what was modern and authentic at that time—singing in classical Arabic, which is understood by all Arabs and giving the song a wider spread throughout the Arab region than would singing in a local (Kuwaiti or Egyptian) dialect.

The songs were one means through which the national day celebrations began to come out from their rigid official frame of focusing on political speeches and ministries' participation. It was in the mid-1960s when the celebrations became open to the public, changing from being a military march performed for distinguished personnel to a celebration open for the public and private sectors. It was primarily through the impetus of the Ministry of Education that the celebrations opened to encourage the public to be both participants and spectators (R. Al-Feeli, personal communication, January 9, 2001). Alongside the various ministries that continued to participate in the public parades, different Arab nationalities paraded in their national costumes, holding their countries' flags alongside the Kuwaiti traditional folk music bands. Also, sport clubs paraded their own young players wearing club uniforms. These parades were held before a large audience that gathered along the Arabian Gulf Road (a main road overlooking the Arabian Gulf and is parallel to downtown Kuwait and several suburban areas; this road is still the place for parades today) to see theme-decorated vehicles with schoolboys and schoolgirls on them waving to the crowd. The public celebrations proceeded into the 1970s as people continued to be eager to participate in such celebrations (M. Al-Sanousi, personal communication, January 15, 2001).

In the early 1970s, a Higher Committee was formed and headed by Mohammed Al-Sanousi, specifically for planning, organizing, and implementing national day celebrations. The committee funding was primarily from the private sector, (M. Al-Sanousi, personal communication, January 15, 2001), making it the people's responsibility to keep alive their patriotism. The committee would send out invitations to all the ministries and most of the private sector encouraging them to participate in the upcoming national day; in turn, each ministry was responsible for allocating budgets for their activities. Al-Sanousi pointed out that there was enthusiasm among both the ministries (i.e., the government) and the private sector to fund and participate in the celebration. The committee's planning for all national activities was year-round (e.g., opening of an annual the National Products Exhibition), but the planning of the national day was the largest event of their year. The committee's goal, Al-Sanousi added was to entertain the people and to revive the market economy and, most importantly, it aimed to build trust in the state and respect for the country. The committee had complete freedom to decide the type of activities for the national day and other occasions. After 15 years, in 1985, the responsibility of planning for the national day was turned back over to the government and an annual budget was allocated for the celebration.

The committee creatively built on the celebrations of the 1960s, which helped the celebration reach a stage of maturity in which national symbols in the form of words (e.g., national songs) and images (e.g., the Kuwaiti flag and the amir and the crown prince's pictures) were used for communicating strong patriotic messages. The maturity of the 1960s in creating and understanding the meaning of symbols led to the development of national concepts, in the 1970s, that were used during national occasions. "Al-usra-al-wahida (The United Family) is one concept created to idealize a myth about old Arab tribal families who lived together, took care of each other, and all lived under the protection of the family patriarch (Tétreault and al-Mughni 1995). Another popular concept was "Waledona al-atheam" (Our Great Father), used to refer to the Amir, who in turn referred to the people as *abnaee* (my children). On the 15th anniversary of the national day, in 1976, the amir, Sheikh Sabah Al-Salim started his speech to the citizens this way:

My dear children. . . . Children, it is my pleasure on this occasion to speak to you as I have always have[*sic*]—as a father talks to his children—to remind you that if it were not for our standing hand in hand we would not have been able to move forward our beloved country to where it stands today. ("Risalt *Amir* al-bilad" 1976)

The picture of the one family with the amir at its head was used to bring the Kuwaitis closer together and to provide respect and allegiance to the state, represented by the leader. When Sheikh Jaber Al-Ahmed was appointed amir in 1977, his annual national day speech was still focused on the family theme, but took a brotherly tone, as he referred to the people as "my dear brothers and sisters." The promotion of the family concept was encouraged by the media as the state's Social Policies Committee put together a media plan to promote and articulate family values of respecting the head of family and the elderly, and caring for the young within the context of the society—by depicting the state as a family (Tétreault and al-Mughni 1995).

The promotion of such concepts contributed to Kuwaitis feeling part of the larger societal family, feelings shown during the national day celebrations. People willingly hung the amir's and the crown prince's pictures in their houses, offices, and classrooms, and the Kuwaiti flag was seen all around the country in various shapes and sizes. Being part of the Kuwaiti family was clearly communicated by hundreds of businesses placing their national day congratulations to the rulers and the Kuwaiti people in the daily newspapers. In its issue published on February 25, 1976, the number of congratulations in *Al-Qabas* increased its average number of pages from 20 to 64, and in the following year it reached 72 pages. In addition to the historical meanings of national day, its festive nature added a further dimension to the meanings of nationalism as people came together to celebrate their history and their nationhood.

With the continuation of the street parades, a new form of celebration was added beginning in 1977. Accompanied by live orchestras, staged performances of national songs and dances by school students, mostly girls, from kindergarten through high school, were attended by the amir or the crown prince, the ministers, and other distinguished people. Nationally televised, it was an evening program that whole families enjoyed. Enthusiastic songs praised the amir, the crown prince, and the country. Among the most memorable songs performed was this one from 1982, which was used over the years for subsequent celebrations:

> We met the most precious days of our lives
> We lived it with happiness filling our hearts
> Our father Jaber [Kuwait's amir] we know his good deeds
> And Abu Fahad [Kuwait's crown prince] he is our pride.

Many songs about Kuwait portrayed it as a being a woman, mostly a mother who nurtured her children (i.e., the people), with goods; therefore, we all need to love our country and protect it from danger and envy:

> We love her with a passion which engrossed us as children
> May God keep her for us and protect her from all evil
> Amen Amen Amen
> She is our mother and she is our land.

These and other songs carried within their words tremendous amounts of love toward the country and showed that one's love of country could be in various forms, ranging from simply educating oneself in order to build the country to being a martyr protecting it.

The unique festive nature of the celebration helped people perceive their country as being bountiful, reflected in their enthusiasm to give back to it during national day in a way that showed their autonomy and social unity. Such public celebrations also inspired citizens with patriotic feeling, or with "civic virtue" (Trachtenburg 1993, 196). Elaborate festivities and the patriotic songs charged the atmosphere with patriotic emotions that were felt even after the celebrations were over. In the 1960s and 1970s, Kuwait utilized its national day to convey political messages to those having doubts about its sovereignty. The occasion also functioned to support its modernization process, and most importantly, they played a role in creating social order as it brought people together during that time. As social and political challenges surfaced in the 1980s, new ways of approaching the national day came into play.

TRIBALISM: NEW POWERS AND NEW WAYS OF CELEBRATING (1980s)

One cannot talk about tribal groups or Bedouins and ignore the reviving Islamic fundamentalist movements in Kuwait, both of which gained strength in the early 1980s as they cooperated in support of each other's conservative ideologies. Neither group is a new phenomenon in Kuwait, as both have existed since the establishment of the country. It is, however, their increasing numbers and their presence in powerful positions in the municipalities of the government that have made them gain recognition and influence in Kuwait.

The tribal affiliation has a long history in Kuwait.[9] But as political and economic relationships began to grow between Kuwait and other countries, tribalism weakened as new customs and city values started entering the country even before oil was discovered. Consequently, people's loyalty and affiliation strengthened toward the country as they realized that for their new land to develop they needed to protect it and put any tribal tension aside.[10]

Bedouins came to Kuwait at different times and for various purposes. The largest group, however, migrated there from the Kuwaiti, Saudi, and Iraqi deserts in the 1950s and 1960s. The prospering country was an appealing destination for these Bedouin tribes, who saw it as an opportunity to settle in the city to take advantage of the modern facilities that were being developed at that time in Kuwait. The government encouraged the migration as it opened various employment opportunities to them. Soon, many of them joined the Kuwaiti army. The government saw in them new allies who would compete with the increasing power of the merchant class and other affluent groups.[11] As their numbers increased in the city, for they are known for high birth rates, they gradually caused what Ghabra (1997) calls "desertization," described as the "transfer of desert customs, traditions, beliefs, dress codes, and mentality into the city" (367). Consequently, he adds, desertization undermined the modern attitude (i.e., liberal outlook toward religion and openness toward modern values) of most of the urban families, including the merchant class.

The Bedouins' social and political power was not realized, however, until the 1980s, when they became a notable majority of the Kuwaiti population and their entity was regarded as an integral part of the Kuwaiti population.

RELIGIOUS FUNDAMENTALISM

The surfacing of the Bedouins as a powerful social group in the early 1980s coincided with the emergence of a new social power under the name of "Islam." These Islamic groups presented their rigid values as the true Islamic teachings (Ghabra 1997). To this day, their political demands, which they paint with a religious façade, serve their ideological aspirations and demands and at the same time cause fragmentation among Kuwaitis and between the Kuwaitis and the government. One Parliament member, Ahmed Al-Rubai, brings attention to the large number of political groups who are fragmenting the country. Specifically, he points to the growing power of political Islamic groups who are gaining control of many governmental institutions and attempt to work their agenda through these institutions to the degree that they began to compete with the state itself (e.g., granting employment for their supporters and exerting pressure on decision makers who do not share their ideology). Therefore, he calls for political groups that ultimately would discourage the division of Kuwait into smaller nations ("Tantheem Al-Mujtamaa" 2000, 32).

The increased number of tribal and religious groups have played a role in changing the way the country celebrates its national day; however, the religious groups were more direct in their interference in the government plans for the national day, and continue to be so. For the tribal groups, it was their increasing numbers that turned the government's attention to them and thus they have been included in a larger part of the celebrations.

This was most evident on February 25, 1986, the 25th anniversary of Kuwait. The celebration for this national day was an elaborate one—it started on February 1 and lasted for the entire month. The government-appointed committee's aim for this particular celebration to revive the people's loyalty and patriotism, which they saw as fading out (I. Al-Shatti, personal communication, December 20, 2000), especially because many people's loyalties were perceived as growing stronger toward their tribes or religious groups. As Ibrahim Al-Shatti, the head of the National Celebration Committee in 1986, points out, the Kuwaiti flag was used as the symbol of the celebrations and the conduit through which loyalty and citizenship was to be communicated to the masses (personal communicaton, December 20, 2000). Thus, all the celebration themes concentrated around the flag, turning it into a lively, majestic symbol full of patriotic meanings. In that year, flags were everywhere one looked, even covering buildings that were 20 stories high. Storeowners used red, green, white, and black lightbulbs, the colors of the Kuwaiti flag, to decorate their stores. The Ministry of Information printed thousands of small paper flags, along with the amir and crown prince's pictures, to give away to citizens at supermarkets.

To mark the official beginning of these celebrations, a flag-raising ceremony was held at the Flag Arena,[12] attended by high officials along with ambassadors, ministers, Parliament members, and thousands of citizens. As the flag was raised, the national anthem was played. At 10:00 A.M., the people around the country stood in their workplaces to salute the flag and to sing the national anthem (I. Al-Shatti, personal communication, December 20, 2000). The ceremony was followed by 25 cannon shots to mark the number of years Kuwait had enjoyed complete independence. Afterward, thousands of balloons were released into the air, and helicopters carrying leaders' pictures flew over the arena, as folk-singing groups performed their traditional sword dances, and Girl Scout troops carried the Kuwaiti flag around the arena ("Alaf al-hanajer" 1986).

Among the festivities that marked that particular year's celebrations were "Yom al-bahar" (Day of the Seaman) and "Yom al-badia" (Day of the Desert). Both cultural themes were designed to bring about remembrance of the Kuwaiti life of the past by showing the country's relation to the land and sea. In Yom al-bahar, which is a permanent, miniature preoil neighborhood along the Arabian Gulf shore, various details are re-created about the city-people's lives who depended on boat building, diving, and pearling to make their living. Old stores, coffee shops, houses, and crafts all were replicated to remind Kuwaitis of their ancestors' harsh life and the long way they have traveled, within a short period of time, since the discovery of oil. Similarly, Yom al-badia, which was held in Al-Jahra (a city in northern Kuwait), populated mostly by Bedouins, went on for a whole week as it exhibited the other side of Kuwaiti history and its connection to the desert. Bedouin culture was celebrated by enacting their traditional way of life. Their dark brown tents, made out of camels' hair, were put on display; men and women demonstrated their crafts; and camels and horses were an integral part of the exhibition (K. Al-Anazi, personal communication, January 15, 2001). The success of this cultural fair encouraged organizers to repeat a similar festival of the Bedouin culture in 1987 at the Red Palace in Al-Jahra. The goal behind such cultural exhibitions was to bring Kuwaitis to contrast their preoil society with the economic, material, and social evolution that took place with the discovery of oil, and to appreciate the role of the state in directing such efforts. Further, tying both the sea culture and the desert culture to the national day is an acknowledgment by the state of the importance of these cultures (city and tribal) in the making of its history, demonstrating its hopes that they would cooperate to contribute to its future.

Such elaborate festivities were a celebration of the country's achievements over a period of 25 years. It was also to show gratitude for a country that offered its people many services and modern facilities, but most importantly, it was a celebration for a country that was able to offer its people peace at a time of turmoil in neighboring countries.

The 1986 celebration marked the beginning of the end for festive national day celebrations, as societal divisions intensified. In addition, the Arabian Gulf region witnessed the beginning of the Iraq–Iran War in 1980, which reached its peak in the mid-1980s. The war substantially affected Kuwait economically and politically throughout the 1980s, and even threatened its sovereignty. Therefore, the 1986 national day was an opportunity to reaffirm Kuwait's autonomous status as a sovereign nation by highlighting its distinct history and cultures. The tension of the war as it reached its climax in the mid-1980s was echoed in a speech Kuwait's crown prince Sheikh Saad Al-Sabah gave in 1986 on the occasion of the national day celebration, which he began by saying, "Our people's history is rich with stories of commitment, sacrifices and patience over hardship. And they have held on to *al-shura*[13] to the letter" (qtd. in "Wali Al-Ahad" 1986). As the country was on military alert, the amir spent the national day with the Kuwaiti troops at the northeastern borders checking military preparation at various defense locations. Similarly, in the subsequent year, the amir was with the troops while the country celebrated the national day. Despite the tense political atmosphere in the region, the country was able to carry on the celebrations that reaffirmed its identity.

Elaborate festivities marked an important period of Kuwait's history; however, they came to an end as the religious groups gained power in society through election to Parliament, enabling them to have more say and to exert direct pressure on the state to stop festive celebrations that involve singing and dancing. These, in the Islamist view, are against Islamic teaching and open the door for degradation in society. In many ways, this dramatically affected the way the country approached the national day, and by 1988, the celebrations at the state level came to a halt.

A NEW NATIONAL DAY: EFFECTS OF THE IRAQI INVASION (1990–2001)

In the early morning of August 2, 1990, Iraqi troops invaded Kuwait, claiming that Kuwait has always been a part of Iraq but was made a country by the British, who divided the world's map to suit their own interests. The invasion was first faced by the Kuwaitis and later by an allied coalition made up of 33 countries, both Arabs and non-Arabs, fighting together for a country that was then unknown to many people in the world. This second Gulf War came to an end with the liberation of Kuwait on February 26, 1991, a date the state declared as a new national day.[14] Called "Liberation Day," it was marked as an official holiday for the whole country. As a Kuwaiti historian Yagub Al-Gunaim (personal communication, January 21, 2001) asserts, this date is much more important than February 25 because it returned life to a country that was brutally attacked by a neighbor. Al-Gunaim adds that the killing of many people and taking Kuwaitis away from their country and loved ones make it unjust to compare the British protection agreement to the aggressive Iraqi invasion.[15] Although the joy of the liberation filled every corner of the country, celebrations were still subdued. Statewide festive celebrations came to a halt as mixed emotions surfaced during the two national days as people remembered the still-captive prisoners of war (POWs) and their terrifying experiences during the invasion. As the celebration changed to accommodate the changes in the local atmosphere, so did the symbols used for the occasion. With such tragedy, two flags were designed: a white flag with a fingerprint colored white, red, black, and green (the Kuwaiti flag colors) that honors those killed during the invasion and the Gulf War and, in commemoration of the POWs, a yellow flag was designed showing arms with the Kuwaiti flag as sleeves pulling apart prison bars. The two flags have gained strong national meaning, and many people regularly include them on national days alongside the Kuwaiti flag.

On February 25, 1992, thousands of people raising flags and posters gathered in a silent parade that expressed their happiness in their newly gained freedom; yet, at the same time, they showed an incomplete joy without the return of their loved ones, who were taken by Saddam Hussein's troops during the war (10 years since the liberation, more than 600 men, women, and children POWs are still in Iraq's prisons). Thus, the celebration was a loud cry for the international community to continue its efforts to bring back the POWs. The silent parade was led by the sons and daughters of the POWs who were, in turn, followed by members of governmental and nongovernmental organizations, school students, and citizens. The parade started at the Ministry of Information and ended at the Flag Arena where the crown prince and other high officials were awaiting their arrival ("Al-eid al-watani" 1992).

On the subsequent year's national days, the state decided that official celebrations had to be brief, out of respect for the POWs and their families. Instead, speeches were given by officials praising the strength and the dedication of the Kuwaitis during the seven-month invasion. As Minister of Defense Sheikh Ali Al-Sabah expressed in his speech during the event,

Kuwaitis have shown a proud example of holding on to their country by their resistance and sacrifices in the face of a brutal invasion. They were able through their minds and wisdom to gather the whole world around their country's just cause. A happening that is the first of its kind in history. ("Al-eid al-watani: Al-ehtifal al-jamahiri" 1993)

On Liberation Day of that same year, hundreds of thousands of Kuwaitis came out to the streets in an unplanned public parade to celebrate the second anniversary of that day ("Al-eid al-watani" 1993). People honked their horns as they drove along the main Gulf Road, raising the Kuwaiti flags from their windows. Some waved the U.S. flag and other allied countries' flags while national songs blared from their radios ("Al-eid al-watani" 1993). The Flag Arena, which has become over the years the place of national celebrations, was used by the people to start their fireworks display in celebration of this day. Such unplanned public events signaled to the government the public yearning for festive national celebrations and desires to replace the sadness of the memories with a cheerful atmosphere. In 1994, the Kuwait News Agency sent out a report on the occasion of Liberation Day that stated, "Three years after liberation there should be a call for change from the depression and the put-downs that resulted from the invasion to adapting an assertive and a positive attitude to serve their country" ("Al-eid al-watani: Tagreer" 1994).

The people's yearning for joyous national days got an answer the following year. The first national musical concert, titled *Al-Kuwait fee aion al-zamen* (Kuwait over the Years), celebrating the liberation was performed in 1994. A number of Kuwaiti composers, songwriters, and singers were asked by the Kuwait Ministry of Information to record this national work that tells the story of Kuwait from its establishment through its preoil and postoil eras, finally focusing on the invasion and eventual liberation ("Oprait" 1994). What makes this work important is that it is a message that reaffirms the sovereignty of Kuwait as it tells its history. For the message to reach a large audience, the songs were written in classical Arabic in order to overcome dialect barriers, a repetition of history from the 1960s when the national songs were sung in classical Arabic.

Similar national musical concerts were performed as part of 1995's celebrations. Such concerts took on an official tone as high officials in the country attended with diplomats, even though only a small number of the public was invited by special invitation. Further, because of the Islamic fundamentalists' pressures to prohibit girls and women from performing in public staged performances, the accompanying dances in these concerts were by men folk dance groups. The concerts were recorded by Kuwait television and aired for the mass audience. There was also a release of the concert on cassette tape, the proceeds from which were set aside for the War Funds ("Al-eid al-watani: Al-thekra 34" 1995). Despite the two-in-a-row national concerts, their songs have been made only for the one-day occasion, and none of the performed songs have gained the popularity of those made in the 1970s. The absence of popular national songs is not confined to national days, but is a year-round phenomenan. Unlike the 1960s and 1970s, when the Ministry of Information played national songs on a daily basis, in the 1980s and 1090, as Al-Gunaim (personal communication, January 21, 2001) rightly sees it, this type of song has become seasonal, and is heard only on national days. Songwriters have thus been discouraged from writing national songs. In the 1970s for instance, songwriters and composers made special efforts to release songs on tapes to be sold during the national day. The songs expressed love and loyalty to the country and mesmerized people about their past and inspired them about the future. Currently, however, the strategy that the Ministry of Information seems to be following, which is the limiting of broadcasting national songs, is slowly killing this type of song.[16] And it is causing a whole generation, those born in the early 1990s, to grow up without having their own national songs, other than the national anthem, to fire patriotism in them.

National songs made especially for the occasion were traditionally an important part of constructing the meaning of national day. However, these official concerts were unable to satisfy the public, who were looking forward to festivities and programs that would include them as active participants and as expressions of their happiness. Therefore, similar to previous years, a large number of the public, especially the youth, gathered along the main Gulf Road celebrating the national day and Liberation Day in their own way.

In 1997 and 1998, for safety reasons, the Ministry of Interior issued a rule prohibiting any public rallies during both the national day and Liberation Day and encouraging the public to follow civic behavior. In 1998, the Public Relations Department at the Ministry of Interior announced, "These days have a great value and meaning to us which we carry in our hearts; therefore, we [the public] do not need to confirm such feelings through public rallies and parades that gives a bad reputation for the occasion, especially under the circumstances [the continual threats from Iraq] the country is going through" ("Al-eid al-watani: Maneaa" 1998).

History repeated itself once again during the 1999 celebration as Saddam Hussein's threats continued, insisting that Kuwait was a part of Iraq. The celebration was a military parade displaying the latest arms owned by the military, including antiartillery weapons, rocket launchers, and various models of armed vehicles ("Al-eid al-watani: 38" 1999). In 1962, a military show was put on to convey a message to Iraq against its allegation of owning Kuwait; the difference in 1999, however, was the presence of children of the POWs and those killed in action walking in the parade, waving the yellow and white flags that commemorated loved ones. The same threats were repeated for the 2001 national days. On Wednesday, January 17, Saddam Hussein's elder son, Uday, renewed claims to Kuwait as being part of a "Greater Iraq." He called for the Iraqi National Assembly to "prepare a map of the whole Iraq, including Kuwait City as an integral part of Greater Iraq" ("Iraq" 2001, 1).

The longing for festive and elaborate celebrations similar to those of the 1970s and the country's slow-growing economy both encouraged a group of investors to initiate a new festival called "Hala Fubraier" (Hello February) in 1999, which starts about a month before the national days. This celebration is important to mention here because its one-monthlong festivities lead directly into the national days program. Even though the Hala Fubraier celebration is organized and supported mostly by the private sector, the government does contribute to it, both directly and indirectly, through the services of its various ministries. For example, Kuwait Television broadcasts live the opening parade of Hala Fubraier. The Ministry of Interior also put its people in the streets to organize different festival events (e.g., musical concerts, photo exhibitions, international exhibitions, and drawing competitions).

The festival has a national flavor to it, as the organizers make it clear that their purpose is to improve the national economy during February, as well as to put Kuwait on the touristic map of the world. The opening parade is very nationalistic as people wave the Kuwaiti flag and the POW flag. Even the songs that have been written for this occasion intertwine the patriotism of the nation with the Hala Fubraier theme celebrations. As one song puts it, "Our Sheikh Jaber, the greatest Sheikh . . . and with Hala Fubraier our happiness is complete . . . I ask God to protect my homeland . . . and our flag remains high." Kuwait Television interviews with those who attended the parades and other festivities have complemented the efforts of the organizers. Many interviewees saw in the festivities a return to a joyful atmosphere to the country. The parade, a genre of Kuwait's national celebrations, reminded them of the parades of the past. Still, such festivities were not appreciated by the Islamic fundamentalist groups who released a statement in the newspapers asking people to boycott the celebrations because they "lead society into moral degradation." Despite their loud protests to stop the festivities, Hala

Fubraier is going into its third year with great success and enthusiasm from the people. In the opening of the 2001 parade more than 40,000 people attended the opening ceremony ("Arbaean alf dsheno" 2001).

With Kuwait chosen as the Arab cultural capital for 2001, the state put extra efforts into celebrating the 2001 national days.[17] Thus, this year's response to Iraq's claim was not one military parade, but a yearlong reaffirmation of the Kuwaiti identity and sovereignty as being one with a long history that produced a unique Kuwaiti culture and identity. For this special year, which marked the 40th anniversary of independence and the 10th anniversary of liberation, Kuwait invited many international high-ranking former officials, who played a major role in Kuwait's liberation in 1991. Among the visitors who participated in the festivities are former U.S. president George H. W. Bush; former U.S. secretary of state James Baker; Norman Schwarzkopf, the commander of allied forces during the Gulf War; and former British prime minister John Major.

Such international gathering added to the importance of the 2001 celebration as it made the festivities a global event with more than 100 news correspondents from around the world covering the events. Furthermore, for the 2001 celebrations, several national musical concerts were produced and performed by renowned actors and actresses. We also find the return of school participation (about 16,000 school students participated in the 2001 celebration). The effort to put on a festive national day did face pressure from the Islamic groups, and the government seems to be considering some of their views. For example, only schoolgirls up to the sixth grade were allowed to participate in the performances (it is thought to be inappropriate for teenage girls to participate in physical performances as they are considered to be women).

One official, who was in charge of organizing the celebration for 2001 national day commented that Kuwaitis are not as free as before to plan their national days; hence, they need to work as if they were walking on eggshells to avoid confrontations with the Islamists. Their pressures have changed the face of national days' celebrations, but only to a certain extent. As past years have shown, as people continue to seek amusement from these celebrations, they will come up with their own way of enjoying them, even if only by raising the Kuwait flag and honking their horns down the Arabian Gulf Road.

RETHINKING NATIONAL DAYS

From the preceding examination of Kuwait's national days, it is clear that both the state and the people treasure the occasions. How it is celebrated, however, is determined by internal and external circumstances of the time. As we have shown, the 1960s and 1970 were decades of intense efforts to build a modern nation that was able to provide its people with a comfortable living, modern facilities, and services. The results of the process were displayed annually during the national day by hundreds of school students, from kindergarten to high school, parading down the street singing national songs, holding up the rulers' pictures, and waving the Kuwaiti flag. The parades were more than a festive opportunity for the participants. They were also a "social vocabulary" (Ryan 1989) that asserted the country's own march toward modernization.

These parades strengthened social unity between the state and the people, seen in the hundreds of thousands of people who sang and danced enthusiastically as if it were a loved one and not a country that was celebrating a special day. National day parading was the focal point of the celebrations during that period. The celebrations were distinctive and echoed a sense of growth in the country, as each year's celebrations over the two decades became more elaborate and creative. National day was used not as a starting point to build people's loyalty and allegiance, but as a space for them to express these feelings. Even though some might view such government-planned activities (e.g., parades and stage performances) as propaganda, they were nevertheless an effort that brought people together and played a part in connecting them to their land. During these two decades, the Kuwaiti person was at the center of the state's efforts to invest in the health, education, and, most importantly, patriotism.

The division of loyalties in the 1980s and 1990s caused confusion and apprehension in Kuwaiti society regarding the country's future, especially with the absence of a long-term public plan or clear direction as to where the country was heading. Meanwhile, the Kuwaiti government appears to be lax in promoting an active national agenda directed toward building a strong sense of nationhood. Unfortunately, Kuwait has failed to use the lesson of the Iraqi invasion as a new starting point from which it can take off toward a newly formulated strong national agenda for renewing people's patriotism and encouraging their coherence. The country was busy cleaning up the war's ruins and rebuilding itself, and in the midst forgot to rebuild the Kuwaiti citizen.

The evolution of national days can tell us something about how national meanings and understandings are created. National days are forms of public speaking through which both the state and the people speak to each other using the same symbols. Therefore, national days are indispensable conduits through which the state can renew itself. They can also, with some smart strategic plans that accommodate what is occurring in society, become a central focus of pride.

The choice of Kuwait as the Arab cultural capital for 2001 encouraged the country to revive its history and culture more elaborately than it had in the past 15 years, and to package them in a creative way to present to its people and to all Arabs. In many ways, the efforts are to reaffirm Kuwait as a sovereign nation with its own identity to those who may have doubts. Such devoted efforts should be the first step toward taking the national days more seriously and viewing them as opportunities to renew people's patriotism.

To sum up, the issue is larger than the need for national songs or parades and it is not confined to national days; rather, it is about making a citizen. What Kuwait needs is a strong national effort in which both the government and the private sector work hand in hand to plan and implement a comprehensible national agenda.

Best would be a plan that would effectively utilize various venues, especially the mass media and the educational system, year round, in order to reach Kuwaiti citizens through a clear and creative national message that literally sells the nation to its people. It would be a message that continually reminds Kuwaitis, including those who have just been granted citizenship, of their rights and responsibilities toward each other and their country. There is no doubt that Kuwaitis do carry patriotic feelings toward their land and their fellow citizens. The Gulf War is a strong, recent example that showed the whole world their love for the land. In reality, however, nationalism and patriotism are not innate, but need to be mediated for the people, while efforts need to be exerted to continually polish them. National days are but one venue in which to do so.

NOTES

1. Amir or emir is the male leader of an emirate. In the case of Kuwait, the head of the country is addressed as His Highness the Amir.

2. The country's small size and location near the Arabian Gulf gave the area its name—Kuwait, which is a minification of the word *Koot*, a large square citadel that is built near the water (river, ocean, or gulf) for ships and boats to purchase from it their food, coal, and other travel needs.

3. Among other "firsts," Kuwait was the first country in the gulf region to employ women in both the government and the private sector (Ghabra 1997).

4. Islam is the second largest of the world's religions. Mohammed is the prophet of Islam and the Quran, Muslim's holy book, is the miracle brought by the prophet. As a religion, Islam is a way of life that offers individuals eternal and day-to-day principles.

5. Kuwait is approximately 6,960 square miles (equivalent to 17,818 square kilometers) (Kuwait Ministry of Information 1999).

6. Radio was the most used medium at that time and very few families had a television.

7. The music of the song is still used today for the opening of news broadcast.

8. Um Kalthoum had noticeable efforts in shaping the identity of Egyptian popular culture and affected the rest of the Arab World. Some of her songs were even played on Radio of Israel to attract Arab listeners. According to Shaheen (1994), Um Kalthoum's songs of love "appealed to the hearts and minds of Arabs. She could sing [one song] for five consecutive hours without stopping. When she died in 1975, the Egyptian government did not release the news for seven days, fearing public chaos. The media [only] transmitted daily reports about her 'illness'" (8).

9. The Bani Khaled and Utub are tribes (groups of related families) themselves from which the founders of Kuwait and its rulers descended (Asiri 1996). Al-Sabah family descends from the Utub tribe, which is a branch of a larger tribe in the Arabian Peninsula named Anaza.

10. For example, in 1760, to face the threats of neighboring tribes, Kuwaitis from various tribes worked together to surround Kuwait City with a wall with four gates, of which parts still stand today as a reminder of Kuwaiti unity.

11. In the 1967 election, the government used this alliance in the parlimant elections and encouraged the Bedouins to vote for the government candidates.

12. The Flag Arena was opened on that day and it is still there today, and Kuwait's flag still stands high in its center.

13. Al-shura means consultation. Islam encourages those in power to consult those with experience and knowledge.

14. A few days after the liberation, thousands of Kuwaitis flocked to the Flag Arena to raise the Kuwaiti flag and declare their freedom ("Al-eid al-watani: Al-ehtifal fee" 1999). Such a move shows what the Flag Arena symbolizes to Kuwaitis.

15. More than 500 were killed during the invasion.

16. Both radio and television are operated by the Ministry of Information (i.e., the government) in Kuwait.

17. The idea of cultural capital was initiated in a conference held in Mexico under the patronage of the United Nations in 1982. The participants decided to adopt a framework that would focus on the celebration of culture and named it the "International Contract for Cultural Development." The European culture cities experiment began in the mid-1980s. In the Arab region, the experiment began in 1996 with Cairo, Egypt, as the first Arab cultural capital. Since then, every year an Arab country showcases its heritage and cultural activities for a whole year.

REFERENCES

Abu-Hakima, A. (1983). *The modern history of Kuwait: 1750–1965.* London: Luzac.

Aidaroos, M. Al-. (1997). *Tarikh al-Kuwayt al-hadith wa al-muaser* [Modern and contemporary history of Kuwait]. Hawaii, Kuwait: Dar al-Ketab al-Jamee.

Alaf al-hanajer rdedt fee kul mkan ams [Thousands sand yesterday]. (1986, February 22). *Al-Qabas,* 2.

Al-eid al-watani [The national day]. (1992, February 25). *Kuwait News Agency,* 1.

Al-eid al-watani [The national day]. (1993, February, 26). *AFP,* 1–2.

Al-eid al- watani: 36 [The national day: The 36th anniversary]. (1997, February 24). *Kuwait News Agency,* 1.

Al-eid al-watani: 38 [The national day: The 38th anniversary]. (1999, February 26). *AFP,* 1–2.

Al-eid al-watani: Al-ehtifal al-jamahiri althi agamtho lajnat al-ehtifal fee sahat al-alam [The national day: The public celebration held by the celebration committee at the Flag Arena]. (1993, February 25). *Kuwait News Agency,* 1–2.

Al-eid al-watani: Al-ehtifal fee sahat alalam al-eid 38 [The national day: The celebration in the Flag Arena for the 38th anniversary]. (1999, February 25). *Kuwait News Agency,* 1–3.

Al-eid al-watani: Al-thekra 34 [The national day: The 34th anniversary]. (1995, February 24). *Kuwait News Agency,* 1–3.

Al-eid al-watani: Maneaa al-masirat [The national day: Prohibiting the rallies]. (1998, February 23). *Kuwait News Agency,* 1.

Al-eid al-watani: Tagreer [The national day: A report]. (1994, February 25). *Kuwait News Agency,* 1–2.

Arbaa maet alf Dinar kulfat al-ehtifal be al-eid al-watani wa eid al-tahreer [400,000 dinar for the national day and the Liberation Day]. (2000, December 8). *Al-Qabas,* 3.

Arbaean alf dsheno Hala Fubraier [40,000 participate in the opening of Hala Fubraier]. (2001, January 25). *Al-watan,* 1.

Asiri, A. (1996). *Al-netham al-seyasi fe al-Kuwayt* [Kuwait's political system]. Shuwaikh, Kuwait: Al-Watan Press.

Ateegi, K. Al-. (2001, January 13). Adat bthakrtha ela zmenal-naserya wa siarat al-wihda [Remembering al-Naserya era and its slogans]. *Al-Qabas*, 11.

Ghabra, S. (1997). Kuwait and the dynamics of socio-economic changes. *Middle East Journal*, *51*(3), 358–72.

Iraq plays to Arab streets in victory spin. (2001, January18). *Arab Times,* 1.

Khalaf, S. (1992). Gulf societies and the image of unlimited good. *Dialectical Anthropology*, *17*, 53–84.

Kuwait Ministry of Information. (1999). *Al-Kuwait hgaig wa argam* [Kuwait's facts and numbers]. Kuwait City, Kuwait: Author.

Kuwait Television (Producer). (n.d.). *Raed al-estiglal* [The leader of independence] [Film]. (Available from the Kuwait Ministry of Information).

Oprait: Al-Kuwait fee eion al-zamn [Kuwait over the years]. (1994, February 25). *Al-Anbaa,* 12.

Rasheed, A. Al-. (n.d.). *Tarihk al-Kuwayt* [History of Kuwait]. Lebanon: Dar Maktabh al-Hayat.

Risalt *Amir* al-bilad [The *Amir*'s speech]. (1976, February 25). *Al-Qabas,* 1.

Ryan, M. (1989). The American parade: Representations of the nineteeth-century social order. In L. Hunt (Ed.), *The new cultural history*. Berkeley: University of California Press.

Saedan, H. Al-. (Ed.). (1993). *Al-mawsuaa Al-Kuwaytia al-mokhtasara* [Abridged encyclopedia of Kuwait]. Mansuria, Kuwait: Murkz al-Bohwth wa al-Derasat al-Kuwaytia.

Sagaf, A. Al-. (1986, February 1). Maa rafea al-alam wa al-nasheed [The flag and the national anthem]. *Al-anbaa,* 1.

Shaheen, J. (1994). *The TV Arab*. Bowling Green, OH: Bowling Green State University Popular Press.

Tamimi, A. Al-. (1998). *Abahath fi Tarihk al-Kuwayt* (Research in Kuwait's history). Kuwait City, Kuwait: Dar Qurtas lee al-Nashr wa al-Tawzi.

Tantheem Al-Mujtamaa. (2000, December 26). *Al-Qabas*, 32.

Tétreault, M., and al-Mughni, H. (1995). Modernization and its discontents: State and gender in Kuwait. *Middle East Journal, 49*(3), 403–19.

Trachtenburg, Z. (1993). *Making citizens: Rousseau's political theory of culture*. London: Routledge.

Wali al-ahad: Msirtna hflat bil tadhiat [Crown prince: Our history is rich with sacrifices]. (1986, February 1). *Al-Qabas,* 1.

New Zealand

Waitangi Day

New Zealand's National Day

Parehau Richards and Chris Ryan

If Michel Foucault has left any clear message for contemporary social scientists, it is to be aware of the silent voice. Yet, New Zealand's Waitangi Day seems to be a veritable Tower of Babel of voices—voices that intertwine, on the one hand, past and present frustrations but differing aspirations for the future, and, on the other hand, indifference. For many New Zealanders, a national day is when New Zealand plays Australia at rugby in the Bledisloe Cup (particularly when victory is to be celebrated) for with its strong sense of the outdoors, its anti-intellectual strain, and its concentration on male values, it is not surprising that sport has become a major component of New Zealand culture. As Laidlaw (1999) has written:

> By the end of the last century the die was effectively cast. As the newspaper *Zealandia* ... pronounced in 1899 with ill-disguised relief: "There is now no danger of New Zealand rearing a nation of milksops, effeminate fops and luxurious dandies ..." it said. Rugby had established itself as perhaps the defining point for the society. It might have been said to be a borrowed suit but it fitted our nationalism very nicely. (24)

Barnett and Wolfe (1989) reiterate the paean to "Plunket, Anzacs, corrugated iron, Swanndris, gumboots, marching girls, meat pies, Sure to Rise and beer" (11). Yet, this comfy "Kiwiana" is challenged by the annual celebration of a treaty signed in 1840 between the British Crown and the Maori chiefs present at the Bay of Islands. To add to the discordant note, the Treaty of Waitangi, as a founding document of the New Zealand Constitution, is by its very nature a treaty between a monarchy distant in relevance and space, and Maori. It presupposes and supports claims of New Zealand being a bicultural society, thereby implying exclusion of the growing population that has no antecedents in either British or Maori society, or indeed in European roots. Asian immigration has been, in recent years, an important component of society in areas of Auckland and elsewhere, and by historical accident is excluded from one of the few written components of what is a generally unwritten constitution. Hence, issues arise as to a national day that commemorates a document that may seem of little relevance to the aspirations of new immigrants. Additionally, by concentrating on the events at Waitangi, the perception has grown that Maori "entered history" on that date, thereby ignoring the history and developments of those peoples prior to the European arrival.

This chapter will briefly describe the historical antecedents of the treaty, and then outline some of the events of the latter part of the 20th century that surrounded these celebrations of the national day—celebrations that have been dogged by controversy and where representatives of the government have, at various times, been deliberately insulted or made welcome by competing groups of Maori, or where the government has chosen to exclude itself from the *marae* (Maori meeting place) at Waitangi. Indeed, one translation of the name Waitangi as waters of sorrow may indeed be pertinent for some. This chapter will also incorporate personal memories of the first author, who was present at two commemorations and is of Te Whanau-a-Apanui and Tainui descent. The second author is tangata tiriti.[1]

THE TREATY OF WAITANGI

As is the case with native peoples in Australia, Canada, and the United States, with the coming of European settlers, Maori in New Zealand suffered significant changes that arose in a context of trade, warfare, dubious land deals, conversions by missionaries, and introduced diseases. Currently, Maori feature strongly in statistics that relate to imprisonment, domestic violence, and other indicators of a society that has suffered significant dysfunctioning at personal and tribal levels. Such data are particularly alarming when considering Tai Tokerau (Northland), which is the region within which Waitangi is located. Nationally, the population figures alone provide evidence of past problems. It is thought that over 150,000 Maori lived in Aotearoa prior to the arrival of Captain Cook (Butterworth 1988), but by the date of the first census in 1858, the official estimation of the Maori population was 56,049. It continued to decline to 42,113 by 1896, and did not recover to its 1858 total until 1921, when the population was recorded as being 56,987. In 1995, those claiming Maori ancestry accounted for approximately 12 percent of the total New Zealand population. Given current demographic trends, by the end of the first decade of the 21st century, that proportion is likely to be over one-third, due to higher fertility rates and a high level of intermarriage between Maori and non-Maori. The health, economic well-being, and status of Maori is thus an important issue for the whole of New Zealand.

Claims for land reparation and compensation under the auspices of the Waitangi Tribunal symbolize competing worldviews. Sharp (1991) argues that the debate has been and continues to be a difficult one, noting:

The inevitability of injustice is due in the case of reparations to the presence of fundamentally distinct and competing ethnic conceptions of what things were (and are) wrong and as to how individual and group identity and responsibility for actions persist through time. Though Maori and Pakeha may (mostly) have recognised a common sovereign state, they did not recognise a common judge on questions of reparations. Nor, in distinguishing right from wrong, did Maori and Pakeha always recognise the same norms as distinguishing right from wrong. (23)

Waitangi Day celebrates the signing of the Treaty of Waitangi on February 6, 1840, a treaty that has been viewed as a piece of political opportunism motivated by the wish of the British Crown to substantiate rights to land in the face of perceived French threats and claims to New Zealand. Certainly, a French fleet did exist in New Zealand waters, but Fountain (1998) notes that the French fleet that sailed to Akaroa delayed its sailing and in any case had more Germans on board than French. That the fleet chose to settle under British rule rather than return to French Polynesia raises some questions as to how real the threat posed to British rule was. On the other hand, both the British naval forces under Captain Hobson and the missionaries who advised him would have been mindful of the earlier Declaration of Independence signed by a confederation of Maori chiefs in 1836, which clearly stated their independence from European influences. Pragmatically, the British had much to gain from stabilizing their position as they then formed a minority of the population. Whatever the motives that lay behind the proposal of the treaty and its subsequent signing, and these remain issues of controversy, there is little doubt that at the time many would have recognized its importance. Evidence from Colonial Office papers of the 1830s and 1840s clearly show that the British government of the day did recognize indigenous peoples as having land rights that were enforceable. In the British view, Maori having land rights could sell land, but concern arose about exploitation through low prices at an early stage. The antislave crusader T. F. Buxton was successful in establishing a Select Committee on the Native Inhabitants of the Empire, and in 1837 this committee reported that:

The native inhabitants of any land have an incontrovertible right to their own soil: a plain and sacred right, however, which seems not to have been understood. Europeans have entered their borders, uninvited, and when there, have not only acted as if they were undoubted lords of the soil, but have punished the natives as aggressors if they have evinced a disposition to live in their own country. ("Report" 516)

Given that subsequently a doctrine of *terra nullius* (land without people) was used to justify the actions of the colonial government in Australia (and New Zealand was at that time governed from British officials based in New South Wales), the Treaty of Waitangi by its very existence gave lie to any such claim being made in the case of New Zealand. Indeed, it went much further, creating a partnership between tangata whenua (Maori, the original people of the land) and tangata tiriti (non-Maori New Zealanders). In the first article of the treaty, Maori ceded sovereignty to the British Crown; in the second, in the English translation:

Her Majesty the Queen of England confirms and guarantees to the Chiefs and Tribes of New
Zealand and to the respective families and individuals thereof the full exclusive and undisturbed possession of their Lands and Estates Forests Fisheries and other properties which
they may collectively or individually possess so long as it is their wish and desire to retain the
same in their possession.

The third article bestowed full British citizenship upon "Natives of New Zealand"
and thus is both unique in the history of early-19th-century British imperialism,
and is all the more notable when in Australia the ruling legal framework was that
Australia was a terra nullius.

There was, however, a second version of the treaty, in Maori, albeit a translation undertaken by missionaries, and this was simultaneously signed. However, the
differences in culture and, consequently, wording between the two versions have
continued to pose problems. The second article in Maori includes the phrase "Ko
te Kuini o Ingarani ka wakarite ka wakaae ki nga Rangatira ki nga hapu—ki nga
tangata katoa o Nu Tirani te tino rangatiratanga o o ratou wenua o ratou kainga
me o ratou taonga katoa" (The Queen of England agrees to protect the chiefs, the
subtribes and all the people of New Zealand in the unqualified exercise of their
chieftainship over their lands, villages, and all their treasures). *Taonga* (treasures)
refers to all dimensions of a tribal group's estate—material and nonmaterial including *wahi tapu* (sacred places), ancestral lore, and *whakapapa* (genealogy)—it
is a term implying cultural integrity, while *rangatiratanga* can be understood as an
exercise of self-determination in one form or another.

Thus, from the outset, tensions existed between British military forces adher-
ing to a Victorian conceptualization of sovereignty whereby power was vested in
the crown and its representatives. On the other hand, Maori, mindful of earlier declarations in 1836, believed that the chiefs continued to possess "unqualified
chieftainship" over lands and traditional matters. Over time, these tensions were to
be transformed in a period of warfare and subsequent land deals whereby, contrary
to traditional joint ownership of lands, the crown effectively provided a recognition of legitimate landownership on the part of Maori individuals who sought to
sell land to the colonial government. The end result was that by the end of the 19th
century, just 60 years after the signing of the treaty, Maori occupied a marginal
position in what had once been their land.

Today, the Treaty of Waitangi appears in over 45 different Acts of Parliament,
is referred to in New Zealand case law, is part of organizational strategic plans and
policies, and many government departments have Treaty Units (Coxhead 1999).
The new public management approach introduced in the 1980s had public sector
organisations "humming a chorus of bicultural goodwill statements that had been
included in charters, mission statements and other documents dedicated to strategic and business planning but not synthesised in policies or practice" (Mataira and
Richards 1993, 11). Thus, for some New Zealanders, especially Maori, the Treaty of
Waitangi is significant. Many of these people seek less planning and talk about the
Treaty of Waitangi and would prefer planning and talk to be synthesized in prac-

tice. For other New Zealanders, the Treaty of Waitangi is not significant and the country treats it far too seriously. Many of these people would like the treaty to disappear and for all to be New Zealanders or "Kiwis." In between these two views are a range of ideas, interpretations, and reactions to Waitangi Day and what it is meant to commemorate.

THE CREATION OF WAITANGI DAY

The anniversary of the signing of the Treaty of Waitangi became a public holiday in 1976 when the government in power decided that the February 6 anniversary was the most appropriate occasion for a day that reflects the cultural heritage of New Zealand. Prior to that date, "New Zealand Day" had been celebrated for a couple of years. Although it had not been an official public holiday, most New Zealanders had been familiar with the February 6 date as a commemoration of the signing of the Treaty of Waitangi between representatives of the crown and representatives of the chiefs of some *iwi* (tribes) at Waitangi. Although representatives of the crown also traveled to other parts of the country where signatures of other iwi and *hapu* (extended family or subtribe of an iwi) representatives were added to copies of the treaty, none of these locations organized national commemorations like those held at Waitangi and none were supported by the government for many years.

A typical weekend of Waitangi Day commemorations has included a range of Maori and crown protocols and ceremonial activities. The protocols of welcomes (on February 4 and 5) are organized by the tangata whenua for mainly hapu, iwi,[2] and pan-tribal groups from around the country. Those initial protocols are followed by a welcome to the official government party on February 6, including the prime minister, the governor-general, and other parliamentary officials. Although the tangata whenua is the host of the commemorations, there is an established organizing committee comprising both representatives of tangata whenua and the crown. Some past programs have included forums where Maori have had the opportunity to air their views and concerns about treaty- and Maori-related matters to the government officials in attendance. Waitangi Day has also included the official ceremony at the Treaty House grounds, where both Maori and state ceremonial cultures have been incorporated into a program including Maori and non-Maori speakers, *kapa haka*,[3] and the New Zealand navy.

WAITANGI DAY—FOCUS OF PROTEST

Over the years, there has been considerable criticism that the commemorations have been used as a platform for Maori protest. Throughout the history of the Treaty of Waitangi, treaty rights, and Waitangi Day, protests and protesters from around the country have been at the forefront of activities that have gained recognition of Maori rights and title to land and resources. One of the disadvantages has been that the crown and the media have tended to focus on negative images of Waitangi Days: the protests. Seldom has there been contextual debate, discussion, or presentation about issues of the day. Protesters have always been welcome at Waitangi marae, but as Pita Paraone, a member of the organizing committee, said, "If they affect the safety of and security of our people, Maori and Pakeha, then they're not welcome" (qtd. in Robertson 1999, 9).

For Parehau Richards, the first listed author of this chapter, two Waitangi Day commemorations remain vivid in her mind: those of 1990 and 1995. The unbalanced reports and the concentration on images of protest presented in the media that followed the events are reasons for remembering those two days in particular. The political context of those two specific events were, first, the fisheries settlement and other badly handled treaty issues that aroused tension and emotion at Waitangi Days between 1990 and 1993. Second, the government's fiscal envelope strategy, international investment, and intellectual property rights caused much of the unrest and concern at Waitangi Days between 1994 and 1998.

Leading up to Waitangi Day 1990, the first author was present at Waitangi for the Aotearoa Maori Festival of Arts that was held on February 3 and 4. A number of events had been organized at Waitangi to celebrate the 150th anniversary of the signing of the Treaty of Waitangi, including the Aotearoa Maori Festival of Arts, the gathering of more than 20 carved *waka*,[4] and a visit by Queen Elizabeth. Several thousand people gathered for the long weekend and many were staying for the formal Waitangi Day celebrations on Tuesday, February 6, 1990.

Parehau Richards includes the following recollection: I remember wondering how patient and relaxed the tangata whenua were leading up to such a big national event. It was evident that they were accustomed to being host of Waitangi Day commemorations and hundreds of people. It seemed that a thousand or so extra people were not making much of a difference. Large tents covered the grounds around Te Tii Marae and the New Zealand army was in attendance, assisting with accommodation and hospitality. The Taumata Kaumatua were at Te Tii Marae welcoming a flow of visiting groups during February 4, 5, and 6, 1990.[5] Those welcomes seemed to flow without any drama even though there were several thousand visitors and extensive accommodation in such close proximity. Several hundred meters away, nearer to the Treaty House grounds, organizers of the festival and Waitangi Day events had erected a large tent with seating and a stage for the kapa haka performances, retail and informational stands, and an ongoing program of entertainment and educational performances. For example, a number of well-known New Zealand actors and actresses had been brought together to reenact the signing of the Treaty of Waitangi. The carved waka were assembling along the beach below the Treaty House grounds guarded by members of their crews. They awaited their important task of accompanying Queen Elizabeth and her barge inshore to the Waitangi Day celebrations.

During the evenings, the tranquil scene of the Bay of Islands, the hum of the crowds, and the silhouettes of waka and crew along the beach was an awesome atmosphere. The bustle of the crowds, both Maori and Pakeha, was proof that the Treaty House grounds, Te Tii Marae, and the bay were well experienced at coping with visitors at this time of the year. Although there was an intense feeling of history and happenings at the Waitangi, I had little knowledge myself of what had happened there. I had not learned much about the treaty, the signing of the treaty, or the history preceding it; however, after the signing, it was obvious as a bystander that so much had occurred in the past 180 years. The bay is now home to many Pakeha people who have very nice homes and holiday homes along the foreshore along from the marae.

At the time I thought, "Wow, what a place to hold a number of events with over 2,000 participants in kapa haka groups and waka crews, as well as several thousand spectators at their busiest time of the year." Parehau Richards concluded her reflection thus: "I have a lot of respect for the tangata whenua of that region. For years now they have commemorated February 6 and during many of those years hosted people from throughout the country, including the crown, protesters, the police, other armed forces, whanau, hapu, iwi, and Pakeha. Over the last decade, protests have seemed more intense based on what media coverage has been presented on the television."

Dominating the news coverage were the scenes of protest described below. In short, what television news dwelled on were highly visual images of "news content"; these images tend to confirm the views of many non-Maori New Zealanders who do not see any need for reparation for past land losses. The visual intensity of violent protest secured prominence over peaceful scenes; additionally, the context of protest is generally not treated in depth, and furthermore is personalized around individuals who may or may not be representative of larger groups. It can also be argued that more radical protesters, being aware of television's seeming need for strong visual imagery, will utilize that need for their own ends, thereby creating a symbiotic relationship between media and protest.

Although there was some goodwill and optimism for 1990 and the future, the treaty issues of the time, such as the fisheries settlement, had not been dealt with in an acceptable way to *all* Maori. The Maori Fisheries Act of 1989 was an interim settlement for Maori fisheries claims. The act provided for the establishment of the Maori Fisheries Commission and also for 10 percent of the total quota to be transferred to the commission. Many Maori believe that iwi never surrendered rights to the fisheries and a meeting of tribal groups from around the country had strongly supported the notion that Maori should share equally the fishing resource with the crown. This was not to be.

Waitangi Day 1990 became an ideal venue for protest. On February 6, 1990, things became intense from some factions of the crowds at Waitangi. A wet black T-shirt was thrown toward Queen Elizabeth, flying close to her face as she traveled in an open car to the Waitangi Day celebration at Waitangi. Thirteen protesters were arrested. It was these scenes that received thorough coverage on television news.

Protests at Waitangi Day commemorations are nothing new. Throughout the 1970s and 1980s, individuals and groups took the opportunity to protest the government. In 1980, Prime Minister Sir Keith Holyoake was involved in a scuffle with protesters at the marae's main gate. In 1982, flares were thrown, smoke bombs lit, and 19 protesters were arrested as 300 protesters demonstrated. In 1983, police arrested 99 protesters, defusing what threatened to be a heated demonstration. In 1985, Maori wardens helped form a close circle around Governor-General Sir David Beattie while protesters staged a noisy demonstration, hurling smoke canisters, flares, and abuse. There was also a strong presence of protesters at both the 1987 and 1989 commemorations although they were quiet during official celebrations.

The Treaty of Waitangi (Fisheries Claims) Settlement Act of 1992 set out the final fisheries settlement for Maori. The problem for many concerned Maori was, as Milroy (2000) stated, "The fisheries settlement provided for the extinguishments of Maori rights, including tino rangatiratanga, in exchange for limited rights under the Quota Management System and the customary fishing regime" (64). To add fuel to the fire, although settlements are being negotiated by *some* Maori, the legislation is binding *all* Maori. The reality is that, in effect, the recognition of Maori rights by the crown, and the implementation of the Waitangi Tribunal, the settlement process, and other treaty issues continues to be driven by the crown and judgments from the courts.

Waitangi Day 1995 was also one of considerable tension and unrest. Although the Waitangi Organising Committee, made up of both tangata whenua and government officials, tried to include all views at the weekend commemorations, many aspects of the planned event were disrupted. For some, like Hone Harawira of Te Kawariki, a leading critic of government policies, the disruption of events was interpreted as a success for the whole of Maoridom.[6] Other Maori were concerned that anger was turning to hatred. Some tribal groups were keen to move forward with the government to settle their claims within the fiscal envelope program. Many Maori tried to make recommendations about ways for the government to deal with treaty claims. Newspapers reported that "protesters showed the depth of their concern for Maori culture and advancement by branding the day with their trademarks of abuse, spittle, bared buttocks and trampling the flag" ("Need" 1995, 6). Media had also grouped all protesters with Te Kawariki although there were many individuals and groups from around the country showing discontent with the fiscal envelope, albeit with different nuances of opinion. Prior to the Waitangi Day celebrations of 1995, the Ministry of Maori Development had organized informational meetings at which the government's fiscal envelope proposal had been rejected by Maori groups throughout the country. For its part, the government had continued to maintain that the $1 billion cap of the fiscal envelope was nonnegotiable.

Prime Minister Jim Bolger stated that protests achieved nothing, and the fiscal envelope package would not be reviewed. Further, he announced that he was also in favor of renaming Waitangi Day "New Zealand Day." In October 1995, the government announced that the official Waitangi Day ceremonies would be moved from the Treaty House grounds in Waitangi to the Government House in Wellington. Some believed that the move would remove the platform for protesters to "spit and hurl insults, but . . . [would] also quarantine the ceremonies off from the majority of participants who traditionally provide so much colour at Waitangi" ("Need" 1995, 6). Dame Catherine Tizard, the then governor-general, said that "despite the unacceptable actions and insults . . . , now was the time for calm in the hope [that] wiser voices would be heard in the future" ("Need" 1995, 6).

By 2001, personal relationships between the new prime minister, Helen Clarke, and Ngapuhi had deteriorated further,[7] partly over past disputes concerning the traditional view that women had no speaking rights at the marae.[8] In 2000, the prime minister celebrated Waitangi Day at Akaroa near Christchurch. During November 2000, there was continued publicity about the possibility of the government not supporting Waitangi Day celebrations at Waitangi, as had been the case for the past 33 years. Northland Maori were angry at the government's withdrawal from Waitangi. Some individuals from the *kaumata* (elders) of the Waitangi Day celebrations at Waitangi warned the Labour Party not to bother campaigning around Northland at the next election. The events at Waitangi in 2001 were also threatened by a funding shortfall. The Waitangi Day Commemorations Committee had drawn up a one-day program costing $80,000, but with the government allocating only $170,000 to distribute for Waitangi Day events nationwide, the committee's allocation were expected to fall short of the amount required.

Subsequently, in December 2000, it was announced that Helen Clarke had refused to go to the historic Waitangi grounds in Northland for Waitangi Day 2001. After an initial announcement that Te Arawa in Rotorua would host the prime minister for millennium celebrations on Waitangi Day, this plan was dropped with some controversy when the plans for the celebration failed to materialize. In consequence, the Prime Minister's Office announced that the prime minister would first attend Waitangi celebrations on the waterfront at Wellington, then go to a multicultural festival at Manukau in South Auckland. The significance of this latter arrangement marks a new chapter in the celebration of Waitangi Day by the New Zealand government. Even prior to the event, newspaper columns were printing letters offering different interpretations of this decision, and of the meaning of Waitangi Day as either a day for creating harmony or discord. It was also announced that Waitangi Day would be used to launch yet another Maori political party to oppose the main parties in the Maori electoral seats. This was accordingly done, although at the very last moment the minister of Maori affairs attended Waitangi in a private capacity so as to later attend a hui convened by two senior figures in Maoridon to discuss the situation of Maori and the nature of celebration of Waitangi in 2040—the 200th anniversary of the signing of the treaty.

Other tensions during 2000 arose for a number of reasons. In May, members of Parliament in Wellington rejected a proposal that could have had a significant impact on the way New Zealand celebrates its history and the relationship between Maori and Pakeha. Parliament voted no to a change in the name of

Waitangi Day. Earlier, in March 2000, a Member's Bill by United New Zealand leader, Peter Dunne, was drawn from a ballot of member's bills. His proposal was to replace Waitangi Day with a new national holiday, Aotearoa New Zealand Day.[9] Mr. Dunne was quoted as saying, "It is time to rekindle the vision of (former Labour Prime Minister) Norman Kirk and establish February 6 as a day on which every New Zealander celebrates with pride . . . the unique gift we all possess by virtue of being New Zealanders" ("Goodbye" 2000, 7). A previous proposal by Mr. Dunne, to rename Waitangi Day New Zealand Day, had struck opposition from within mainly Maoridom. This was not a first. The New Zealand Day Act of 1973 changed the name of Waitangi Day to New Zealand Day and made it a public holiday. Due to strong opposition from the New Zealand Maori Council to the change of name, the Waitangi Day Act of 1976 changed the commemoration day back to the original name.

On April 6, 2000, a conference entitled "Building the Constitution" was convened in Wellington to provide a forum to hear ideas about governance suggestions for the country. Suggestions included a separate Maori state within a state, or Maori self-government of one province (located in the upper North Island) out of four. The leader of the Australian Capital Territory political party, Richard Prebble, was most concerned that many of the options being debated were "heavily weighted in favour of change and do not defend New Zealand's Westminster-based system. In short, he said, if it ain't broke why fix it?" (Armstrong 2000, 8). One of the Maori presenters, the Honourable Justice Eddie Durie, proposed the incorporation of the Treaty of Waitangi into a written constitution.

In February 2000, the Aotearoa Traditional Maori Performing Arts Festival was held at Turangawaewae Marae during Waitangi Day weekend. The National Organising Committee and the Waikato Host Committee took the opportunity to organize an event for Maori to celebrate not only cultural arts but Waitangi Day as well. There are a number of reasons why Maori groups have celebrated Waitangi Day away from Waitangi. Although a number of Maori protest groups have found public protest at Waitangi a useful strategy to further their political causes, many other Maori do not make the journey north for a number of reasons. First, some do not want to be seen to support an event that is strongly influenced by the crown and well attended by crown officials; second, others disagree with the forms of protest; and, third, others agree with protest but believe that a media circus does little to add to creative dialogue. Additionally, many Maori would wish to celebrate the signing of the treaty in other ways as many Maori are not from Waitangi or Ngapuhi and their ancestors signed the Treaty of Waitangi on different dates during 1840, in different parts of the country. For example, four of Parehau Richard's Te Whanau-a-Apanui ancestors signed the Treaty of Waitangi on June 14, 1840, at Te Kaha. Thus, a fourth reason is that many believe it is more appropriate to stay home to commemorate the treaty and not intrude on the way the Waitangi tangata whenua carry out their commemorations. Finally, pragmatic reasons of distance and cost of travel make it difficult for many Maori to travel to Waitangi.

WAITANGI—A REFLECTION OF DEVELOPMENT?

It can thus be easily shown that Waitangi Day has become simultaneously a focus of aspiration and of conflict, a day for claiming harmony, a day for celebrating diversity, and a day of contention. It highlights a past treaty that was notoriously forgotten for much of the 19th century, and then used as a means to legitimize Maori aspirations in a resurgence of their culture and economic well-being that occurred in the final half of the 20th century. The treaty itself is not a homogeneous document. From the outset, the two versions, in English and Maori, were not consistent with each other, and other changes occurred as the British signed other treaties over the next decade with other iwi. From one perspective, the treaty was born from a context of acts of political pragmatism on the part of the British authorities—the colonies had but small populations, were initially dependent on Maori goodwill for their survival, and the British government was sensitive to the presence of other European powers in the Pacific. On the other hand, to simply decry the treaty as a paper legalization of colonial powers is to ignore the context of debate in the Westminster Parliament, and the dictates of a Colonial Office of the time in its instructions to governors. As evidenced by the work of reformers such as William Wilberforce and Sir Thomas Buxton in the 1830s and beyond, there did exist a genuine desire on the part of some to provide a proper framework of recognition for "native inhabitants." However, as the colonies such as New Zealand and Australia became more populated with Europeans, the desire for self-government, combined with factors such as distance and slow communications, meant that political action increasingly fell under local jurisdiction. In the case of New Zealand, this led to an increasing marginalization of Maori by the latter part of the 19th century.

By the end of the 20th century, when reparation to Maori began, history had also moved in other ways. Increasingly, and particularly in the centers of population in the north part of North Island where almost 40 percent of the country's population resides, New Zealand is no longer bicultural but multicultural. A day that celebrates a treaty between two ethnic groups by its nature excludes other groups. One perspective on this is to perceive New Zealand as a young nation with a history of being independent of the former mother country being but little over a century. Since the 1880s, the world has seen rapid change in technology and society. It is difficult against such a background of change to simultaneously correct problems caused by very different perceptions of the world as it existed in the 19th century while also dealing with the realities of a more diverse society in a former colony in the early 21st century. Many in Pakeha and Maori society recognize the process of globalization and the tensions that it brings. On the one hand, New Zealand is not divorced from wider global trends by reason of distance—it is increasingly interdependent on a global economy and the networks of the knowledge economies. Yet, as in many other countries, globalization leads to a desire to celebrate diversity and difference even while taking advantage of and partaking in global movements. Maoridom, unique to New Zealand, has a rich, vibrant culture and an economic force, and to deny its past would be a rejection of much that has shaped New Zealand. The debate is about identity, and the recognition not of necessarily competing identities, but, to use a Canadian expression, the creation of a mosaic of identity whereby each identity retains its color as it is weaved into the fabric that is New Zealand. As yet, being a new country, the act of weaving is difficult. It is accompanied by tensions, but demographic and social trends are creating their own realties and each generation is reinventing its own relationships. At the basis of these relationships lie the issues of economic, social, and political power, and the reality of Waitangi Day will, in the final analysis, depend on Maoridom having a secure economic future whereby it can celebrate difference without a need to use difference and past wrongs as a means of legitimizing claims for economic well-being. Only then, perhaps, will Waitangi Day be perceived as a day of celebration by all New Zealanders.

NOTES

1. Within Maori society, much emphasis is laid upon a statement of *whakapapa* in any formal meeting, or writing. While this might be seen as a noting of genealogy, it goes beyond this as being an identification of self with place, that is, with the land of ancestors and of those to come. Thus, for a Pakeha to declare himself or herself as being tangata tiriti, it means they are a people of the treaty that relates to New Zealand, and a recognition of partnership.

2. Tangata whenua is a term that can be applied to all Maori as the first people of New Zealand, but each iwi can claim to be tangata whenua of that region where it is based. Thus, Ngapuhi are the first people of Waitangi.

3. Kapa haka is a performance of dance and song, couched within traditional idiom, but increasingly using modern performance techniques, wherein comment might be made on contemporary issues, whether social, political, or popular.

4. Waka is the generic name given to canoes. In this instance, the specific reference is to *waka taua*, large oceangoing canoes in which Maori arrived in New Zealand in the early 14th century. For example, the waka Nga Toki Matawhaorua is 35.7 meters long and up to 2 meters wide and can carry 80 paddlers plus 55 passengers. It was named after the famous vessel in which Kupe discovered Aotearoa, and rests at Waitangi.

5. The Taumata Kaumatua are the elders entrusted with welcoming guests by reason of their status and authority.

6. Te Kawariki is a group committed to enactment of tino rangatiratanga (Maori self-determination), and as such organizes protests at many locations. For example, on October 28, 2000, the group sought to reclaim Te Oneroa a Tohe Beach (90-Mile Beach) as a commemoration of the 165th anniversary of the Declaration of Independence.

7. Ngapuhi is the iwi whose traditional lands include Waitangi.

8. Practice varies between iwi as to whether women have speaking rights at *hui* (formal meetings) at the marae (meeting places). For example, for iwi on the east coast of North Island, women have traditionally held equal rights with men as to speaking rights, but this is not the case for Ngapuhi.

9. Aotearoa is generally perceived as being a Maori name for New Zealand. Translated it means "land of the long white mist." However, there too is controversy as to the "authen-

ticity" of the title as initially it would appear that the early Maori settlers may not have had a name for the whole of the country.

REFERENCES

Armstrong, J. (2000, April 6). Politicians upset by "elitist" forum. *New Zealand Herald.* Available: http://www.nzherald.co.nz/storydisplay.cfm?thesection=news&thesubsection=&storyID=129666

Barnett, S., and Wolfe, R. (1989). *New Zealand! New Zealand! In praise of Kiwiana.* Auckland: Hodder and Stoughton.

Butterworth, G. V. (1988). *Aotearoa 1769–1988: Towards a tribal perspective.* Wellington: Department of Maori Affairs.

Coxhead, C. (1999). *Lecture and tutorial notes for legal systems course.* Waikato: Law School, University of Waikato.

Fountain, J. (1998). Beyond the brochures: An examination of the history and process of place image construction in Akaroa. *Proceedings of New Zealand Tourism and Hospitality Research Conference: Part One.* Lincoln, NZ: Lincoln University.

Goodbye Waitangi Day . . . hello Aotearoa NZ Day? (2000, March 24). *The Dominion,* 7.

Laidlaw, C. (1999). *Rights of passage: Beyond the New Zealand identity crisis.* Auckland: Hodder Moa Beckett.

Mataira, K., and Richards, P. (1993). Old wine in a holy wine skin—The re-organisation of racism in corporate New Zealand. In *Confronting Racism Conference Proceedings.* Sydney, Australia: University of Technology.

Milroy, S. (2000). The Maori fishing settlement and the loss of rangatiratanga. *Waikato Law Review, 8*(1), 63–85.

Need for a truly national day. (1995, October 27). *The Dominion,* 6.

Report from the select committee on Aborigines. (1836). In *British parliamentary papers* (vol. 7, no. 538).

Robertson, C. (1999, January 13). Women get to speak, but not during powhiri. *The Evening Post,* 9.

Sharp, A. (1991). *Justice and the Maori: Maori claims in New Zealand political argument in the 1980s.* Auckland: Oxford University Press.

Waitangi Organising Committee. (1990). *Programme of events for the 150th anniversary of the Treaty of Waitangi, 6 February 1990.* Waitangi: Author.

NIGERIA

Nationalism, Mass Media, and the Crisis of National Identity in Nigeria

Mohammed Musa and Ayo Oyeleye

Nigeria became an independent state on October 1, 1960.[1] As is usually the case, other icons of nationalism were created in preparation for the dawn of nationhood and were thus ushered in as symbols of the new Nigerian State and of a new Nigerian national identity. Notable among such icons were the national flag and a new national anthem that came to replace the Union Jack and the anthem of the colonial empire—the "God Save the Queen" chorus.

In the euphoria of becoming an independent nation and the desire to set about filling the masterly roles formerly occupied by the colonial rulers, the new political elite quickly formed a cabinet-style government, fashioned after the parliamentary system of their colonial lords. Colonial institutions of administration were not transformed or reoriented to suit the specific needs of the new Nigerian nation but simply occupied by the new indigenous political masters.

Every new development in the early days of the postindependence era hailed the celebration of independence as a collective national gain that would bring hope, self-determination, and prosperity to the newly liberated peoples of Nigeria as the new national anthem indicated:

Nigeria we hail thee
Our own dear native land
Though Tribe and Tongue may differ
In brotherhood we stand
Nigerians all are proud to serve
Our sovereign motherland

O God of all creation
Grant this our one request

Help us to build a nation
Where no man is oppressed
And so with peace and plenty
Nigeria may be blessed.

The significance of the birth of the nation, and the struggles that led to it, were symbolized by declaring October 1 as the national day (Independence Day). Notable patriots who participated in the struggles and negotiations for independence had monuments erected in their honor, public buildings or streets named after them, or their photographs emblematized on currency.

Subsequent commemoration of October 1 would feature events and activities ranging from public parades by schoolchildren, the armed forces, and the police; public lectures and symposia in universities and colleges; drama performances; and a host of other pageantry. In the continued effort to construct Independence Day as symbolic for all Nigerians, successive governments have made it a tradition to deliver important national policy statements on October 1 every year.

For the next 25 years or thereabouts, Nigerians really did celebrate Independence Day, although the euphoria felt by most Nigerians of being part of a newly independent nation had mostly peaked by the time of the first military coup in 1966. The colonial authorities did not properly address certain fundamental questions about Nigeria's nationalism in the run-up to independence. Key among these questions was, first, whether Nigeria, as cobbled together for colonial administrative convenience, would be viable as a single independent nation. Second, there was the issue of the type of sociopolitical structure that was put in place to ensure that the various cultural units could coexist peacefully within the framework of a new single nation-state. While the nationalist elite recognized the potential problems that these issues would pose in the new nation being proposed, their greater desire to attain independence from Britain seemed to have forced them to capitulate to the colonial authorities on these issues. The specter of these unresolved issues came back to haunt the political process in the early period of Nigeria's independence and has remained an albatross in the life of the nation ever since.

Once the euphoria of independence was over and the political elite settled down to the business of running the nation, the whole process was soon engulfed in a power struggle between the various, but especially the three largest, cultural units in the country.[2] This led first to a military posse in 1966 and subsequently to a civil war in 1967.[3]

General Yakubu Gowon's regime succeeded in arresting the attempted breakup of the country by the secessionist move to create a separate Biafran Republic when federal troops finally regained the eastern territory.[4] Moreover, General Gowon's administration sought to reunite the country by making a number of conciliatory gestures to rehabilitate the disenchanted east after the internecine war between 1967 and 1970. These two developments gave a great boost to popular belief in the possibility of a united Nigeria. Subsequently, each successive national day in Nigeria has been celebrated as proof of the strength of unity and federalism that exists in Nigeria. While many of the fundamental issues that gave rise to the civil war in the first place remain unresolved, the state machinery continued blithely on in the tradition of celebrating an erroneous national unity on every national day.

LOSS OF SIGNIFICANCE OF THE NATIONAL DAY

Alas! The annual pomp and pageantry that surrounds the celebration of Nigeria's nationhood has long ceased being the symbol of hope and opportunity for millions of disaffected and disenfranchised Nigerians; instead, it has become a farcical road show, put on only for the benefit of the political elite, the state apparatchiks, and the diplomatic community. Contradictions in the emerging postcolonial social order had turned earlier optimism into disillusionment. The struggle for power and privilege among the emerging elite in postcolonial Nigeria ushered in its own form of contradictions where exploitation earlier meted on colonial subjects by the colonialists is now meted on citizens by the indigenous elite.

First, the civilian government of the first republic woefully failed the test of political leadership and failed in their ability to deliver the promised land to the people of Nigeria. Then, the military, through a succession of coup d'états, failed to be the corrective regimes they purported to be; instead, they turned out to be massively corrupt and, not surprisingly, inept at running the affairs of state. The hopes and dreams of Nigerians for a better life, of a nation that would be a land of opportunity, and of a nation that would provide all its citizens an equal chance to realize their potentials have been deeply shattered by the experiences of a new national reality. In this new reality, nationalism is no longer encompassing but sectional (indeed, it had not been since the early wave of cultural nationalism that petered out in the early part of the 20th century). The Nigerian nation as an "imagined community" (Anderson 1991) seems to no longer invoke the spirit of a single, united conglomeration of cultural units or ethnic groups who have found a core of common values and ideals upon which to build a future together. Thus, the checkered history of Nigeria's struggle for nationhood since independence has made the national day significant in more ways than one on the national conscience.

National day commemoration in Nigeria has a symbolic dichotomy. There is an official one in which the national day continues to be a wholly farcical and fanciful affair. Here, the usual nationalist rhetoric is uttered about how a strong and united nation is being built, enjoining all Nigerians to be patriotic and to continue to give of their best to their motherland. This official celebration of the national day simply fails to connect with the reality on the ground and continues to ignore the real concerns of the wider public. Then, there is the unofficial, but by far more significant, commemoration by ordinary Nigerian citizens, social movements, workers' unions, and other progressive elements that take stock of the failed opportunities by the political elite to deliver on the promises of nationhood, on the failed opportunities to tap Nigeria's abundant potentials for the benefit of the whole nation. In this other commemoration, Nigeria's national day has come to symbolize a day of reflection and of apathy in which Nigerians ask searching questions about their troubled nationality. Thus, in the past two decades or so, and with increasing intensity as each year goes by, Independence Day in Nigeria is not so much a day of celebration but of soul-searching and critical appraisal.

Trade union organizations, students, academics, market women, and the like take to the streets with placards that voice frustration, protest, and defiance. Public lectures are held to assess the postindependence predicament of the Nigerian nation. For most Nigerians, the national day is simply meaningless, and so they remain in their homes or go about their normal business but they certainly do not celebrate. There is nothing to celebrate. Nigeria as a nation, through the provisions of the state to its citizens, has simply not touched the lives of many Nigerians.

Increasingly, the state (especially under military regimes) has felt more insecure on national days, being well aware of the strength of the people's feeling against a ruling elite of usurpers. As a result, the level of policing on major streets during national day celebrations is increased. Such heavy policing has turned the national day from a symbol of freedom to a symbol of oppression whereby the police and the armed forces are deployed against the citizen lest there be any public protest.

UNDERSTANDING THE CRISIS OF NATIONAL IDENTITY IN NIGERIA

To understand the crisis of national identity that has beset Nigeria since independence, one has to start from an analysis of her political history. This political history is born largely out of the confluence of a number of factors including a complex ethnic composition of different traditional sociopolitical structures, which were incorporated into the colonial administrative framework at different times and in different modes.

The formation of the Nigeria nation reflects the well-established historical process of the sociopolitical structures of traditional societies being ruptured in the wake of imperialist encroachment. This fact has a historical significance for understanding a great deal of the problems of nationalism and national identity that reemerged across the world in the last quarter of the 20th century. Each society that has had this experience in its history will have its own specific local inflection of the phenomenon. This recognition of the role of external forces in the volatile nationalism that exists in many parts of the world today should not necessarily be seen as harking back to the past to blame all the problems of national development on exogenous factors. The fact remains that the very nature of how many modern nations have been created through their historical encounter with external forces does entail the bringing together of certain deep-seated social as well as cultural components that do not always gel together very well. Such is the nature of the antipathy between these social and cultural elements that they can create a general structural instability that continues to hamper any real chance of national unity for a very long time.

Discussions about the problems of national development, especially within the development literature, have entered into a phase of introspection whereby commentators have turned their analytical gaze at endogenous factors (especially the actions of the national elite) for explanations of the lack of progress on national aspirations. Quite rightly so! But such introspection must ride on the back of an understanding of how the nation came into being, its place within an international system of unequal relations between nations, and the particular history of the conjuncture of local social and cultural systems with the international system.

We will take as our starting point Gellner's (1983/1997) definition of nationalism as "a political principle, which holds that the political and the national unit should be congruent" (52). Thus, we can proceed to argue that for many countries that are caught in the middle of nationalist and ethnic conflicts today, a primary cause is the ambition of nationalist leaders to achieve this conflating goal (Angus 1997; Christie 1998). In the specific case of Nigeria, it has been well recognized that the merging of the two erstwhile protectorates of northern and southern Nigeria in 1917 was born more out of administrative convenience for the colonial authority than for any consideration of, or respect for, the preexisting ethnic and sociopolitical structures of the colonized territory (Coleman 1958; Guibernau, 1996; Post and Vickers 1973). It is precisely this feature of the Nigerian nationality that holds the key to understanding the problems of nationhood and national identity. It may well be argued that Nigerians ought to rise above the constraints of the factors that separate them in order to forge a national unity that will benefit all the constituent groups in the country. It is necessary, however, to recognize that many of the distinctive ethnic and sociopolitical structures that prevail among the numerous (but in particular the three largest) ethnic groups in Nigeria are of a constitutive nature to the social existence of each group. So much so that these differences have not only played a significant part in the failure to evolve a common national identity for Nigerians, but they have also become absolutely crucial to any attempt to readdress the vexed question of the form of existence that a continued Nigerian nationality should take.

THE PROBLEMS OF NATIONALISM AND NATIONAL IDENTITY IN NIGERIA

In his seminal study of nationalism and national identity Anthony Smith (1991) argued that questions about the origins of nations can be usefully pursued through three related questions:

1. Who is the nation? This raises questions about the ethnic composition of a particular nation;

2. Why and how does the nation emerge? This raises questions about the combination of factors leading to the emergence of a nation, as well as the mechanism of "nation-formation";
3. When and where did the nation arise? This affords insight into the specific sets of ideas, persons, and places that led to the formation of a nation. (19)

In posing these questions with regard to the Nigerian nation, a good starting point is to establish that Nigeria is what Post and Vickers (1973, 11) have termed a "conglomerate society." Our use of this term is that of a society made up of disparate cultural groups that have diverse and often unrelated interests brought together to form a single national entity by the forces of history. This conglomerate nature of Nigeria has been well captured by Coleman (1958, 15) in his seminal study of the preindependence Nigerian society. Drawing on various official statistical records available at the time, as well as other relevant works, Coleman noted that there are approximately 248 linguistic groups contained within the boundaries of Nigeria. Following which, Coleman, drawing on a number of linguistic studies at the time, also noted that Nigeria is a major linguistic crossroads of Africa. While such a staggering number of linguistic diversity contained within a single sociopolitical space is of a certain significance on its own, it is not this sheer number as such that is most significant for an understanding of Nigerian society and polity. Rather, it is the pattern of distribution of these cultural groups in terms of size, geographical location and concentration, traditional social structure, and religion.

Thus, Diamond (1998) noted that "nothing can be understood about Nigeria until its pattern of ethnic diversity is delineated" (21). Many of the 248 cultural groups are fairly small in size (Coleman [1958] noted that the sizes range from units of less than 700 to ones with more than 5 million people). Such disproportionate distribution of ethnic groups, having created the context for the development of ethnic nationalism in Nigeria for numerical power, easily translates into political power. Three major ethnic groups have emerged as dominant in the scheme of things in Nigeria: the Hausa-Fulani, the Igbos, and the Yorubas. Crucially, there is a pattern of regional concentration in the distribution of these three major ethnic groups. Moreover, none of these groups enjoys total control of the geographical space so occupied, or, for that matter, complete internal harmony of kinship.

The Hausa-Fulani are concentrated in the northern region, while the Yoruba and Igbo are concentrated in the western and eastern regions, respectively. This regional distribution of the three largest ethnic groups encouraged the development of ethnic nationalism in Nigeria for it added a territorial dimension to the cultural and political-structural factors that cleaved the Nigeria society into different nationalist aspirations. The particular form that this territorial divide took served to exacerbate the problem of ethnic balance of power and the ensuing power struggles among the various ethnic groups. While the western and eastern regions of the country are approximately equal in size, the northern region is vastly larger. This disparity in regional size, both in terms of land and population (the latter claim being highly contentious for many southerners), has had an important implication for the distribution of national resources. The different traditional cultures and social structures of the various ethnic groups in Nigeria have been the key factor of cleavage in Nigerian nationalism. The peoples of northern Nigeria (principally Hausa-Fulani, Kanuri, and Nupe) have had a long-established and strong contact with Islam as well as a traditional, cephalous social structure of large-scale, centralized authoritarian states.

The middle-belt region of Nigeria is the most ethnically diverse region of the country, containing most of the over 200 linguistic groups to be found in Nigeria. The largest ethnic group in this region is the Tiv. Other key groups include the Igala, the Igbirra, the Idoma, and the Birom. Crucially, although this region has often been geographically grouped together with the "North," many of the cultural units that make up the middle belt of Nigeria had quite a distinct history and cultural identity as recent agitations indicate. The internal diversity of this region was well captured by Kirk-Greene (1967) when he described the region as containing "vigorous concentrations of Christianity among groups of resolute animists" (6).

Southern Nigeria was far less influenced by Islam, and by the highly centralized traditional social structure of the North than it was by Christianity and early European contact. This created a North–South dichotomy in terms of worldviews, nationalist aspirations, and social identities. Still, the South was by no means a homogeneous block before independence. In the West, the Yoruba were the major ethnic group, comprising over two-thirds of the population of this region. They also had a highly developed, cephalous social structure though less centralized and not organized into a single traditional state. Indeed, the other principal ethnic group within the western section of the country—the Edo— demonstrate a similar pattern of state-building by way of the Benin Kingdom. Christianity and Islam have both had about an equal amount of incursion among the Yoruba. However, the widespread take-up of Islam among the Yoruba has not necessarily engendered an interethnic religious alliance between them and the Muslim North because Islam was heavily inflected by other Yoruba traditional cultural values and practices. In this way "Islam took a less encompassing form in the South" (Diamond 1988, 25). Similarly, Young (1976) noted that "Hausa and Yoruba pray at different mosques, and Islam does not function as a crosscutting interethnic solidarity structure" (278). The Edo, given their own strong political and cultural heritage, have evolved their own cultural identity and so resist any attempt of assimilation by the Yoruba. Furthermore, the Yoruba have not always had the easiest of relations among themselves as witnessed by a long history of intraethnic clashes and warfare. Largely, the Igbo populate the eastern part of the country. The traditional political structure of the Igbo is even more distinctive from the cephalous patterns developed by the Hausa-Fulani and the Yoruba, underscoring the diversities in culture and society of the cultural groups brought together to form the Nigerian nation. This distinctiveness was instrumental in the construction of larger-scale group identities in the emergence of ethnic nationalism that developed in the post–World War II era.

The Igbo nation had an acephalous and decentralized political system that, for the most part, did not afford the building of kingdoms and empires. Coleman (1958) has noted, for instance, that the Igbos were historically fragmented into subgroups and clans that spread over some 500 relatively autonomous villages. Underlying this pattern of fragmentation however are the unifying structures in religion (Igboland is virtually all Christian), culture, and political and economic organization that made possible the formation of a pan-Igbo consciouness in the rise of ethnic nationalism. Further, in a passing reference to the Igbo culture, Coleman noted a "strong evidence of a cultural emphasis upon individual achievement affecting rank status" (28).

Other principal groups in this part of the country are the Ibibio and the Efik. Both groups have resisted cultural unification with the Igbos and have developed cultural resistance to each other despite sharing virtually the same language.

The foregoing, thus, is a brief sketch of the scale and diversity of political organization achieved by the major ethnic groups in Nigeria. This sketch also indicates the presence of a certain amount of cultural resistance by other significant cultural groups within each of the three regions that were brought together to form the Nigerian nation.

The significance of the foregoing for understanding the problem of nationalism and the lack of a single national identity in Nigeria can be explored by drawing on Smith's (1965) propositions about "plural societies" and their cultural ramification. Smith contends that not all societies follow the Parsonian pattern of being made up of individuals and groups sharing a consensus about some central values. Rather, he observed that some societies (referred to as "plural societies") are constituted of mutually exclusive cultural units. His concern that such societies, due to their organization and composition, are unable to integrate provides a useful framework for analyzing the sociopolitical character of nationalism in Nigeria. It is worth quoting relevant sections of Smith's proposition at some length here:

My argument derives from the general anthropological finding that the core of a people's culture and system of social relations is to be found in their major institutional systems, namely, kinship, religion, economy, education, government, and recreation. Each institutional system consists of patterned activities, modes of social relation, rules, values, and ideas. Accordingly, institutional differences distinguish differing cultures and social units. When groups that practise [sic] differing institutional systems live side by side under a common government, the cultural plurality of this inclusive unit corresponds with its social plurality. Institutional pluralism involves corresponding cultural and social pluralism. In a culturally divided society, each cultural section has its own relatively exclusive way of life, with its own distinctive systems of action, ideas and values, and social relations. The institutional system that forms the cultural core defines the social structure and value system of any given population. Thus, pluralism consists in the co-existence of incompatible systems. (5)

Smith (1965) identifies three modes that constitute a plural society: cultural pluralism, social pluralism, and structural pluralism. Cultural pluralism essentially refers to the existence of institutional differences (such as we noted earlier), among the various sections brought together under the same political administration. Social pluralism refers to the state where institutional distinctiveness converges with clearly defined social segments such as to give rise to virtually distinct and inclusive social sections. Smith's definition of the third mode of pluralism—structural pluralism—is worth quoting at length:

Structural pluralism consists . . . in the different incorporation of specified collectivities within a given society and corresponds with this in its form, scope, and particulars. It institutes or presupposes social and cultural pluralism together, by prescribing sectional differences of access to the common public domain, and by establishing differing contexts and conditions of sectional coexistence, segregation and subordination. Such conditions preserve or generate corresponding institutional pluralism by fostering diverse sectional adaptations to their distinctive situations and promoting divergent and sectionally specific collective domains for their internal organization and intersectional relations. Such an order of structural pluralism may be instituted in one of two ways: by the total exclusion of subordinate sections from the inclusive public domain, which is then the formally unqualified monopoly of the dominant group; or alternatively by instituting substantial and sufficient inequalities of sectional participation in and access to this sector of the societal organization. (440)

In a number of ways, this brief account of plural societies shows some promise in its relevance for examining the problem of nationalism and national identity in Nigeria. In particular the notion of "differential incorporation" of de-similar cultural sections into a single political/administrative framework, and the ensuing competition and struggles for supremacy among them would strike many Nigerians as an apt description of the main problem that has beset the country since independence.

Some weaknesses in Smith's (1965) position have been noted by critics, thus making it necessary to reformulate what is generally a perceptive analytical model in order to make it even more useful for our analysis of the Nigerian political situation. Mckenzie (1966), criticized Smith for offering a rather deterministic notion of cultural affiliation where all behavior is assumed to refer back to the existence of cultural sections in plural societies. Post and Vickers (1973) noted two problems that such cultural determinism present: first is the need to provide a careful distinction between all the different kinds of behavior possible within a cultural section, and second, it cannot be assumed that people always behave as conscious members of a cultural section. It seems more likely that certain factors tend to trigger behavior as a conscious awareness of membership of cultural sections. Furthermore, for Smith's model to be usefully applied to our analysis of the nationality problem in Nigeria, it is necessary to modify his concept of the "cultural core," which has been criticized for not sufficiently distinguishing between the cultural and the structural aspects of social actions (Morris 1967, 171).

The central feature of Smith's (1965) model of a plural society is one in which human behavior is linked with, or determined by the membership of cultural sections. Picking up on this proposition, Post and Vickers (1973) argue that a finer distinction ought to be made between the cultural and the structural aspects of social action. In this way, "structures" (which they defined as "relationships which bind clusters of social roles together") can be distinguished from "culture" (which they defined as "the beliefs associated with the clusters of social roles") (16). By so doing, Post and Vickers showed that when Smith's model is applied to the study of precolonial societies of Nigeria, there are no easy fits between social action, social structures, and cultural sections.

For one thing, Post and Vickers (1973) argued that cultural sections in precolonial Nigerian societies did not have structures that embraced the social roles of all members of the section. Furthermore, in relation to cultural values, they noted that while the cultural sections shared, to a large extent, common cultural values, there nonetheless existed variations (either in language or other properties) within these cultural sections that served to modify any notion of cultural unity. Thus, they argued that cultural sectionalism is more about how individual behavior is based on consciousness—"the extent to which an individual actually identifies explicitly with the values of his cultural section" (17)—than it is about social structures. They then proposed a distinction between "relatively latent" and "relatively manifest" cultural sections; and that members of a cultural section begin to behave in terms of their membership only as the section begins to become manifest, whereupon new structures may develop that incorporate all members of the section.

Thus, the question at this point is, What or who was responsible for setting in motion the transition of precolonial Nigerian societies from a latent to a manifest cultural section, and thus the emergence of sectional consciousness among members of these cultural sections? A crucial part of the answer must be the colonial administrative strategy that Smith (1965) refers to as "differential incorporation." The colonial administrative framework that forcibly brought these disparate cultural sections together created a new political space in which they all had to come in closer contact with one another. It inevitably paved the way for the rivalry, rancor, and mutual distrust that marked both the post–World War II nationalist struggle and the post–independence efforts at nation-building.

Principally, the incorporation of different sections of the country into the new political framework, that came to be known as Nigeria, at different points in time created an imbalance within the various sections in terms of access to Western education and the paraphernalia of colonial administration. Further, the mode of incorporation was also not uniform such that the colonial administration of the northern protectorate was by indirect rule where most of the colonial contact was restricted to the traditional rulers. By contrast, the administration of the southern protectorate was by direct rule. For the southerners, this had two consequences: first, a far greater degree of colonial encroachment with its attendant social rupture and deep incorporation into the Western cultural system, and second, it led to a clear advantage in terms of access to the political, cultural, and economic capital that inevitably became vital for operating in the new political dispensation ushered in by colonialism.

Thus, this differential incorporation into a new political framework brought the various cultural sections in Nigeria into an intense interaction with one another. As such, the mobilization of these various sections toward social transition and nationalist struggle from the 1930s up to and after independence in 1960 was marked by a feeling of identification with a cultural section, rather than with a Nigerian nation.

MEDIA TRANSFORMATION AND NATIONAL IDENTITY IN NIGERIA

The role of the Nigerian press in the history of the nationalist struggle and in the construction of a national identity can be said to be ambivalent. It has vacillated between campaigns for a united Nigerian nation and a common national identity, and one that has not only lent support to sectionalism, but has actively taken part in the construction of interethnic rancor and suspicion. The Nigerian press of the early- to mid-20th-century period was largely influenced by the prevailing pan-Africanist movement and so characterized by a strong, cultural nationalism fervor (Sobowale 1985; Omu, 1978).

In this period, the struggle for nationalism was constructed in terms of an us versus them discourse where the "us" referred to a multistaged cultural enclosure with a reference point that ranged from West Africans to Africans and finally to black people. The "them" referred, of course, to the colonialists. The type of nationalist discourse that characterized the journalism of this period is evident in the following extract from John Payne Jackson's *Lagos Weekly Record* of February 26, 1910:[5]

West Africans have discovered today what the Indians . . . discovered 35 years ago, that, placed as they were under the controlling influence of a foreign power, it was essential to their well-being that they should make a common cause and develop a national unity. . . . We hope the day will soon come when . . . Hausas, Yorubas, and the Ibos will make a common standard and work hand in hand for their common fatherland.

The Nigerian press of the post–World War II period up until about the 1980s was far less united in the construction of a common national identity. Although many of them, with the particular example of Nnamdi Azikwe's *West-African Pilot*,[6] continued the struggle for a broad-based nationalism as can be gleaned from the name of the newspaper, they all eventually succumbed to a narrow-based variant. This new phase of nationalist journalism not only began to define nationalism within the geographical boundaries constructed by the colonial powers but more disastrously began to define it along ethnic boundaries as well.

This descent of the nationalist struggle in Nigeria from the heights and aspirations of the pan-African nationalism of the earlier period to one of interethnic rivalry emerged from a phase when the continued struggle for independence was channeled through the vehicle of panethnic political organizations. Such political movements include the Egbe Omo Oduduwa for the Yorubas, the Ibo Federal Union for the Igbos, and the Jam'iyyar Mutanen Arewa for the peoples of northern Nigeria.

These various ethnic-based political organizations transformed the nature of nationalist struggle by making membership of a cultural group the basis for political affiliation and the platform on which nationalist struggle and cultural identity are fought and constructed, respectively. Invariably, such developments also influenced the role of the press during this period as the various newspapers became the platform for voicing ethnic-based aspirations as well as for launching often vitriolic attacks on "other" ethnic groups.

To be fair, none of these cultural–political organizations was deliberately set up to foster disunity and interethnic antipathy in the nationalist struggle. It seems, however, that through a combination of the actions and pronouncements of key individuals within these organizations as well as the inevitable attempts by the various groups to respond to the structural imbalances created by the colonial authorities, these were the outcomes of the creation of such organizations.

The Nigerian press of this era was not so much a business as it was an essential political tool for galvanizing nationalist activities and sentiments among the few, but growing class of, literate city dwellers. Indeed, many of the publishers, newspaper owners, and journalists of this period had gone into the newspaper business in order to establish a platform for pursuing the nationalism project, but one which often also led to the formation of caucuses for venting ethnic inflections of the overall nationalist ambition. A third era in the relationship between journalism and nationalism in Nigeria can be dated from the 1980s to the present. The actual makings of the journalism of this era can be traced back to developments from the post–Civil War period of the early 1970s. The reconciliation and national reconstruction initiatives of the period brought in a wave of changes in the federal structure as well as in government policies. One of the areas in which such significant developments occurred, and continue to do so, was in the media and communication sphere. To comprehend and appreciate this transformation requires understanding the changing relationships between the postcolonial state, the mass media, and capitalism in Nigeria. The economic boom of the period that issued from the large-scale exploration of Nigeria's oil reserves gave added confidence to the military regime of Generals Murtala Mohammed and Olusegun Obasanjo to embark on a project of nationalization of key institutions. The period, in the mid-1970s, was especially noted for an economic boom and prosperity that also saw an expansion in other sectors such as education, manufacturing, import, and export. The new, emergent elite class, who had enormous exposure through travel and education, made the climate conducive for a new, more diverse and robust kind of journalism that would serve the elite's taste as well as the taste of the burgeoning educated working class. For this, as well as the return of party politics, the 1980s saw huge media growth in Nigeria. The most significant development in the press was the birth of *The Guardian* in 1983 and *Newswatch* in 1985. Jointly established by a famous entrepreneur—Alex Ibru—and a famous academic—Stanley Macebuh, who had established himself as a top journalist with the *Daily Times* newspapers—*The Guardian* transformed Nigerian journalism through an intellectualization of the editorial board and columnists.

Within a brief period, the successes recorded by *The Guardian* sent a signal that there was a market for high-quality journalism in Nigeria. This led to the emergence of newsmagazine journalism as a specialization within the print media industry. The pioneers in this trend, such as *Newswatch*, clearly marked a departure from what used to be known about previous efforts in this genre. For whereas *Newswatch* appeared with political consciousness and investigative ethos, early magazines in Nigeria in the 1950s and 1960s, such as *Drum*, *Trust*, and *Spear*, were known more for their entertainment content than the articulation of progressive political consciousness.

Newswatch and other similar magazines that came on the Nigerian media scene during this period cultivated a niche for investigative journalism as well as the promotion of debate that were hitherto not associated with magazine journalism in Nigeria. Indeed, the commitment to investigative spirit is widely believed to be the reason behind the murder of the first editor and cofounder, Dele Giwa, by "unknown" assailants, via a parcel bomb in 1986. The culture of in-depth investigation and promotion of debate with which *Newswatch* was known endeared it to the Nigerian public for whom it symbolized its quest for freedom and transparency. It is to that extent that Dele Giwa's murder was mourned as a national tragedy.

Newswatch's success led to the emergence of rival magazines, such as *The African Guardian*, the *African Concord*, and the *Citizen*, that had the same ethos of investigative journalism that strove to ride above ethnic politics and premodial loyalty in their handling of delicate issues of nationality and national unity. By far the most crucial factor at work in this period was the emergence of a new breed of business-oriented, private media proprietors who not only offered competition against state-run newspapers, but provided the conducive environment for the new breed of journalists to evolve a more diverse content and a professionalized type of journalism.

The development of broadcasting in postindependent Nigeria revolved around three major factors: government, party politics, and capital. At independence in 1960, the central government saw broadcasting as one of the icons of nationalistic establishments that it was duty bound to establish. At that time, the remnants of a BBC broadcasting culture became the nucleus from which radio broadcasting was established. Indeed, training for early Nigerian broadcasters was mostly done through the BBC, which hosted Nigerian trainee broadcasters in an in-house training program. At other times, BBC experts were sent to Nigeria to provide the training. The regionalization of party politics meant that right from independence Nigeria took off with three regional broadcasting stations, one each for the three constituent parts or regions. The dissolution of Nigeria's regional structure and its replacement by state structure in 1970 meant that each of 12 states then had a radio station of its own. All of these state stations, though, hooked up to the federal radio station for national network news and other national programs. At each time such national network programs or news were relayed, it meant the entire nation was united in the consumption of a common broadcasting diet. What is national about these programs is not only their target audience being the entire nation but also that their themes and highlights are often intended to be of national rather than local interest and concern. The return to party politics in 1978 after a long period of military dictatorship marked a very significant period in Nigerian broadcasting history. For under the American-style presidential system of democracy that Nigeria adopted, it was the case that political parties different from the one controlling the central or federal government were in power in some states. Before 1978, however, television broadcasting was a monopoly of the federal government, which had also established a station in each of the states that made up Nigeria. Much of what was shown on television was national network programs originating from the headquarters of the Nigerian Television Authority. From 1979, all such state governments ruled by political parties different from the one controlling the federal government felt insecure in continuing to rely on television broadcasts from the authority. Each of the states went ahead and established a rival television station, thus making the number of television stations in its domain two. Overall, this situation brought the number of television stations in Nigeria to about 30. The return of the military to governance of Nigeria through the military coups of 1983 and 1985 did not reduce the number of broadcasting stations but actually raised it because the military-led government of General Badamosi Babangida loosened the government's monopoly on broadcasting by allowing for private ownership of radio and television stations in the country. The National Broadcasting Commission was established in August 1992 as the supervisory agency empowered to grant or revoke broadcasting licenses and set ethical and technical standards in broadcasting, as well as entertain complaints and apply sanctions. After its establishment, the commission conceived of and put into effect the National Broadcasting Code that spelled out the details regarding standards of broadcasting in Nigeria as well as procedures for applying for a broadcasting license. By 1995, therefore, by courtesy of the decree, there was a major explosion in the number of television and radio stations in Nigeria.

The emergence of private broadcasting at that time must be seen, though, in the context of the relationship between capitalism and the state. The 1990s was generally a period when most countries in Africa were going through the Structural Adjustment Programme of the World Bank and the International Monetary Fund. The prescription to most African countries by these twin institutions of finance capital was that they embrace the ideology of deregulation and privatization necessary for the integration of their societies into the global capitalist framework as well as opening such societies for capital investment and regeneration.

Such free movement of capital that was envisaged under the structural adjustment needed a deregulated media environment both for the transmission of symbolic goods as well as a major investment outlet. This development therefore implied that such developments in Nigerian broadcasting that saw significant changes in ownership structure were dictated not by the needs of citizens but by those of capital. The implication of this new development is yet to be fully realized, however, because even the assumption that state-controlled broadcasting services necessarily cater to the needs of the public is a dubious one.

A common take by critics of the commercialization and privatization of public communication is that such a development portends bad things for the public especially in terms of their communication, cultural, and political needs. While we share many of the genuine concerns that are raised in this line of thinking and so do not wish to dismiss it altogether, we take the view here that such a position requires a qualification and modification especially with respect to non-Western social and national contexts.

Limited space here prevents a detailed exposition of this argument but we would initiate it summarily by noting that in pre- or nondemocratic societies such as Nigeria, where the media, especially broadcasting, is usually monopolized and centrally controlled by the state, commercialization and privatization may, indeed, offer some benefits to the public.

Ironic as it may seem, in such societies, a commercialized and privatized media may be a better guarantor of the public's needs than a public media that is usually no more than a megaphone of autocratic governments. The debate in the West about public versus private media, in terms of their respective benefits and pitfalls, must take an expanded dimension when brought into the analysis of the media in emerging societies. In these societies, the notion of "public," and the principles that underpin it, is not yet the same as implied in developed, liberal democracies. In many of these emerging societies, the principle of public institution is used as an excuse by a small ruling elite to control the resources of the state not for the benefit of the public but for the furtherance of the narrow interest of the ruling class.

Thus, in the Nigerian experience, the media became far more dynamic in terms of the range of content, cross-sectional audience reach, appeal, fearless editorial comments, and coverage of political events and actors when they became more diversified through private ownership. And this explains why there have been more private media journalists who have fallen victim to state repression and harassment than those in the so-called public media.

CONCLUSION

Nigeria's national day occupies a significant place in the history of the country. It symbolizes the dismantling of the structures of British colonialism and the realization of the people's agitation and right to self-determination. The mass media have played a central role as the informational arm of the struggle that culminated in independence on October 1, 1960, and subsequently in the continued struggle for national unity and the construction of a national identity. In this role, however, the media (or at least sections of it) have often been used as a platform for venting sectional, and other nonnationalist, interests. The negative transformation of the significance of national day has its roots in the emerging appropriation of the country's independence by the new elite who, sensing the prospects of independence from Britain, "began to break up into ethnic and religious camps and regroup around ethno-regional cleavages to better utilize ethnic symbols in their competitive bid for advantageous political niches in the independent nation state of the future" (Agbaje 1993, 459).

Intraclass struggle among the new elite combined with the long-standing interethnic rivalry to create a complex political battleground where the nationalist aspirations and promises of the precolonial struggle were often subordinated to class and sectional vested interests as well as personal aggrandizement. In this situation, a viable national rallying point has failed to materialize, thus leading to a clamor for restructuring of Nigeria into more local councils, more states, and even separate countries.

NOTES

1. Nigeria, the most populous country in Africa, has the largest concentration of black people anywhere in the world (approximately 126 million by a 2001 estimate). It is located in West Africa, bounded by Benin to the west, Niger to the north, Chad to the northeast, Cameroon to the east, and the Gulf of Guinea to the south. It was formally colonized by Britain from the early 20th century to 1960.

2. There are some 250 ethnic groups in Nigeria with the three largest being Hausa-Fulani, Yoruba, and the Igbos.

3. The first military interregnum in Nigeria took place in 1966 due to the culmination of the highly divisive politics of the postindependence civilian government. The military administration was headed by Major-General Johnson Aguiyi-Ironsi, an Igbo. Inevitably, Nigeria drifted into a civil war in 1967 as the postindependence struggles for the spoils of the colonial administration and the problems of nation-building spun out of control. The military establishment became embroiled in the ethnic rivalry that marked the postcolonial polity so much so that they became part of the problem rather than the solution to the problems started by the politicians. As a result of a tit-for-tat killing of prominent persons among the political elite and the military establishment on the basis of ethnicity that led to a massive killing of the Igbos in northern Nigeria, there was a move for secession by the Igbos. The attempt by the Igbo military and political elites to create a republic of Biafra was resisted by the federal government, thus leading to a civil war between 1967 and 1970.

4. General Yakubu Gowon was the compromise candidate who emerged as the head of state in the second military coup that northern army officers staged as a reprisal to oust Aguiyi-Ironsi's military government.

5. John Payne Jackson was one of the great pioneers of the journalism and newspaper business in Nigeria in the early 20th century. In particular, his brand of journalism was of the anti-imperialist type aimed at forging a cultural–nationalist movement across West Africa and beyond. Born in Liberia, for 25 years, between 1890 and 1915, he was regarded as the most outstanding journalist in the entire West African subregion.

6. Nnamdi Azikwe was the proprietor of the *West-African Pilot* that represented a second wave of journalism in Nigeria from about the 1940s. He was to later become the first president of Nigeria in a parliamentary-style government that was formed after independence in 1960.

REFERENCES

Agbaje, A. (1993). Beyond the state: Civil society and the Nigerian press under military rule. In *Media, culture and society*, vol. 15.

Anderson, B. R. O'G. (1991). *Imagined communities: Reflections on the origins and spread of nationalism*. London: Verso.

Angus, I. (1997). *A border within: National identity, cultural plurality and wilderness*. Montreal, QC: McGill-Queen University Press.

Billig, M. (1995). *Banal nationalism*. London: Sage.

Calhoun, C. (1997). *Nationalism*. Buckingham, UK: Open University.

Christie, C. (1998). *Race and nation*. London: Tauris.

Coleman, J. (1958). *Nigeria: Background to nationalism*. Berkeley: University of California Press.

Diamond, L. (1988). *Class, ethnicity and democracy in Nigeria*. London: Macmillan.

Edelstein, J. C. (1974). Pluralist and Marxist perspectives on ethnicity and nation-building. In W. Bell and W. Freeman (Eds.), *Ethnicity and nation-building*. London: Sage.

Gellner, E. (1997). *Nations and nationalism*. Oxford, UK: Blackwell. (Originally published in 1983)

Guibernau, M. (1996). *Nationalisms*. Cambridge, UK: Polity Press.

Hobsbawm, E. J. (1990). *Nations and nationalism since 1780: Programme, myth, realty*. Cambridge, UK: Cambridge University Press.

Kirk-Greene, A. H. M. (1981). *Nigeria since 1970: A political and economic outline*. London: Hodder and Stoughton.

Mckenzie, H. I. (1966, March). *The plural society debate. Social and Economic Studies, 15*(1).

Mustafa, A. R. (1986). The national question and radical politics in Nigeria. *ROAPE, 37*.

N.B.C. Decree No. 38 of 1992. (1992). Federal Republic of Nigeria.

Omu, F. (1978). *Press and politics in Nigeria, 1880–1937*. London: Longman.

Post, K., and Vickers, M. (1973). *Structure and conflict in Nigeria, 1960–65*. London: Heinemann.

Rex, J. (1995). Ethnic identity and the nation-state: The political sociology of multi-cultural societies. *Social Identities (1)*1, 21–34.

Smith, A. (1991). *National identity*. London: Penguin Books.

Smith, M.G. (1965). *The plural society in the British West Indies*. Berkeley: University of California Press.

Smith, M. G., and Kuper, L. (Eds.). (1969). *Pluralism in Africa*. Berkeley: University of California Press.

Sobowale, I. A. (1985). The historical development of the Nigerian press. In F. O. Ugboajah(Ed.), *Mass communication, culture and society in West Africa*. Munich, Germany: Zello.

Young, C. 1976. *The politics of cultural pluralism*. Madison: University of Wisconsin Press.

NORWAY

Norway's 17th of May

A Historical Date and a Day of National Celebrations

Knut Mykland

In 1319 Norway was linked with Sweden in a union with over 400 years as a self-governing and independent realm. In 1380 Norway and Denmark were united under the same king, a union which eventually led to Norway's being integrated in a Danish-Norwegian single unified state with Denmark as the realm's dominant partner and Copenhagen as the unchallenged capital of the kingdom. It was not until 14 January 1814, the date of the Treaty of Kiel, that the Danish-Norwegian dual monarchy was dissolved and King Fredrik IV of Denmark was forced to cede Norway to the King of Sweden.

It is true that from the middle of the 18th century there had been a certain amount of discontent in Norway over the fact that the country's interests were disregarded to Denmark's advantage and, above all, to the advantage of the dual monarchy's capital, Copenhagen. There were repeated Norwegian requests that the country should have its own university and its own bank, but it was not until 1811 that the demand of a university was finally met. The demand for a bank continued to be rejected out of fear that the dual monarchy could break up if Norway were to acquire a separate and independent monetary system.

When Denmark-Norway was drawn into the whirlpool of the Napoleonic wars in 1807, Fredrik VI opted for alliance with France and war with England. His choice was determined exclusively out of consideration to the Realm's continental portion, Denmark and the two duchies of Schleswig and Holstein. As far as Norway was concerned the war with England meant blockade, crisis and hunger. In this situation there were clear signs of a growing separatist movement in

This chapter is reprinted with the compliments of the Royal Norwegian Consulate General, New York, with the Norwegian Information Service in the United States (http://www.Norway.org).

Norway and increasingly disenchantment with the existing regime and the union with Denmark. Some Norwegians, among them Count Wedel Jarlsberg, went so far as to advocate Norway's separation from Denmark and the establishment of a union with Sweden. However, this discontent never reached such proportions as to threaten the existence of the dual monarchy. When Norway was separated from Denmark by the Treaty of Kiel on 14 January 1814, this came not as a result of dissatisfaction in Norway, but rather as a consequence of the policies Napoleon's former marshal, Jean Baptiste Bernadotte, had pursued after he was elected Crown Prince of Sweden in 1810 and as heir-presumptive to the Swedish throne adopting the name Carl Johan. Norway was the reward of the victorious commander in the field, in return for his and Sweden's support to the allies in the final reckoning with Napoleon.

From the spring of 1813 the young heir-presumptive to the Danish-Norwegian crown, Prince Christian Fredrik, resided in Norway as "Stattholder." At the end of January, when he received news of the Peace signed at Kiel and the cession of Norway to Sweden, he decided to prevent the realization of the cession of the Kingdom by placing himself, as the head of a Norwegian independence movement, with reunion with Denmark as his unexpressed secret hope. King Fredrik VI of Denmark was well aware of the Prince's plan, was in sympathy with it, and himself supported the independence movement in Norway by supplying large quantities of grain.

When Christian Fredrik incited the Norwegians to fight for their independence, he was in no doubt that he enjoyed the support of large sectors of the population. The Norwegian independence movement received encouragement from many different traditional sources: the attachment to the old royal house, hopes for reunion with Denmark, anti-Danish feeling, recollections of bygone days and fear of a union with Sweden. From these vague and confused dreams, there developed in Norway, during the winter and spring of 1814, a powerful and heady desire for independence: Norway was once again to join the ranks of independent states as a free, self-governing realm, as she had been many centuries earlier.

There was one point on which Christian Fredrik's political plans after the Treaty of Kiel were frustrated by the desires and hopes of the upper stratum of society. After the news of the Treaty of Kiel and cession of the Kingdom reached Norway, Christian Fredrik had the intention of ascending the Norwegian throne by virtue of his alleged right of inheritance and of governing the Kingdom as the only rightful absolute monarch. However, many prominent office-holders and other citizens nourished a strong desire for a free constitution, a desire to which the Prince would have to give way if he were to bring his policy of independence to a successful conclusion. On 10 April 1914 the popularly elected National Assembly met at Eidsvold Iron Works outside Christiania (Oslo) for the purpose of giving the country a constitution. As one of the representatives described this Assembly: "Here was to be seen a selection of men from all parts of the realm, of all ranks and dialects, men from court circles as well as land-owners come together in no set order for the sacred purpose of laying the foundations for the rebirth of the nation." Six weeks later, on 17 May 1814, the National Assembly had completed its work on the Constitution, and on the same day closed its proceedings by electing Prince Christian Fredrik King of Norway. The solemn proceedings ended with a short and powerful speech by the President, Georg Sverdrup, linking the old free Norway to the Norway which was now emerging: "Thus within Norway's boundaries is resurrected Norway's ancient seat of Kings, which was graced by Athelstans and Sverres and from which, with wisdom and might, they ruled over Norway of old."

The fact that Christian Fredrik was able to unite the Norwegians in the struggle for independence and, in cooperation with the National Assembly, to organize the government of the new state in the course of a few hectic weeks prior to the 17th of May, was due to Carl Johan's continued involvement on the Continent with the main Swedish army. But after Napoleon was forced to abdicate at the beginning of April, the Crown Prince of Sweden had fulfilled his obligations to his allies and, towards the end of May 1814, he was able to return to Sweden with the Swedish army. Despite bombastic statements from Norway, and despite the declaration "Death before slavery," after a short war Norway was forced into a union with Sweden, the union became effective when the Storting (the Norwegian Parliament) elected Carl XIII of Sweden as King of Norway on 4 November 1814. But the constitutional form of the Kingdom was in all main respects such as was laid down in the Constitution of 17 May, and the union with Sweden was so loose that it could be dissolved in 1905 without either kingdom being seriously affected as a result.

There are therefore good grounds for regarding 17 May 1814 as the pre-eminent date in Norway's history. After centuries as a dependency Norway once again joined the ranks of free states as an independent realm, and the new union with Sweden proved only to be an intermezzo, with no influence on the inner development of the country. From being subjected—at least in theory—to a most extreme form of despotism, the country emerged with a more liberal Constitution than any other contemporary state. While other free constitutions in Europe, drawn up during the Revolutionary and Napoleonic eras, were rescinded and substituted by more authoritarian regimes, the Norwegian constitution remained standing.

As early as the 1820s people started to celebrate the 17th of May, and since then this day has been established as Norway's National Day, Norway's Liberation Day, even though the celebrations have in the course of time changed their character and form. The history of the 17th of May celebrations in Norway reflects in many ways the main features of the country's history from 1814 until today.

When Carl Johan, as the victor of 1814, accepted the 17th of May Constitution as the basis for government in Norway, within the framework of a union with Sweden, there were many reasons for this policy: hope of once again being able to play a role in French politics, fear of a Gustavian restoration in Sweden, fear of a winter war in Norway, the desire to win the Norwegians over to the idea of a union with Sweden through concessions and a policy of appeasement. Among these motives, there was one which had the future in mind: the hope of later winning back what he had been obliged to give up in 1814. It was this last motive which formed the basis for Carl Johan's policy *vis a vis* [*sic*] Norway after becoming King in 1818. Deliberately and systematically he pursued a policy aimed at restricting the powers of the Storting such as they were prescribed in the Constitution, extending the powers of the Crown and creating a closer union between Norway and Sweden. Norwegian policy in the 1820s was characterized by a struggle to defend that which had been gained in 1814, the defense of the Constitution which formed a bulwark for national independence. These events also formed the background for the 17th of May celebrations in the 1820s. They took the form of an outer manifestation in support of the national liberation efforts of 1814 and for the will to defend the Constitution and national independence. It is significant that the slogan "Guard the Constitution" was the running theme of the banners used in the first 17th of May processions.

Around 1830 Carl Johan changed his policy on Norway. In reality he gave up the idea of a thoroughgoing revision of the Constitution, and his successors to the throne were to follow the same line of policy. Thus the 17th of May celebrations took more and more the form of a national day of celebration. The defensive watchdog attitude which characterized the first 17th of May celebrations was superseded by a form of celebration characterized by a feeling of springlike optimism, by the joy of having a free constitutional government, by a people seeking to stress their own identity. It is a characteristic feature of the change that, in addition to the solemn procession of the citizenry, the children's procession was introduced, which, in time would come to be the most striking and colourful feature of the Norwegian 17th of May celebrations.

It was above all the holders of "embete," or higher office, who were responsible for creating the Constitution of Eidsvold. It was this group which stood guard over it against Carl Johan's encroachments in the 1820s. It was also this group which in fact ruled the country during the first two generations after 1814. From the 1830s the farmers began to awaken and became conscious of the power given them under the Constitution, and the 1870s and '80s were characterized by the fierce political struggle between the old ruling class—the senior office holders and bourgeoisie—on the one side, and the farmers and the liberal urban citizenry on the other. The conflict erupted into a bitter and uncompromising struggle in the Storting, which led to impeachment, the victory of parliamentary government and the establishment of the two political parties, the Conservatives (Hoyre) and the Liberals (Venstre). In this situation the 17th of May celebrations again changed character. The day was no longer regarded as a day of national unity, but a day of strife, when conservatives and liberals voiced their political standpoints in town after town, each with their own 17th of May speakers and their own 17th of May processions.

On 7 June 1905 the union with Sweden was dissolved by a decision passed in the Storting. The dissolution was supported by a united population, more united perhaps than at any time before or since. This attitude was also to be reflected in the 17th of May celebrations. The differences between the parties were to give way to the feeling of unity. The 17th of May processions were now characterized by a feeling of fellowship and of rejoicing that the country had at last gained full independence.

But time brought changes. In the 1880s and the 1890s, the Norwegian political scene had been marked by the struggle between the Conservatives and the Liberals, between the old regime of officialdom on the one hand and on the other the alliance of farmers and urban liberals. In the 1920s and '30s the clash of interests between the middle class and the working class formed the main area of conflict in Norwegian political life and this state of affairs was intensified by unemployment, strikes and labour unrest. The bourgeois parties put full emphasis on the national element in politics. As far as the working class was concerned, politics centered on international fellowship in tune with the slogan "Workers of the world, unite." This conflict-ridden situation was also to set its stamp on the 17th of May celebrations. While the middle class celebrated the day with massed processions in the towns, processions often featuring slogans directed against the workers' internationalism, the working classes largely avoided the 17th of May celebrations altogether. "It is not in cooperation between the classes, but in the class struggle to the bitter end that the answer is to be found—on 17 May as on the other days of the year," wrote Martin Tranmael, editor of the Labour Party's main organ. The Labour party [sic] and unions in Oslo supported the party line in a declaration in which they urged the workers not to take part in "the bourgeois celebrations of 17 May. Boycott the arrangements of bourgeoisie."

During the German occupation of Norway from 9 April 1940 until 7 May 1945, the feeling of national fellowship predominated. The Nazi regime, with all its terror, imprisonment and torture, united the population. During the German occupation, the 17 of May celebrations were strictly forbidden, but there can scarcely have been any time when the day occupied a more important place in the national consciousness than just then in the occupation period, as the writer Nordahl Grieg phrased it in a poem which was soon the common property of all Norwegians:

Now stands the flagpole bare
Behind Eidsvoll's budding trees,
But in such an hour as this,
We know what freedom is.

The bitter conflicts which had marked the 17th of May celebrations in the 1920s and '30s were replaced after the way by a feeling of fellowship resembling that of the years around 1905. But there was a difference. Then, it was on full national independence that the 17th of May celebrations and the public rejoicing were centered. In the post-1945 period, the main stress was laid more on democratic rights, constitutional government, freedom of the press, and law and order, in contrast to what had been experienced in the war years—violence, terror, concentration camps and dictatorship.

The discussion of Norwegian membership in the EC in 1971 and 1972 again led to a major split in public opinion. The Norwegian population found itself divided into two main factions: the supporters of membership and its opponents. The hostile feelings were just as intense as in the 1880s and the 1930s. This dissension was at the same time a struggle over the national symbols, a struggle where traces were visible in the 17th of May celebrations in 1972. But after the question of membership had been decided by a public referendum of 25 September 1972, antagonism gradually faded, and in the years that followed the feeling of fellowship was again to come to the fore.

If the 17th of May celebrations in Norway are viewed in the long-term perspective, one is struck by the manner in which the annual celebrations have changed in character and content over the years. The 17th of May has been a day of strife, as well as a day when the people rallied around the Constitution, national independence and democratic rights. Viewed against this background, the question inevitably arises: despite all this, how is [it] that the National Day has managed to retain its central position in the public consciousness and remain Norway's great ceremonial day? One reason is to be found in the physical features of the country.

The 17th of May has remained the great spring festival in Norway, in a country with a winter that is both long and cold. For this reason the 17th of May has more and more taken on the character of a children's festival. The children's procession has become the colourful focal point in the celebrations, from the most remote coastal settlements to the capital city where literally thousands of schoolchildren, marching along behind their school bands and banners, file past the Royal Palace in salute to the King.

Another reason for the central position the 17th of May celebrations have occupied and continue to occupy in Norway is to be found in the country's relationship with other countries. From 1814 to 1905 Norway was joined in a union with Sweden, and although the country held an independent position in this union, nevertheless in the Norwegian consciousness the union always represented a potential danger, able to arouse feelings of nationalism and lead to closing of ranks around the national symbols, as in the 1820s and the period around 1905.

Jumping from the time of the Union to our own globally-minded era, a similar tendency may be seen. The German occupation during World War II provided evidence of the fate which could befall a small country in a world ruled by the great powers. Experiences from that time have been kept alive in people's minds in the post-1945 cold war, in which the small states were often treated as no more than pawns in the great powers' ruthless game. There are still many countries which have not yet attained national independence. There are still many peoples who continue to live under dictatorship and despotic forms of government. Viewed against such a background, the ideals from Eidsvoll still retain their relevance and significance, representing values which are able to give the 17th of May celebrations a deeper meaning.

ROMANIA

The Romanian Way

From Nationalism to Privatism

Sorin Matei

In 1990, one year after putting an end to their totalitarian Communist regime, Romanians decided to move their national day from August 23 to December 1. This was an attempt to replace a symbol of popular subservience with one of national pride. On August 23, 1944, Romania abandoned its wartime ally, Germany, and peacefully allowed Russian troops to occupy the country, marking the beginning of the Communist regime. On December 1, 1918, Transylvania, a Romanian-majority province of Hungary, proclaimed its desire to leave the Austro-Hungarian Empire and be united with the Romanian Kingdom. Yet, despite the fact that December 1 is for many Romanians their country's "finest hour," each post-Communist attempt at making the new holiday truly popular has failed. Each year the official celebration is an object of political infighting; all major political parties try to use it for scoring the most propaganda points possible. Local and individual involvement is sporadic or nonexistent. Most Romanians take advantage of the day off to tend to their private affairs.

Why is the Romanian national day so ineffectual in mobilizing the nation and why is it so politicized? Although the self-interest of the political class, which often puts its need for cheap political capital ahead of national pride, should not be discounted, I would propose the alternative view that the failure of establishing a credible national day after 1989 is the symptom of a deeper crisis in Romanian culture and society, a crisis of the public spirit. This is produced by a resurgence of privatism and individualism, which sap the Romanian people's efforts to rediscover new forms of communal commitments.

This chapter is adapted from *Problems of Post-Communism*, 51, no. 2 (March-April 2004): 40–47. Copyright © 2004 by M. E. Sharpe, Inc. Used with permission.

FROM AUGUST 23 TO DECEMBER 1:
HISTORICAL BACKGROUND

The haste with which the Romanian Parliament decreed a new national day in 1990 was understandable and predictable. The Communist August 23 celebrated the beginning of the Communist regime and, to add insult to injury, it did so in a fraudulent way. In August 1944, a coalition of monarchist–constitutionalist, liberal–democratic, and pro-Communist leftist forces (in this order) deposed through a military coup the wartime dictator, General Ion Antonescu, who had assumed power in 1940. He had allied the country with Germany in November 1940, shortly after Russia had invaded and occupied one-third of the country. For the first three postwar years (1944–47), August 23 was a symbol of a new political beginning. Still, the Romanian national day remained May 10, commemorating the proclamation of the Romanian Kingdom in 1881.

After the Communists forced the Romanian king, Michael I, to abdicate in 1947, August 23 was proclaimed the new Romanian national day, which was now rebranded as the day celebrating the "anti-fascist, popular insurrection of national liberation" supposedly led by the Communist Party. During the following 40 years (1947–89), August 23 became an Orwellian exercise in political regimentation. "Popular" parades were organized in cities large and small. All employed people were forced to attend, either as celebrants or as spectators, under the threat of losing their jobs. All children, between the ages of 5 and 18, were trained for months by their schools to create "living pictures": squadrons of youth would be arranged on the parade ground to write with their squatted bodies the Communist Party acronym PCR (Partidul Communist Roman—Romanian Communist Party).

Everyone in Romania seemed to agree after the 1989 events that although August 23 could remain a reason for legitimate remembrance, it was too laden with the painful memories of public humiliation the Romanian people were subjected to for 40 years to keep it as a national holiday. Surprisingly, the Parliament having to decide on the new day—a heterogeneous group of intellectuals, surviving prewar politicians, second-rank former Communist Party administrators, and a good number of demagogues—did not have a hard time coming to a satisfactory solution. After minimal debate, it was decided that the new national day would be December 1, celebrating the unification in 1918 of the pre–World War I Romanian Kingdom with Transylvania.

The new national day seemed to be, at least for the superficial observer, a good choice. The day marks the fulfillment of a national dream, which no patriotic Romanian has ever contested—a unitary state containing most of the Romanian-speaking groups in the Carpathian basin. This was accomplished by diplomatic skill and military bravery at the end of World War I. Romania, a traditional ally of France, entered the war against Austro-Hungary and Germany in 1916 and initially was defeated on the battlefield after fierce resistance. In March 1918, after its eastern ally, Russia, had collapsed in the wake of the Bolshevik coup against the Kerensky government, the Romanian government signed a humiliating separate peace with Austria and Germany, which preserved it as a state entity but transformed it into a German vassal state. However, the time the peace bought was invaluable. Six months later, an exhausted Germany declared itself defeated on November 11, 1918, signing the Compiegne cease-fire. The Romanian army resumed its operations against Austro-Hungary and the Transylvanian Romanians, acting on U.S. president Woodrow Wilson's call for national self-determination, proclaimed on December 1 their desire to be united with the Romanian Kingdom. The Versailles peace treaties of 1919 gave international recognition to this act.

A great victory for Romania, December 1 has always had a special place in the Romanian national calendar, even during the Communist years. Yet, as the very first anniversary of this date as a national day in 1990 demonstrated, Romanians do not have the same feelings for their past or for the significance of their national unity as they used to. Their most pressing concerns and desires seem to be disconnected from their fate as a nation and much more in tune with their private lives. The profound changes in the collective consciousness of the Romanian people produced by Communism seemed to be too deep to be mended by a simple change in the calendar. Analyzing the Romanian national day is not just a way to learn how a people could come together but also how far it has fallen apart.

THE POLITICAL TRIBULATIONS OF
DECEMBER 1 AS NATIONAL DAY

At the December 1, 1990, celebration, all Romanian political forces sent their representatives to Alba-Iulia, the Transylvanian city where the unity act was proclaimed in 1918. The event was expected to be nonpartisan and an opportunity for national reconciliation between those in power, who preserved strong connections with the former Communist regime and the opposition, made chiefly of pre–World War II politicians imprisoned by the Communists for many years. The location itself was symbolic. The Transylvanian host city, located in the middle of the country, was considered removed enough from the passions of the capital city, Bucharest, to foster a climate of national concord. Yet, as soon as the leader of the center-right opposition, Corneliu Coposu, a pre–World War II politician whose party was directly involved in the 1918 event, began his address, a group of pro-government sympathizers started booing him. Petre Roman, prime minister at the time, just a few yards away from the old statesman, started waving approvingly at the hecklers. The celebration ended up in a fiasco.

At the time, there was great animosity between the democratic, pro-Western forces led by Coposu and the nationalist–statist inheritors of the Communist regime, then in power. Although Coposu's party, the National Peasant Christian Democratic Party, had good patriotic and democratic credentials, it was viewed with anger and jealousy by the leaders of the country. Because of their connections to the previous Communist regime they lacked the historical legitimacy enjoyed by Coposu and his party. To compensate for this situation, the regime embraced a strident nationalistic and xenophobic ideology. This was meant not only to best the opposition at the national game but also to replace its own intellectual vacuum left by the collapse of Communist ideology.

PUBLIC PERCEPTIONS OF DECEMBER 1

During the following eight anniversaries of December 1, the power and the opposition never appeared together at the national celebration, not even after the nationalist–statist regime was replaced by a pro-Western government in 1996. December 1 has brought, each year, an increasing feeling of alienation from the national day. Leading national newspapers have constantly made note of this phenomenon: "Instead of celebration . . . the 80th anniversary of the National Day finds us in an unprecedented state of fragmentation. Each of us hangs together with his clique and his ideas, none of us ready to stand by his fellow men in commemorating an event we all claim as ours" (Evenimentul 1998). The dominant feeling, notes Boari (personal communication, February 26, 2000), a leading political scientist, is that each political group is treating the anniversary as an opportunity for self-aggrandizement.

On the other hand, December 1 does not have a life of its own, outside military parades and political speeches. According to a noted *Curentul* columnist, the local pride in organizing and participating in December 1 or celebrations outside Bucharest are almost nonexistent (Pepine 1998). For the public at large, the national day is a *state* not a *popular* holiday; it is kept alive by the central government only for political reasons.

Yet, the failure of the Romanian national day should not be seen only from a political perspective. There seems to be deeper forces at work. According to Chelaru (personal communication, February 19, 2000), a BBC World Service (Romanian Department) journalist, ordinary people are entirely disconnected from the event: "The . . . people are happy they have a day off. Nothing else. Nobody perceives it as a holiday that brings the nation together. You never hear anyone wishing one another 'Happy First.' In fact, besides Christmas, New Year, and Easter there are no other celebrations to unite the nation." More incisive, and closer to the point of this chapter, is Ghiu's (1998) opinion that the Romanian national day has become "a roll-call in an empty room. . . . Our collective celebration has been for a long time one of free days [word play: days off], days marked vacant in the calendar, domestic days, days that are strictly private. The day that should be the most intensely public has become the most privatized day possible."

Ghiu's comment emphasizes the fact that whatever the mistakes of the political class there is an even more alarming side of the story: the resistance of a good part of the Romanian population to public involvement. In view of this, I advance the hypothesis that the causes of this opposition are the devastating effects of Communism on the peoples' attitude to involvement in public life. The prevalent mentality emphasizes the private aspect of one's life, at the expense of the public one.

The emergent Romanian social ethos in general,[1] and the work ethic in particular, have been modified by the totalitarian effort of the Communist state to confiscate the peoples' right to be autonomous social agents. Totalitarianism suspends the right to a legitimate public life outside governmentally sanctioned institutions such as the state company, the Communist Party, its affiliated organizations, and the state bureaucratic apparatus. These are the only places where citizens are expected to live an officially acceptable public life, a constraint that can have profound social-psychological implications. The natural desire for conducting a public life is introverted, colonizing the private space. A new social ethos emerged in Romania, performing an ambiguous social role. On the one hand, it impelled people to live for the sake of their own personal or family benefit; on the other hand, it made their social involvement an exercise in extending their private lives into the public world, remaking it in the semblance of their personal relationships.

Under these conditions, the point I would like to make in this chapter is that no matter what the national day, the level of public response to it will be low. This is due to the fact that Romanian public spirit is dying. To support these ideas, I will bring two kinds of evidence. First, based on ethnographic observation, I will show that the Romanian orientation to work is characterized by an attitude that turns all public obligations into private pursuits. This is generally identified in the prevalence and social valuation of sinecures. Second, based on sociological survey data, it will show that many Romanians are confined to a narrow circle of private life, where social honor and social investments are conceived only in terms of the closest family members.

ROMANIAN WAY OF LIFE AND PRIVATE GOALS

One of the most obvious consequences of the emergence of the new Romanian ethos is treating one's official duties as an honorary sign of social distinction for which no or little work is required. Many Romanians treat their jobs as sinecures. Old social phenomena, quite prevalent in traditional societies, sinecures are paid jobs and official positions that do not require any labor or obligations on the part of those occupying them. Not a new thing in this Balkan country, either, sinecure-holding has acquired unexpected characteristics during the Communist years and has become an unconscious social norm. Living off a sinecure constitutes a positive lifestyle model; it is an attempt to incorporate neither a private nor a public type of social ethos into socially acceptable behavior.

A sinecure has become, after 1989 in Romania, not just a moral deficiency of particular individuals but an anthropological syndrome characterizing the depth structures of Romanian culture. To yield honor or income from a job for which you are not doing anything is not just a way of supporting oneself materially, it is a social signifier of status. Moreover, the social satisfaction of being the holder of such an office/function/job is not complete if one does not publicly display it. The social value of such a position increases the more one shows his or her friends or admirers how little effort he or she spends on it.

Usually, the sinecure is seen as a survival of the not-so-long gone—at least in Romania—feudal society. But sinecure-holding, at least in my opinion, is not just a historical survival, but a creative tool of social bricolage that originates in the traditional patrimonial society but not resumed to its heritage.

Historians and sociologists have traditionally emphasized historical continuities between traditional Romanian cultural attributes and characteristics of the Romanian "modern" ethos (Dobrogeanu-Gherea 1910; Jowitt 1978; Radulescu-Motru 1910). Modern Romanian political culture is frequently associated with the patrimonial bureaucratic state of oriental origin. Researchers point to the fact that traditional Romanian principalities relied heavily on sinecure as a tool for creating and maintaining political loyalty among members of the ruling class.

The traditional Romanian state was ruled through dispensation of "prebends," social and political positions granted for life, with which admission in the noble class was usually associated (Weber 1946, 207). Significantly, prebend-holders or wealthy people, in general, were and still are—especially in the countryside—designated with a special phrase "oameni cu stare" (men with good standing). Although linguists have not come to a definitive agreement on the origin of this Romanian phrase, I advance the hypothesis that it reflects the fact that wealth and social distinction are a consequence, not a cause, of one's social standing. "Standing" here signifies not position in the economic system but membership in a selected group of people, sanctioned by the state or its ruler.

The Romanian *stare* can be identified with the English *estate*, the French *etat* or the German *Stand*. *Stare* is, in fact, rank, but in a different manner than this term is understood in Western traditional society. Filitti (1925–26), a much ignored historian and sociologist of Romanian traditional society, makes a very astute observation:

The main difference between Romanian aristocracy and the Western one was that as long as for the later nobility was an attribute of the person, existing in certain situations without the need to own land, and which could not be lost with losing one's fief . . . for the former admission to the noble class was not done by induction into knighthood but by being granted a piece of land by the Prince. (326)

The Romanian estates of the realm were not legitimated by a personal nobiliary title, but by having temporary use of a fief granted by the prince, who was the real and sole owner of the whole country's land. Landownership was conditioned by admission into the aristocratic class. During the 18th century, this was institutionalized by registering the title holder in the *arhondologie*, the official record of the estates of the realm. Thus, the noble person became an "employee" of the feudal state, with no hereditary rights on the title or the land given in his use. Wealth, honor, or rank—all were derived from being granted land by the prince. Romanian traditional society was a typical patrimonial bureaucracy (Weber 1946).

Modernization of the Romanian state has only partially changed this state of affairs. The slow pace of social mobility during the first decades of modernization is an indication of the degree to which partimonialism survived modernization. Janos (1974) notes that between 1866 and 1888, 77 percent of state ministers were of "noble" origin. More importantly, access to lucrative contracts with the state, social promotion, and job opportunities were tremendously increased if one were connected to members of the political class or civil service. University professorships, managerial positions at state-owned companies, direct personal financial support from the state, or fortunes made from contracting with the government were many avenues to social promotion. Radulescu-Motru, a keen contemporary observer of these phenomena, noted in 1910 that "public services and institutions have become from means destined for achieving the public good, means for achieving personal interests" (1910, 3).

Conservative critics, known as "Junimists" (The Youth) carried a long and partially successful battle against the all-embracing state. One of them, Ion Luca Caragiale (1965), a prominent writer and journalist, diagnosed the situation at the end of 19th century with remarkable accuracy:

[Our young modern] state, founded in such circumstances, quickly demanded a society. The improvised state, instead of keeping the balance between various social forces at a given point in time, is seeking to be the substance and the origin of these forces. The state, which is naturally the result of society, has become the artificial progenitor of society. The improvised state, feeling a gaping void under its foot, has invented a point of support for it. (71)

Several authors, inspired by neo-Marxist theory (Badescu 1984; Chirot, 1976; Janos 1978; Jowitt 1974) propose another way of looking at sinecures. Believing that modern Romanians' preference for state employment resides in the relationship of dependency that the world capitalist system has imposed on Romania, they thought that it was the world system of production (Wallerstein 1974) that has created in Romania a parasite class of "comprador bourgeoisie." Later on, the sinecure-seeking class of pre-Communist Romania was directly inherited by the Communist and post-Communist regimes. Although partially true, this model is vitiated by economic determinism inspired by Marxist theory. It ignores the fact that each social and political regime has its own cultural patterns, which remodel social values and behaviors, above and beyond class or economic arrangements.

Post-Communist sinecures are not just "negative" adaptations to the world system, but are, in fact, cultural phenomena with perceived positive values for those seeking them. Holding a sinecure and valuing private life above all aspects of one's existence is now part of the Romanian ethos in a constructive way, although with potentially destructive secondary effects. It is constructive because it contributes to bringing meaning to personal lives; yet, it is destructive because it can blur the difference between the private and the public ego.

EVIDENCE OF ROMANIAN PRIVATISM

The cause of these transformations is the traumatic Communist experience. Totalitarianism has forbidden the Romanian people to conduct autonomous public lives. Their public ego has been limited in its degrees of freedom and ultimately pushed back over, or worse, confounded with the private self. People have increasingly ceased making a difference between the two sides of their selves, public and private, living their lives with a privatized ideal in mind, even when trying to assume public roles. To clarify this process, let me present two ethnographic observations and several findings of recent public opinion polls.

M.O. is a young and successful Romanian journalist.[2] Energetic and sedulous, he has a good job with a foreign media organization paid in hard currency. This provides him a salary of several hundred dollars a month; a nice income, at least compared to what other Romanians earn working for state companies. He is quite well-known in Romanian intellectual and media circles for his series of articles about the Communist secret service, to whose archives he had privileged access due to his employment with the foreign media organization. However, he made it no secret to me that his current job, to which he owed his relative prosperity and fame, is of no importance to him. His secret goal, he confessed, is to officially work as little as possible. Working for your private goals and ideas is the only way of finding satisfaction in life, M.O. believes. He made his point by telling me that he put a good part of the money he earned into a private foundation that supports his true passion: archaeology. The foundation provides money for an archaeological dig in Romania. He takes pride in the fact that the beneficiaries of his charitable acts, who also are his friends, call him "The Sponsor."

M.O.'s attitude about work reveals what is new about the post-Communist sinecure-seeking behavior in Romania: its symbolic value. Although a sinecure provides a means of subsistence, even more important is the fact that it provides a reason to live, or something to take pride in, which paradoxically is not the job itself but the fact that one is able "to beat the system." This also indicates that the space where you really matter is the one where your friends and family are.

This attitude contributes to and changes the social ethos of Romanian society, the central idea being that Romanians' social identity cannot be gained in the public sphere because this is not where "real" life is. A public position in the work or other environment is to be exploited for the benefit of one's private goals, but it is not something to boast about—other than how little you do for earning your keep. This draws a very sharp line between sinecure as a lazy man's dream and the way in which Romanians see this phenomenon. They are quite industrious people, interested in success when the goals they are trying to achieve in their official capacities are personal; however, public work and duties are subjects of disdain and neglect when they provide no immediate benefit in the private realm. In social-psychological terms, this represents a reversal of the roles performed by the private and the public selves (Goffman 1959; Triandis 1989).

A second example might illuminate this phenomenon better. D.M. is a physician who has participated in several medical training programs in the United States. After completing them, he told me that in America "everything is upside down." What shocked him the most was the fact that "you have to dress up when you go to work and to dress down when you go to parties." This code of behavior violated what he took for granted in Romanian society. In describing how people dress when they go to work, he used the Romanian expression "ca la nuntā," which loosely translates to "as if invited to a wedding." In contrast, the informal dress code of the private parties he attended in the United States violated another assumption: that you dress up for celebrations, not for everyday pursuits, such as your job. This type of thinking betrays an important distinction the new Romanian ethos makes between what is to be valued and what is to be deprecated in one's life. Social space is divided into two areas: one of distinction, elevation, and pleasure—the private space of parties and of "good life"—and one of toil and effort—the public space of work. We can find this type of distinction in M.O.'s way of looking at what matters in his life. His private hobbies, like archaeology, are the only form of finding a public meaning for his life.

Mixing the two spaces in the Romanian ethos is the result of the Communist power's seizure of all public spaces and roles, which has reduced people to islands of privatized self-interest. Contrary to what is currently believed—that Communism has created or reinforced a collectivist ethos—Marxist totalitarianism has, in fact, depreciated and destroyed any serious belief in collective action. Compromising the very idea of social participation, which meant collaboration with a suppressive and criminal regime, Communism has pushed people into a lonely existence, confining them to their private parameters. It has led to what Durkheim (1984) calls anomic individualism, destroying all solidarities of locale, class, and group and creating a type of personality interested solely in its own private happiness.

Thus, seeking a sinecure in the Communist or the post-Communist world is completely different from seeking positions of social distinction and honor in traditional society. For example, Jowitt (1978) is right when he points to the fact that during the first attempt at modernization in Romania from 1859 to 1944, wealth obtained from public positions was used for demonstrations of power in a world of scarcity. The ethos that animated this behavior was ultimately social because it was made to be displayed in public.

In Communist regimes, all social groups not controlled by the state are destroyed. The only ones allowed to survive are kin and immediate friend networks. Destroying all public spaces where people used to display their wealth and signs of social prestige, the Communist regime has forced them to use the private space for the same reasons. However, even these spaces are partially delegitimated as social environments. The individual is left more or less alone. Social life for most people alternates between a form of brutish individualism and diffuse social groups. It is a mixture of collectivism and individualism without individuality, such as the one described by Zinoviev (1984). Most acts of social exchange and social signification take place in these privatized spaces. Social distinction is measured by the amount of wealth or prestige "looted" from the public space and displayed in the private sphere. This creates a new social reality, where public and private are mixed together.

An indication of the emergence of this space is the new way of addressing mature, socially influential women. Titles such as Doamna Mimi or Doamna Jeni (Mrs. Mimi or Mrs. Jeni) mix a public title (Doamna /Mrs.) with a person's first name, often in a diminutive form. They show that a person, even when she is important, is isolated from her social circle (family), which used to give her identity. On the other hand, they also show that women have increasingly entered public life, even though this happens in the "underground." Traditionally, women were relegated to the private space. But, since this space has become an area of public interest through emergence of privatism, women have been forced to enter the public limelight too. Yet, this meant not conquering a new social territory but becoming actors in a liminal space (Gennep 1909; Turner 1969), a space of transition between public and private life, where they can perform roles of power intermediaries.

Because private relationships are now of paramount importance in conducting social transactions, their traditional mediators, women, have become key players in social life too. As circles of friends and kinship networks replace the civic structure of society, women become more and more important in the "secondary polity" that has emerged around them. Many connections and influence networks go through these "Mrs."

SOCIOLOGICAL EVIDENCE OF THE NEW PRIVATISM

Recent sociological surveys, such as the biannual Public Opinion Barometer (a General Social Survey-like poll), seem to support the idea that Romanian society is a highly privatized society. According to the June 1997 survey, 45 percent of Romanians declared that their best friends are their relatives and 22 percent their neighbors. Another 56 percent indicated that their relatives are also the people they rely on the most to accomplish instrumental goals; 21 percent that they rely on their neighbors for the same goals. This indicates that Romanians not only live surrounded by tightly knit communal and kin networks but that also their social horizon is incredibly narrow. One can easily infer from these figures that most Romanians live a life almost entirely privatized (Public Opinion Barometer 1995–98).

The "introversion" of Romanian society is also confirmed by its attitude toward money. Asked what would they or their families do if they won at the State Lottery 100,000,000 lei ($14,000 or the equivalent of an average household income for 10 years), 17 percent of Romanians (the second largest response group) answered that they would give the money to their children. More refined statistical analysis performed by myself by logistic regression reveals that those who are more likely to make what seems to be a nonpublic investment in their immediate family are people who also seem to be the most invested in the arrangements of the statist socioeconomic regime created by Communism.[3]

For example, urban retirees, whose only income is Social Security payments, have 27 times greater odds of giving such a great amount of money to their children than the self-employed. Clerical and middle management personnel, another group heavily invested in the statist-industrial apparatus, have 11 times greater odds to use the money in the same way compared to the reference group. In contrast, Romanians who are not integrated in statist social structures, either because they are at the beginning of their mature lives, like university students, or because they are engaged in professional occupations, or even those who have lost their jobs as a consequence of the privatization process (the unemployed), are no different from the entrepreneurial class in terms of their attitude to money.

DISCUSSION AND CONCLUSIONS

In this chapter, I have tried to describe and interpret the way in which the "Romanian way" has changed under the impact of totalitarian Communist social practices. Romanians have increasingly become involved in a privatized universe, their private selves and life-ideals having taken the place of many publicly sanctioned goals. The fall of Communism has affected this to a very little degree, because the Romanian character was affected in its very core cultural beliefs and values by Marxist totalitarianism. Although influenced by traditional social behaviors and values, inherited from the feudal society, modern Romanians have "reinvented" sinecure-seeking and privatism. These are not just dysfunctional phenomena, for many have become "positive" life-ideals, as confirmed by ethnographic observation and data provided by sociological surveys (Public Opinion Barometer, 1997). Romanians today often sacrifice their public life and obligations, especially those work related, for satisfying their private hobbies. They also live in extremely narrow social circles whose centers are one's kin networks, centered around their children.

The Romanian ethos forged after the Soviet occupation in 1944 seems to be very resilient and overreaching. One of its effects is the popular disconnection from public engagements. Disengagement from work or nonfamily-related social groups should be seen as part of a larger outlook. This considers all nonpersonal social events instrumentally. This leads both to the political class' view of public/civic events as simple political footballs and to that of the populace, who takes the national day to be a simple day off from the chore of daily duties. Ten years after the downfall of Communism, there is evidence that Romanians are still engaged in social and cultural patterns of life characteristic to the Communist period. The main challenge of any process of reform in Romania seems, at least in my opinion, to be changing these "habits of the heart" before trying to hastily implement changes in the national day calendar.

NOTES

1. Ethos is used here in the way employed by Weber (1904–5/1992) and Geertz (1973). The ethos of a culture is its tone and style, its way of framing the major issues of life. It is the set of rules and values that shape the way in which people imagine their model of social life. It is a personal and social life-ideal. Each social formation has its specific ethos or ethoses. European feudalism has generated several such models: the nobility was inspired by bravery, honor, and social signs of distinction; and the clergy was inspired by

renunciation to formal links to secular society and by education. In classical Chinese civilization, there was a mandarin ethos, which valued a complex system of social norms and secular erudition. But probably the most famous ethic/ethos in contemporary academic literature is the Protestant one, described by Weber (1904–5/1992).

2. Initials are used to preserve anonomity. This section is based on informal interviews conducted in the summer of 1997 for a study on the new Romanian ethos and its media representations.

3. The response category "I would give the money to my children" was transformed into a dummy variable with two values; 1 if the respondent selected this option and 0 if he or she did not. Logistic regression indicates the odds ratio for a series of independent variables to be associated with the occurrence or nonoccurrence of the values of the dependent variable. The independent variables entered in the model were occupation and gender. Education and nationality had no significant effect. The analysis was performed specifically for this study.

REFERENCES

Badescu, I. (1984). *Sincronism european și cultura critică românească: contribupii de sociologie istorică privind cultura modernă românească* [European synchronization and Romanian critical culture: Contributions to the historical sociology of modern Romanian culture]. București: Editura Științifică și Enciclopedică.

Caragiale, I. L. (1965). In A. Rosetti, Șerban Cioculescu, and L. Călin (Eds.), *Opere* [Works], vol. 4. București: Editura pentru literatură.

Chirot, D. (1976). *Social change in a peripheral society: The creation of a Balkan colony*. New York: New Academic Press.

Dobrogeanu-Gherea, C. (1910). *Neoiobăgia: studiu economico-sociologic al problemei noastre agrare* [Neo-serfdom: An economic and sociological study of our agrarian problem]. București: Editura Librăriei Socec.

Durkheim, E. (1984). *The division of labor in society* (W. D. Halls, trans.). New York: Free Press.

Evenimentul. (1998, November, 30). Sărbătoarea însingurării [A holiday of solitude]. *Evenimentul zilei.* Available at: http://www.expres.ro/arhive/1998/noiembrie/30/editorial/30nov98.html

Filitti, I. C. (1925–26). Clasele sociale în trecutul românesc [Class in Romanian history]. *Arhiva pentru știinpa și reforma socială, 5–6*(3–4), 326–45.

Geertz, C. (1973). *The interpretation of cultures*. New York: Basic Books.

Gennep, A. v. (1909). *The rites of passage* (M. B. Vizedom and G. L. Cafee, Trans.). London: Routledge and Kegan Paul.

Ghiu, B. (1998, December 4–10). Unu', Decembrie (semnat indescifrabil) [December first (signed anonymous)]. *Dilema.* Available at: http://www.algoritma.ro/dilema/305/ghiu.htm

Goffman, E. (1959). *The presentation of self in everyday life*. New York: Anchor Books/Doubleday.

Janos, A. (1974). Modernization and decay. In K. Jowitt (Ed.), *Social change in Romania, 1860–1940*. Berkeley: Institute of International Studies, University of California.

Jowitt, K. (1978). The socio-cultural bases of national dependency. In K. Jowitt (Ed.), *Social change in Romania, 1860–1940*. Berkeley: Institute of International Studies, University of California.

Pepine, H. (1998, December 3). Utopia unei sărbători [Utopian holiday]. *Curentul*. Available: http://curentul.logicnet.ro/curentul/arhiva/03dec98/120398/op02.htm

Public Opinion Barometer. (1995–98). *Joint database for [public opinion] barometers carried out between 1995–1998*. Bucharest: Soros Foundation for an Open Society. Available at: http://www.osf.ro/pob/joint.zip

Radulescu-Motru, S. (1910). *Cultura română și politicianismul* [Politicking and Romanian culture] (ed a 3-a). București: Editura Librariei Leon Alcalay.

Triandis, H. (1989, July). The self and social behavior in differing cultural contexts. *Psychological Review, 96*(3), 506–20.

Turner, V. (1969). *The ritual process*. New York: de Gruyter.

Wallerstein, I. (1974). *The modern world-system*. New York: Academic Press.

Weber, M. (1946). *From Max Weber: Essays in sociology* (H. H. Gerth and C. W. Mills, Trans.). New York: Oxford University Press

Weber, M. (1992). *The protestant ethic and the spirit of capitalism* (T. Parsons, Trans.). London: Routledge. (Originally published in 1904–5)

Zinoviev, A. (1984). *The reality of communism* (C. Janson, Trans). New York: Schocken Books.

SINGAPORE

Reading Singapore's National Day

A Case Study in the Rhetoric of Nationalism

Linda K. Fuller

While the "Singapore Success Story" continues to be recounted and recycled, a subcutaneous examination of the rhetoric surrounding its nationalism offers invaluable clues to understanding that development. Background information on the Republic of Singapore is provided as a contextual base for trying to understand how the concept of "Singapore-ness" has evolved, including brief descriptions of its history, geography, economics, politics, and sociocultural climate, with special emphasis noted on the country's communications industry. Next, Singapore's symbols of nationalism will be described; and finally, a number of prominent national days from 1966 to the present are featured.

BACKGROUND

Origins of this city-state can be traced to the 7th century A.D., when it was known as Temasek (sea town), a trading center of Sumatra's ancient Srivijaya Empire. Over the next few centuries came struggles for the country from Java and Siam and the Dutch, the Portuguese, and the British—but history was made in 1819 when Sir Thomas Stamford Raffles selected it as a British maritime base, developing Singapore as a free port. It remained under British colonial rule for 110 years, until defeat in 1942 by Japanese forces. In 1946, the country demanded self-determination, and as of 1959, it became a self-governing state, joining with the Malaysian Federation in 1963. On August 9, 1965, the Republic of Singapore became an independent republic (See Appendix 1 for the proclamation). It is the annual celebration of National Day on that date for this young, political entity that informs this chapter.[1] Its strategic location, at the southern tip of the Malay Peninsula, about 85 miles (137 kilometers) north of the Equator, makes Singapore an important crossroad route for East–West trading. Recently, it has achieved the distinction of being the world's busiest port—trading mostly in tin, rubber, coconut, oil, rice, timber, jute, spices, and coffee. Singapore's ideal situation also puts the small island (616 square kilometers, or 235 square miles) in a time zone that allows for global telecommunications transactions from London to Tokyo in a working day.

The economy of Singapore can best be typed as one of free enterprise. While it began as a trading center for spices and other agricultural commodities for export to Great Britain, the first oil refinery was established in 1961, and today its philosophy of international networking helps it maintain a competitive edge in a number of modern industries. More than 4,000 multinational corporations, mainly from the United States, Japan, and Europe, have operations here, making it an offshore location with one of the highest concentrations of foreign investors. In addition, Singapore's massive banking system numbers among the world's key financial centers. As a free port poised to deal with the outside world, residents here have long been made aware of people and practices from many varying cultures.

Politically, the avowedly anti-Communist People's Action Party (PAP) has been in control of the government since 1959, mainly associated with the current senior minister Lee Kuan Yew. Describing that legacy, Milne and Mauzy (1990) state, "A high degree of state control has been possible because the government knows what it wants and takes steps to get it, in conjunction with an efficient civil service, a tightly organized party, extensive grass-roots organizations, periodic 'campaigns' on particular issues, and control of the mass media" (176). From the start, the PAP has wisely constructed itself as belonging to all, but none in particular. "The movement of the Singapore polity from one with a highly mobilised and engaged citizenry to an administrative state has been attributed to the redefinition of politics of the ruling PAP leadership. Popular sentiments have been shifted away from politics and redirected towards economy and accumulation of material wealth," notes Ooi (2000, 200). Today, the government considers itself as having a mandate from the people. Consider: failure to vote in elections is punishable by fine—as is littering ($500—explaining why the country is so clean), congesting downtown traffic without a paid permit, jaywalking (a $50 fine), and smoking in public places ($250); the penalty for drug dealing, the arriving tourist is warned, is death. "The government is strong, efficient, non-corrupt, and unabashedly paternalistic," comments Professor Eddie C. Y. Kuo (1992, 243), dean of the School of Communications at Nanyang Technological University. "The dominance of the state is overwhelming."[2]

Above and beyond tending to its own domestic pursuits, the new independent Singapore was also interested in regional cooperation, best exemplified by its activities with the Association of South-East Asian Nations (ASEAN), which was formed in 1967, as well as global contacts, both bilaterally and multilaterally. For the first time in its history, it also had to develop its own military defense system. "Internally, the introduction of National Service in February 1967 was a significant step in the building up of both a substantial defense capability over the next two decades, and a sense of common national responsibility, loyalty, and destiny," wrote historian Ernest C. T. Chew (1991, 364). "The prior introduction of such symbols as a state national flag, anthem, pledge of loyalty, and the like contributed to a spirit of nationhood."

Education in Singapore has been a top priority since the founding of the republic three decades ago, where not only knowledge but also ideology is imparted. From the start, nationalistic rituals such as flag raising and singing of the national anthem were introduced. The national pledge, which previously was recited in four languages, was now delivered only in English—the lingua franca for the new government, law, and commerce, and eventually a major contributor to the "mainstreaming" of the educational system. Early in the 1980s, a curriculum stressing more education was put forth (see, for example, Tay 1982), including an emphasis on Asian values and the teaching of religion, with Confucianism as a base.[3] While this was later rescinded, it is obvious that the main control for nationalism comes from economic and political spheres.

Probably nowhere was the effect of the PAP government's success more noticeable, or more likely to help gain loyalty, than in its public housing policies. In an effort to mix various ethnic and religious groups together, as a means of preventing antagonism among groups, it established a quota system that has become a model for other societies. The maintenance of racial harmony here can best be explained by shifting the emphasis from ethnic to national identity. Willmott (1989) cites how, while the purpose of integrating different ethnic groups in the high-rises may have been for integration, a more important result of the housing policy has been the provision "for citizens of all income levels the opportunity of owning a flat and therefore of 'having a stake in the country'" (589).

Singapore's nearly 3 million people represent a multiracial, multiethnic, multireligious, and multilingual combination of Chinese (76 percent), Malay (15 percent), Indian (7 percent), and other ethnic groups; yet, most citizens think of themselves as Singaporeans first—a fact that is central to this discussion (see also Chua 1995, 1998; Fuller 1998, 1999; Rahim 1998; Teo and Ooi 1996).[4] The country has often been called "Instant Asia" (Gupte 1988; Sutton 1989) because these various cultures and peoples display such a sense of racial harmony and national unity. The Singapore family system is strong, with cooperation, loyalty, respect for elders, and unity all highly valued concepts. Singaporeans enjoy freedom of worship (approximately 40 percent are Buddhist, 30 percent secular, 15 percent Moslem, 10 percent Christian, and 7 percent Hindu), and are encouraged to be tolerant of others' religious choices. Sesser (1992) has made this observation: "From economics to food, Singapore is a nation of contradictions. Except for Japan, it has the best-educated, most knowledgeable, and most worldly-wise society in Asia, but the government still tries in many ways to regulate its citizens' lives" (40). While Singapore-born citizens may now be the norm, it is important to recall that when the Republic was first developed in 1965, most people here had immigrated from other homelands, and had other allegiances; hence, conceptions of nation-building and national identity had to be built from scratch.

COMMUNICATIONS

Singapore is considered the telecommunications center of Southeast Asia, with 24-hour telex, telephone, telegram, and facsimile services connecting to all parts of the world. Further, the country's businesses enjoy these comprehensive services at prices that are among the lowest in the world. In the "Globalization Index" measuring level of integration in developed countries and key emerging markets worldwide, Singapore ranks number 1 (Naim and Laudicine 2001).

Enjoying a high literacy rate (84 percent), Singaporeans are active media participants. *The Straits Times*, a 150+-year-old newspaper with a circulation of around 300,000, leads all others in readership and is widely recognized as the leading English-language newspaper in the Far East. It is published by Singapore Press Holdings, which also owns *Business Times* (circulation of 21,000, in English), *The New Paper* (an afternoon English newspaper of 65,000), *Berita Harian* (Malay, 43,000), *Murasu* (Tamil, 5,400), and two Chinese newspapers: *Lianhe Zoabao* (187,000) and *Lianhe Wanbao* (85,000).

Broadcasting, like its print counterpart, is mainly under governmental purview (Wong 2001). Radio services are available daily in Singapore in both English and Chinese from 6:00 A.M. to midnight, and in Malay and Tamil at selected times. Television began in 1963, telecasting 28 hours a week; today, programming is provided nearly 160 hours weekly in the country's four languages: English, Chinese, Malay, and Tamil. From the start, television was charged with providing not just entertainment, but educational and informational programming as well. Its arrival coincided with great upheaval in the country regarding Singapore's breaking off from the Malaysian Federation, and "was seen as a channel which could set out the issues and arguments of the day and forge a consensus on the Singapore its people wanted. It projected what the government was doing for the people in terms of employment, social services, health, and education" (Singapore Broadcasting Corporation 1988, 12). In other words, television has been viewed since its inception as a powerful propaganda tool of the government.

Considering the fact that Singaporeans are adjudged to be the most ardent moviegoers in the world, it is surprising that the country remains without government patronage for a national cinema (Fuller 1991a, 1994). Yet, some encouraging signs are emerging (Fuller 1996b; Tan and Soh 1994): there is a Singapore Film Society; the Economic Development Board has a Film Task Force; the Copyright Act of 1987 has helped curb circulation of pirated videotapes; there are capabilities for transnational satellite linkups; Tang Dynasty Village has appropriate scenery for period films; production courses are offered at local colleges and universities; the Singapore Film Festival operates successfully; and there have been recent announcements of filmmaking prospects here.

The Telecommunication Authority of Singapore, boasting one of the world's most advanced infrastructures, has kept prices so low that it has been able to return several billion dollars to its customers. Aided by modern satellite and submarine cable systems, Singapore is linked globally to almost all its ASEAN neighborhoods, as well as to the Middle East, western Europe, Hong Kong/Taiwan, and Australia/ Indonesia. By telephone, it is connected to 300+ destinations. And it is an Internet pioneer.

The role of the Singapore government in its press, broadcasting, and telecommunications industries figures into its means of celebrating National Day. For example, for the 24th celebration in 1989, at which I had the opportunity to be a participant-observer (Fuller 1991b), *The Straits Times* ran a special four-section National Day publication, "Singapore Close-Up" featuring (1) Surprising Faces, (2) Surprising Images, (3) Surprising Portraits, and (4) Surprising Journey. Its front-page articles dealt with the country's selective immigration policy, an announcement of Singapore's 9.1 percent economic growth, a message of congratulation from the Malaysian king, and National Day awards to individual Singaporean citizens. It seems instructive to quote the prime minister during that time, Lee Kuan Yew, from a feature article on how "to make up for losses from emigration and shortfall in babies. . . . Selective immigration (is) for [the] long-term good":

People must feel that Singapore is worth being part of and worth defending. Otherwise, we cease to exist. We cannot close our doors to prevent Singaporeans from leaving. But we can make Singapore a vibrant and thriving society, with opportunities for a rewarding and fulfilling life. We can keep Singapore a healthy and safe place where parents can bring up their children with traditional morals and values. We owe it to ourselves and our children to make sure that they need never leave Singapore because of a fear that the future is bleak. And we shall do this best by continually attracting talented and dynamic people to join us in Singapore.

As might well be imagined, nearly every article in National Day's 102-page newspaper ("National Day" 1984) was about the country and the day. There were positive and persuasive reactions to the prime minister's announced immigration policy attempting to draw skilled workers ("the keenness to succeed on the part of people like them that gave Singapore its competitive edge . . . in the spirit of the people, passed on from Singapore's migrant forefathers to their children"); reactions to Singapore's statement to allow U.S. bases there; and reactions to what fund managers had to say of the government's new tax scheme for unit trusts. Also, consider articles such as:

- Build a Sound Mind in a Healthy Body: Dr. Tan
- N-Day Joy in Schools with Grandmas' Tales, Food, Floats
- Chok Tong [first deputy prime minister] Leads Countdown to National Day
- 8,000 Converts Celebrate Double Joy [National Day and school's anniversary]
- Orchid Grower Reaps a Star [award from Ministry of Community Development]
- Ministries Mark Event with Special Ceremonies

- ND Honours List [distinguished service order, meritorious service medal, public service bar and star, public administration and military medals]
- Singapore Must Continually Attract Talented People
- Miss Singapore Wins Best Legs Award at Supermodel of the World Contest
- SBS [bus service] to Introduce Recorded Messages for Passengers
- National Solidarity Party Shares Nation's Joys [a statement that "Singapore continued to enhance her economic status on the world platform through the hard work and dedication of her people both at home and abroad"]
- Ensure Equal Status for All, says PM

In addition to many more articles, there were reports on soccer, hockey, tennis, snooker, cycling, golf, hurdles, bowling, baseball, and cricket. Also an interesting tidbit on sport psychology was included. Dr. Seet Ai Mee, minister of state for Community Development and Education told 400 delegates at the opening of the 7th World Congress in Sport Psychology: "The outcome of applying a psychological method or technique on a person is not always predictable (because) of outcome and the competing demand for time and commitment."

A particularly telling *Straits Times* editorial in the 102-page issue, "Success Has a Sober Lining," compared the country to any 24-year-old taking stock as any young adult might to future considerations. "If a multi-racial population looks back to its polyglot past, can it move forward in unity?" it wondered. In this country that is boastful about its safety, there were two crime-related articles: "Hold-Up Victim Bites Off Tip of Robber's Finger" (about a vegetable seller who bit an assailant who robbed him of $1,000, complete with a photo of the victim showing the unfortunate finger and an appeal to anyone who spotted someone needing treatment); and "Man Ordered to Pay Lawyer $35,000 for Defaming Him" (emphasized an unabashedly favored legal system). There were at least 100 more Singapore-specific articles in the four Close-Up sections, most of them light and humorous, all undoubtedly interesting for citizens. One of the more intriguing cartoons details "The Way We Were," showing an evolution from Matamata and rickshaw puller to modern dress. Emphasis in most of the articles was on culture, fashion, how-tos, the role of labor, history, architecture, people, and family—particularly the elderly.

For advertisements, the numbers speak for themselves in terms of sheer quantity, each one congratulating the country, and most bridging an alliance with it. Television also played a large role in the National Day celebrations. The previous evening, dancing, singing, and fireworks displays were all telecast in what came off as quite a professional four-hour show. On the actual day, there was live coverage of events, which were held in the National Stadium. Since only 85,000 people could be accommodated in the stadium, the rest were reportedly glued to their television sets.

Quite obviously, this is a citizenry heavily involved in its country; at the same time, it is a country whose media operate in constant awareness of governmental regulations and expectations. Communications, combined with strong national symbols, all contribute to an ongoing nation-building. Using a conceptual framework based on Michel Foucault that sees Singapore and Singaporeans as discursive objects, Chua and Kuo (1992) state, "Singapore as an 'independent nation' refers not to the geographical feature of the island as such; similarly, 'Singaporeans' in a discourse of national identity refers not to the biological being—as such" (2) The key here is that Singapore's national identity was foisted on it by circumstances beyond its control contrary to the development of most nationalistic identities.

SYMBOLS OF SINGAPOREAN NATIONALISM

As such a young country, Singapore took up the process of nation-building with a determination and dedication that has marked much of its success.[5] Here, as Willmott (1989) has pointed out, "The state preceded the development of nationalism rather than emerging as its political consequence, and the state itself became the first major symbol of national identity. Since independence, it has set out to create others" (581). One of the key parts of that process has included designing and implementing usage of its own unique symbols, such as its own national flag, national coat of arms, national animal (the [Mer]lion), national flower, and national anthem.

The National Flag

Consisting of two equal horizontal sections, with red on the top and white on the bottom, the upper left section is inscribed with a white crescent moon next to five white stars that form a circle. The red portion is said to symbolize universal brother and the equality of man, the white a pervasive and everlasting purity and virtue. The crescent moon is meant to represent a young nation on the ascendant, while the five stars illuminate ideals of democracy, peace, progress, justice, and equality.

The National Coat of Arms

The white crescent moon and stars on a red background are repeated in the country's coat of arms, with the shield supported by a lion on the left and a tiger on the right, and the republic's motto "Majulah Singapura" (Let Singapore Flourish) emblazoned across a banner. While the tiger represents historical linkages with Malaysia, the lion has come to represent Singapore itself, as the country's national symbol. Historian John Drysdale (1984) has called the animal representations from both countries "a collection entirely consonant with the aspirations of Singapore's new and energetic government" (237).

The National Symbol: The (Mer)lion

According to the legendary Malay annuals called "Sejerah Melayu," a ship-wrecked Sumatran prince named Sang Nila Utama, who landed on this island, encountered a ferociously odd appearing creature that he believed was a lion. When his fortunes encouraged him to settle here, he named it "Singa Pura," or "Lion City," in honor of that majestic beast. The creative rationale for the lion symbol is based on notions of courage, strength, and excellence. Depicted in solid red against a white background, in line with the colors of the national flag and coat of arms, the mane divided into five segments, meant to represent the nation's five ideals: democracy, peace, progress, justice, and equality. *Singapore Facts and Pictures* (1991) states: "The lion's tenacious mien symbolizes the nation's single-minded resolve to face any challenges and overcome any obstacles" (6).

The National Anthem

Singapore's national anthem is composed of Malay lyrics, also translated into English. Written in 1959 by Zubir Said in celebration of the country's becoming a self-governing state, "Majullah Singapura" is proudly sung by all the citizenry, even though only a handful might know its exact "Onward Singapore" translation. Citing a survey from 1991 in which most people reported singing the song with pride, despite not knowing its literal meaning, Birch (1993) states:

What it might mean, for the most part, lies not with its individual words exhorting a migrant, postcolonial, people to success through unity, but with its powerful association with a carefully constructed national identity which signals the idea of belonging; of finally being "home." The anthem has media-tised the rhetoric of aspiration into a powerful mythology of "anchoring"; its often wordless voice [is] a reminder that Singapore is home and therefore worth protecting and improving, worth staying in and developing. (2)

The National Pledge

The national pledge, a daily recitation by the schoolchildren of Singapore and, of course, an expected part of all-country events such as National Day, reads as follows:

We, the citizens of Singapore
Pledge ourselves, as one united people
Regardless of race, language, or religion
To build a democratic society
Based on justice and equality
So as to achieve happiness
Prosperity and progress for our nation.

The National Flower

Named for a flower that bloomed in the garden of Miss Joaquim in 1893, the "Vanda Miss Joaquim" is a hybrid between Vanda teres and Vanda Hookeriana. Bearing some five to eight flowers, each about 7 centimeters tall and 6.5 centimeters across, it is marked by purple petals with crimson spots and pale purple, almost white lateral sepals.

National Songs

Probably nothing can stir a country's sentiments better than melding voices together in song. Music, as we are continually learning, can bind people together across cultures, whether we all know and/or sing the same words or even interpret them the same way. Examine closely the words to these songs, sung each National Day, which Mutalib (1992) points out "were given catchy lyrics and up-beat tunes to enable both the young and old to pick them up easily in a sing-along fashion" (77).

"We Are Singapore" relates the story of how this country has had to overcome odds ("There was a time when people said that Singapore won't make it / But we did"). These verses, in their very simplicity, best represent the rhetorical success of the country's messages. Just as one can understand the stirring of emotions from certain pro-Nazi chants, consider the effects of thousands of people chiming in on this repeated stanza: "This is my country / This is my flag / This is my future / This is my life / This is my family / These are my friends / We are Singapore / Singaporeans." Or consider just the titles of some other national songs like "Count on Me Singapore" ("We can achieve, we can achieve") and "Stand Up for Singapore" ("Be prepared to give a little more"; "Do it with a smile"). *Sing Singapore* (1988), published by the republic's Psychological Defense Division under the Ministry of Communications and Information, prefaces the volume with this statement:

Singing the songs will bring Singaporeans together, to share our feelings one with another. It will bring back shared memories of good times and hard times, of times which remind us of who we are, where we came from, what we did, and where we are going. It will bring together Singaporeans of different races and backgrounds, to share and to express the spirit of the community, the feeling of togetherness, the feeling of oneness. (i)

"Sing Singapore 2000" had as its aim discovering and promoting original songs written by Singaporeans for Singaporeans; that process brought some 23 songs in different moods and styles, available online at http://www.singsingapore.org.sg/songhome.htm. One of the winners was "Where I Belong," with music and lyrics by Tanya Chua: "Morning comes around and I / Can't wait to see my sunny island / In its glorious greenery / Whether rain or shine, it's still beautiful / Bright lights shine on the streets at night / Guiding me closer to home / To a place where I'll be safe and warm / Where I belong."

"It was hoped that these expressive symbols and slogans, regularly repeated in mass and joyful settings, such as the National Day celebrations, could help instill virtues and values in the hearts and minds of the citizenry," according to Hussin Mutalib (1992, 77). "Perhaps, from the perspective of these authorities, these national songs and slogans could help people externalize and broaden their otherwise insular horizons to embrace one that is Singaporean in orientation." Perhaps, indeed; by any standard.

AUGUST 9: SINGAPORE'S NATIONAL DAY

Depending on which history book you read, Singapore separated of its own accord from Malaysia on August 9, 1965, to become a sovereign, democratic, independent nation of its own accord, or it was evicted[6]; by whatever means, that date marks the moment when its nationhood became a reality. Commenting on what he called the "political divorce," Chew (1991) stated: "At that moment of history, there was little enthusiasm over the proclamation of Singapore as 'forever a sovereign democratic and independent nation,' founded upon the principles of liberty and justice and ever seeking the welfare and happiness of her people in a more just and equal society" (363). Who at that juncture could have foreseen what the fruits of the many adjustments that had to be undertaken would reap. Surely, there is a lot for this nation-state to celebrate.

Bringing all Singaporeans together each year on August 9 to commemorate its anniversary of independence, National Day is spectacular. Although there are festivities leading up to and following the actual public holiday, the highlight, unequivocally, is the parade, where representatives from various schools, community and cultural groups, bands, martial arts associations, and military troops provide creative and colorful presentations. Flags, flash cards, and flares combine with song and dance to confirm this country's uniqueness. After all the speeches and spectacle, the ending to the day is punctuated by laser displays and impressive fireworks displays.

While the ritual of the National Day parade remains basically within a constructed frame, the venue has been moved around and various themes and subthemes have been played out. As can be seen in Appendix 2 of this chapter, parade themes tend to emphasize productivity, togetherness, excellence, education, and achievements.

Proudly, Singapore's military forms a foundation for each National Day profile. Army and navy join forces with police, civil defense, and nonmilitary groups, reassuring the citizenry that they are in good hands. While the content of the celebrations has not changed appreciably over the years, as Devasahayam (1990) points out, "Its semantic evolution is inextricably related to ideological issues" (49).

In 1966, in honor of Singapore's first year of independence, a parade took place on the morning of August 9, reviewed by President Yusof bin Ishak and viewed by some 23,000 Singaporeans. Although the emphasis was on military prowess, several members of the People's Action Party were part of the march-past, as reportedly providing, "an exemplary model for Singaporeans to participate in national events." Pride of independence has long continued; the 1968 National Day souvenir magazine read, "Indeed, a certain amount of pride arises when the word Independent is used, inasmuch as to be independent is to be self-governing, self-controlling and self-reliant. These are the points on which Singapore progresses today." Marking the 150th anniversary of the founding of modern Singapore by Sir Stamford Raffles, a change took place in the 1969 parade in that civilian contingents joined their military counterparts. The finale consisted of a dance performed by 90 lions and 6 dragons—a feat so impressive that it has become de rigeur for subsequent celebrations. A particular honor for this year was the presence of Princess Alexandra, a member of the British royal family.

By 1975, emphasis was on decentralization, with smaller parades taking place at 13 different educational settings. By the next year, however, it was decided to bring everyone together again, and the National Stadium was selected as the site. "A Time to Celebrate, A Time to Stand Up for Singapore" was the underlying theme measuring out 25 years of nation-building in 1984. Sporting the theme of "Together . . . Excellence for Singapore," the 1986 souvenir booklet for the 21st National Day opened with messages from President Wee Kim Wee and Prime Minister Lee Kuan Yew, and then had quotations interspersed throughout from the ministers for defense, home affairs, law, trade and industry, finance, health, national development, communications and information, foreign affairs, community development, and the NTUC secretary-general. The colorful brochure, opening with an aerial pan of the city juxtaposed against its busy port, had the statement "No Vision Too Bold." This was followed by pictures of work and workers under the signifier "No Goal Too Far," plus some images from the transportation and construction industries underscored as "No Task Too Big." Keeping to the major theme of togetherness, the following monikers surrounded yet other photos of the country and its hardworking but happy citizenry:

> Together . . . We Achieve ("Our Goal Is to Become a Developed Nation")
> Together . . . We Trade [regional financial networks]
> Together . . . We Build [social and economic growth]
> Together . . . We Communicate [international telecommunications]
> Together . . . We Live [festivals and fun]
> Together . . . We Care [hospitals and home care]
> Together . . . We Take Pride ("Teamwork, Co-Operating with Peers")
> Together . . . We Learn [education and experience]
> Together . . . We Excel ("Count on Me Singapore")
> Together . . . We Celebrate [the National Day Parade Programme]

Simultaneous themes continued in 1987, "Total Defense and Independence" being the foundation theme, and "Vibrant Society with Citizens Developed to the

Fullest" designated as the hope theme. By 1988, the parade's souvenir magazine listed five educational messages strongly influenced by concerns for defense:

- Singapore is our homeland. This is where we belong.
- Singapore is worth defending. We want to keep our heritage and our way of life.
- Singapore can be defended. United, determined and well-prepared, we shall fight for the safety of our homes and the future of our families and children.
- We must ourselves defend Singapore. No one else is responsible for our security.
- We can deter others from attacking us. With Total Defense, we can life in peace.

By this year, according to Milne and Mauzy (1990), the celebrations "seemed to indicate that the PAP leadership has become more fun-minded" (178). A "Swing Singapore" party conveniently held a few days before the elections attracted some 250,000 people.

Reportage from 1989 comes from my perspective as a participant-observer of Singapore's National Day. Yet, to be honest, it was not until the time of the event itself that I realized what a unique opportunity had been offered me. First, some background on my getting there. Since I had been in touch with Lim Heng Tow, then head of public relations for the Singapore Broadcasting Corporation, regarding audience data for my book on *The Cosby Show* (Fuller 1992), we made an appointment to meet while I was visiting the country to deliver a paper for the World Communication Association. Not only did he give my husband and me a tour around the incredible facilities of SBC, he also arranged for us to get tickets to the stadium for National Day—which we later discovered was quite a feat, since only Singaporeans were issued tickets, and then on a lottery basis. There was not even a black market means for getting tickets.

We were warned to get to the stadium well in advance of the ceremony's 5:00 P.M. start, and so arrived midafternoon. There were no fewer than a half dozen checkpoints that we had to pass, each time presenting our tickets for proof of identity. The seats, it turns out, were in the VIP section. We met the choreographer, whom we had first seen at SBC, and he was most gracious in introducing us to key personnel. One person we met was Major Gerard Ong of the Singapore Army, who was in charge of logistics for the parade; he ended up sitting and talking with us throughout the events. As might be expected, everything was precision. Dignitaries were greeted extremely seriously, and everyone—even the babies—sat immobilized. When the prime minister arrived, he was given a 21-gun salute. And for the president, spectators were instructed to wave enormous green and orange "Big Hands" that had been issued at the turnstiles. It was a most impressive sight.

Said to be representing "all walks of life," five different people were selected to recite the Pledge to the Nation: a restaurant captain, a choreographer, a doctor, a clerk, and a businessman; in addition, a signer was on hand for the hearing impaired. Next came a *feu du joie* (fire of joy), marked by some 480 men of the Guard-of-Honor, firing "1,400 rounds in three crackling volleys," as reported by *The Straits Times*. Right on schedule, at 5:40 P.M., the march-past of the Guard-of-Honor began, with the song "Step-by-Step" sung rapturously by the gathering. "La Bamba," chosen to signify Singapore's strong and vital young people, blared as some 1,000 schoolchildren moonwalked and break-danced to the accompaniment of 120 musicians. Another school band played on while pom-poms were mass distributed to the crowd by mini-skirted undergrads from Singapore Polytechnic. Soon, colored gloves joined, cheerleader style, with candles and balloons and colorful costumes and masks worn by Singaporeans of so many different ethnicities. Another highlight of the "Education and Good Health" activities occurred when some 900 girls from the Nicheron Shoshu Buddhist Association frisked aerobically to the refrains of "The Heat Is On" and "Breaking Out," followed by 800 representatives of the Sports Council and the Singapore Taekwando Federation. But there was more. Soon, 700 soldiers, attired in their red and blue martial arts outfits, took center stage to demonstrate their own forms of discipline and glory. And yet more dislays:

1. *Vibrance and Vitality*—264-strong main bands, a 320-strong band, and a 200-strong percussion band performed drills
2. *Happy Birthday Singapore*—school bands formed a symbolic "24" of two large banners with the Singapore seal of lions' heads
3. *Sports and Study*—People's Association Youth Movement, Community Centre Activity Groups, and Manjusri Secondary students in precision
4. *Staying in Shape*—930 young ladies doing gymnastics
5. *Daring and Discipline*—800 Taekwondo exponents
6. *Vigour and Victory*—battalion guards and infantry regiments present a symbolic attacker-defender display
7. *Heights of Harmony*—Grand Finale, when all participants return "in spiral formation to depict a nation growing together in harmony and reaching for greater heights" (1–10)

In the end, of course, everyone came together, joining as one for Singapore—with the finale a foreshadower of the "real" social experiment that was going on then and there. Another telling insight into the government's use of rhetoric to reinforce its programs and policies can be found in President Wee Kim Wee's Address to Parliament of January 9, 1989, reprinted in the National Day program:

If we are not to lose our bearings, we should preserve the cultural heritage of each of our communities, and uphold certain common values which capture the essence of being a Singaporean. These core values include plac[ing] society above self, upholding the family as the basic building block of society, resolving major issues through consensus instead of contention, and stressing racial and religious tolerance and harmony.

The next year, 1990, was the big one: 25 years of independence, with the anticipation for "Another 25 Years of Achievement." The operative slogan was "One People, One Nation, One Singapore." Indeed. With visions aimed internationally, 1991–94 had underlying slogans of "My Singapore," adding on "My Home" as a reminder. Other, wider geographics were considered, as ASEAN and notions of Singapore as a world city began to appear in the rhetoric.

Looking back on "30 Years of Nationhood," National Day 1995 had some new features: the first woman gun positioning officer, who was in charge of commanding the presidential 21-gun salute, plus 1,000 fighting men of the army contingent running (or "doubling") in step to demonstrate their strength and unity. Further, the "Magnificent Men in Their Flying Machines" added the phrase "and women," as it allowed the first-ever female pilot to participate in a National Day parade fly-past. Added to a photo in the commemorative brochure, next to 540 musical instruments and 900 dancers was this comment: "Tomorrow these young people will run the economy, heal the sick and defend the nation. But for today, they're going to show us how to party." Prime Minister Goh Chock Tong delivered this apt statement as part of his annual address to the nation:

We must strengthen the unique characteristics of our society, which root Singaporeans here—the festivals, the atmosphere, the food, the warmth of human relationships among extended family members, schoolmates, friends, and neighbours. . . . I urge Singaporeans to take stock of how much we have achieved and build on these solid foundations.

A theme of "Discipline, Cohesion, Unity, Consolidation and Progress" continued the emphasis on regionalism in 1996, moving toward the new millennium. From there, the celebrations have gone into cyberspace, Singapore's National Day being a very popular Web site, with live Web casting drawing numerous visitors (listing 91,444 hits on July 24, 2001). Tickets for the 35th anniversary parade in 2000 were being scalped for $200 each, much to the chagrin of various citizens, and growing commercialism is clear as businesses increase tie-ins and promotions relative to National Day. This chapter was finished prior to 2001, but the theme "Strong Families, Opportunities for All; Every Singaporean Matters" both continues a key tradition and encourages growth for the future.

CONCLUDING COMMENTS

It seems particularly instructive to return to the topic of core values. While they might sound like pie in the sky to some people, and while Singapore has been classified as a cross between Disneyland and Switzerland, nevertheless they add to the dialogue the government has begun since this country became independent. "The constant reiteration of the state's values and objectives throughout the years has played a significant role in the parade," writes Theresa Wilson

Devasahayam (1990, 88). "It draws out a whole host of experiences of the participants, specifically emphasizing state-definition of identities. The result is a transformation of character and social relationships which essentially pertains to a clearer distinction of 'self' from 'other' in the social experience of Singaporeans." Emphasis continues on the secular nature of the state, as it now can tally quite some shared heritage and history.

Whether approached as ritual or rhetoric, Singapore's National day parade provides a fascinating communications case study, exemplifying the resultant extension of this young nation's social order. It boggles the mind that within three short decades this is a nation that has developed a list of its prioritized "shared values" and, in the process, has been able to implement its own planned national ideology. The hegemonic key is control, so knowing how to dissect the product becomes a first step in appreciating all the intricacies in this multicultural mosaic. Review the country's successful modernization and distinguish it from other examples, in that the government not only did not abandon tradition but instead actually drew on its Confucianism and eschewed Western values. Milne and Mauzy (1990) conclude: "Observers of this experiment in elitism are usually either enthusiastic admirers or, less often, resolute critics. Few can fail to be moved, one way or the other, by the Singapore story" (181).[7]

APPENDIX 1

Prime Minister's Office,
Singapore

Proclamation of Singapore

WHEREAS it is the inalienable right of a people to be free and independent;

AND WHEREAS Malaysia was established on the 16th day of September, 1963, by a federation of existing states of the Federation of Malaya and the States of Sabah, Sarawak and Singapore into one independent and sovereign nation;

AND WHEREAS by an Agreement made on the seventh day of August in the year one thousand nine hundred and sixty-five between the Government of Malaysia of the one part and the Government of Singapore of the other part it was agreed that Singapore should cease to be a state of Malaysia and should thereupon become an independent and sovereign state and nation separate from and independent of Malaysia;

AND WHEREAS it was also agreed by the parties to the said Agreement that, upon the separation of Singapore from Malaysia, the Government of Malaysia shall relinquish its sovereignty and jurisdiction in respect of Singapore so that the said sovereignty and jurisdiction shall on such relinquishment vest in the Government of Singapore;

AND WHEREAS by a Proclamation dated the ninth day of August in the year one thousand nine hundred and sixty-five the Prime Minister of Malaysia Tunku Abdul Rahman Putra Al-Haj Ibni Almarhum Sultan Abdul Hamid Halim Shah did proclaim and declare that Singapore shalll on the ninth day of August in the year one thousand nine hundred and sixty-five cease to be a state of Malaysia and shall become an independent and sovereign state and nation separate from and independent of Malaysia and recognised as such by the Government of Malaysia.

Now I LEE KUAN YEW Prime Minister of Singapore, DO HEREBY PROCLAIM AND DECLARE on behalf of the people and the Government of Singapore that as from today the ninth day of August in the year one thousand nine hundred and sixty-five Singapore shall be forever a sovereign democratic and independent nation, founded upon the principles of liberty and justice and ever seeking the welfare and happiness of her people in a more just and equal society.

Prime Minister, Singapore

Dated the 9th day of August, 1965

APPENDIX 2
SELECTED SINGAPOREAN NATIONAL DAY CELEBRATION THEMES/SLOGANS

1966   Reported in the *Straits Times* as "a demonstration of national pride and confidence in the future."

1967   Building a Rugged and Vigorous Singapore

1968   Youth and Ruggedness

1969   150th Anniversary of the Founding of Modern Singapore

1970   Work for Security and Prosperity

1972   Productivity and Progress

1976   Self-Reliance

1978   Unity and Harmony

1979   Save Energy

1980   March into the Past

1981   Teamwork

1983   Each center had a different theme

1984   25 Years of Nation-Building
       Slogan: A Time to Celebrate, A Time to Stand Up for Singapore

1985   Building a Better Tomorrow—The Vision for 1999

1986   Foundation theme: Productivity, Discipline, and Hard Work
       Hope theme: Vibrant Society with Citizens Developed to the Fullest
       Slogan: Together . . . Excellence for Singapore

1987   Foundation theme: Total Defense and Independence
       Hope theme: Vibrant Society with Citizens Developed to the Fullest
       Slogan: A Nation for All

1988   Foundation theme: Social Cohesion, Commitment, and Compassionate Society
       Hope theme: Refined Living and Cultural Excellence
       Slogan: Excellence Together/Singapore Forever

1989   Foundation theme: Education and Good Health
       Hope Theme: Interesting and Purposeful Living
       Slogan: Excellence Together . . . Singapore Forever

1990   Foundation theme: 25 Years of Achievement
       Hope theme: Another 25 Years of Achievement
       Slogan: One People, One Nation, One Singapore

1991   Foundation theme: Productivity, Discipline, Diligence and Determination
       Hope theme: Singapore International
       Slogan: My Singapore

1992   Foundation theme: Social Cohension, Loyalty, Commitment, and Caring Community
       Hope theme: Singapore in ASEAN
       Slogan: My Singapore

1993   Foundation theme: Sound Education and Good Health in a Clean Environment
       Hope theme/slogan: Singapore—My Country, My Home

1994   Foundation theme: National Sovereignty and Total Defense
       Hope theme: Singapore—World City
       Slogan: My Singapore, My Home

1995   Foundation theme: 30 Years of Nationhood, Values for the Future
       Hope theme: The Challenges of New Frontiers

1996   Foundation theme: Discipline, Cohesion, Unity, Consolidation, and Progress
       Hope theme: Singapore, Growing with the Region

1997   Diary of a Nation

1998   Recollections

1999   Our People

2000   36 years of nationhood—Singapore in the New Economy (live Web cast) Strong
       Families, Opportunities for All; Every Singaporean Matters

2001   36 Years of independence

2002   A Caring Nation

2003   A Cohesive Society

2004   A Progressive Society: Celebrate NDP04

NOTES

I would like to acknowledge the help of the following individuals in the preparation of this chapter: Dr. Phyllis G. L. Chew, Quah Swee Bee of the (Singapore) Ministry of Information and the Arts, and Tan Kheng Boon, Eugene.

1. For an in-depth discussion of Singapore's history, see Barber (1978); Bloodworth (1986); Chew and Lee (1991); Corr (1979); Drysdale (1984); Jossey (1979); Marshall (1971); Moore and Moore (1969); Ow (1984); Pearson (1985); Pluvier (1974); Sheppard and Tan (1982); Singh and Arasu (1984); Turnbull (1977); You and Lim (1984).

2. For an in-depth discussion on the politics of Singapore, see Bellows (1970); Buchanan (1972); Chan (1971, 1976); Chen (1984); Fong (1979); Milne and Mauzy (1990); Pang (1971); Quah, Chan, and Seah (1985); Rodan (1989, 1993); Schein (1996); Seow (1998); Yeo (1973).

3. See Willmott (1989, 588–89) for a good discussion on the rationale and response to introducing Confucianism in the curriculum.

4. For an in-depth discussion of Singapore's multiculturalism, see Ah (1995); Benjamin (1976); Chew (1987); Kapur (1986); Vasil (1995); Wilson (1978).

5. The purpose of this chapter is not necessarily to deconstruct the concept of Singapore's nation-building per se, but rather to try to understand its message management. For an in-depth discussion of Singapore's nation-building, see Beng-Haut and Kuo (1995); Chan (1971a); Chan and Evers (1978); Chew (1991); Hill and Lian (1995); Mutalib (1992); Nair (1976); Shaw, Chen, Lee, and Thomson (1977); Willmott (1989).

6. The *National Geographic* of July 1966 is reported in Ow (1984, 376) as referring to the new independent Singapore as a "reluctant nation."

7. As this book goes to press, preparations are in place for Singapore's National Day 2004 (see www.ndp.org.sg). The organizers have sponsored a Web site contest, launched a music video for the occasion, posted reviews of past parades and ceremonies, offered e-ticketing and e-coupons, and are featuring mobile phone downloads for the occasion. Pins are available that say "Have a heart." There is an opportunity to be on the National Day e-mail list, and participants can vote for their favorite National Day parade song from the following choices: "One United People," "We Will Get There," "Where I Belong," "Shine, Together," or "Home."

REFERENCES

Ah, E. L. (1995). *Meanings of multiethnicity: A case study of ethnicity and ethnic relations in Singapore*. Kuala Lumpur, Malaysia: Oxford University Press.

Barber, N. (1978). *The Singapore story*. Singapore: Fontana.

Bellows, T. J. (1970). *The People's Action Party of Singapore: Emergence of a dominant party system*. New Haven, CT: Southeast Asia Studies, Yale University.

Beng-Huat C., and Kuo, E. C. Y. (1995). The making of a new nation: Cultural construction and national identity. In C. Beng-Huat (Ed.), *Communitarian ideology and democracy in Singapore*, 101–23. New York: Routledge.

Benjamin, G. (1976). The cultural logic of Singapore's multiculturalism. In R. Hassan (Ed.), *Singapore society in transition*, 115–33. Oxford, UK: Oxford University Press.

Birch, D. (1993). *Singapore media: Communication strategies and practices.* Asia Paper 1, Asia Research Centre, Murdoch University. Melbourne, Australia: Longman Cheshire.

Bloodworth, D. (1986). *The tiger and the Trojan horse.* Singapore: Times Books.

Buchanan, I. (1972). *Singapore in Southeast Asia.* London: Bell.

Chan, H. C. (1971a). *Nation building in Southeast Asia: The Singapore case.* Occasional Paper 3. Singapore: Institute of Southeast Asian Studies.

Chan, H. C. (1971b). *Singapore—The politics of survival, 1965–1967.* Oxford, UK: Oxford University Press.

Chan, H. C. (1976). *The dynamics of one-party dominance: The PAP at the grassroots.* Singapore: Singapore University Press.

Chan, H. C., and Evers, H.-D. (1978). National identity and nation-building in Singapore. In P. S. J. Chen and H.-D. Evers (Eds.), *Studies in ASEAN sociology*, 117–29. Oxford, UK: Chopmen.

Chen, P. S. J. (Ed.). (1984). *Singapore: Development policies and trends.* Oxford, UK: Oxford University Press.

Chew, E. C. T. (1991). The Singapore national identity: Its historical evolution and emergence. In E. C. T. Chew and E. Lee (Eds.), *A history of Singapore*, 357–68. Oxford, UK: Oxford University Press.

Chew, E. C. T., and Lee, E. (Eds.). (1991). *A history of Singapore.* Oxford, UK: Oxford University Press.

Chew S. F. (1987). *Ethnicity and nationality in Singapore.* Athens: Ohio University Press.

Chiew S.-K. (1983). Ethnicity and national integration: The evolution of a multi-ethnic society. In P. S. J. Chen (Ed.), *Singapore development policies and trends*, 29–64. Oxford, UK: Oxford University Press.

Choi, A. (1999). Press coverage of a social problem in Singapore: An analysis of content, modes and styles of communication. *Asian Journal of Communication,* (1), 129–47.

Chua, G. H. (1995). *Communitarian ideology and democracy in Singapore.* London: Routledge.

Chua, G. H. (1998). Culture, multiracialism, and national identity in Singapore. In K.-H. Chen (Ed.), *Trajectories: Inter-Asia cultural studies*, 186–205. London: Routledge.

Corr, G. H. (1979). *The war of the springing tigers.* London; Osprey.

Devasahayam, T. W. (1990). *Happy birthday Singapore: An analysis of "identities" in the National Day parade.* Unpublished master's thesis, Center for International Studies, Ohio University.

Drysdale, J. (1984). *Singapore: Struggle for success.* Singapore: Times Books.

Fong, S. C. (1979). *The PAP story—The pioneering years.* Singapore: Times Books.

Fuller, L. K. (1991a, July). *Singapore cinema: Case study of a burgeoning industry.* Paper presented at the World Communication Association Conference, Jyvaskyla, Finland.

Fuller, L. K. (1991b, March). *Singapore's 24th National Day: A participant-observer's analysis of August 9, 1989.* Paper presented at the Intercultural and International Communication Conference, Miami, FL.

Fuller, L. K. (1992). *The Cosby Show: Audiences, impact, implications.* Westport, CT: Greenwood Press.

Fuller, L. K. (1994, October). *Entertainment entrepreneurship: Singapore cinema*. Paper presented at the Ohio University Film Conference on Asian Cinema, Athens, OH.

Fuller, L. K. 1996a, June). *Developing grassroots community media in Singapore*. Paper presented at the Asian Mass Communication Research and Information 25th Anniversary Conference, Singapore.

Fuller, L. K. (1996b, February). *The motion picture industry, from Hollywood to Singapore*. Paper presented to the Rotary Club of Marina-City, Singapore.

Fuller, L. K. (1998). The role of dominant ethnicity in racism: Reportage on Chinese rule in multi-racial Singapore. *The Edge: The E-Journal of Intercultural Relations, 1*(3). Available at: www.hart-li.com/biz/theedge

Goh, C. T. (1986). *A nation of excellence*. Lecture delivered by the First Deputy Prime Minister and Minster for Defense at the Alumni International Singapore, Ministry of Communications and Information.

Goh, C. T. (1994). *Moral values: The foundation of a vibrant state*. Address by the Prime Minister for National Day Rally 1994. Ministry of Information and the Arts, Singapore.

Gupte, P. B. (1998, August 22). Instant Asia (Singapore). *Forbes, 142,* 104–5.

Hill, M., and Lian, K. F. (1995). *The politics of nation-building in citizenship*. New York: Routledge.

Jossey, A. (1979). *Singapore: Its past, present and future*. Singapore: Eastern University Press.

Kapur, B. K. (Ed.). (1986). *Singapore studies: Critical surveys of the humanities and social sciences*. Singapore: Singapore University Press.

Koh, T. T. B. (1991). Singapore in 1990: Continuity and change. In J. Tan (Ed.), *Singapore 1991*. Singapore: Ministry of Information and the Arts.

Kuo, E. C. Y. (1992). Communication scene of Singapore. In A. Goonasekera and D. Holaday (Eds.), *Asian communication handbook*, 243–45. Singapore: AMIC.

Kuo, E. C. Y. (1994). Singapore. In E. Noam, S. Komatsuzaki, and D. Conn (Eds.), *Telecommunications in the Pacific Basin: An evolutionary approach*, 265–85. New York: Oxford University Press.

Kuo, E. C. Y., and Chen. P. S. J. (1983). *Communication policy and planning in Singapore*. London: Kegan Paul International.

Kuo, E. C. Y., Loh, C. M., and Raman, K. S. (1990). *Information technology and Singapore society: Trends, policies and applications*. Singapore: Singapore University Press.

Kwek, I. (1998). *Visualized nation: An analysis of photographs in National Day supplements, 1966–1996*. Unpublished master's thesis, Nanyang Technological University.

Marshall, D. (1971). *Singapore's struggle for nationhood, 1954–59*. Singapore: Eurasia Press.

Milne, R. S., and Mauzy, D. K. (1990). *Singapore: The legacy of Lee Kuan Yew*. Boulder, CO: Westview Press.

Moore, D., and Moore, J. (1969). *The first hundred years of Singapore*. Singapore: Donald Moore Press and Singapore International Chamber of Commerce.

Murray, G. (1996). *Singapore: The global city-state*. New York: St. Martin's Press.

Mutalib, H. (1992). Singapore's quest for a national identity: The triumphs and trials of government policies. In Ban Kah Choon, A. Pakir, and Tong Chee Kiong (Eds.), *Imagining Singapore*, 69–76. Times Academic Press.

Naim, M, and Laudicine, P. A. (2001, February 28). Sizing up global integration. *Christian Science Monitor,* 11.

Nair, C. V. D. (Ed.). (1976). *Socialism that works . . . The Singapore way*. Singapore: Federal Publications.

A nation for all: Together . . . excellence for Singapore. (1987). National Day Souvenir Magazine. Singapore: Educational Publications Bureau.

150 years of progress: Singapore National Day. (1969). *The Straits Times.*

Ooi, G.-L. (2000). Civil society, democracy and the role of media in Singapore.*Media Asia, 27*(4): 200+.

Ow, C. H. (1984). Singapore: Past, present, and future. In Y. P. Seng and L. C. Yad (Eds.), *Singapore: Twenty-five years of development*, 366–85. Singapore: Nan Yang Xing Zhou Lianhe Zaobao.

Pang, C. L. (1971). *Singapore's People's Action Party: Its history, organization, and leadership.* Oxford, UK: Oxford University Press.

Pearson, H.F. (1985). *Singapore: A Popular History.* Singapore: Times Books International.

Pluvier, J. M. (1974). *Southeast Asia from colonialism to independence.* Oxford, UK: Oxford University Press.

Quah, J. S. T. (1985). *In search of Singapore's national values.* Singapore: Institute of Policy Studies.

Quah, J. S. T., Chan, H. E., and Seah, C. M. (Eds.). (1985). *Government and politics of Singapore.* Oxford, UK: Oxford University Press.

Rahim, L. Z. (1998). *The Singapore dilemma: The political and educational marginality of the Malay community.* Kuala Lumpur, Malaysia: Oxford University Press.

Rodan, G. (1989). *The political economy of Singapore's industrialisation: National, state and international capital.* London: Macmillan.

Rodan, G. (Ed.). (1993). *Singapore changes guard: Social, political, and economic directions in the 1990s.* Melbourne, Australia: St. Martin's Press.

Schein, E. H. (1996). *Strategic pragmatism: The culture of Singapore's economic Development Board.* Cambridge, MA: MIT Press.

Seet, K. K. (1990). *Singapore celebrates.* Singapore: Times Editions.

Seow, F. T. (1998). *The media enthralled: Singapore revisited.* Boulder, CO: Rienner.

Sesser, S. (1992, January 13). A nation of contradictions. *New Yorker, 37+.*

Shaw, K. E., Chen, P. S. J., Lee, S. Y., and Thomson, G. G. (1977). *Elites and national development in Singapore.* Tokyo: Institute of Developing Economies.

Sheppard, M. and Tan S. D. (Eds.). (1982). *Singapore: 150 years.* Singapore: Times Books.

Singapore Broadcasting Corporation. (1988). *On television in Singapore: 1963–1988.* Singapore: Author.

Sing Singapore. 1988. Singapore: Psychological Defense Division, Ministry of Communications & Information.

Singh, D. and Arasu, V. T. (Eds.) (1984). *Singapore: An illustrated history, 1941-1984.* Singapore: Ministry of Culture.

Sussman, G. 1991. The "Tiger" from Lion City: Singapore's Niche in the New International Division of Communication Information. In G. Sussman and J. A. Lent (Eds.), *Transnational communications: Wiring the third world*, 279–308. Newbury Park, CA: Sage.

Sutton, H. (1989). Instant Asia: A stewpot of Far Eastern flavors, squeaky-clean Singapore, its towers soaring skyward, has become the Big Apple of the East, *Endless Vacation*, 41–49.

Tan, J. (Ed.) (1991). *Singapore 1991.* Singapore: Ministry of Information and the Arts.

Tay, E. S. (1982). Some Issues on Education. In *Issues facing Singapore in the eighties: Talks by ministers at the National University of Singapore*, 71–99. Information Division, Ministry of Culture.

Teo, P. and Ooi, G. L. (1996). Ethnic Differences and Public Policy in Singapore. In D. Dwyer and D. Drakakis-Smith (Eds.), *Ethnicity and development: Geographical perspectives.* West Sussex, UK: John Wiley.

Thumboo, E., Wong, Y. W., Koh, B. S., Maaruf, S., and Elangovan, T. (Eds.). (1990). *Words for the 25th: Readings by Singapore writers.* Singapore: Ministry of Education.

Tsu, L. A. (Ed.). (1998). *Nation-state, identity, and religion in South East Asia.* Singapore: Singapore Society of Asian Studies.

Turnbull, C. M. (1977). *A history of Singapore, 1819–1975.* Oxfore, UK: Oxford University Press.

Twenty-five years of independence, another twenty-five years of achievement. (1990). Singapore: National Day Parade Executive Committee.

Vasil, R. K. (1995). *Asianizing Singapore: The PAP's management of ethnicity.* Singapore: Heinemann Asia.

Wai-Teng, L. (1995). Consuming the nation: National Day parades in Singapore. Unpublished paper, Sociology Department, National University of Singapore.

Wee, K. W. (1989). A meaningful life for all. Presidential address to Singapore Parliament.

Willmott, W. E. (1989). The emergence of nationalism. In K. S. Sandhu and P. Wheatley (Eds.), *Management of success: The moulding of modern Singapore.* Singapore: Institute of Southeast Asian Studies.

Wilson, H. E. (1978). *Social engineering in Singapore: Educational policies and social change, 1819–1972.* Singapore: Singapore University Press.

Yeo, K. W. (1973). *Political developments in Singapore, 1945–1955.* Singapore: Singapore University Press.

Yong, M. C. (Ed.) (1992). *Asian traditions and modernization: Perspectives from Singapore.* Singapore: Times Academic Press.

You, P. S., and Lim, C. Y. (Eds.) (1984). *Singapore: Twenty-five years of development.* Singapore: Nan Yang Xing Zhon Lianhe Zaobao.

SOUTH AFRICA

(Re)Building a Nation

South Africa's Heritage Day as a Site of Renaming, Reimaging, and Remembering

Scott M. Schönfeldt-Aultman and Gust A. Yep

On 9 May 1994, Nelson Mandela addressed the people of South Africa on the occasion of the opening of the new Parliament. He did not speak of "the people" or "the nation." As he stood on the balcony of the Cape Town City Hall with the majestic Table Mountain as his backdrop, he pointed to the landscape on which the "beginning of the fateful convergence" of Black and White had begun. . . . South African identities cross-cut each other in multiple ways and in multiple contexts. . . . A Muslim, or a Coloured, may span many religious, political, social and cultural contexts and thus link them together into a social universe. . . . On the other hand, these differences are also seen as the principal source of conflict in South Africa.

—Robert Thornton, "The Potentials of Boundaries in South Africa"

As the ANC, we must seek to provide people with the space to express their multiple identities in ways that foster the evolution of a broader South Africanism as their primary identity. . . . The ANC and government should develop a programme around Heritage Day which celebrates diversity and unity, and promotes respect for cultural identities in a manner that contributes to welding a sense of nationhood among our people.

—African National Congress, *Resolution on Building the ANC—The National Question*

In postapartheid South Africa, personal and collective identities are rapidly shifting and changing (Alexander 1997a; Mattes 1997a; Thornton 1996). Such identities intersect along racial, religious, political, social, and cultural contexts and they are overtly and covertly threatened and negotiated (Greenstein 1998). A site of these identity negotiations is South Africa's recently established holiday,

Heritage Day, created by an Act of Parliament in 1994 (Public Holidays Act 1994) and strongly supported by the African National Congress (ANC) as a day for recognizing unity, diversity, and respect for cultural identities.

The South African government employs this public holiday to foster national unity via renaming, reimaging, and remembering. In its renaming efforts, we see a shifting emphasis on national days and locations as these renamed holidays and sites often diverge from previously established histories and interpretations. For instance, Shaka Day, still recognized in KwaZulu-Natal, to remember the assassination of King Shaka of the Zulus on September 22, 1828, is now practically renamed and replaced countrywide as Heritage Day is celebrated on September 24.[1] This renaming or reconceptualizing is accompanied by the reimaging of the meaning and history behind commemorative events and locations. For instance, Heritage Day celebrations have renamed and reimaged parks, roads, and prisions. These changes in calendar and representation are demonstrated in the rituals of remembering the "heritage" of South Africans, which often serve to promote an awareness of the history and heroes of the Black liberation struggle. Such changes were not surprising.

As many predicted and expected, there have been multiple renaming efforts (of roads, airports, buildings, bridges, and so forth) since the ANC came into power in 1994 (Brink 1998; Golan 1994; Malan 1994; van Rooyen 1994; Welsh 1991). Often the new names replace names of leaders affiliated with apartheid with those of liberation heroes. One such case is the renaming of John Vorster Bridge in East London and the Sanlam Building in Port Elizabeth after Stephen Bantu Biko (ECN 1997; Political Reporter 1997). The renaming of the public holiday the Day of the Vow or the Day of the Covenant (December 16) as the Day of Reconciliation also plays down the formerly Afrikaner-specific memories and interpretations of the undergirding event, commonly known as the Battle of the Blood River.

Using Benedict Anderson's (1991) notion of the nation "as an imagined political community" (6), this chapter examines how the South African government works toward (re)building South Africa as a nation as it engages in renaming, reimaging, and the rituals of remembering. To accomplish this task, we argue that the ANC's current program of nation-building undergirds the renaming, reimaging, and the rituals of remembering, simultaneously highlighting forgotten history and "heritage" and obscuring others (Renan 1882/1990) while (re)minding the public of the black liberation struggle and calling for reconciliation for past wrongs. In this chapter, we first examine the concept of nation as an imagined community and provide a brief history of the ANC's nation-building project, then discuss the sites and identity negotiations associated with renaming, reimaging, and the rituals of remembering Heritage Day, and conclude by exploring how the ANC's project of nation-building might have suppressed certain voices and representations through forgotten histories in the name of national unity.

THE NATION AS AN IMAGINED COMMUNITY

The concept of nation is fairly new in history (Anderson 1991; Brennan 1990; Hobsbawm 1990; Nairn 1977/1994; Renan 1882/1990). In a lecture delivered at the Sorbonne in 1882, Renan (1882/1990) asserted that "a nation is a soul, a spiritual principle" (19). This principle is constituted by a common legacy of memories and "the desire to live together, the will to perpetuate the value of the heritage that one has received in an undivided form" (19). In other words, nation and national identity are powerful collective constructs with very "real" consequences.

According to Hutchinson and Smith (1994), the concept of nation has been contested in two ways. First, although there is a plethora of conceptualizations of the term, there appears to be no agreed-upon definition. After a comprehensive examination of nation and nationalism, Seton-Watson (1977) concluded that "no 'scientific definition' of the nation can be devised" (5). Second, nation is conceived as a type of collective identity that rivals other forms of collective identities such as race, class, gender, and religion. Although it is generally understood that national loyalties and identities are more powerful and primary than those of race, class, and gender, there is little agreement over the role that ethnicity, will and memory, and territory and language play in the shaping of this identity.

In his groundbreaking book *Imagined Communities*, Anderson (1991) argues that the notions of nation and nation-ness are cultural productions. Calling the volume the most influential and heuristic theoretical formulation of nationalism in recent years, Chatterjee (1993) writes that "Anderson demonstrate[s] with much subtlety and originality that nations were not the determinate products of given sociological conditions such as language or race or religion; they had been, in Europe and everywhere else in the world, *imagined into existence*" (4; emphasis added). In Anderson's words, the nation "is an imagined political community—and imagined as both inherently limited and sovereign" (6). He further elaborates on his conceptualization, emphasizing his key points:

It is *imagined* because the members of even the smallest nation will never know most of their fellow-members, meet them, or even hear of them, yet in the minds of each lives the image of their communion . . . the nation is imagined as *limited* because even the largest of them, encompassing perhaps a billion living human beings, has finite, if elastic, boundaries, beyond which lie other nations . . . it is imagined as *sovereign* because the concept was born in an age in which Enlightenment and Revolution were destroying the legitimacy of the divinely-ordained, hierarchical dynastic realm. . . . Finally, it is imagined as a *community*, because, regardless of the actual inequality and exploitation that may prevail in each, the nation is always conceived as a deep, horizontal comradeship. Ultimately it is this fraternity that makes it possible, over the past two centuries, for so many millions of people, not so much to kill, as willingly to die for such limited imaginings. (6–7)

In spite of the pretension and appearance of representation, a nation never fully or adequately reflects the individuals and the lives of diverse people living in it. To understand a nation as a collective identity, and a representative symbol of unity and communal existence, the concept of the nation must be naturalized (Ono 1998). It is through this process of making the nation a taken-for-granted and normalized component of daily existence that this socially imagined space called "nation" becomes a social cement that compels people to live and die for it. Through this lens, we first provide a brief historical context of the ANC's nation-building program and then examine Heritage Day as a site of renaming, reimaging, and remembering in the collective social imaginary of South Africans.

THE ANC'S NATION-BUILDING PROGRAM

The ANC has historically had a varying notion of nation and nation-building than the former ruling government of South Africa, the National Party (Anonymous 1988; E.D. 1990; Giliomee and Schlemmer 1989a, 1989b; Greenstein 1995, 1998; Grundlingh 1991; Jordan 1988; Marks and Trapido 1987; Schreuder 1994; Sharp 1988; Sizwe 1979; van Diepen 1988; Welsh 1991). Only recently, since being voted into power, has it been able to publicly and powerfully propagate its version of the "nation-state" (Giliomee and Schlemmer 1989b) and to make concrete efforts to build this new South African nation. Its sense of nation, as Welsh (1991) and Giliomee (1991) have argued, is indicated in the Freedom Charter of 1955 and the ANC Constitutional Guidelines from 1988.

In short, this "nation" and thus the ANC's program of nation-building are grounded, at least philosophically, in a nonracialism that seeks to incorporate equally every South African individual (Giliomee and Schlemmer 1989a, 1989b; Greenstein 1998). In practice, the ANC attempts to build a unified South African nation by (re)cognizing, (re)incorporating, and (re)presenting those members of society who were excluded in the old regime—namely, through its speeches, public statements, metaphors (for example, rainbow nation), images, renaming efforts, Constitution, organizations, departments, public calendar changes, and celebrations. For purposes of this chapter, we suggest that the ANC's efforts of renaming and reimaging and its rituals of remembering, especially during celebrations of Heritage Day, serve its nation-building program.

This objective seems clear in the ANC Resolution cited at the beginning of the chapter. Moreover, in another resolution from the 50th National Conference, concerning arts and culture, ANC members recognized the Department of Arts, Culture, Science, and Technology's "comprehensive national policy on arts and culture." They also recognized that arts and culture "can play a crucial role in nation-building, reconciliation and the development of a new national identity and ethos reflective of our new democracy," as well as "play a pivotal role in the moral renewal of our society" (African National Congress 1997b). They resolved, then, to

support the government's efforts to correct the distortions and imbalances in our heritage landscape through the creation of new monuments, museums, the naming of places, and generally affirming the neglected history and culture of the majority of South Africans [and to] support government efforts to encourage, promote and support all cultural activities that celebrate the rich and diverse cultural heritage of all South Africans. (African National Congress 1997b)

One of the clearest indications that the ANC uses Heritage Day in its nation-building is Nelson Mandela's (1996) statement during a 1996 Heritage Day speech honoring Enoch Sontonga, author of the first verse and chorus, as well as composer, of "Nkosi Sikelel' iAfrika" (which makes up part of the current national anthem along with "Die Stem van Suid Afrika":

When our first democratically-elected government decided to make Heritage Day one of our national days, we did so because we knew that our rich and varied cultural heritage has a profound power to help build our new nation. We did so knowing that the struggles against the injustice and inequities of the past are part of our national identity; they are part of our culture. We knew that, if indeed our nation has to rise like the proverbial phoenix from the ashes of division and conflict, we had to acknowledge those whose selfless efforts and talents were dedicated to this goal of non-racial democracy. Enoch Sontonga stands tall and distinguished among these luminaries, as the architect of our ode to joy and pain, a builder of the nation just born.

RENAMING

As was noted earlier, how a nation comes into being is a complex system of cultural production and signification (Anderson 1991; Bhabha 1990). One of the ways of "linking fraternity, power and time meaningfully together" (Anderson 1991, 36) is through the process of renaming to create a language that highlights national unity and communion and shared historical memories. With the advent of new communication technologies, this new national consciousness expands and reinforces the naturalized myth of an imagined community of South Africa. The emphasis on heritage presupposes a past that is materialized in the present through a desire to continue a common life (Renan 1882/1990).

One familiar with the history and political tensions surrounding celebrations of Shaka Day, or even the underlying factors, would not have been surprised by the ANC's establishment of a concurrent national holiday, Heritage Day (Christopher 1995; Correspondent 1996; Golan 1991, 1994; Hamilton 1998, Hlongwa 1997; Makhanya 1996a; Marks and Trapido 1987; Mathieson and Attwell 1998; Spiegel and Boonzaier 1988). In fact, the ANC renamed Shaka Day as Heroes Day when it choose to celebrate it in KwaXimba in 1993, a move that Mathieson and Attwell (1998) suggest was an effort at redefining the day as a multicultural event rather than one fostering Zulu nationalism and identity.

Similarly, the instituting of Heritage Day seems intended to neuter or obscure an exclusive nationalism while promoting a broadened, inclusive one, such that it is generally perceived as a "neutral day to which each community in South Africa can attach its own significance and which will foster a spirit of accommodation" (East London's Online Calendar 1999; Heritage South Africa 1999). Consequently, the day is intended to serve as a site for diverse populations to celebrate "heritage," diversity, identity, and unity within one country and to work toward "respect for cultural identities in a manner that contributes to welding a sense of nationhood" (African National Congress 1997a). Perhaps due to this celebration of one's own heritage, the ANC gives little attention or promotion, for instance, to what might be considered the Zulu or Afrikaner nations within South Africa.

Heritage Day also provides the ANC opportunities to rename public sites. One such occasion was the 1996 celebration at Braamfontein Cemetery in Johannesburg when Nelson Mandela eulogized Enoch Sontonga. During the ceremony on Heritage Day 1996, Sontonga's formerly unmarked grave was declared a national monument, and the Order of Meritorious Service (Gold) was bestowed on him posthumously. The program included praise poetry, a biographical narrative, Sontonga's music played by the National Symphony Orchestra, Mandela's speech, and the unveiling of a bronze memorial plaque on Sontonga's gravestone (Mlangeni 1996; Walker 1996). Gauteng premier Tokyo Sexwale renamed Braamfontein Park as Enoch Sontonga Memorial Park while Johannesburg mayor Isaac Mogase renamed Showground Road as Enoch Sontonga Avenue (Mandela 1996; Mlangeni 1996; Salgado 1996).

The rhetoric surrounding the event seems to suggest that this renaming/ recognition ceremony was intended to work toward building a unified nation with a collective sense of belonging and toward remembering the forgotten past. For example, Mandela (1966) said that in honoring the once-obscure, unappreciated, and nearly forgotten teacher-poet Sontonga "we are recovering a part of the history of our nation and our continent" and contributing to the "re-awakening of the South African nation." He recognized Sontonga as a "builder of the nation just born," while noting the historical irony that "like the relics of our more distant past, the grave of Enoch Sontonga lay neglected and unseen, even as his words and music nourished the soul of our nation." A writer for the National Monument Council penned that Sontonga was a man "who wrote a song almost 100 years ago that, unbeknown to him, became one of peace and healing for the Rainbow Nation of South Africa" (Walker 1996). In a similar vein, a statement from the Ministry of Arts, Culture, Science and Technology claimed, "Within a broader social and political context, the day's events in Braamfontein are a powerful agent for promulgating a South African identity, fostering reconciliation and promoting the notion that variety is a national asset as opposed to igniting conflict" (Makhanya 1996b). Both of these statements suggest that the cultural production and signification by the ANC government is intended to meaningfully connect history, power, and fraternity, to foster unity, community, and remembering, and ultimately to image a unified South African nation. The ANC's efforts also acknowledge the value of heritage in recognizing, reclaiming, and actualizing individual and national identities, though there seems a greater emphasis on cultivating national identity.

REIMAGING

Along with renaming, a new national biography emerges. Anderson (1991) reminds us that nations have no clearly identifiable births, and that their deaths, if they should occur, are never "natural." Because of this, national biographies become inversions of conventional genealogy, that is, they start with the originary present. Contemporary South Africa is characterized by tremendous changes at multiple levels (Alexander 1997a, 1997b; Hamilton 1998; Louw 1998; Mathieson and Attwell 1998; Mattes 1997a; Nuttall and Coetzee 1998; Schuster 1997). However, Anderson (1991) notes that "all profound changes in consciousness, by their very nature, bring with them characteristic amnesias. Out of such oblivions, in specific historical circumstances, spring narratives" (204) and these narratives are set in homogeneous, serial time. The awareness of this serial time, which simultaneously implies continuity and the "forgetting" of such continuity, creates the need for a narrative of a national identity. In this section, we focus on those current expressions and narratives of national identity that reimage the meaning and history associated not only with Shaka/Heritage Day but with "heritage" sites as well.

Since the beginning of annual Shaka Day celebrations in the 1970s, the ANC has voiced challenges to the conveyance of the Zulu versions of "tradition" and history during the events, particularly by Inkatha Freedom Party (IFP) leader Gatsha Mangosuthu Buthelezi (Golan 1991, 1994; Hamilton 1998; Mathieson and Attwell 1998; Spiegel and Boonzaier 1988). As Golan (1991, 1994) notes, these tensions between the ANC and the IFP (as well as some intra-Zulu tensions) are grounded in power struggles, control of resources, governing methods, the significance of ethnic division within the black community, use of symbols, and historical interpretation. They also concern different imaginings of "nation" and identity (Christopher 1995; Golan 1991, 1994; Hamilton 1998; Mathieson and Attwell 1998; Spiegel and Boonzaier 1988).

The 1993 ANC Shaka Day celebration in KwaXimba was "one of the first, tentative steps in actually engaging with Zulu ethnicity" (Mathieson and Attwell 1998, 113), a step the ANC likely saw as necessary given its rise to power, the need to dialogue with those historically not identifying with its policies and political agenda, and the potential for civil conflict (Mathieson and Attwell 1998). In 1996, the platform of speakers during the Heritage Day celebration at King's Park Stadium in Durban seemed another step toward reconciliation and (re)imaging of relations between the ANC and some Zulus, as well as what appeared the telling of/calling for a new narrative. It is important to note, however, that while there seemed a sense of reconciliation between the ANC and King Goodwill Zwelithini during this time, relations between the ANC and Buthelezi (that is, IFP) were not as peaceful at this point. Moreover, there were intra-Zulu struggles and differing opinions about affiliating with the ANC, as observed in the tensions between Buthelezi and Zwelithini and in Buthelezi's disapproval of Zwelithini's alignment with the ANC (Correspondent 1996; Golan 1991, 1994; Hamilton 1998; Hlongwa 1997; Makhanya 1996a; Mathieson and Attwell 1998).

Despite such differences, a reimaging, reconciliatory narrative still seemed evident in those speaking at the King's Park Heritage Day event. Zulu king Goodwill Zwelithini advocated tolerance and the end of violence between the IFP and the ANC. KwaZulu-Natal premier Frank Mdlalose of the IFP urged for tolerance of others' religion, culture, and heritage. ANC provincial leader and self-professed Zulu Jacob Zuma suggested that the diversity of the province was representative of the South African nation (Anonymous 1996a; Brown, Phosa, and Masipa 1996). This and other Heritage Day celebrations, as well as the actual establishment of Heritage Day, as we have suggested, still challenge Zulu-oriented histories and representations, as do the occasional ANC officials' appearances at Shaka Day gatherings, if only by playing down Zulu nationalism and commemorating nation-builders other than Shaka. In essence, there are now new storytellers weaving alternative narratives on a day that has usually been one affiliated with Shaka stories.

Heritage Day also provides a venue for the ANC to engage identities other than Zulu. One of the most publicized and well-documented accounts is the 1997 by-invitation-only Heritage Day ceremonies on Robben Island and the opening of the Robben Island Museum (Friedman 1997). While some criticized the gathering as an ANC promotional event and questioned its funding (Duffy and Edmunds 1997), the narrative it constructed reimaged Robben Island, as well as addressed the history and identities of South Africans. In a speech on the island, Mandela (1997) said that the new museum was a beginning to countering the tradition of representation that perpetuated and preferenced "mainly white and colonial history." He spoke of his "great joy" that "we can all come as free South Africans . . . to Robben Island" and that "we are gathered to celebrate our joint heritage as a nation, to acknowledge this heritage in the context of our commitment to Democracy, Tolerance and Human Rights." He referenced those who in the past had to celebrate their heritage outside of the established structures and instead in craft, music, festivals, carnivals, and the like. The Robben Island Museum, he argued, now brings those heritages into the mainstream, noting that the island "is a vital part of South Africa's collective heritage." He spoke of how it had formerly been known as a "place of pain and banishment for centuries and now of triumph." He continued by highlighting some of the issues concerning the island's future and its role in representation:

How do we look at the histories of different people who lived here, through various ages: lepers, prisoners, jailers all together; leaders of resistance? . . . How do we give expression to these diverse histories as a collective heritage? How do we reflect the fact that the people of South Africa as a whole . . . turned one of the world's most notorious symbols of racist oppression into a world-wide icon of the universality of human rights; of hope, peace and reconciliation? How do we represent the tradition of intense political and academic education that the Island has come to symbolise?

In answer to these questions he stated his confidence that

we will together find a way to combine the many dimensions of the Island, and . . . we will do so in a manner that recognises above all its pre-eminent character as a symbol of the victory of the human spirit over political oppression; and of reconciliation over enforced division. In this way we will help strengthen the ethos of heritage as a binding force, rather than a divisive one.

He concluded by urging listeners to "recommit" themselves to constitutional ideals, those "which were shaped in the struggles here on Robben Island and in the greater prison that was Apartheid South Africa." In short, Mandela called South Africans to a common purpose and task, making reference to what seems a common human heritage, as well as a common national one.

Robben Island has often been an important symbol in South Africa and for national identity (Deacon 1998). Clearly, Mandela works toward a new image of the island and of those former prisoners and workers of the liberation movement by dissociating them with the image of outcast and lawbreaker and (re)imaging them as heroes and builders of a free nation. In the process, Robben Island (especially with the establishment of a museum and the elevating and privileging of former prisoners' narratives) becomes (re)imaged as a place of joy, triumph, education, inclusion, liberation, unity, and celebration rather than one of despair, loss, neglect, exclusion, imprisonment, division, and tragedy. Herein, of course, can lie the danger of forgetting and the struggle of representation. The tensions over the future of the island and the debates about it becoming a tourist attraction are certainly indications of these concerns—a reflection of the varying memories, experiences, and meanings associated with the island and the contested nature of national and subnational identities (Deacon 1998; Dlamini 1997).

REMEMBERING

According to Renan (1882/1990), forgetting is critical in the creation and maintenance of a nation. National unity is typically achieved by brutality and tragedy and the need to "forget" them appears to be a primary contemporary civic responsibility. However, Anderson (1991) reminds us that "having to 'have already forgotten' tragedies of which one needs unceasingly to be 'reminded' turns out to be a characteristic device in the later construction of national genealogies" (201). In this section, we focus on the dynamic tensions between memory, remembrance, and forgetting of the tragedies and "heritages" surrounding Shaka/Heritage Day and its celebration.

As we have already implied, the celebrations of Heritage Day often tend to downplay the tragedies of the past, except perhaps to springboard off of them for purposes of unity and highlighting heritages that had formerly been forgotten or absent in national narratives. Recent Shaka Day celebrations, while still Zulu specific, have included multiparty platforms and stressed reconciliation and unity among Zulus and between the IFP and the ANC (Correspondent 1996; Hlongwa 1997; Makhanya 1996a; Sapa 1998a). For instance, in 1996, Buthelezi called on Zulus to be "brutally honest with ourselves and recognise that for a long time now,

Zulu people have died at the hands of their Zulu brothers" because of "the weakness of the Zulu nation owing to our internal divisions" (qtd. in Correspondent 1996). In 1998, King Goodwill Zwelithini claimed that Zulus "are one of those nations in Africa which should take a lead in the campaign to revive our African heritage and all those things that gave us dignity and respect in our humanness as Africans" (Sapa 1998b). At the same celebration, KwaZulu-Natal Tourism and Economic Affairs member of the Executive Committee Jacob Zuma urged Zulus to respect their chiefs and to lead in Africa's rebirth. In 1996, this provincial ANC leader asked Zulus to unite and work out their differences, saying "Difficult a task as it is, we have to succeed because the alternative is to destroy ourselves. We must bring about peace and stability. Let us unite and be proud of our nation-building. It is the task we have to perform" (qtd. in Correspondent 1996). There seems, however, an ambiguity in Zuma's statement: is the "nation" in the nation-building Zuma calls for a reference to the Zwelithini's or Buthelezi's Zulu nation, or to one grounded in an ANC nationalism? Whichever "nation" is intended, what seems indisputable is that Shaka Day celebrations now provide the ANC specific occasions to address Zulu and national identities directly, the former of which they seem to do little of during Heritage Day celebrations.

On Heritage Day, the ANC has chosen to take an inclusive approach by celebrating many cultures and identities. While they have included Zulu representatives such as King Goodwill Zwelithini in events, the rhetoric those representatives have employed has focused primarily on recognizing "common heritage and cultural values" (Brown, Phosa, and Masipa 1996). Other celebrations such as those at Sontonga's memorial and Robben Island (re)claim, (re)image, and (re)member a forgotten past, while simultaneously "forgetting" a former privileged past and calling for national unity and community. Other celebrations also demonstrate this call and multiple heritages. For instance, in 1996, Minister of Environmental Affairs and Tourism Dr. Pallo Jordan, at a ceremony in Kruger National Park that marked the opening of the 16th century stone-walled citadel of Thulamela, said that the people of Thulamela had a culture that was "inclusive" and was a "past we must recapture" (qtd. in Allen 1996). In 1997, celebrations remembered District Six in Cape Town (Jordan 1997) and Robben Island veterans (Friedman 1997; Mandela 1997; Mellin 1997). In 1998 and 1999, days of sport, arts, dance, drama, unity parades, museum displays, a visit to a Paramount chief's kraal, play productions, speeches, musical entertainment, praise-singing, honoring of liberation leaders and victims of forced removals, and a National Monument Council poster urging people to claim their heritage were planned in such places as Alice, Bizana, Butterworth, Cape Town, Contralesa, Cradock, East London, Macleantown, Port Elizabeth, Pretoria, Sterkspruit, Umtata, and Zwelitsha and at the North West Cultural Calabash Festival (Anonymous 1998a, 1998b, 1999; DDR 1998a, 1998b, 1998c, 1998d, 1998e, 1998f, 1999; Kakaza 1998; Mpondwana 1998; Mxotwa 1998; Ngani 1998; Sapa 1998a; Zifo 1998). Often, it seemed that these celebrations and cultural productions forgot the specific brutality and tragedy of past atrocities (the Truth and Reconciliation Committee has done much of this work) and instead sought to remember and celebrate forgotten pasts and promising futures, that is, to create and maintain a certain sense of history, nation, identity, heritage, unity, and community.

One example of this focus was East London's 1998 Heritage Day festivities. There were traditional garment displays, art exhibitions, speeches, and traditional and modern dance and music. Cultural groups were invited to wear the national attire of their "country of origin" and to sell traditional cuisine (DDR 1998d). One of the speakers, Mayor Lulamile Nazo, wearing traditional dress, said that the festivities were intended to address the past wrongs of the former regime by high-lighting forgotten history and achievements and symbolizing various identities and sense of place (DDR 1998d). In a speech, Gay Khaile from the Office of the Premier of the Eastern Cape, the communications directorate, emphasized the importance of nation-building, of forming relationships between different cultures, and of re-membering those like Sontonga and writer Sol Plaatjie on Heritage Day (DDR 1998c). Following the events, one writer criticized one of the speakers, the Educa-tion member of the Executive Committee Sheps Mayatula, for only paying lip service to his native Xhosa language when he addressed a predominantly Xhosa-speaking crowd at Orient Beach mostly in English (Mxotwa 1998). In Sterkspruit, Sotho-, Hlubi-, and Xhosa-speaking individuals, as well as government officials, were on the tourism-promoting program planned by the Department of Sports, Arts, and Culture (DDR 1998f).

REFLECTIONS

We have attempted in this chapter to demonstrate how the ANC approaches nation-building via Heritage Day and its efforts of renaming, reimaging, and for remembering. Nation-building is a task that has often been viewed as "all but impossible" (Giliomee 1991), "hopeless [and] damaging" (Degenaar 1995), in-herently ambiguous and potentially exclusive (Sharp 1997), and problematic given South Africa's diverse communities and cultures (Louw 1998; Simpson 1994). The metaphors and symbols a government employs during the nation-building process may, at times, seem inappropriate, ambiguous or imbued with variant meanings (Adam 1994; Hall 1998; Sharp 1997; Welsh 1991). Such has been the case with the metaphoric imaging of South Africa as a "rainbow nation" (Anonymous 1997a, 1997b, 1997c, 1997d, 1997e; Davis 1995; Robins 1997), which prompted Alexander's "Gariep nation" (Alexander 1996, 1997a, 1997b; Davis 1995).

Even so, the ANC persists with its program of building a strongly unified na-tion, often through its renaming, reimaging, and rituals of remembering. Through such efforts, it seemingly participates in what Brink (1998) sees as the fabrication of metaphors "in which, not history, but imaginings of history are invented" (42). These imaginings, of course, represent some identities and heritages while "for-getting" or downplaying others, particularly those associated with the apartheid era or reflecting ethnic nationalism. These imaginings also seem intended to serve as the social cement of a South African nation, as is suggested in the first line of a Reuters (1998) story: "Cracks were appearing in South Africa's post-apartheid sense of identity . . . President Mandela said yesteday." Whether such a South African nation exists or can even be created has been debated for some time—primarily because of the diversity in ethnicity, sense of nation, ideology, memory, rituals, language, culture, history, heritage, class, gender, race, region, socioeconomics, and so on (Adam 1994; Degenaar 1995; Filotova 1994; O'Malley 1994; Randall 1998; van Rooyen 1994).

In spite of such debates, the ANC continues creating new collective memories and interpretations of history, which as Hasian and Frank (1999) argue are "contested terrains [which] help create our individual and collective identities, maintain our traditions, and allow us to forget" (97–98). Still, creation of collective memory in a country marked by diversity can be problematic given such varied experiences and identifications (Nuttall 1998; Robins 1998). For instance, while the ANC participates in nation-building through the "politics of memory [where the] past is uncovered for the purposes of political reconciliation in the present" (Minkley and Rassool 1998, 89), Robins (1997) maintains that the ANC's efforts to build a "new nationalism" ignores or submerges differences among people and forgets not only the support apartheid received from "ordinary civil servants and millions of white voters" but the continuing living conditions of "poverty and misery that apartheid produced." In this sense, then, the ANC's (re)membering of people as part of the South African nation, that is, their attempted making of members of the nation of those formerly excluded, seems not to have been fully achieved as of yet. Still, the ANC continues to imagine a community, a community of South Africans as a diverse and unified nation.

As we have noted, the celebration of "heritage" plays a primary role in this imagining. Since its beginning, however, some have wondered what the "Heritage" of "Heritage Day" means.[2] It has been described as "obscure" (Anonymous 1995), ambiguous (Bunsee 1997), and "amorphous" (Anonymous 1996b). Indeed, it would seem that the ANC deliberately created a day that would be open to multiple meanings and, consequently, to some confusion and uncertainty about what and how to celebrate and whether the day actually fosters unity or division (Anonymous 1997f, 1997g, 1998c; Editorial Opinion 1998; Patten 1998).

No doubt, achieving national unity in today's South Africa is a complicated and complex objective, and perhaps only possible in the imagination (Anderson 1991). Just as difficult to create is a strong sense of national identity, particularly given the multiple identities people possess. Still, debates arise in the public press about the sense of "we-ness" among South Africans (Giliomee 1997; Mattes 1997a, 1997b; Roefs 1997; Robins 1997). Polls are conducted to determine if respondents identify as or are "proud" to be "South African" (Anonymous 1997b; Mattes 1995, 1997b). There are, of course, always varying opinions and mixed responses, which indicate that nation-building can be a complicated endeavor. For instance, Mattes (1997b) argues that if the nation is conceived in a "political or civic sense, rather than in a cultural or ethnic one," the "essential pre-condition" exists for nation-building.

Giliomee (1997) and Robins (1997), who note people's varying values, historical interpretations, economic inequalities, resource competition, poverty, gender, class, and so forth, disagree. Robins (1997) has written about the "tremendous diversity of meanings that South African national identity has for citizens of different class, gender, race, education, occupation and language backgrounds." Giliomee (1997) states, "Certainly there is no sense among South Africans that they already form a nation." Thaver (1996) claims that "as South Africans we have very little sense of a nation." One journalist writes that "we still do not identify strongly with one another or see ourselves as one people" (Anonymous 1997b). Thornton (1996) contends that there exists "no fundamental identity that any South African clings to in common with all or even most other South Africans. South Africans have multiple identities in common contexts, and common identities in multiple contexts" (150). One journalist went so far as to say, "Simply put, South Africans have no clue who they are" (Mda 1997). Even Mandela, in a recent address to Parliament, referenced "a certain weakening in the sense of common national identity that we have been building since we began our negotiated transition" (qtd. in Reuters 1998).

Ultimately, these perceptions seem centralized around the actuality and strength of subnational identities (accompanied by a plethora of other particularities) and their relationship with the holding of national identity (Alexander 1996, 1997a, 1997b; Anonymous 1997a; Davis 1995; Giliomee 1997; Mattes 1997a, 1997b; Robins 1997; Roefs 1997; Welsh 1991). Alexander (1996), thus, argues that "we have to create a sense of national unity while at the same time making space for the expression of self-defined sub-national identities as long as these do not undermine or negate that national unity." Acknowledging the multiple, socially constructed and contested identities people have, Alexander (1997a) suggests that contemporary South Africa is "faced with a situation that calls for rapid and often dramatic shifts of identity or, in some cases, for the consolidation of inherited identities. To mention only a few, the categories of 'African,' 'Afrikaner,' 'coloured' and 'Zulu,' among others, are being hotly contested." Thus, he (1997b) argues that the rainbow nation metaphor is inadequate and should be replaced with a more appropriate, "dynamic" and "indigenous image" such as the "Gariep nation," which references what was formerly known as the Orange River—a river traversing all of South Africa with tributaries that have catchment areas throughout the country. He goes on to say that the Gariep image

accommodates the fact that at certain times of our history, any one tributary might flow stronger than the others, that new streamlets and springs come into being and add their drops to this or that tributary even as others dry up and disappear, and, above all, it represents the decisive notion that the mainstream is constituted by the confluence of all the tributaries, that is, that no single current dominates, that all the tributaries in their everchanging forms continue to exist as such, even as they continue to constitute and reconstitute the mainstream.

That the ANC has seemingly questioned the appropriateness of the rainbow nation metaphor, as may be indicated in their affirming of the validity of the "general approach" of the 1997 ANC conference paper *Nation-Formation and Nation Building: The National Question in South Africa* (Anonymous 1997e), which briefly examines the metaphor, makes one wonder whether it will vary its approach to nation-building (African National Congress 1997a). Whether it does or not, what does seem evident, as we have suggested, is the observation that Welsh (1991):

Building a South African nation will not be an easy task. . . . Nearly 50 years ago G. H. Calpin wrote a book entitled *There Are No South Africans.* The pessimistic verdict implied by the title remains substantially true, but at least the elapse of time and the pressure of events may just have succeeded in producing a new generation of South Africans who are determined to prove the opposite. (567)

Such a stance, and its accompanying ambiguity, seem clear in the words of one writer with a "mixed cultural background" when reflecting on Heritage Day: "So can anyone tell me exactly what my South African heritage is? What does someone like me do on Heritage Day? . . . But this I can say with confidence: no matter what my 'heritage' is, I am wholly South African" (Anonymous 1997g).

NOTES

1. Golan (1994) notes that the first Shaka Day celebration was a three-day commemorative event held in 1954 by King Cyprian Bhekuzulu. She mentions that in 1970 the KwaZulu government named September 24 "Zulu National Day," that in 1972 a public ceremony was held at Shaka's grave at Stanger, and that the annual mass gatherings (Shaka Day celebrations) began in 1978. While it can be argued that Shaka Day has not been replaced or "renamed," especially given its continued celebration within the province of KwaZulu-Natal, that the ANC chose to create a national holiday (Heritage Day) so close to Shaka Day seems for most intents and purposes to rename the day, at least in the general consciousness. Some newspaper reports even imply that Shaka Day has been renamed (Anonymous, 1998c; Sapa, 1996). However one chooses to argue, what does seem clear is that Heritage Day overshadows, broadens, and practically replaces or reconceptualizes Shaka Day, at least for much of the country.

2. One interested in investigating South African heritage projects, sites, organizations, and legislation can find innumerable resources on the Internet. Some of these are the web pages affiliated with the Department of Arts, Culture, Science, and Technology (http://www.dacst.gov.za), the National Heritage Council Act (http://www.govdocs/legislation/1999/act11.pdf), the National Heritage Resources Act (http://www.govdocs/legislation/1999/act25.pdf), Heritage South Africa (http://www.heritage.org.za/hsa1.htm), the National Trust of South Africa (http://www.heritage.org.za/ntsa/ntsa93.htm), the National Monuments Council (http://www.nmc.intekom.com/a.htm), the Southern Africa Environment Project (http://saep.org/subject/heritage/culture.html), and *Mail and Guardian* links to 50 must-see heritage sites (http://www.mg.co.za/mg/africa/feb97/23sep-heritage.html).

REFERENCES

We have drawn from many Internet resources for this chapter, mostly from online newspaper archives and government document sources that often post materials anonymously or credit them to press associations (for example, Sapa) or generic reporters (for example, DDR). While we have drawn from such sources in large part due to reasons of inaccessibility, and in part to better assess public perceptions within South African society, the practice does seem to be an increasingly accepted one in recent writings on South Africa (see, for example, Louw, 1998), particularly by those outside of the country with little or no access to South African media sources. Given these circumstances and our intent, authorial anonymity of some of our sources is unavoidable.

Adam, H. (1994). Nationalism, nation-building and non-racialism. In N. Rhoodie and I. Liebenberg, (Eds.), *Democratic nation-building in South Africa*, 37–51. Pretoria: HSRC.

African National Congress. (1997a, July). *Resolution on Building the ANC—The National Question adopted at the ANC 50th National Conference, Mafikeng*. Available: http://www.anc.org.za/ancdocs/history/conf/conference50/resolutions2.html#National Question

African National Congress. (1997b, July). *Resolution on Social Transformation—Arts and Culture adopted at the ANC 50th National Conference, Mafikeng*. Available: http://www.anc.org.za/ancdocs/history/conf/conference50/resolutions3.html#Arts

Alexander, N. (1996). Rainbow people but no pot of gold. *Cape Times*. Available: http://www2.inc.co.za/Archives/1996/9607/26/sarainbow.html

Alexander, N. (1997a, October 29). Colours of the rainbow do not necessarily always mingle well. *Cape Times*. Available: http://www2.inc.co.za/Archives/1997/9710/29/alec.html

Alexander, N. (1997b, October 27). In the Great River of South African life, each tributary is important. *Cape Argus*. Available: http://www2.inc.co.za/Archives/1997/9710/27/lx.html

Allen, A. (1996, September). Pallo Jordan calls for cultural inclusivity. *The Star*. Available: http://www2.inc.co.za/Archives/1996/9610/11/thulaa.html

Anderson, B. R. O'G. (1991). *Imagined communities: Reflections on the origin and spread of nationalism*. London: Verso.

Anonymous. (1988, December 20). Building a nation. *Die Burger*. Available: http://www.naspers.com/cgi/nph-bwcgis/BURGER/burger/alg/storie/DDW?W%3DOPSKRIF%20PH%20IS%20%27building%20a%20nation%27%26M%3D1%26K%3D322767%26R%3DY%26U%3D1. Or to find by Search: http://www.naspers.com/argiewe/soek.html

Anonymous. (1995, September 22). Seven Days. *Weekly Mail and Guardian*. Available: wysiwyg://62/http://web.sn.apc.org/wmail/issues/950922/wm950922-52.html

Anonymous. (1996a, September 25). Zulu king calls for peace. *Electronic Mail and Guardian*. Available: http://www.mg.co.za/mg/news/96may/25sep-pastnews.html

Anonymous. (1996b, September 24). Leader: What is heritage? *The Star*. Available: http://www2.inc.co.za/Archives/9610/07/lead2409.html

Anonymous. (1997a, October). The rainbow notion is great, but the nation needs more. *Cape Argus*. Available: http://www2.inc.co.za/Archives/1997/9710/24/rain.html

Anonymous. (1997b, May 23). Rainbow nation is a myth, survey finds. *Saturday Star*. Available: http://www2.inc.co.za/Archives/1997/9705/27/marki.html

Anonymous. (1997c, February). Race and identity behind protests. *The Star*. Available: http://www2.inc.co.za/Archives/1997/9702/15%20Feb/mala1.html

Anonymous. (1997d, April 28). Hundreds phone in: Special report sparks rainbow of responses. *Cape Times*. Available: http://www2.inc.co.za/Archives/1997/9705/20/pollop.html

Anonymous. (1997e, July). *Nation-formation and nation building: The national question in South Africa*. Paper presented at the 50th National Conference of ANC, Mafikeng. Available: http://www.anc.org.za/ancdocs/discussion/nation.html

Anonymous. (1997f, September 24). Today's leading stories—24 September. *The Star*. Available: http://www2.inc.co.za/Archives/1997/9710/2/le1.html

Anonymous. (1997g, September 29). Can anyone tell me whose heritage we are talking about? *Cape Times*. Available: www2.inc.co.za/Archives/1997/9709/29/loph.html

Anonymous. (1998a, September 24). Butterworth bash. *Dispatch Online*. Available: http://www.dispatch.co.za/1998/09/24/entertainment/butterwo.htm

Anonymous. (1998b, September 24). Cultural pride. *Dispatch Online*. Available: http://www.dispatch.co.za/1998/09/24/easterncape/apride.htm

Anonymous. (1998c, June 27). SA's milestone days are ignored. *The Star*. Available: http://www2.inc.co.za/Archives/1998/9806/27/19lead2.html

Anonymous. (1999, September 24). Colourful parade marks Heritage Day. *Independent Online*. Available: http://www.iol.co.za

Bhabha, H. K. (1990). Introduction: Narrating the nation. In H. K. Bhabha (Ed.), *Nation and narration,* 1–7. London: Routledge.

Brennan, T. (1990). The national longing for form. In H. K. Bhabha (Ed.), *Nation and narration*, 44–70. London: Routledge.

Brink, A. (1998). Stories of history: Reimagining the past in post-apartheid narrative. In S. Nuttall and C. Coetzee (Eds.), *Negotiating the past: The making of memory in South Africa*, 29–42. Cape Town: Oxford University Press.

Brown, B., Phosa, P., and Masipa, M. (1996, September 25). Heritage Day marked by culture and rallies. *The Star*. Available: http://www2.inc.co.za/Archives/1996/9609/27/herage.html

Bunsee, B. (1997, October 21). Our story becomes a history junket. *Cape Times*. Available: http://www2.inc.co.za/Archives/1997/9710/21/naom.html

Calpin, G. H. (1941). *There are no South Africans*. London: Nelson.

Chatterjee, P. (1993). *The nation and its fragments: Colonial and postcolonial histories*. Princeton, NJ: Princeton University Press.

Christopher, A. J. (1995). Post-apartheid South Africa and the nation-state. In A. Lemon (Ed.), *The geography of change in South Africa*, 3–17. London: Routledge.

Correspondent. (1996, October 4). Peace reigns at Shaka Day celebrations. *The Star*. Available: http://www2.inc.co.za/Archives/1996/9610/04/zlu.html

Davis, G. (1995, August 25). In search of the Great Gariep. *Weekly Mail and Guardian*. Available: wysiwyg://45/http://web.sn.apc.org/wmail/issues/950825/wm950825-22.html

DDR. (1998a, September 23). Heritage Day for senior citizens. *Dispatch Online*. Available: http://www.dispatch.co.za/ddisp/1998/09/23/easterncape/heritage.htm

DDR. (1998b, September 22). Heritage Day features cultural smorgasbord. *Dispatch Online*. Available: http://www.dispatch.co.za/ddisp/1998/09/22/easterncape/day.htm

DDR. (1998c, September 22). Diverse cultures "to forge identity." *Dispatch Online*. Available: http://www.dispatch.co.za/ddisp/1998/09/22/easterncape/identity.htm

DDR. (1998d, September 25). Cultural preservation essential says Nazo. *Dispatch Online*. Available: http://www.dispatch.co.za/ddisp/1998/09/25/easterncape/cultural.htm

DDR. (1998e, September 22). Dispossessed remembered. *Dispatch Online*. Available: http://www.dispatch.co.za/ddisp/1998/09/22/easterncape/disposse.htm

DDR. (1998f, September 24). Sterkspruit to celebrate Heritage Day. *Dispatch Online*. Available: http://www.dispatch.co.za/1998/09/24/easterncape/celebrat.htm

DDR. (1999, September 24). Parades, games to mark Heritage Day. *Dispatch Online*. Available: http://www.dispatch.co.za/1999/09/24/southafrica/day.htm

Deacon, H. (1998). Remembering tragedy, constructing modernity: Robben Island as a national monument. In S. Nuttall and C. Coetzee (Eds.), *Negotiating the past: The making of memory in South Africa*, 161–79. Cape Town: Oxford University Press.

Degenaar, J. (1995, May 9). Multi-kulturele SA moet nie 'n nasie probeer bou nie [Multicultural South Africa must not try to build a nation]. *Die Burger*. Available: http://www.naspers.com/cgi/nph-bwcgis/BURGER/burger/alg/storie/DDW?W%3DOSKRIF%20PH%20IS%20%27multikulturele%20SA%20moet%20nie%27%26M%3D1%26K%3D662796%26R%3DY%26U%3D1

Dlamini, J. (1997, September 25). Robben Island council set up. *Business Day Online*. Available: http://www.bday.co.za/archive/97.html

Duffy, A., and Edmunds, M. (1997, September 26). Heritage bash cost R1-million. *Weekly Mail and Guardian*. Available: wysiwyg://38/http://web.sn.apc.org/wmail/issues/970926/NEWS1.html. Also can be found at http://www.mg.co.za/mg/news/97sep2/26sep-heritage.html

E.D. (1990, March 1). 'n Prikkelende bydrae tot debat oor SA se toekoms [A stimulating contribution to debate over South African's future]. *Die Burger*. Available: http://www.naspers.com/cgi/nphbwcgis/BURGER/burger/alg/storie/DDW?W%3DOPSKRIF%20PH%20IS%20%27Prikkelende%20bydrae%20tot%20debat%27%26M%3D1%26K%3D78365%26R%3DY%26U%3D1

East London's Online Calendar—Public Holidays. Accessed April 29, 1999. Available: http://www.eastlondonsa.com/ddcal/public.html

ECN. (1997 August 15). Steve Biko's house to be national monument. *Cape Argus*. Available: http://www2.inc.co.za/Archives/1997/9708/15/iko.html

Editorial Opinion. (1998, September 29). Heritages. *Dispatch Online*. Available: http://www.dispatch.co.za/ddisp/1998/09/29/editoria/aopinion.htm

Filotova, I. (1994). The awkward issue: Some comments on the South African debate on nation-building and ethnicity. In N. Rhoodie and I. Liebenberg (Eds.), *Democratic nation-building in South Africa*, 52–59. Pretoria: HSRC.

Friedman, R. (1997, September 27). Launching the Robben Island Museum. *Cape Times*. Available: http://www2.inc.co.za/Archives/1997/9709/27/cul.html

Giliomee, H. (1991). Nation-building in a post-apartheid society. In W. S. Vorster (Ed.), *Building a new nation: The quest for a new South Africa*, 30–50. Pretoria: University of South Africa.

Giliomee, H. (1997, April 3). We are not simply one "we" in SA. *Cape Times*. Available: http://www2.inc.co.za/Archives/1997/9704/Apr%2007/giliomee.html

Giliomee, H., and Schlemmer, L. (Eds.). (1989a). *Negotiating South Africa's future*. Johannesburg: Southern Book.

Giliomee, H., and Schlemmer, L. (1989b). *From apartheid to nation-building*. Cape Town: Oxford University Press.

Golan, D. (1991). Inkatha and its use of the Zulu past. *History in Africa, 18.* 113–26.

Golan, D. (1994). *Inventing Shaka: Using history in the construction of Zulu nationalism.* Boulder, CO: Rienner.

Greenstein, R. (1995). *Genealogies of conflict: Class, identity, and state in Palestine/Israel and South Africa.* London: Wesleyan University Press.

Greenstein, R. (1998). Identity, race, history: South Africa and the pan-African context. In R. Greenstein (Ed.), *Comparative perspectives on South Africa,* 1–32. New York: St. Martin's Press.

Grundlingh, A. M. (1991). Nation-building and history in South Africa: Probing the pitfalls and prospects. In W. S. Vorster (Ed.), *Building a new nation: The quest for a new South Africa,* 15–29. Pretoria: University of South Africa.

Hall, M. (1998). Stories of history: Reimagining the past in post-apartheid narrative. In S. Nuttall and C. Coetzee (Eds.), *Negotiating the past: The making of memory in South Africa,* 180–200. Cape Town: Oxford University Press.

Hamilton, C. (1998). *Terrific majesty: The powers of Shaka Zulu and the limits of historical invention.* Cape Town: Philip.

Hasian, M. Jr., and Frank, R. (1999). Rhetoric, history, and collective memory: Decoding the Goldhagen debates. *Western Journal of Communication, 63*(1), 95–114.

Heritage South Africa. Accessed April 29, 1999. Available: http://www.heritage.org.za/hsa1.htm

Hlongwa, W. (1997, September 26). A royal row over Shaka Day. *Mail and Guardian.* Available: http://www.mg.co.za/mg/news/97sep2/26sep-shaka.html

Hobsbawm, E. J. (1990). *Nations and nationalism since 1870: Programme, myth, reality.* Cambridge, UK: Cambridge University Press.

Hutchinson, J., and Smith, A. D. (1994). Introduction. In J. Hutchinson and A. D. Smith (Eds.), *Nationalism,* 3–13. Oxford, UK: Oxford University Press.

Jordan, B. (1997, September 28). Picking up hope from the broken pieces of the past. *Sunday Times.* Available: http://www.saep.org/forDB/CHdistsixST971128.html

Jordan, P. (1988). The South African liberation movement and the making of a new nation. In M. van Diepen (Ed.), *The national question in South Africa,* 110–24. London: Zed Books.

Kakaza, P. (1998, October 2). Finding the culture of the kraal. *Weekly Mail and Guardian.* Available: wysiwyg://49/http://web.sn.apc.org/wmail/issues/981002/ARTS55.html

Louw, E. (1998). "Diversity" versus "National Unity": The struggle between moderns, premoderns, and postmoderns in contemporary South Africa. In D. V. Tanno and A. González (Eds.), *Communication and identity across cultures,* 148–74. Thousand Oaks, CA: Sage.

Makhanya, M. (1996a, October 25). Unique show of unity as all parties honour Shaka. *The Star.* Available: http://www2.inc.co.za/Archives/1996/9610/25/shakas.html

Makhanya, M. (1996b, September 21). Composer's grave to be declared a monument. *The Star.* Available: http://www2.inc.co.za/Archives/1996/9609/21/heris.html

Malan, C. (1994). Symbolic unity: The role of cultural symbols in nation-building. In N. Rhoodie and I. Liebenberg (Eds.), *Democratic nation-building in South Africa,* 182–89. Pretoria: HSRC.

Mandela, N. (1996, September 23). *Speech by President Mandela at the unveiling of the monument to Enoch Sontonga on Heritage Day.* Johannesburg, South Africa. Available: gopher://gopher.anc.org.za:70/00/govdocs/speeches/1996/sp0923.01

Mandela, N. (1997, September 24). *Address by President Mandela on Heritage Day*. Robben Island. Available: http://www.anc.org.za/ancdocs/history/mandela/1997/sp0924a.html

Marks, S., and Trapido, S. (1987). The politics of race, class and nationalism. In S. Marks and S. Trapido (Eds), *The politics of race, class and nationalism in twentieth century South Africa*, 1–70. New York: Longman.

Mathieson, S., and Attwell, D. (1998). Between ethnicity and nationhood: Shaka Day and the struggle over Zuluness in post-apartheid South Africa. In D. Bennett (Ed.), *Multicultural states: Rethinking difference and identity*, 111–24. London: Routledge.

Mattes, R. (1995). *The election book: Judgement and choice in South Africa's 1994 election*. Cape Town: Institute for Democracy in South Africa (IDASA) Public Information Centre.

Mattes, R. (1997a, July 14). The meaning of national identity. *Cape Times*. Available: http://www2.inc.co.za/Archives/1997/9708/1/matters1407.html

Mattes, R. (1997b, March 27). No lack in sense of "we-ness," nationhood. *Cape Times*. Available: http://www2.inc.co.za/Archives/1997/9704/Apr%2009/attes.html

Mda, L. (1997, December 23). Has the rainbow faded forever? *Mail and Guardian*. Available: http://web.sn.apc.org/wmail/issues/971223/NEWS19.html

Mellin, R. (1997, September 25). *Dispatch Online* [Heritage Day pictures]. Available: http://www.dispatch.co.za/1997/09/25/page%2010.htm

Minkley, G., and Rassool, C. (1998). Orality, memory, and social history in South Africa. In S. Nuttall and C. Coetzee (Eds.), *Negotiating the past: The making of memory in South Africa*, 89–99. Cape Town: Oxford University Press.

Mlangeni, B. (1996, September 24). High notes for composer of Nkosi' hymn. *The Star*. Available: http://www2.inc.co.za/Archives/1996/9610/07/santa.html

Mpondwana, Z. (1998, September 25). Tree-planting marks Macleantown Heritage Day. *Dispatch Online*. Available: http://www.dispatch.co.za/ddisp/1998/09/25/easterncape/herit.htm

Mxotwa, T. (1998, September 28). Politico clings to British heritage. *Dispatch Online*. Available: [http://www.dispatch.co.za/ddisp/1998/09/28/editorial/lp.htm

Nairn, T. (1994). The maladies of development. In J. Hutchinson and A. D. Smith (Eds.), *Nationalism*, 70–76. Oxford, UK: Oxford University Press. (Originally published in 1977)

Ngani, P. (1998, September 22). Contralesa hails noted liberators in history. *Dispatch Online*. Available: http://www.dispatch.co.za/ddisp/1998/09/22/easterncape/history.htm

Nuttall, S. (1998). Telling "free" stories? Memory and democracy in South African autobiography since 1994. In S. Nuttall and C. Coetzee (Eds.), *Negotiating the past: The making of memory in South Africa*, 75–88. Cape Town: Oxford University Press.

Nuttall, S., and Coetzee, C. (Eds.). (1998). *Negotiating the past: The making of memory in South Africa*. Cape Town: Oxford University Press.

O'Malley, K. (1994). A neglected dimension of nation-building in South Africa: The ethnic factor. In N. Rhoodie and I. Liebenberg (Eds.), *Democratic nation-building in South Africa*, 77–88. Pretoria: HSRC.

Ono, K. A. (1998). Problematizing "nation" in intercultural communication research. In D. V. Tanno and A. González (Eds.), *Communication and identity across cultures*, 193–202. Thousand Oaks, CA: Sage.

Patten, J. (1998). Public holidays still a problem. *Cape Times*. Available: http://www2.inc.co.za/Archives/1998/9807/13/media1906.html

Political Reporter. (1997, September 11). Big celebrations to salute Steve Biko 20 years on. *The Star*. Available: http://www2.inc.co.za/Archives/1997/9709/11/ram.html

Public Holidays Act, 1994. Act of Parliament No. 36 of 1994. (1994, December 7). Available: http://www.polity.org.za/govdocs/legislation/1994/act94-036.html

Randall, E. (1998, August 13). Parliament tries to figure out the sum of South Africa's parts. *Saturday Argus*. Available: http://www2.inc.co.za/Archives/1998/9808/13/herit.html

Renan, E. (1990). What is a nation? (M. Thom, Trans.). In H. K. Bhabha (Ed.), *Nation and narration*, 8–22. London: Routledge. (Originally published in 1882)

Reuters. (1998, April 24). Mandela warns of cracks in S[outh] African society. *The Star*. Available: http://www2.inc.co.za/Archives/1998/9804/24/mandy.html

Robins, S. (1997). Rainbow nation: Is it a myth or reality? *Cape Times*. Available: http://www2.inc.co.za/Archives/1997/9705/2/robins.html

Robins, S. (1998). Silence in my father's house: Memory, nationalism, and narratives of the body. In S. Nuttall and C. Coetzee (Eds.), *Negotiating the past: The making of memory in South Africa*, 120–40. Cape Town: Oxford University Press.

Roefs, M. (1997, April 15). An "outsider" adds to the "we-ness" debate. *Cape Times*. Available: http://www2.inc.co.za/Archives/1997/9704/Apr%2017/roefs.html

Salgado, I. (1996, September 24). Mandela eulogises Enoch Sontonga. *Business Day Online*. Available: http://www.bday.co.za/archive/96.html

Sapa. (1996, September 23). Mandela eulogises Sontonga. *Cape Times*. Available: http://www2.inc.co.za/archives/1996/9610/08/herile.html

Sapa. (1998a, September 19). Got any rock art sites in your back garden. *Dispatch Online*. Available: http://www.dispatch.co.za/ddisp/1998/09/19/southafrica/garden.htm

Sapa. (1998b, September 28). King urges Zulus to lead renewal. *Dispatch Online*. Available. http://www.dispatch.co.za/ddisp/1998/09/28/foreign/renewal.htm

Schreuder, D. (1994). The power of colonial nationalism in shaping post-colonial South Africa. In P. B. Rich (Ed.), *The dynamics of change in Southern Africa*, 52–70. New York: St. Martin's Press.

Schuster, L. (1997). *Gautvol in paradise* [Album]. Johannesburg: EMI Music SA.

Seton-Watson, H. (1977). *Nations and states: An enquiry into the origins of nations and the politics of nationalism*. Boulder, CO: Westview Press.

Sharp, J. (1988). Ethnic group and nation: The apartheid vision in South Africa. In E. Boonzaier and J. Sharp (Eds.), *South African keywords: The uses and abuses of political concepts*, 79–99. Cape Town: Philip.

Sharp, J. (1997). Beyond exposé analysis: Hybridity, social memory and identity politics. *Journal of Contemporary African Studies*, 15(1), 7–21.

Simpson, M. (1994). The experience of nation building: Some lessons for South Africa. *Journal of Southern African Studies*, 20(3), 463–74.

Sizwe, N. (1979). *One Azania, one nation: The national question in South Africa*. London: Zed Books.

Spiegel, A., and Boonzaier, E. (1988). Promoting tradition: Images of the South African past. In E. Boonzaier and J. Sharp (Eds.), *South African keywords: The uses and abuses of political concepts*, 40–57. Cape Town: Philip.

Thaver, B. (1996, December 5). Inclusion in SA is part of coloured identity. *Cape Times*. Available: http://www2.inc.co.za/Archives/1996/9612/05/id.html

Thornton, R. (1996). The potentials of boundaries in South Africa: Steps towards a theory of the social edge. In R. Werbner and T. Ranger (Eds.), *Postcolonial identities in Africa*, 136–61. London: Zed Books.

van Diepen, M. (Ed.). (1988). *The national question in South Africa.* London: Zed Books.

van Rooyen, J. (1994). Forces inhibiting the making of a South African nation. In N. Rhoodie and I. Liebenberg (Eds.), *Democratic nation-building in South Africa*, 205–12. Pretoria: HSRC.

Walker, G. (1996). *Enoch Mankayi Sontonga.* South African Government of National Unity Web site: http://www.polity.org.za/people/sontonga.html

Welsh, D. (1991). Can South Africa become a nation-state? In D. J. van Vuuren, N. E. Wiehahn, N. J. Rhoodie, and M. Wiechers (Eds.), *South Africa in the nineties*, 551–68. Pretoria: HSRC.

Zifo, M. (1998, September 10). Heritage Day fest for B'worth. *Dispatch Online.* Available: http://www.dispatch.co.za/ddisp/1998/09/10/easterncape/heritage.htm

SPAIN

National Days throughout the History and the Geography of Spain

Ignacio Molina A. de Cienfuegos and
Jorge Martínez Bárcena

THE INTRICATE SPANISH NATIONAL IDENTITY AND ITS SYMBOLS

Spain is one of the few countries in the industrialized and democratic world—perhaps together with Japan—where most of its inhabitants associate their official national symbols with a political regime that is largely and even formally reviled. The links between Franco's conservative dictatorship (1939–75) and Spain's national day, flag, or anthem have created an extremely particular state of mind as regards their use or celebration, still surviving after 25 years of democracy. This association between the recent authoritarian past and Spanish symbols is politically subjective, rather than historically objective. It is true that the Constitution of 1978 did not abolish "Hispanity" Day—the name the celebration was known by at the time—as did neither the flag nor the anthem, which were used during the military regime. October 12, commemorating the Spanish transatlantic endeavor known as the "Discovery of America," had been commemorated in the 19th century. Franco did not invent either the two-colored flag or the "Royal March" because, although they had been replaced during the democratic period of the Second Republic (1931–39), they actually date back to the reign of Charles III in the 18th century, one of the few periods of Spanish history that enjoys a general positive judgment. Besides, the origin of these symbols does not withstand a great nationalist burden, as happens in other countries.[1] Anyway, 40 years of Franco's stigmatization have been stronger than a likely traditional and apolitical nature of the historic events and images linked with the idea of Spain.

The fact that current national symbols are unable to mobilize and integrate Spaniards cannot be solely explained by a split between authoritarian conservatism and democratic liberalism. Besides the historical cleavage confronting different ideological conceptions about the country—and turning eventually the common symbols as right wing—political tensions provoked by geographical pluralism must also be taken into consideration. This approach refers to the opposition between those considering Spain as a nation-state and peripheral nationalists who deny such national character, reacting against the excessive, and at the same time inefficient, association between the political and the geographical center of Castile. This second source of disaffection with the symbols of national identity is more usual in other politically and economically developed countries, such as Canada or Belgium, that also face ethnoterritorial conflicts. What makes the Spanish case particularly complex and interesting is the confluence of both kinds of political tensions, ideological and territorial, toward the nation and its official symbols.

This chapter examines the difficult relationship between Spaniards and their symbols, focusing particularly on national festivities. The aforementioned peculiarities of the Spanish case led us to carry out a historical and geographical analysis including, on the one hand, the origin and evolution of not only the October 12 commemoration but also other commemorations promoted by the political center—although some of them, strongly associated with the specific ideology of past regimes, are not commemorated today. On the other hand, it is necessary to consider the territorial diversity of Spain, nowadays divided into 17 autonomous regions, with a federal-like self-government, paying special attention to recently established regional official festivities. To make this study more complicated, we must consider the *changing* and *heterogeneous* ways in which both political dimensions—progressivism versus conservatism and center versus periphery—have been combined: (1) Changing because, up to the end of the 19th century, peripheral protonationalisms tried to defend the privileges and charters of the ancien régime as opposed to the modernizing centralism. However, from then on, the Spanish liberal nationalism was increasingly substituted by a rather conservative standardizing approach linked to military governments that denied rights to everyone. Therefore, liberal and left-wing democrats started to become sympathetic to federalism and, sometimes, to political movements of local assertion in, for example, Catalonia or the Basque Region. (2) Heterogeneous because, whereas a solid—and persistently hostile to the center—nationalism has emerged in these two regions, in some other peripheral parts of Spain regionalisms arose that only oppose a uniform and authoritarian conception of Spain, if not the decentralized and democratic country in which it was transformed during the 1970s. We will analyze, from a historical and geographical point of view, how these complex combinations have given visible form in the commemoration of national days in Spain.

THE HISTORICAL DIMENSIONS OF NATIONAL DAYS IN SPAIN

This first section of the chapter deals with the evolution of the national identification feeling of Spaniards with their country, influenced by the use and manipulation of past experiences by political and social powers. All through history, public authorities and cultural elites have tried to impose, regardless of their degrees of success, different national days that should be ardently observed every year by everybody. Depending on the event to commemorate, a different political trend will be favored, aiming at either the symbolic integration of all inhabitants into their country or the identification of just those professing a certain ideology. As mentioned earlier, this also means a certain understanding of the ethnoterritorial diversity of the whole country.

The first legends emerged in the Middle Ages in the northern Christian areas of an Iberian Peninsula mostly dominated by Muslims since the 8th century (see map). The inhabitants of these north territories, who consider themselves to be descendants of Roman-Visigoths, embarked on what they called the "Reconquest" of the ancient Roman Hispania. During that military campaign that lasted more than seven centuries, although with long periods of truce, it is said that Christian warriors, while fighting against Muslims, were miraculously helped by saints who had died many centuries ago. The supposed incursion of ghosts with cuirasses, swords, and a name (St. James, St. George) allowed them to build the symbols of each kingdom. A certain day was established to celebrate those myths, according to the calendar of saints' fetes established by the church, in order to keep religious spirit alive. At the beginning, they were not national days, but Christian feasts. Late in the 19th century, with the appearance in Spain of a real modern nationalism, such feasts would become a perfect material for symbolizing patriotic exaltation.

Between the 15th and the 16th centuries, several important events took place giving birth, now and not before, to Spain. The wedding of Isabella of Castile and Ferdinand of Aragon (the Catholic monarchs) in 1469 would be the basis for the unification of the two most powerful peninsular kingdoms, the resulting entity taking advantage of the incorporation of the Canary Islands and Navarre. Besides, it managed to assert its preeminence over Portugal or France and, above all, it terminated the Christian Reconquest with the occupation of Granada in 1492, the last Muslim bastion. On October 12 of that year, Columbus landed in America and, on behalf of both monarchs, he started the continent's reconnaissance and conquest. Despite the prominent role of Castile in such an adventure, this would be a key event to reinforce, even retrospectively, the incipient unity of the new state. The overseas empire would be the best complement to hegemony in Europe, and both parallel processes finally consolidated the embryonic Hispanic monarchy. There was no doubt about the real and symbolic significance of such a date, even though it was institutionalized much later.

In fact, Catholic religion, not patriotic motivations, would continue to impose festivities during the following three centuries. For example, the Cortes, the parliament of the absolutist regime, worshipped the Immaculate Conception in 1760. The contemporary idea of nation would not come into being until the 19th century, when real popular demonstrations started to take place. A good example is the uprising of May 2, 1808, when Madrid's inhabitants rose

CAPITAL LETTERS	: The four Christian kingdoms in the Iberian Middle Ages (Portugal, Castile, Navarre and Aragon).
UNDERLINED/Underlined	: The five founding kingdoms in the Spanish Coat of Arms (Castile, Leon, Aragon, Navarre and Granada).
CAPITAL LETTERS	: The current Autonomous Regions.
———————➤	: Road to Santiago.
	: Crown of Castille in 1512.
― ― ― ― ― ― ―	: Evolution of borders between Islam and Christian Kingdoms throughout different centuries.

CANARY ISLANDS and cities of Ceuta and Melilla (Northern Africa) not showed up in arms to repel Napoléon's occupation. Although there was not a national-ist motivation in those days, since promoters tried to protect tradition and Catholicism, such a date would start to be remembered some years later as a symbol of heroism. Late in the century, mass nationalization would be more ob-vious; however, the turbulent alternation of long periods of conservative constitutionalism and short democratic periods—according to the European and 19th-century meaning of democracy—hindered the consolidation of real national days. As constitutions or constitutional projects were passed and abol-ished (up to 10 times between 1808 and 1876), national days changed during the century.

Early in the 20th century, the split between the "two Spains" definitively crystallized, and the long process of radicalization of both conceptions about the nation—the conservative and centralist one versus the progressive and fed-eralizing one—came to an end. The monarchy, unable to coexist with a real liberal parliamentarianism, led to an ephemeral republican period in 1931, with its own symbolic paraphernalia. In that occasion, the substitution of symbols not only affected the national day or some part of the shield, as used to happen in the 19th century, but also, the flag and the anthem, identifiable in those days with the monarchs' conservatism and the military intervention in Spanish pol-itics, were altered.

This progressive and widespread manipulation of symbols reached its peak in 1936, when the left-wing government suffered a coup d'état promoted by the most conservative sector of the armed forces, significantly self-labeled as the "Na-tional" army. The choice of such a name was not trivial, and the 40 years of dictatorship that followed the Spanish Civil War marked the end of the process, ini-tiated in the previous century, of identifying the Spanish nation with centralist authoritarianism. As expected, the Republican official aesthetics was fully altered in 1939 by the victorious General Franco whose regime, originally based on an ide-ological combination of fascism and historical traditionalism, adopted an eclectic rhetoric. Several symbols were invented and, at the same time, the ancient monar-chical ones were restored, being thus condemned to an (almost) definitive stigmatization (Fusi 2000, 30). With the restoration of the Bourbon dynasty and the subsequent transition to democracy (1975–81), the purely Francoist symbolic attributes, such as the shield or some songs and emblematic dates, were abolished. On the contrary, those elements that were previous to the dictatorship, such as the flag, the anthem, or October 12, remained alive.

Nowadays, together with the new Constitution Day (December 6), these are the national symbols in force. Many Spaniards politically identified with the Left or, above all, with the peripheral regions where they live, hardly accept these sym-bols as their own. After all, these official emblems are different from those of the Second Republic, they had been used by General Franco; and in any case, they per-sonify Spain, a concept considered by a large amount of the population as conservative and centralist in itself.

The Christian Reconquest of the Iberian Peninsula: St. James and St. George

In Roman times, the concept of "Hispania" as a unitary entity was already in use and, after the Barbarian invasions, the christianized Visigoths again reunified the peninsula, both politically and religiously. Some nationalist excesses, mostly focused on geography, date back to those ancient times in establishing the foundation of Spain; however, even traditional approaches prefer to point toward the Reconquest. A very long process started shortly after the Arabs and African Berbers conquered almost all the territories of the peninsula (711–720). Northern Christian redoubts managed to contain the Muslims, who were slowly obliged to withdraw until they were finally defeated in 1492, the date traditionally considered as the real origin of Spain.

One of the first sources of resistance, located in Asturias, soon dominated the northwest of the peninsula. Later known as the Kingdom of Leon and, although it was unable to avoid the split of Portugal, it later became the powerful Crown of Castile, which wanted to lead the Reconquest adventure. Its will of hegemony among Iberian Christianity was counterbalanced, however, by the existence of other kingdoms in the Pyrenees. Thus, from the present Basque Region to the north of Catalonia, several Christian communities emerged that were incorporated into either the Kingdom of Navarre or the Crown of Aragon. From the 12th century on, the north of the peninsula was therefore divided into four kingdoms (see map) with different languages, institutions, and markets but also with a powerful religious and geographical shared objective: to expel Islam from the peninsula.

Early in the 16th century, once the Reconquest had finished, only three of the four kingdoms came together. This can be interpreted as a sign of the incidental origin of Spain or as the relative predetermination of the peninsula to merge into a single state—with Portugal, annexed to Spain shortly after but fully independent since the mid-17th century, an exception. The Spanish nationalism re-created the second interpretation and, obviously, the Portuguese contribution to the Reconquest was forgotten. On the contrary, special attention was paid to the two other important crowns: Aragon, which is the origin of four of the present 17 autonomous regions, and Castile, above all, the basis of the other 12 autonomous regions—or 13 including Navarre, whose ancient and small kingdom was incorporated into Castile in 1512, although respecting its charters and being considered as a formal cofounder of the Hispanic monarchy.

In Castile, in which in the Galician section it is said that the apostle Saint James is buried, is found one of the first antecedents of a protonational feast. There, during the 11th and the 12th centuries, the French monastic movement of Cluny claimed the authenticity of the tomb, to control their own pilgrimage spot far from papal Rome: the Road to Santiago de Compostela (see map). The successful worship of St. James, coinciding with the Crusades, would encourage a new spirit of holy war as a Christian offensive against the Muslim south. The saint, dead from the 1st century, reappeared 1,000 years later not like a peaceful Galilean fisherman but like a "moors-killer" and the symbol of Castilian Reconquest (Álvarez Junco 2001, 41–44). The legend also triumphed in Navarre and Aragon, the two accesses to the Road to Santiago from France, and St. James was subsequently chosen as Spain's patron saint. Such festivity, commemorated on July 25, loses part of its functionality after the end of the Reconquest.[2] Still, other days more related with a modern nationalism would substitute St. James as a patriotic festivity. Although July 25 continued to be always commemorated, nowadays it has become advisable to reduce the holiday's official nature, due to the exploitation of this symbol by Franco and maybe due to its anti-Muslim political incorrectness. In most regions of Spain, it is now a working day, and even the king, who should make a traditional offering to the saint, delegates his duty as head of state to a representative. Curiously, as the apostle reduces his Spanishness, a peripheral nationalism takes advantage of such a situation to remember the Galician spirit of Santiago de Compostela. Based on popular devotion and the links of the saint with Galician regionalism in the last century, Saint James has become today the official Day of Galicia, one of the autonomous regions with their own language.

St. James also has close links with the Aragonese and Catalan sections of the old Crown of Aragon. However, devotion to the increasingly Castilian St. James was shared there with devotion to a patron of their own: Saint George. There is no doubt that there is a parallel between both saints: both emerged as celestial knights in the Reconquest battles and, despite embodying patriotic essences, they came from Asia, one of the most remote areas of the world known in those days. Fervor for St. George of Capadocia spread all over Europe in the Middle Ages; for example, in England, thanks to the legend of his fight against a dragon and the description of his martyrdom, he was religiously commemorated on April 23. Assuming that he really existed, the saint-knight could not have close links with Aragon, but the legend arrived there in the 11th century and later became a festivity. St. George has also been Catalans' patron saint since the 17th century, acquiring a strong regionalist burden two centuries later, thanks to the cultural movement of the Renaixença, which was looking for an emblematic date. Moreover, on April 23, a Catalan bourgeois tradition—the exchange by couples of books with roses—was born, surreptitiously implying a specific territorial identity, different from that of Spain. The rather literary than political nature of such festivity was doubly useful, since it outlined the importance of Catalan language and culture and reduced the possibilities of repression from the central government. As Llobera (1996, 199) has suggested, the nature of such a date (popular, universalist, present oriented, and civic) was opposed to the values that Catalan nationalists preferred to underline (heroic, particularist, past oriented, and ethnic) during the 1970s and therefore, as we will discuss, was not chosen as the official day of the autonomous region. St. George is still commemorated in Catalonia, although it is a working day coinciding with Cervantes's anniversary and the Book's Day all over Spain. On the contrary, just after being granted self-government in 1983, the neighbor region of

Aragon brought the medieval festivity back in as the Day of Aragon. The commemoration, now with a regionalist flavor, thus tries to connect the new autonomous government with a symbol of the ancient homonymous crown.

Territorial Unification and Arrival in America: Spain Emerges (October 12)

Given the historic and symbolic significance of the Reconquest, it was expected that historians in the 19th century adopted its end (1492) to commemorate the nation's birthday. When Isabella of Castile and Ferdinand of Aragon married, there were still four different kingdoms east of Portugal, one of them being a Muslim. However, the Catholic monarchs, during their reign between the 15th and the 16th centuries, managed to end up dominating a single and powerful state whose boundaries were strikingly similar to those of contemporary Spain. In any case, the symbolic holiday chosen would not commemorate either the unification of both crowns or the end of the Reconquest, but, instead, the territorial spread that immediately followed it. Historians eventually resolved that Spain emerged on October 12, 1492, in the Caribbean, which is the most representative date to commemorate the country's spreading to Europe and America.

The commemoration of the arrival of Columbus's ships to America allowed idealization of the most influential and universal period in Spain's history. This also allowed the most conservative and centralist sectors of society to remember the past, evangelizing imperialism and emphasizing the role of Castile, as opposed to that of Aragon that scarcely took part in such a venture. It was Menéndez Pelayo who, by means of the journal *Raza*, developed late in the 19th century, when Spain lost its overseas empire, the nationalist and Catholic version of what became known as Hispanity Day. He spread this name, adopted by the Right in the 20th century, to overwhelm the more cosmopolitan view of October 12 adopted by progressive liberal circles (Santoveña 1994).[3] In any case, the official commemoration of October 12 was established much later, showing the weak development of Spanish nationalism and its subordination to Catholicism. In fact, the first official calendar of annual festivities, very similar to the present one, established in 1867 that all festivities should have a religious basis, St. James being the only one who would maintain a certain patriotic nature. As late as 1892, coinciding with the 4th centennial of the discovery of America, Hispanity Day was finally created. According to Serrano (1999), the 3rd centennial was not commemorated, but "a century later the situation has dramatically changed. The king does not hold exclusively the sovereignty and the new citizen consciousness requires a more appropriate representation of the Nation, with a civil liturgy allowing its celebration" (314).

In 1888, a liberal government initiated preparations for a public-spirited modern celebration, as opposed to the traditional Catholic feast in which saints concealed men's endeavors. But in 1892, the conservative Right was again in power and they did not pay much attention to promoting a popular ceremony that should be more politically than religiously oriented. The budget for the programmed festivities was reduced, and they became just formal ceremonies, without a massive influx of people (Serrano 1999, 314–16). Although Queen María Cristina declared October 12 a public holiday, it was not until 1918 that a law institutionalized this festivity with the ambiguous name of "Race Day." This name does not imply any attempt at ethnic supremacy; however, it acquired conservative overtones, since it was promoted by Menéndez Pelayo and was then enthusiastically defended by General Franco. Consider the coincidence of such a day with the commemoration of the Day of the Virgin of Pilar, a devotion that replaced the aforementioned copatron saints and that would remain, together with St. James, as the divine protector of the whole nation. The Civil Guard, the militarized force responsible for policing duties, also chose this virgin as its religious dedication. Interestingly, the coincidence of both festivities shows the problems faced by Spanish nationalism to appear as secular and civil. It is not only that a part of official iconography is delegated to the church, but also that the general symbols of the state become mixed with those strictly connected to public order and, hence, repression.

With Franco's dictatorship, the imperialist nostalgia and official Catholicism helped underline the military and religious connotations of October 12. Only with the recent democratization has its conservative slant started to be removed, and somewhat antiquated terms such as *race* or even *Hispanity* have been replaced by cosmopolitan terms, without ideological overtones. Considering the fulfillment of these premises, the successive democratic governments have expected that reluctance to this commemoration would start to be removed. In the end, it is the most important event in Spain's history, with repercussions all over the world. Furthermore, celebrating the discovery of America helped underline that, despite all the problems faced by Spaniards in the historical meantime, that the country had positively started and finished a cycle of 500 years. In 1987, after having spent 10 years wondering whether Constitution Day might perhaps be a most appropriate national holiday, democratic authorities determined that the best option was the somewhat more popular and remote October 12. After all, there were too many precedents during the 19th and the 20th centuries of rootless national holidays just linked with a specific event, normally violent, or a certain political regime, normally short-lived.

Spanish Nationalist Feasts during the 19th Century

It is possible to argue that there has existed a Spanish state since 1492, but it is very difficult to admit that there was a Spanish nation before the 19th century.[4] Only when the masses entered into history, coinciding with bourgeois revolutions and the beginning of the so-called Contemporary Age, were nationalist movements developed; in case they were successful, nations would appear. In Spain, the nationalist ideology and movement appeared a bit later but, emulating other European cases, soon created its own symbols and official commemorations. Inversely to the ancient régime, in which public matters were just related with religion, the crown, and traditional laws, it was necessary to re-create the existence of the nation itself as a new subject that would be the basis of the state sovereignty. New symbols emerged with the aim of being applied to all Spaniards, who should have to become citizens. As a national festivity, it was decided to commemorate a recent event that could be easily remembered; moreover, in order to include as many Spaniards as possible, such events provide for a common enemy that comes from abroad. Hence, in the first half of the 19th century, the festivity of May 2 emerged, commemorating resistance in the streets of Madrid in 1808 to Napoléon's invasion. But soon after, and all over the century, liberal and especially conservative regimes succeeded each other at a dizzying pace. With them, constitutions and patriotic commemorations were constantly replaced, acquiring inevitable partisan overtones according to the government that promotes them. This would reach its paroxysm in the next century.

Whereas the remote October 12 was established as a festivity late in the 19th century, May 2 was the first event that tried to promote Spanish nationalism. No more than six years after this historic episode, which happened early in the century, the parliament recommended its celebration. From the beginning, it was idealized as national liberation or "independence," which was rather an anti-French xenophobic uprising, in favor of the continuity of the Bourbon dynasty (Álvarez Junco 1996, 91–93). However, this event was very important, since it marked the emergence of the masses in Spanish politics, the real seed of modern nationalism. Besides, this uprising soon spread all over Spain, leading to the appearance of a protonational identity able to mobilize the masses and even to start a guerrilla war in a territory wholly occupied by French soldiers, except in the city of Cadiz.

It was precisely there where a liberal constitution, the first in Spanish history, was drawn up, stating that "sovereignty is essentially vested in the nation," which implied the existence of a Spanish nation. Shouts of "Viva Spain" could be heard in Cadiz for the first time, whereas in the uprisings of May 2, only the traditional "Long life to the king" could be heard, together with "Death to French people" and "Death to Napoléon." From then on, the original identity based on belonging, as subjects, to the Hispanic monarchy or, as Catholics, to the common religion, would hardly start to be replaced by a Spanish national identity. This would not be fully accepted, given the weakness of a state lacking the resources required to consolidate this new collective identity. Soon, the commemoration of May 2 decreased its strength, becoming a religious worship, which

could not embody the national feeling nor become the symbol of the whole nation, as expected by the soft but triumphant liberalism. The celebration maintained some plebeian elements, markedly linked to Madrid and, for all those who supported the political model of the neighboring Republic, had a high degree of anti-French feeling. Therefore, the authorities never supported it, nor gave it the required popular luster. (Serrano 1999, 317)

During the second half of the 19th century, not many years after its introduction, this festivity was doomed to decline, showing that Spanish nationalism was not able to turn into a mass ideology. Also weak, although somewhat more socially relevant, the embryonic workers' movement started to commemorate, in 1889, May 1. Such a date was prone to re-create a symbolic confrontation between the internationalist May 1 and the patriotic May 2 (Guereña 1986).[5]

The Independence War and the festivity of May 2 not only implied the birth of a growing national feeling leading to a rejection of foreign elements. It also implies the seeds of a domestic confrontation between two conceptions of Spanish national identity, liberal-progressive versus conservative (Álvarez Junco 1996, 102), where enemies were also Spaniards. During the turbulent, often tragic, Spanish 19th century, constitutions were changed along with ephemeral festivities supposedly destined to perpetuation, although they were only maintained during a short-lived regime. Although Spanish nationalism was liberal in 1812, and again in other brief periods (1820–23, 1837–45, and 1868–74), conservatism would eventually dominate the political spectrum. Early in the 20th century, the idea and symbols of Spain were already linked with the authoritarian Right and repression. Both workers' internationalism and regionalist feelings were repressed because Spanish governments, in view of the threat of the even more reactionary Carlism (a movement claiming privileges granted by traditional charters that was particularly strong in non-Castilian rural environments), finally identified periphery with opposition. From a liberal nationalism, Jacobin but more prone to take into account the country's pluralism, Spain ended up experiencing a centralist and repressive conservatism without any capacity of ideological or territorial integration.

The "Two Spains" of the Civil War

The biggest evidence of this historic failure is the emergence of two extreme conceptions of the country. After a new attempt in the 1930s to establish a plural and nonconservative project of Spain, Civil War broke out, ending with the triumph of an alliance of the military, traditionalists, and fascists. Such radically different ideas of nation implied their own reciprocally irreconcilable symbols.

On April 14, 1931, the Republic was proclaimed in Spain. Since the two-colored flag or "Royal March" was identified with the monarchical, oligarchic, and authoritarian Spain of the previous era, there were no attempts to maintain these symbols and to remove such connotations. In turn, the Republicans' flag and anthem became the official symbols: the three-colored (red, yellow, and purple) flag, and the antiabsolutist march of General Riego. April 14 would become the national day, but it was maintained just until the new right-wing Franco regime, which triumphed in 1939, again adopted the traditional symbols. The reestablishment by military dictatorship of the red and yellow flag and the Royal March reinforced the definitive loss of their original liberal, or at least apolitical, meaning.

Besides, although October 12 had been commemorated during the Republic without an imperialistic rhetoric, Franco decided to reinforce Hispanity Day in 1940. However, it was not chosen as a national holiday, because the nationalist aesthetic developed by Franco not only recovered 19th century and Catholic symbols but also incorporated new ones. Such paraphernalia included a pretentious coat of arms or the commemoration of July 18 as the day of the "National Uprising" against the Republican government, to substitute the commemoration of April 14. Including the term *national* in the name of this festivity and the Francoist single party itself showed the desire to appropriate the patriotic feeling, without paying attention to that such date (July 18, 1936), actually meaning the beginning of a tragic civil war. To consolidate the celebration, apart from adding Catholic overtones, the regime decided to establish an extra month's salary in summer for all workers, to be paid exactly on that day.

SPAIN AND THE CONSTITUTION OF DECEMBER 6, 1978

In accordance with Franco's plans, a monarchy was reestablished in 1975. But Juan Carlos I relinquished authoritarianism and favored the recovery of democracy, the regional decentralization and the drawing up of a constitution in 1978 that was approved by referendum on December 6. From the beginning of transition, Spanish authorities were aware of the importance and sensitivity of establishing renewed national symbols. On the one hand, all citizens should be at least identified with Spain; on the other hand, since there was not a formal breaking-off between Franco's regime and the monarchy, authorities did not want to incite the army, which was still identified with dictatorship in the 1970s and self-perceived as the guardian of national symbols. Those symbols entirely connected with the Franco era, such as July 18, were quickly abolished. However, those that had been in force during previous monarchical periods, such as the flag or the anthem, remained.

No new national symbols were created, because they could be excessively identified with the new democratic regime and, taking Spanish history into consideration, that could prove to be reckless. Furthermore, a new aesthetic could be also interpreted as a snub to the notion of monarchy. In fact, authorities tried to take advantage of the synthesis of symbols offered by the parliamentary monarchy itself, an institutional combination of conservative and democratic values. Finally, traditional symbols were just reoriented through, for example, their use together with European and regional ones, the only real novelties in the official symbols of the 1980s. At the local level, great symbolic controversies appeared in relation to the substitution or maintenance of the street names and statues reminiscent of the Franco era. On the contrary, at the national level, the government continually tried to get around this issue by officially scorning in parallel the emblems invented in the 20th century by each of the two Spains. However, admitting that the change of regime led to political and socioeconomic policies that substantially transformed the country, bringing it closer to the secular and liberal goal of moderate Republicans, the supposedly neutral politics of symbols actually meant a certain acquiescence to the "national" rightists. Thus, the anachronistic Franco coat of arms was not replaced by the Bourbon one until 1981, and the humiliating Victory Day on April 1—commemorating, with a military march, the end of the civil war on that day in 1939—was only surreptitiously transformed during the 1970s into an aseptic day of the armed forces, which has been observed on a spring Sunday until a few years ago.[6]

To declare the national day, this conservative and conciliatory strategy with regard to the establishment of official symbols led to the arrangement of a compromise consisting in, on the one hand, promoting October 12 to the status of national day and recovering the ancient monarchical practice of feting the king in his saint's day; on the other, December 6 was considered a new festivity: Constitution Day. The symbol of democracy thus resulted, to some extent, being subordinated to the traditional festivity remembering the discovery of America, but it is also true that the imminent celebration of the 5th centennial (1992) was taken into account as well. In any case, and apart from the particular circumstances of the 1980s, wisdom suggested adopting the most politically neutral (that is, historically remote) symbols as possible. Maybe the historical background of constant failures in the attempts to establish symbols linked with new, and often divisive, regimes advised not to give December 6 the highest rank. It is true that consensus between all political parties in drawing up the 1978 constitution distinguished the young democracy from the previous sectarian governments. But it was precisely such consensus, with its pros and its cons, that implied this sort of decisions.

At any rate, present commemorations of the national day and Constitution Day are very similar, due to their institutional nature and the little enthusiasm they have aroused. It is true that October 12 has a conservative slant and now it even receives the new stigma of political incorrectness, associated with the controversial clash of the Western and the pre-Columbian cultures that followed to the so-called discovery. However, today, the biggest enemy of both festivities is the lax attitude of Spaniards, who do not take to the streets with flags nor attend patriotic events. Sober official receptions take place on both days and on October 12, since 2000, the Day of the Armed Forces as well. People can attend a military parade in Madrid, but attempts to distinguish those days have failed. Significantly, Spaniards know these festivities as "Pilar's long weekend," in the case of the national day, and "Immaculate's long weekend," in the case of Constitution Day—after the name of the two Catholic holidays that coincide with both patriotic feasts. The nationalist civil religion seems to have failed in Spain. Such apathy toward symbols and other objects of the Spanish political system is the result of a psychological collective process, influenced by the incidental historic events in the 19th and 20th century, the little participative behavioral patterns that were socialized during the Franco era and territorial conflicts.[7] Furthermore, in its periphery, combative regionalist or nationalist movements, which are visibly hostile to the state, help remove the charm and self-confidence of Spanish rites and symbols.

THE GEOGRAPHICAL DIMENSIONS OF
NATIONAL–REGIONAL DAYS IN SPAIN

Nowadays, together with the eight official festivities at the national level—October 12, December 6, May 1, and five other Catholic feasts such as, among others, Good Friday, All Saints' Day, and Christmas—there are six other public holidays established by local and regional authorities. Such a high percentage stresses the significance of subnational traditions that, in some local cases, date back to the 13th century.

Towns and cities enthusiastically celebrate festivities of religious or rural meaning, although some of them commemorate local episodes of historic events such as the Reconquest or the Independence War. More political, and also more recent, several regional festivities have been established, after the territorial decentralization and the emergence of 17 autonomous regions (see map). The constitution itself, with the opposition of the most conservative Right, officially recognized regional symbols, which should be showed together with those of Spain.

Since then, national symbols lost their official status uniqueness, which could be also interpreted as an advantageous starting point for a policy of integration. After all, the Spanish flag, anthem, or day, being shown or commemorated together with those of the different regions, could become collective and plural. Anyhow, regional symbols will enjoy a greater popularity than national ones in some cases (Fusi 2000, 261). In such achievements they were helped by the stigmatization, even with the constitution already passed, of Spain's concept and the temporal coincidence between recovery of freedoms and regional devolution. The strong nationalist movements of Catalonia and the Basque Region indeed supported their symbols, but even in other regions with a weaker subnational identity, their recently established—and sometimes completely invented—symbols quickly spread. As official days are concerned, the difference between regions with a higher or lower degree of political identity led, in the first case, to the commemoration of historic events implying hostility against the center of Spain and, in the second case, to festivities stressing the prominent role or the peculiarities of a region in the context of the whole nation.

The National Diada in Catalonia

Catalanism is an extremely successful political movement that emerged in 1860, only 50 years after the appearance of modern Spanish nationalism. Sharing with the latter its passion for historicism and foreign enemies, Catalan nationalism re-created past episodes in which the Catalan people heroically withstood their neighbors' invasions. Thus, an episode of the Independence War against France (the victory of a Catalan guerrilla in the Bruc skirmish) would be mythicized, and so it was a couple of uprisings against Castilians (that is, Spaniards). These marked two historic events in their fight against the centralism of kings and for the defense of Catalan traditional rights and privileges: a rural uprising in 1640 (re-created by the anthem of *Segadors*, or harvesters) and the occupation of Barcelona on September 11, 1714. That day, King Phillip V of Bourbon, supported by the territories of the ancient Crown of Castile, dealt a harsh blow to the other pretender to the throne: Charles of Hapsburg, the candidate preferred by the ancient Aragonese kingdoms, in the War of Spanish Succession.

After Phillip V's victory, as punishment for supporting the enemy, he decided to abolish the Catalan charters and such a day was chosen as the *Diada Nacional* of Catalonia, in which the loss of self-government was commemorated and therefore its recovery was claimed. The day would not start to be commemorated until almost two centuries had passed since the event (Llobera 1996, 197), but a new feeling of collective identity was then built, even stronger than that of Spain as a whole. A booming bourgeoisie created pro-Catalan associations and managed to spread enduring symbols that did not suffer the controversies surrounding their Spanish equivalents. Both the *Senyera* (the flag), with the traditional bars and colors of the Crown of Aragon, and the anthem, composed in the 19th century, found higher degrees of popular acceptance, as compared with the popularity of the Spanish flag and anthem among Spaniards. The Diada was forbidden during the most repressive periods of Spanish centralism, above all in the Franco era. However, it was very popular in the Republican era and it is still indeed in the present democratic regime. This day has a great popular impact: flags invade the streets, the anthem is sung, and several concerts are held as compared to the scarce attractiveness of October 12 and December 6.

Aberri Eguna: Day of the Basque Homeland

As had happened before with the punishment to the ancient kingdoms of the Crown of Aragon, the charters of the Basque territories were also restricted, in 1875, as a consequence of capitulation. Those charters, which implied significant tax privileges, had been in force since the Middle Ages when Basques broke away from Navarre to join Castile. It was in 1875 when the Spanish army finally defeated the Carlists, an armed movement in favor of the ancien régime legal system, that enjoyed a great influence on the rural world in the Basque Region and Navarre. Some years later, Carlism would develop into Basque nationalism, starting to claim the recovery of self-government and traditionalism. Therefore, the Basque nationalist movement emerged as a sociopolitical project of the right-wing radical and catholic bourgeoisie (Hobsbawm 1990, 120). It is a reactive movement driven by Sabino Arana, founder of the Basque Nationalist Party, who took advantage of the high self-esteem of the Basque people—based on their long-established social higher condition—and transformed it into a reaction against the Spanish society, claiming their ethnic purity and the supremacy of Basque people over Castilians.

Since 1879, this nationalism started commemoration of festivities to defend their folklore and language: the Basque language Euskera. But the first Aberri

Eguna (the Day of the Basque Homeland) was not commemorated by the Basque nationalists until March 27, 1932, in Bilbao, at the starting point of the Second Spanish Republic. The first democratic elections of that period revealed the strength of the pro-Basque movement and, taking Irish nationalism as inspiration, they decided to commemorate the feast of the Easter Sunday and, at the same time, the 50th anniversary of Sabino Arana's evolution from Carlism to a pro-independence stance.

The subsequent Franco dictatorship tried to avoid the celebration of this day, that would only be freely commemorated again thanks to the return of democracy and self-government. The Basque Nationalist Party gained access to the first regional government and established its own symbols—the flag, *Ikurriña*, the anthem "Gora ta gora," and the Aberri Eguna—as their official ones. Unlike the remaining autonomous regions, and due to its partisan origin and the climate of violence and political extremism today characterizing the Basque Region, the official day has not been recognized as a true celebration by a high number of citizens living there. Nonnationalist Basque people, almost half of the total population, consider this day too sectarian, and claim the establishment of a festivity supported by a larger majority. Also, regarding the Basque Region and its neighbor Navarre, where there is a minority who speak Euskera, must be mentioned the absolute rejection of Spanish symbols by the most radical nationalists. This circumstance, much less common in Catalonia, often led to altercations in the streets during the national or regional festivities, including the burning of two-colored flags or, curiously, the establishment of October 12 and December 6 as working days in some Basque towns governed by the radical nationalist party.

Other Autonomous Regions

In the other 15 autonomous regions, official days are not fueled by an anti-Spanish nationalism. However, all of them—especially Galicia, Andalusia, the Canary Islands, and the ancient non-Castilian kingdoms—have promoted a regionalism requiring their own symbols. Flags, anthems, and festivities are fully invented or re-created, recovering supposedly ancient traditions.

In some cases, they tried to distinguish the recently acquired self-government by choosing a very remote event to commemorate, even if the feast itself is absolutely recent.[8] Other cases have avoided historicism, due either to a real conviction or the impossibility of finding in the past a common regional day to mythicize; instead, they preferred to commemorate the recent acquisition of self-government. For example, Andalusia celebrated a referendum on February 28, 1980, that allowed access to full self-government as soon as Catalonia, the Basque Region, or Galicia. Precisely on February 28, the regional Day of Andalusia is commemorated. Four other autonomous regions admitted the novelty of their regionalism, and accordingly, they decided not to celebrate past-oriented commemorations. Thus, on June 9, 1982, the Statutes of Autonomy of two tiny regions were passed, becoming the

Day of La Rioja and the Day of Murcia. In the case of the Canary Islands and Castile–La Mancha, the constitution of the first Regional Parliament in 1983 is the event commemorated on May 30, the Day of the Canary Islands, and May 31, the Day of Castile–La Mancha.

Finally, other autonomous regions have decided to establish a traditional religious feast as an official regional day,[9] and in this category, it is worth considering the remarkable case of Cantabria, where authorities strove to invent its own tradition and its symbols. There, the regionalist feeling is particularly scarce, and there was not even a deeply rooted historic or Catholic event, but it was decided to give a local virgin's devotion, celebrated on September 15 only since the beginning of the 20th century, the official status of Day of Cantabria (De la Cueva 2001). It seems that the regional government just intended to identify the regional character with religion, a policy previously put into practice by the Spanish traditionalism. Such a strategy is obviously linked with a weak territorial identity, and it may be oriented to avoid the emergence of modern nationalism or, if not, to support its most conservative version.

CONCLUSIONS

In the definition of collective identities in Spain, it should be underlined that there was an irregular process for the creation of national symbols during the 19th and the 20th centuries. Its previous history was scarcely significant, since it was only taken into account by a small cultural elite. Since then, the nationalization of the masses by means of a wide range of symbols easily recognized by everybody, regardless of their cultural level, failed. The lack of popularity and continuity of festivities is proof of such a situation. Spain very soon defined itself as a state, but much later and poorly as a nation. The inability to consolidate common symbols contributed both the weakness of the national ideological project that, in addition, had to compete with strong peripheral identities, and the inefficiency of the state in the 19th century to provide social services, education, or infrastructures. The 40 years of Franco's dictatorship ended up decisively corrupting the nation's days and other symbols. Because of this, Spaniards found it very difficult to identify with symbols that had been for a long time monopolized by an authoritarian, reactionary, and centralist regime. Furthermore, whereas the Right appropriated Spain's symbols, the Left has preferred an alternative iconography and peripheral nationalisms rejecting any kind of Spanish symbols.

From the Constitution of 1978 on, the democracy and the ambitious process of territorial decentralization achieved much more harmony between the Spanish State and its sociological and historical reality. At the same time, those few missing Franco's regime lost their enthusiasm for a country that is now very different from that of dictatorship. These political progresses, together with the strong economic growth and the development of a welfare state, have helped Spaniards leave behind their pessimistic view of history. However, when studying the scant popular appreciation for national symbols, we can observe that Spaniards have not become so reconciled to their past. At the most, since the 1990s, there is just a relative balance for most people who accept national symbols as institutional ones but do not consider them as festive—nor, certainly, as part of their domestic life. The flag may be visible only at some religious or sporting events, something that is not very helpful to promote its inclusive nature. Thus, it is never used in leftist demonstrations and is rejected by wide sectors of the Catalan and Basque population. Maybe, with the passing of time, the embryonic constitutional patriotism could convince left-wing and Catalanist leaders—this being much more difficult in the Basque case—so they can adopt as their own symbols of a democratic, Europeanized, and decentralized Spain.

In any case, neither the rejection and reservations of these groups nor the solemn and unrealistic rigidity with which, in turn, the central institutions should act in symbolic matters (Rodríguez-Aguilera and Vernet 1993, 155) project an accurate image of the collective reality. As regards the anthem, the flag, or national days, the general opinion in Spanish society is rather marked by disaffection that leads to apathetic behavior in their use or commemoration. Apart from combative minorities in one direction or the opposite, most Spaniards have ended up considering national symbols—always manipulated, often variable, and dominated by disdain and controversy—as superfluous or embarrassing. That is, Spaniards tolerate their symbols, although they hardly identify with them and, certainly, they do not use them for mobilization.

While patriotic festivities do not rouse popular enthusiasm, this does not mean that Spaniards are ashamed of being Spaniards, or that they necessarily consider their nation as reactionary and without a national identity that goes beyond the mere juxtaposition of parts. According to polls, the majority of citizens consider that they have close affective links with Spain, but are skeptic about its official expression.[10] In turn, national identification is shown, in a more latent than manifest expression, through a traditionalism that reacts against peripheral nationalisms. It is characterized by certain premodernist features that can be observed, for example, in the love for conventional customs or the belief of a higher standard of living in Spain.

Spaniards are very proud of being Spaniards,[11] but they neither need, accept, nor know how to translate such patriotic feeling into a mobilizing political idea, neither constitutional nor reactionary in nature. On the one hand, pessimistically, we can conclude that there is still a difficult relationship between Spaniards and their history. The idea of nation that, from a civic perspective, could unite the community, create social capital, and provide self-esteem remains alienated as a consequence of the manipulation by the few and the slackness by the many. On the other hand, optimistic conclusions can also be obtained and state that, in fact, Spaniards have learned from nationalist excesses in the past, some of them being still committed by nationalists in certain Spanish regions. According to this interpretation, the somewhat cynical approach of Spaniards toward their symbols would allow a high degree of Europeanism and spending long weekends in autumn, yet far from the altars of the homeland, when October 12 and December 6 arrive. Choosing one or the other conclusion is not the aim of this examination.

NOTES

1. The flag was designed with the prosaic aim of making Spanish vessels visible in the distance, and the national anthem, composed in Prussia, lacks lyrics, which limit its use in patriotic demonstrations (Menéndez Pidal, O'Donnell, and Lobo 1999). October 12, the date of Spain's current national holiday, may seem more chauvinistic; however, this date has a cosmopolitan character, which is unusual in other national festivities. Consider: Most countries in the Americas officially commemorate October 12, 1492, when the Genoese (that is, non Spaniard) Columbus disembarked in what is today the Anglophone Bahamas.

2. In 1627, when political and religious interests consisted of fighting against the Protestant Reformation in Europe and when southern Spanish bishops had become more powerful than northern Spanish ones, the very Catholic Santa Teresa de Ávila, who was born in central Castile, was chosen as copatron saint of Spain (Álvarez Junco 2001, 163n47).

3. The mere fact of choosing a historic date as national day—unlike the religious and absolutist practice of commemorating the saint's day of the king—allowed a civic and secular view of such a festivity.

4. There was perhaps an affective feeling, above all among elites, coexisting with the regional or local protonationalisms that had emerged—in Castile, in different areas of the ancient Crown of Aragon, or in Basque territories such as Vizcaya—even before the 16th century. For example, Castile was the first European kingdom that could be called a nation-state (Hobsbawm 1990, 16). This pioneering character in the emergence of national feeling, since it was linked with certain parts and not with the whole nation, was detrimental to the emergence of a modern nationalism covering the whole territory of the state.

5. May 2 is only commemorated nowadays in the capital city of Spain and its province, as Day of Madrid, after its creation as an autonomous region in 1983.

6. Furthermore, to satisfy those sectors reluctant to democratize and decentralize, the Penal Code, in force until 1995, punished in a rigid and dramatic way the offenses against the Spanish flag (Rodríguez-Aguilera and Vernet 1993, 152–54).

7. On the reasons of this certain cynicism characterizing Spanish political culture, see Montero, Gunther, and Torcal (1997).

8. In the Balearic and Valencian regions, whose territories belonged together with Catalonia and Aragon to the Crown of Aragon (see map), Reconquest events were chosen to commemorate regional festivities. Thus, King Jaime I, after expelling the Saracens in 1230 granted Majorca a Chart of Population on May 1 (nowadays commemorated as the Day of the Balearic Islands) and, eight years later, entered in Valencia on October 9 (commemorated today as the Day of the Community of Valencia). For its part, the regional Day of Castile and Leon (April 23) commemorates the martyrdom suffered in 1521 by the leaders of the Comuneros, which is a rebel movement promoted by the low nobility and an incipient bourgeoisie in Castile opposed to the centralization plans of Emperor Charles V.

9. Thus, on September 8, the Day of Asturias and the Day of Estremadura are commemorated, coinciding respectively with the feasts of Covadonga and Guadalupe. These are two Sanctuaries to the Virgin Mary that have close links with the initial and final stage of Castilian Reconquest, and the Christianization of the peninsula and the New World. The Day

of Navarre is commemorated on December 3, the feast of Saint Francisco Javier, a Catholic missionary from that region.

10. According to Moral (1998), 85 percent of Spaniards are very or quite proud of being Spaniards. However, such national identity coexists with—apart from a strong support of European integration—a weak affinity with the state authority, both civil and military. For example, there is a lack of willingness to defend the country with arms and a high aversion to politicians and bureaucrats. Curiously, this is not incompatible with a great attachment to democratic institutions and a strong statism in socioeconomic matters.

11. The degree in which citizens are proud of being Spaniards is reduced in Catalonia and, above all, the Basque Region, to 68 percent, and 36 percent respectively. However, the percentage of those in favor of independence is only 20 percent in Catalonia and 29 percent in the Basque Region (Moral 1998).

REFERENCES

Álvarez Junco, J. (1996). The nation-building process in nineteenth-century Spain. In C. Mar-Molinero and A. Smith (Eds.), *Nationalism and the nation in the Iberian Peninsula*, 89–106. Oxford, UK: Berg.

Álvarez Junco, J. (2001). *Mater Dolorosa: La idea de España en el siglo XIX* ["Mater" Dolorosa: The idea of Spain in the 19th century]. Madrid: Taurus.

De la Cueva, J. (2001). Inventing Catholic identities in twentieth century Spain: The Virgin Bien Aparecida, 1904–1910. *The Catholic Historical Review, 87*, 624–42.

Fusi, J. P. (2000). *España: La evolución de la identidad nacional* [Spain: The evolution of the national identity]. Madrid: Temas de Hoy.

Guereña, J. L. (1986). Del anti-Dos de Mayo al Primero de Mayo: Aspectos del internacionalismo en el movimiento obrero español (From the anti-second of May to the first of May: Traits of internationalism in the Spanish workers' movement}. *Estudios de Historia Social, 38–39*, 91–103.

Hobsbawm, E. J. (1990). *Nations and nationalism since 1780*. Cambridge, UK: Cambridge University Press.

Llobera, J. R. (1996). The role of commemorations in (ethno)nation-building. The case of Catalonia. In C. Mar-Molinero and A. Smith (Eds.), *Nationalism and the nation in the Iberian Peninsula*, 191–206. Oxford, UK: Berg.

Menéndez Pidal, F., O'Donnell, H., and Lobo, B. (1999). *Símbolos de España* [Symbols of Spain]. Madrid: Centro de Estudios Políticos y Constitucionales.

Montero, J. R., Gunther, R., and Torcal, M. (1997). Democracy in Spain: Legitimacy, discontent and disaffection. *Studies in Comparative International Development, 32*(3), 124–60.

Moral, F. (1998). *Identidad regional y nacionalismo en el estado de las autonomías* [Regional identity and nationalism in the Spanish state of the antonomous regions]. Madrid: CIS.

Rodríguez-Aguilera, C., and Vernet, J. (1993). Cuestiones simbólicas y Constitución Española [Symbolic issues and the Spanish constitution]. *Revista de Estudios Políticos, 79*, 139–60.

Santoveña, A. (1994). *Menéndez Pelayo y las derechas en España* [Menéndez Pelayo and the right wingers in Spain]. Santander: Librería Estudio.

Serrano, C. (1999). *El nacimiento de Carmen: Símbolos, mitos y nación* [The birth of Carmen: Symbols, myths and nation]. Madrid: Taurus.

TURKEY

Nation and Celebration

An Iconology of the Republic of Turkey

Halil Nalçaoglu

O ne of the most significant characteristics of modern nationalism is a retro-spective gaze that is, in essence, an act of remembering. Remembering, in turn, can be understood as an act of colonization or reappropriation of the past. It can be claimed that what nationalism reappropriates is an imaginary situation that is supposed to have existed before an intermediary regime and its corresponding discursive hegemony. Depending on specific circumstances, the dark period before the arrival of nation could be (re)formulated as "colonial period," "dark ages," "bar-barian invaders," and the like. In nearly every case, though, there exists a "golden age" to be remembered and cherished, an ultimate "national objective" to be re-captured. The constructed object of remembrance and reappropriation bears, at the same time, the magical tool of disclosing that deep essence, high character, or supreme morality of the group of people who make up the nation. Remembering sometimes presents us temporal jumps consisting of thousands of years; to regis-ter this retroactive identity formation, the nation-builder sometimes takes a certain mythological event as the zero point for the so-called rebirth of nation. As an es-sential ideology, nationalism rejects social change or transformation, and in this respect, a former era cannot be the precursor of a current one. Nevertheless, the current era cannot, in turn, be rootless. Nationalism thus claims that national iden-tity has always been present as it is today, albeit suppressed or obstructed by some (mostly constructed) accidental or external forces—colonialists, a Sultan, old habits, imperialism, external enemies, and the like.

The history of Turkish nationalism bears similar marks or acts of remem-brance. In a paradoxical way, its history is fueled by an opposite: forgetfulness. In nearly all popular or official narrative, the rebirth of Turkey as a republic has been turned into a discursive sponge clearing away more than 600 years of history of the Ottoman Empire. The point zero for the history of Turkish nation is an exact date: October 29, 1923, which has been celebrated as the republic holiday ever since. A substitute for the loss or lack that emerged out of this discursive operation has naturally been various forms of "Turkisms." Joining the forces of remembrance and forgetfulness, the substitute discursive formation writes the history of the Turkish nation from scratch, in an act of emphasis mainly underlining "Turk-ness" of the peoples who have lived in a given geography. Naturally, the years of the War of Independence (1919–23), and a couple of decades prior to this period, were years of eye-averting from the enemy Europe and from the Arab-Islam world in a search for Turk-ness. Central Asia, where a great number of diverse Turkic people live, has been the "epicenter" of turmoil for early Turkish nationalism, while the actual war fought against the imperialist forces shrank the pan-Turkist dreams of "greater Turkey" (known as "Turan Land") and the final victory drew the borders of the Turkish motherland on the Anatolian Peninsula.

There might be various ways of writing the history of the Republic of Turkey, as there are multiple ways with any history. The aim in this chapter is neither to (re)write that history, nor to formulate a history in any general sense of the term; rather, it will focus on the joint operation of remembrance and forgetfulness in this particular history. In doing so, it relies on the discourse of celebration over a 75-year period, focusing on three moments of celebration: the 10th, the 50th, and the 75th anniversaries. This does not reflect an arbitrary choice.

The 10th-year celebration (1923) was the most vividly remembered "big event" of the period. It was, in a sense, a republic's coming-of-age. In the words of historian Arzu Öztürkmen (1996), the 10th-year celebrations became a "model" for the following years. The "Tenth-Year March," commissioned and composed for this occasion in 1933, is still considered irreplaceable. It is sung during every occasion where "national feelings" are high, such as in party congresses, on television shows, at soccer games, and so on.

The 50th-year celebrations (1973) mark a turning point in terms of loosing the spirit and enthusiasm in celebrations. The mid-1970s were years of social turmoil, and the celebrations of 1973 were shadowed by heavy economic problems. These years are also remembered as those of the beginnings of social unrest (for example, street fights among enemy political factions and political assassinations claiming nearly 5,000 lives), which was to die off by the 1980 September 12 Military Coup. One acute indication of loosing the spirit might be found in the "iconification" of celebrations. During the 1970s, Turkey's historically rooted social project of Westernization had begun to adopt an increasingly formal attitude that could be expressed in terms of the rise in the iconic value of national symbols such as the national flag.

By the 1990s, national icons (especially the Turkish flag, founder Mustafa Kemal Ataturk's portrait, and the map of Turkey) reached their highest ever degree of abstractness, prevalence, and commodification, which can be read as an indicator of a total loss of original national sentiments—the enthusiasm, the joy, and the spirit of republican reforms. How can we read such a transformation? What is the significance of such a high degree of iconification? Finally, how can we explain the coexistence of a massive nationalism with the fact that Turkish national day celebrations have lost much of their original spirit and enthusiasm?

Needless to say, such questions can be answered on a number of different theoretical levels. For instance, one may rightfully tie the loss of spirit with the cultural ramifications of globalization. Nevertheless, what immediately casts doubt on and complicates the argument of cultural effects of global capitalism is the phenomenon of the rise of a new nationalism throughout eastern Europe, including Turkey. Ironically, as 75-year-old national sentiments turned into mere surfaces, there was undeniable popular support for the nationalist political parties and groups in Turkey. Are these two phenomena conflictuous? I don't think so. It would be naïve to argue that the general social and cultural investment in iconification of the principles of the republic is only understandable in terms of triggering mass nationalistic hysteria. Icons address the eye, but they do not require in-depth thinking. In the following pages, I would like to base my argument partly on how the process of "superficialization" is related with another process: the preference of icons in place of writing in spreading national ideas. The argument that icons have replaced writing has deeper theoretical connotations that might be the subject for another work; however, the notions of loss, lack, and substitute, as well as the question of writing versus image (icon) opposition, immediately bring to mind recent contributions of psychoanalysis and deconstruction.

One can think of the notion of "golden age" placed in the beginning of the fantastic history of nation in terms of the concept "Nation-Thing," developed by Slavoj i ek on the footprints of Jacques Lacan. In a similar vein, the same notion links up with the idea of "lost presence" that surfaced in the critique of Western metaphysics by Jacques Derrida. Within the limits of the aforementioned historical and theoretical topography, what follows is a summary of the overall purpose as an attempt to understand the role of national icons in the nation-building process. Chosen are the critical moments (three celebrations on 1923, 1973, and 1998) in the 75-year history of the Republic of Turkey to guide this effort.

NATION-THING: THE LOGOS OF NATION

The act of remembering is significant not in the sense of recovery of a lost object, but in terms of constant reconstitution. As indicated earlier, in the case of nationalism, remembering is reappropriation of what is declared to be lost. The object of reappropriation, in turn, can be said to be a "golden past." Nation, in this sense, is a construct that can stay erect only under conditions of recollecting "that thing" that existed once upon a time. In nationalistic discourses, the proof of the existence of a golden past is abundant. It is fair to argue that especially the late 19th-century "social scienctific" endeavor is loaded with such evidence by "scientists" of race, language, and history. It is fair to say that contemporary historical narratives, as well as symbols in massive everyday use are products of the "invention of tradition":

It is clear that plenty of political institutions, ideological movements and groups—not least in nationalism—were so unprecedented that even historic continuity had to be invented, for example by creating an ancient past beyond effective historical continuity either by semi-fiction . . . or by forgery. . . . It is also clear that entirely new symbols and devices came into existence . . . such as the national anthem, . . . the national flag, . . . or the personification of "the nation" in symbol or image. (Hobsbawm and Ranger, qtd. in Brennan 1990, 49)

The object of reminiscence in the fantastic history of nationalism can give identity to a group of people as "us." i ek (1993) calls this object the "Master Signifier," or the "Nation-Thing," a concept that overlaps with the Lacanian "object of desire" in the sense that it has a reference to a "lost object." The loss under consideration is not a static attribute; on the contrary, loss is a dynamic force behind what one might call "active remembering," or that what is believed to be lost is under constant threat of being lost again.

The definition of Nation-Thing as an object of desire problematically draws Lacan into the field of philosophy while at the same time pulling philosophy into the field of life determined by an "economy of desire."[1] The nationalistic desire to return, to reappropriate, and to reclaim the lost past can be seen as an analytical bridge bringing together philosophical psychoanalysis and deconstruction in the context of critique of origins. By following this thought, we can get closer to an understanding of the so-called paradox expressed in terms of "nation being a modern phenomenon" while nationalism is woven with irrational myths of origin.[2] The fantasy object of nationalism resembles the Lacanian *objet petit a*,[3] and it also reminds us of the famous "first term" of deconstructionist's binary oppositions: it is both "lost" and "primary," it both "refers to past" and is "constitutive of present." Whether it is, as i ek prefers, constituted as a result of symbolic castration (the original loss) or is, as Derrida would have formulated, an attempt to reappropriate lost presence, the idea/l of national identity cannot be conceptualized without reference to an imaginary past community, an "arche-nation." Arche-nation is the logos of modern nationalism, ever motivated by a perplexed blending of moving forward and turning back to the golden past. In this respect, we can argue that far from being a paradox, the combination of the terms *modern* and *nation* is but a necessary mix. Nations held together with the ideology of nationalism could have only been possible with a general sense of loss, a twin process of the general excess of modernity.

This thesis can also be read in terms of the cultural consequences of capitalism, the loss–excess balance of which relies on the advance and spread of capitalism and the parallel development of communication media. From the perspective of unity of people under a single name, capitalism can be said to have played a double role: on the one hand, with increasing individualization, capitalism made face-to-face association less and less feasible; on the other hand, it created a myth that such an association is, and has in fact once been, possible. Capitalism destroyed community along with a discourse crowned by "community values." This double role of capitalism had a perfect alibi: the advance of communication media.

As the key marker of modernization, the spread of communication media "improved" exchange between individuals (and groups), yet every move toward perfection in mediated communication has also meant downcasting "real" exchange among people. This fact may very well be extrapolated to incorporate a theoretical problematic involving modernity and nationalism. Recalling McLuhan (1964), it is possible to argue that various "extensions of man"—print, radio, film, and television—improved the common understanding of people with the desire to share common (national) values; yet, at the same time, they took them further away from the imagined golden past. In view of the emergent atomization among the members of nation, the functional response of nationalism would be nothing but mobilization of ideological mechanisms of reminiscence. A nation, in this sense, can only remain as a nation when it is constantly kept alert against current (capitalistic or whatever) conditions, and against external and internal enemies who willingly or unwillingly deteriorate the national texture. National texture, in turn, finds its spirit in ancient times during which those factors of deterioration were supposedly nonexistent. The concrete strategy of nationalism, then, is expected to be both spiritual and emotional, addressing hearts rather than minds. Such a strategy would revive the symbolic universe as accurately as possible given the irreversible damage done by the modern. The choice of icons as "objects of uncritical devotion" cannot be a coincidence in the modern era.

What, then, gives meaning to icons in national context? This question is deeply related to the constituted nature of identity, be it national or otherwise. Like all other identity formation processes, national identity needs contestation in the form of a threat posed by a "non-we" or "the Other." In the context of national identity, I refer back again to i ek, opening a passageway to the relationship between national identity and national iconology; for him, the desire for a fixed national identity, an identity marked by a proper name, is connected to the way in which that unique "Thing" marks "us" off from the "others." It can be argued that national icons are special visualizations of Nation-Thing formed throughout the symbolic topography of arche-nation. i ek (1993) states:

National identification is by definition sustained by a relationship toward the Nation qua Thing. This Nation-Thing is determined by a series of contradictory properties. It appears to us as "our Thing" (perhaps we could say *cosa nostra*), as something accessible only to us, as something "they," the others, cannot grasp; nonetheless it is something constantly menaced by "them." (201)

In this sense, what i e k calls Nation-Thing cannot be understood as national icons per se; neither could it be said that such icons stand for fixed objects of desire. Rather, Nation-Thing is the gap left behind the "original loss," generating a productive loss–excess economy powered by the circulation of icons which, in this economy, are (like) commodities with no use value yet augmented by excessive symbolic value that can only be attained through circulation and expansion through various media. More icons in circulation means an increased need for icons, reminding us of the iconic value of commodities in the capitalist market: consumption calls for more consumption, not fulfilment.

No example better depicts what is conceptualized in these lines than the experience of the bloody overturn of the Ceauşescu regime in Romania; in this turbulent period, rebels waved the national flag with the red star, the symbol of the Communist Party, cut out. So, writes i e k (1993), "nstead of the symbol standing for the organizing principle of the national life, there was nothing but a hole in the center" (1–2). What is witnessed in those days in Bucharest and other cities of Romania was a brief moment of passage from one discourse to another, when

the hole in the big Other, the symbolic order, become visible. The enthusiasm which carried them was literally the enthusiasm over this hole, not yet hegemonized by any positive ideological project; all ideological appropriations (from the nationalistic to the liberal democratic) entered the stage afterwards and endeavored to "kidnap" the process which originally was not their own. (1–2)

It is obvious that the current unstarred Romanian flag would not signify the complex semiological trajectory to be found in its concrete history; rather, it would simply signify the identity of the Romanian nation.

Looking at another example, a semiological struggle of the similar sort (in the form of a "war over reminiscence") marked a contemporary political history of Japan, fought over the meaning of Japanese flag and national anthem. It might strike some as surprising that the Japanese flag—a red disc on a white rectangular field—and the "Kimigayo" ode, was voted by the upper house of Japanese parliament to become official symbols of the nation only in August 9, 1999. Until then, in spite of popular use of these symbols, they were not official due to bad memories (for example, Japanese atrocities during World War II and the defeat of Japan) in the public consciousness. Debate around the adoption of national symbols as official symbols of the Japanese nation have taken place between politicians fostering nationalistic sentiments and intellectuals defending democratic values; however, from a semiological standpoint, the debate itself had become an interesting testing ground for imagination in the risky business of assigning meanings to icons and symbols. Even written signifiers such as the lyrics to the Japanese "national" anthem have been subject to semiological negotiation. A *New York Times* author, Nicholas D. Kristof (1999), stated that the Japanese national anthem, whose lyrics are 900 years old, is considered by some as "inappropriate for a democratic, modern Japan," since it is basically praising the emperor. Therefore, in order for it to be appropriated as the national anthem, the government had to push the lyrics to mean "just about everything but what they seem to." What is striking about the search for meaning, or rather negotiation of meaning, is that its end product is toward confusion rather than clarity as Kristof rightly observes: "Even as its meaning gets muddier and muddier, the song itself is getting closer to adoption as the official national anthem" (6).

THE RHYTHM OF CELEBRATIONS

National days are typically days of "adornment," celebrations in which national symbols, especially national flags, adorn streets, buildings, parks, entire cities, and entire countries. Even the poorest nations or nations during their poorest times do not spare money for celebrations and adornment. Adornment is not mere orna-mentation. Nor is it ever innocent.

Modern ornamentation can function for mass identification and declaration of status. It can be argued that at the crossroads of nationalism and modernity, ornamentation for adornment gives way to ornamentation for something else. Or-nament becomes the signifier of a concept larger than the status or privilege of its bearer. In the age of mass identification, ornamentation becomes the organizing principle of an entire national identity. In her analysis of American and Australian national identity formation processes through commemorations of centennials and bicentennials, Spillman (1997) observes that invoking any particular symbol in both cultures meant expressing these cultures' "world position" or "internal inte-gration," or both. What is striking in the overall analysis and the comparison of the centennials and bicentennials in Spillman's analysis is that the referents of symbolic actions change in the course of 100 years. For instance, in Australia, the emphasis placed on "founding moment" during centennial celebrations has become in-significant in bicentennials. In a similar vein, the aspect of "internal recognition" seems to fade away as we move from centennials to bicentennials in the United States.[4] The dialectic of remembrance and forgetfulness is certainly in operation here just as it is in other national identity formation processes cited so far. These examples also demonstrate that despite their overall historical orientation, the func-tioning of symbols (national celebrations and icons alike) are constitutive of present as much as they represent the past.

A classic symbolic dislocation can be observed in the history of celebrations of the Republic of Turkey. An analysis of the critical moments of celebration re-veals that there are significant shifts and breaking points in themes and iconography among them; hence, it is meaningful to begin this analysis from the very periodization of "critical moments" mentioned in the beginning of this chap-ter. The 10th-, 50th-, and 75th-year moments of the celebration of the Republic of Turkey seem somewhat too frequent when compared with celebrations of cen-tennials or bicentennials. Thinking analytically, one would expect the periods to expand as time goes by, instead, the expanding rhythm as we move from zero to 10 and from 10 to 50 makes a sharp turn at 75. Why? This, above all, reminds one that analytical thinking falls short when concrete histories of nations are in ques-tion. Within the particular history of the Republic of Turkey, the 10th-year had a tremendous significance in many respects. First of all, founder Mustafa Kemal Ataturk (1881–1939) was a living symbol of the republic and was certainly at the center of attention in 1933.[5] Second, the 10th-year was a declaration to the world and the nation itself as a kind of landmark, indicating that the "sick European" had won its war with death; the triumphant 10 years of progress showed that

Turkey was a healthy young republic. Last but not least, the 10th-year was a time when memories of war and independence were alive with firsthand witnesses so that there was virtually no need for the remembrance–forgetfulness dialectic to operate. Nothing to remember: marks of victory won against "the reverse fate" of a nation were everywhere.

It seems that the 50th-year celebrations in 1973 were not at all as bright. It would not be an exaggeration to claim that economic and social problems experienced during the 1970s clearly dissolved Turkey's national self-confidence. The aura of the 10th-year celebrations had all gone along with the organic coherence between official and civil experiences. Many sources cite the early years of the republic as times when there was a strong unity among the state, military, and ordinary people. A single-party regime was ruling the country, relying on people's enormous trust toward the military leadership that, by 1923, had transformed itself into a civil leadership. Since 1950, Turkey has become a multiparty parliamentary democracy. This regime, however, had been interrupted by military interventions every other decade until 1980; thus, there was a loss of spirit: the discursive monopoly of strong nationalistic forces of the early years gave way to divisive forces like political Islam and Kurdish nationalism in the years following the 1950s.

The 10-year period following the 1980 coup d'état is generally remembered as the decade of oppression, during which military methods were utilized for the elimination of "state internal enemies."[6] In line with the global ideological polarization between "democracy" and "communism," these were years of oppression of the Turkish Left. Then, by the 1990s, winds changed again in harmony with global ideological and economic currents, such that antinationalistic forces seemed to be diffused and global. Celebrations covering the entire year of 1998 as the 75th anniversary of the republic brought about a novelty: the national symbols (the flag, Ataturk, and the map of Turkey) colonized everyday life. Despite the omnipresence of national symbols in the form of icons, it would be fair to argue that those symbols' referent was so diffused that it became impossible to conceive of them as "unifying" in any sense of the term.

Now we can interpret the sharp turn in the rhythm of celebrations as we approach the 75th year. Two significant transformations have caused the way in which the declaration of Turkey as a "republic" has shifted status. Over a period of 75 years, first the monopoly of state over national identification lost its force, becoming formal and superficial. Parallel to this transformation, national identification became heavily dependent on the dialectic of remembrance and forgetfulness, with the nationalistic activity of the early years giving way to the nationalistic iconography. The concrete successes of the republic in the fields of education, transportation, health, economy, and agriculture all ceased to be symbols of the republic; instead, iconic symbols were invented to remind the people of the organizing principle of the nation: Turk-ness. Ironically, attempts toward filling the gap left behind by a dissolved Ottoman Empire proved to be far from unifying. Divisive forces along religious and ethnic lines have always challenged the idea of Turk-ness in the form of uprisings and underground organizations, as well as legitimate political establishments within the multiparty parliamentary regime. As the forces against single national identity gain strength, symbols promoting such an identification got shallower and shallower.

TURKEY'S MAJOR CELEBRATIONS

The 10th Year (1933): The Republic's Coming-of-Age

One of the most striking characteristics of the 10th-year celebrations can be found in the representational regime dominant in the production of visual signifiers, determined by a "one-to-one-correspondence" logic present between images and writing as well as images and historical narrative. A second striking characteristic was the reliance on writing as a mode of communication deemed trustworthy. In the 10th-year celebrations, nearly all iconic representations were supported by writing. A third characteristic concerns the symptomatic lack of icons that dominated decades to come. During the early years of the Republic of Turkey, those who shaped the ideological and representational aspects of identity formation did not feature the national flag, Ataturk's portraits, or the map of Turkey as dominant figures.[7]

The representational regime dominant in the 10th-year celebrations was marked by an attempt to describe nearly every item of material reality in pictorial forms and illustrations. Such an attempt was vital in the sense that it functioned toward narrowing down the field of contingency in the process of signification. This practice is most visible in an examination of front-page illustrations of Turkish newspapers published on October 29, 1933. The illustration that appeared on *Hakimiyeti Milliye*'s entire front page consists of drawings of buildings, railways, and bridges, as well as symbolic figures of factory workers and peasants, making it clear that the entire illustration was designed to represent the achievements of 10 years within one-to-one-correspondence logic coupling images and historical reality.[8] This, however, does not refer to a realistic aesthetic in the sense that there exists a photographic realism in the images; on the contrary, images attain more symbolic value than being realistic. Trains symbolize the railways, planes the air force, docks the maritime, turbines the electricity, and so forth. It is striking that the entire front page was filled with images, with little empty space left. From a semiological standpoint, one can argue that this illustration was trying to meet the challenge of describing the reality in its entirety and, when faced with the impossibility of such a project, it reverted to a form of symbolism. On the upper left corner is the ruling CHF (*Cumhuriyet Halk Fırkası*; Republican People's Party) party flag with six arrows. It might be said that this icon is the only abstract item in the entire illustration. Needless to say, the meaning of each arrow is inscribed underneath the flag, as if the illustrator has noticed the contradictory representational strategies that emerge out of the fact that pictorial representations of reality and a pure symbolic form—the flag—cannot stand on the same analytical plane.

Written explanation indicating what each arrow means eliminates this contradiction along with any possibility for imagination.

One of the "brightest innovations" that shaped the 10th-year celebrations was the ritual of picking a handful of soil from "every corner of the country," then presenting it to "Ghazi" Mustafa Kemal.[9] A similar logic of complete representation can be found in this ritual as well. The unifying practice of picking the soil had been extended to subprovince levels and some villages. It is important to note that a perfect organizational arrangement made it possible to join all these sealed bags of soil and present them to Ataturk on October 29, 1933, when considering the naturally weak communicational and transportational means at that time. But this organization was certainly fueled by a deep sense of gratitude toward Ghazi, who not only "saved the country from its enemies," but also "gave it back to its people" by declaring it a republic. The logic running through this ritual is, again, that of a one-to-one correspondence. The saved country is given back to its real owners—the citizens who now are symbolically paying their debt to their savior.

As has been indicated here, according to the dominant representational logic, even the most obvious icons such as CHF's six arrows were usually accompanied by a script telling what each arrow meant: republicanism, nationalism, populism, statism, secularism, and revolutionism. Another medium on which the republic's wisdoms were inscribed was the paraphernalia produced and distributed for the memory of the 10th year, recording that tens of thousands of cigarette packs were produced and distributed free for this special day, with tiny leaflets inserted with slogans such as "Republic Is Wisdom." It should be noted that the entire program and activities of celebrations were organized by a single High Commission for Celebrations, which was formed by the state. CHF carried out the heavy task of preparing and distributing banners containing pictures representing the 10-year achievements as well as brief scripts reiterating them. During the 1933 celebrations, nearly 200,000 banners were printed and distributed all over the country, and were described on the front page of the October 29, 1933, issue of Hakimiye-i Milliye as follows:

The banners which sum up to 200 thousand items, vividly and meaningfully show how the Turkish nation destroyed institutions unfitting to its body and alien to itself, how it moved forward with a national leap by eliminating the bad inheritance of past, and the successful results that have been achieved. A significant and outstanding aspect of these banners was that in their preparation, pictorial representations were not solely relied on, and Great Ghazi's words and addresses, which have always been a source of excitement and forward movement, have been given a place of first priority.

The years of establishment were the years when the experience of nation-building was too concrete to leave any space for imagination or thinking. The nationalist ideology joined forces with the strong state, controlling everyday life in its entirety.[10]

It has been indicated here that a hegemonic nationalist and statist discourse was prevalent during the early years. The sole strategy of hegemony was not bent on suppression and silencing; on the contrary, the 10th-year celebrations were marked by an interesting practice called the "people's platforms," which were formed in town centers so that citizens could deliver speeches on the successes and wisdom of the republic and its reforms. As the newspapers reported, this initiative was received with great enthusiasm all over the country. Numerous men and women over the age of 18 registered to give speeches mostly "to tell our people the goodness brought about by the republican regime and to spread the national feelings" (*Hakimiyet-i Milliye*, October 27, 1993, 4). In one instance, a speaker began to speak about the caliphate, a topic that had been taboo since one of the first reforms of the new regime, by secular laws.[11] As expected, the speaker was forced off the platform and arrested. This action vis-à-vis the ideas deemed against the regime should be accepted only as "normal" in its time, yet the way it is reflected as a news item illustrates how the monolithic discourse of dominant ideology would only let us see its actual working through cracks in its otherwise solid structure. That is, the information regarding the underlying structure of the ideology could only surface through unconsciously formulated discourses of justification such as describing an act of resistance as an accident or mishap. The article stated that " retired major Dr. Suleyman Efendi has been forced to leave the platform when he, *under the influence of a temporary insanity*, started to speak nonsensical claims about the caliph right after he mentioned the wisdom of the republic" (*Hakimiyet-i Millige*, November 4, 1933, 5; emphasis added). These lines indicate that the tenth-year celebrations were carried out under strict ideological supervision of the state, such that even the slightest remark against the dominant ideology might be ruled out. As the example demonstrates, the dominant discourse (necessarily) fails to identify a talk about the religious leadership (caliphate) as a political opposition and defines it as a mishap by medicalizing it ("temporary insanity").

The 1920s and 1930s were the years during which the memory of imperialist invasion, the War of Independence, and the declaration of Turkey as a republic were quite vivid. Ataturk, the national hero, was, in a sense, a living icon of the nation, and there was no need for iconification for nation-building, as is observed in the present work as the prime force behind the superficialization of republican reforms. A second major characteristic was the enormous emphasis given to public indoctrination. This was mainly achieved by the use of oral and written communication rather than iconification. Ataturk's 10th-year address was disseminated via live radio broadcasts connected to loud speakers in major town centers. Where radio broadcasting was technically impossible, leaflets and banners were centrally distributed to every corner of the country. It is important to note that when images were used for the purpose of indoctrination, it was basically perceived as supplements to writing. It would not be a mistake to argue that images have not yet reached the status of icons. Pictures and illustrations were basically seen as instrumental in transmitting the desired message. Quite often, icons such as the CHF party flag were accompanied by an explanatory inscription. A third characteristic found in the 10th-year celebrations is the hegemonic articulation of the young state's secular and nationalistic ideology that, under the circumstances of a single-party regime, was understandable. The strategy of exclusion utilized by this hegemony was far less dependent on the dynamics of remembrance–forgetting, since the state apparatus was omnipresent and thus basically taking care of everything. Even a minor deviance from the rule was declared unthinkable and, as the last example illustrates, declared to be outside the boundaries of reason.

The 50th Year (1973): Loosening of the Spirit

Only a few days remained for the 50 Year Celebrations. It became visible from today that in the works for the celebrations we are yet to come across with any tangible, visible and really sincere outcome which is to make one remain startled with its contemplative aspect.
— Turgut Etingu, "50th Year and Our True Friends"

These words by essayist Turgut Etingu, on the celebrations of the 50th year in 1973, were written on the same day that İlhan Selçuk, a prominent columnist, compared the 10th-year celebrations with the 50th: "We had a higher self-esteem and self-confidence and there was not a single thought criminal and political prisoner in our dungeons as well" (1). While these voices represent oppositional rhetoric, then-president Fahri Korutürk, in his public message of celebrations stressed a national unification reflex against the "dangers" threatening the unity of "our nation." In 1973, the official rhetoric was almost completely composed of references to Ataturk. In newspapers published during the week of celebrations, "being loyal to Ataturk's principles," "the feeling of gratitude toward him," "realizing the wish of Ataturk," and the like were the prominent motifs. It would not be an exaggeration to say that these years had been those of lifting national symbols to the level of icons. Ironically, all three military coups that have taken place (in 1960, 1971, and 1980) based their legitimizing rhetoric on the grounds that the existing parliamentary political system diverged from the "principles of Ataturk."[12]

It should be noted that both the official discourse usually dominated by center-right governments and, with a rough categorization, the center-left discourse, exemplified in the words of the two journalists cited in the beginning of this section, played a similar role in the iconification of Ataturk. While Etingu's (1973) discourse was inviting everyone in "national unification against internal and external enemies" in order to stay in line with Ataturk's ideals, Selçuk (1973) accentuated the need for a more secular and democratic regime—again, in the name of Ataturk. The fact that Ataturk's name is heavily employed by both the left and the right wings of the legal political scene indicates some form of "uncritical devotion" in how the term is used to define "icon." It is also possible to argue that Ataturk's name became an unquestionable reference point, single-handedly rendering legitimate all political discourses and actions. These years can be cited as those elevating his name to a rhetorical status of unquestionable reference point, rendering any discourse legitimate, including that of military interventions as indicated earlier.

Cumhuriyet, a newspaper that began its publication in 1924, had a November 29, 1973, special celebration supplement that deserves attention. Compared to the aforementioned cover page of *Hakimiyet-i Milliye*, the most striking difference is that *Cumhuriyet*'s 50th-year issue consisted of a single image: a photograph of Ataturk in suit and necktie. The choice of his photo not in military uniform is obviously telling. It might also be noted that the compulsory passage to a "civilized, Western way of dressing" was one of the significant reforms that have taken place during the early years of the republic, bearing a rhetorical value in the Turkish discourse of modernization. Thus, the choice of this photo of Ataturk in a suit has an iconographical value defining the Republic of Turkey as a modern and secular state. The lack of any other image on the front page is also very significant in terms of the overall argument being developed here. In addition to the newspaper's "iconistic" approach, the writing-image relation also represents a significant break from the representational regime described for the 10th-year celebrations.

In the 50th year, the primary characteristic of icon-writing relations can be described as abstraction and detachment. It can be argued that in the 50th-year celebrations, the icon of Ataturk represented only abstract notions of national identity, loyalty in and gratitude to Ataturk rather than actual achievements of the 50 years. The dominant script in this cover is a short poem entitled "Mustafa Kemal's Age," which describes Ataturk as immortal. The relationship between the poem and the image diverges from the one-to-one-correspondence principle observed in the newspapers 40 years ago, with words and images staying separate, the former having no direct explanatory relation to the latter. It is possible to substantiate this judgment by a number of other examples involving script-image relationship. The front page of *Hurriyet*, another leading Turkish national newspaper known for consistently high circulation and liberal tendencies, is another case in point. On the cover of its November 29, 1973, issue is a full-page special illustration consisting of Ataturk's portrait, the Turkish flag, and two other drawings representing the first and current Turkish Grand National Assembly (parliament) buildings. The center of the illustration is reserved for the overimposed images of Ataturk and the Turkish flag, while the top left and the bottom parts of the illustration are for the drawings of two buildings. No script accompanies the illustration except for "50 Year" in block capitals at the bottom. The overimposition of these images is significant in the sense that such a configuration demonstrates abstraction, a primary characteristic of iconicity; in fact, it is possible to observe the same attitude in an intensifying trend for years to come. Images have come to bear meanings in themselves without reference to an apparent external reality. It is interesting to note that the 50th-year celebrations were also marked by an emblem: a logo composed of five crescents (each representing 10 years) forming a circle, with a star in the middle. Obviously, in this invention we can still follow the trend of abstraction.

Realism in national icons goes hand in hand with abstraction. The choice of photographs or illustrations with painstaking realism are primary characteristics of the visual material printed in newpapers. One can argue that the more national symbols become abstract icons, the more "realistic" they can become. One striking initiative was the attempt to establish a wax museum of the leaders of the republic. Ataturk's wax statue, of course, was the central piece. In the words of the sculptor, the wax statues were "loyal to the originals at every point, for this reason, giving a sense that they are alive" (Hurriyet, November 27, 1973). At first sight, the coexistence of the notions of detachment/abstraction and realism might seem contradictory. However, the realism effective here is a "symbolic realism" based on the effective reduction of historicity to iconicity. That is, while abstraction and detachment is effective on the historical level, realism is on the aesthetic. Icons such as the Turkish flag, the map of Turkey, and Ataturk gain significance over the years, producing a strict sense of realism as they are cut off from their historical significance. The logic behind this symbolic realism is something like this: nothing else stands for Turkey but its map; likewise, nothing may correctly represent Ataturk but a realistic portrait or a wax statue. As these examples suggest, one-to-one correspondance is between the "work of art" and its object. In contrast with the representational regime dominant during the 10th-year celebrations, no attempt was made in the 50th year toward completing the representation by interpolating icons with writing in order to produce historical, didactic, and explanatory discourse.

Examining the details of the celebration program and comments here, it is possible to observe a significant degree of detachment and formalization. Above all, one can see far less emphasis on celebrations in national newspapers compared with detailed nationwide celebration programs published in 1933, that clearly were considered a matter of protocol. For instance, the president of Ankara Bar, representing the body of lawyers, declared that they would boycott the official ceremony because the bar was given a secondary place with respect to professional associations. Needless to say, parallel to the iconistic formalization, debates on the formal protocol in the official parades occupied the agenda in the following years; for example, should the chief of the general staff be in front of opposition leaders? should the mayor be next to the governor? Overall, the formalistic attitude in the celebrations of the 50th year was acquired at the expense of public enthusiasm. It would not be a mistake to claim that they and the ones that were to follow almost completely lacked public enthusiasm. In small towns, for instance, celebrations were limited, with official organizations such as visiting Ataturk monuments, school ceremonies, and routinized official visits among military and civil authorities. Perhaps the words chosen by the newspapers to describe celebrations illustrate what is meant by the lack of enthusiam: "From the smallest towns and villages of Anatolia, to the largest cities of the country, the 50 year celebrations has been very bright *within their own limits*" (*Cumhuriyet*, November, 1973; emphasis added). The limits, of course, refer to a comparison with the 10th-year celebrations.

75th-Year (1998): Commodification

When I was a child, the flag used to symbolize the nation. Then we realized that it was symbolizing nationalism. Now it became clear that the flag is the indicator of something even more vague and mysterious than nation and nationalism. If we don't discover what his mysterious thing is and what rules are governing it, many more people will get hurt for the sake of flag.

—Orhan Pamuk, "The Flag"

To understand nation-building strategies dominating the 75th-anniversary celebrations of the Republic of Turkey, one needs to expand the contextual circle to the global level, primarily because the 1990s have been years during which Turkey has begun global integration in both economic and cultural terms. Turkey's global integration, which no doubt deserves being the subject of another study, had a significant impact on the way in which Turkish national identity and its cultural signifiers were shaped. Global integration meant, first and foremost, an acceleration in the pace of capitalism, marked by an increase in overall national production, proliferation of domestic and import goods circulating in the market, and strong intentions toward deregulation and privatization.

On the cultural level, these processes found their counterpart in improved channels of communication such as the introduction and proliferation of private television channels, a steady increase in the number of radio stations on both national and local levels, and the introduction and popularization of new communication technologies such as the Internet and mobile telephones. From a symbolic point of view, these developments meant a tremendous shift both quantitatively and qualitatively in the status of visual signifiers and the representational regime in general. Turkey, in a sense, has become paradise for the sociologist of social and cultural change. Needless to say, the way national symbols are circulated and utilized for national identify formation purposes have been affected by so-called market forces. One can argue that the process of abstraction and detachment described in the context of the 1970s reached its pinnacle during the 1990s. National symbols, mostly in the form of icons, found themselves as a previously unheard-of media of circulation. Being the prominent signifier of nationalism, images of the Turkish flag have been "logo-ized" and traveled well beyond flag poles. Nonetheless, as the quotation in the beginning of this section indicates, the significatory power of national symbols has not been limited to nation or nationalism at all.

Even a superficial observation would reveal that the Turkish flag, along with the map of Turkey and Ataturk's portrait, inscribed itself onto the corners of television screens, bumper stickers, electricity bills, and even on special lemon bags one could find in a grocery store. In this process, the decision that 75th-year celebrations should be extended over the entire year of 1998 had a significant contribution. The 75th-year logo, a skewed drawing of the Turkish national flag complete with the crescent and star, was ordered to be inscribed on all official letters and documents, thus creating a sense of abundance. It has become almost a necessity to use the logo flag in every context in and out of the frame of national feelings. All these developments relied on a superficial formulation of national feelings and gained a moral/political bearing in terms of an exclusionary scheme that had far-reaching

connotations. In a sense, the old slogan "Turkey Belongs to Turks" has been transformed into a visual statement declaring who is in and who is out. The fact that the
1990s were the years of internal political troubles "threatening our national unity"
strengthened this tendency and exploded its potential. The Turkish flag has become
the undeniable signifier of being Turk, being secular, being Kemalist.[13] Further, it
has been used for such distinct purposes as indicating sexual preferences, or utilized as a shield to protect one from being prosecuted, or blocking authorities from
demolishing one's illegal building.[14]

Turkey celebrated the 75th year of the republic in such an economic, political, and cultural atmosphere during 1998. From a public relations perspective, the
celebrations were certainly successful: the idea that Turkey as a republic has reached
its 75th year with success (perhaps with a few bruises!) was made extremely popular, a success that could be attributed to a first-ever quality of organized
celebrations. For the first time in the history of the republic, the organization of celebrations is commissioned by a civil organization: the Turkish Historical
Foundation, which solicits the help of scientists, academicians, and private public
relations firms. The foundation started its efforts by publicizing its good intentions,
perhaps the most striking of which was the principle of inclusion that, for the first
time, openly declared that no section of society and no part of history (referring to
the Ottoman period) would be excluded.

The flip side of the coin, however, showed signs of extreme superficialization
in the core values of being a republic, despite the "good intentions" of the foundation. National symbols have become commercial icons, circulated like commodities
with a padded exchange value. The concept of commodification refers not only to
the fact that national symbols are turned into marketable goods, but can be used
in metaphorical terms to analyze their formal functioning. For one thing, to perform any form of content analysis of such icons would not make much sense simply
because they are devoid of any positive content. It can be said that they gain semi-
otic value simply by circulation and are applicable to almost any situation for a very
wide range of political legitimation and ideological justification purposes. For instance, as was mentioned earlier, radical political Islamic groups generally known
to be against the fundamental principles of the republic, particularly that of secularism, waved the Turkish national flag in some of their demonstrations. On the
other hand, there have been records of "flag-burning actions" by groups with similar ideological stances.[15] In a similar fashion, the Turkish flag has even been utilized
to say "We are against transvestites!" while, as the famous Turkish novelist Orhan
Pamuk reports (1997, 16–17), on the same street after midnight, flags also functioned to indicate which apartments might be inhabited by transvestite prostitutes,
the apartments without a flag began to signify the possibility of prostitution.

Apart from the "fuzzy" ideological content of icons, their formal functioning
also provides us with significant clues toward understanding the notion of commodification. First, national icons have begun to be inscribed on nearly every
medium in a wide range of forms. Second, they have begun to be inscribed on top
of each other as if to join forces to transmit a "message" even more strongly.

Especially during 1998, this phenomenon of overlapping became quite visible. From cheap coffee mugs sold in supermarkets to the standard statues standing in the main gates of military complexes, Ataturk's portrait, the Turkish flag, and a logo-ized map of Turkey appear inscribed together. National holidays, of course, provide a fertile ground for the overimposition of national icons. It has become an "invented tradition" for every state and private television channel to broadcast a combination of these icons in a corner of the television screen.

In perfect harmony with iconization, abstraction/detachment, and commodification, the 75th-year celebrations may be remembered with television and print advertisements placed by private companies. Even a cursory glance at newspapers published a week before and after November 29, 1998, shows that there are as many "prestige ads" as news items with the same subject matter: Republic Day.[16] It is, in fact, important to compare the contents of news items and advertisements, for there is a visible divergence in terms of their rhetoric. Overall, it can be said that the news items describing national day celebrations employed an exaggerated rhetoric emphasizing their magnificence. Rhetoric employed by the private sector, however, seems to shoulder the function of controlling "damage" done to the republican ideal by existing political currents stringently in the fight with the state. In ads, the "chic" rhetoric of a booming advertisement industry emerges, using every trick to invite the Turkish nation to celebrate "wholeheartedly," "to claim and protect" the republic while, at the same time, promoting company names. One bank advertisement came out with the slogan, "We Meet at Republic, We Celebrate Republic," and in finer print contained the following lines publicizing special postcards issued by a civil organization for education for this occasion: "Enlivening our Republic is only possible by claiming its every aspect. Let's celebrate our Republic Day sincerely and with a real 'holiday enthusiasm.' By sending these postcards to friends and business milieu, let's repeat our commitment to Republic and contribute to our country's international education efforts."

In a full-page ad, an electronics technology firm employed the 75th-year logo under a half-page photo of Ataturk, between which the two it reads "'He' is Unique." In another full-page ad, one of the country's largest banks (Is Bank) used the Turkish flag as the background upon which Ataturk's words were inscribed: "Tomorrow, we shall announce republic." In finer print, a relatively extended text for an ad seemed to reiterate the message given by many similar ads:

With this decision, the people who were the subjects of an empire, woke up as the free citizens the next day.... Tomorrow, as we enter into the 76th year of our liberty, we would like to thank all those brave men, first and foremost to Ataturk, who gave us this republic as a present. We know that the best way to thank them is to protect and claim this tremendous asset more than ever.

It is possible to include more examples of this sort, but there are also more that go beyond the celebratory rhetoric. Another full-page advertisement has a textile company (Sarar), specializing in menswear, asking the following question, printed right above a photo of Ataturk: "It is not difficult to dress up like him. . . . But what about thinking like him?" A major pharmaceutical firm went a step further in combining the Ataturk icon with its area of specialty to a modified photo of him in a surgeon's mask and cap. Next to the photo in which only the eyes of Ataturk were visible, the ad asked: "Wasn't he whom healed the 'sick European' seventy-five years ago?" One of the leading companies of the country (Sabanci), with 30,000 employees active in areas ranging from automotives to banking and tourism to textiles, preferred in its ad to include a lengthy description of the holding's achievements. Its script-based ad bore the title "We Wholeheartedly Hugged Our Republic." In the middle of the ad, the 75th-year logo flag was imprinted on top of a map of Turkey as the main visual element.

In contrast with the taken-for-granted news rhetoric, which was almost completely devoted to passing the message that the republic had been accepted and internalized by the masses, ads of business companies sensed the rhetoric of damage control and invited people to "reclaim" and "protect" Turkey. It does not require a detailed discourse analysis to understand the underlying suspicious perspective in both categories of printed material, but it can be argued that while most of the news items employed the strategy of covering up the sense of suspicion by a "grandiose rhetoric," the ads published in the same newspapers mostly preferred a "rhetoric of protection."

It is possible to argue that the exaggerated emphasis put on "protection" of the republic's central principles has been, in fact, a reaction to an underlying suspicion held by some segments of the population. For instance, the suspicion that the regime of the republic has been turned into a regime of oppression of Islamic views was the main subject matter of an article series that was published in the Islam-oriented newspaper *Zaman* in November 29, 1998. The title of the series summarizes its content: "Republic of 60 Millions, Or? . . ." The question mark indicates that the republic has been the "Republic of *some*, not *all*," while overall, the article concentrates on the claim that the discourse and practice of celebrations are contradictory. Despite the well-intended rhetoric of "inclusion," the article aims to demonstrate that practices such as the exclusion of certain intellectuals from panels and conferences, or certain groups with Islamic view from the celebrations, and so forth, this rhetoric is, in fact, bogus.

CONCLUSIONS

Turkey's chronic political instability, its global economic integration, and the dominant cultural trend summarized in terms of superficialization, commodification, and abstraction were determining macroparameters in the 75th-year celebrations. From the perspective of dominant logic of representation, these parameters can be seen as fertile ground on which a new representational regime ends the search for truth. By the end of the 10-year period, celebrations were heavily dependent on junctions linking the idea of celebration to positive achievements of the republic. Sentences like "We are proud, because we did these . . ." represented a "structure of feeling" dominant then. When the republic reached its 50 years, confusion and lack of direction could be adjectives describing its situation. Sentences like "We should be proud, why are we so depressed?" might be representative of the structure of the feeling. The year 1998, during which 75th-year celebrations took place, can be understood as the time when the representational regime presented 25 years ago reached its full maturity. It is hard, though, to summarize the dominant structure of feeling in one sentence for the 75th year. The hardship involved is completely consistent with the mode of celebrations in 1998 because, parallel to the process of commodification, national symbols are converted into tools of legitimation and ideological support for just about any political project. National symbols, instead of representing national feelings rooted in real or constructed achievements of the nation, transformed into empty tools awaiting, in the words of Slavoj i ek (1973), to be "kidnapped" by some form of ideological appropriation.

It would be a mistake, however, to deny the role played by national icons floating freely in a postmodern attitude contributing to a process of demystification. Their very superficiality seems to have given many a distressing lesson that the "pedagogic" aspect of national identity formation is giving way to a "performative" aspect in the balance. Bhabha (1990) employs these terms in explaining what he calls "the writing of nation":

The scraps, patches, and rags of daily life must be repeatedly turned into the signs of a national culture, while the very act of the narrative performance interpellates a growing circle of national subjects. In the production of the nation as narration there is a split between the continuist, accumulative temporality of the pedagogical, and the repetitious, recursive strategy of the performative. It is through this process of splitting that the conceptual ambivalence of modern society becomes the site of *writing the nation*. (297)

Turkey, by opening its gates to the world and by realizing the importance and the concomitant responsibility of being a "respectful" member of the so-called international community, has entered into a cultural mode in which the performative aspect of identity formation is becoming dominant. From a sociological perspective, this means that groups marginalized by the state discourse are beginning to question the pedagogical aspect of "writing the nation" with an increasing tone of voice. The marginalized voices in question here are by no means limited to intellectuals speaking from an Islamic perspective. It is certainly possible to question the marginality of Islam in a country whose population is predominantly Muslim. What is underlined here is the counterhegemonic articulation of a number of oppositional groups including, but certainly not limited to, Islamic political currents. For instance, from the mid-1980s on, an intellectual current established by the proponents of the Second Republic, mostly left-wing intellectuals, did not hesitate to form alliances with Islamic intellectuals in matters like democratization.[17]

This chapter has attempted to bring together a number of theoretical positions in order to understand changes in the way Turkish national day celebrations have taken place. Change is argued to have taken place in a sense of reality pertaining to the spirit of celebrations. The question that guided this investigation has been this: What has caused the loss of spirit or dwindling of sincere enthusiasm in celebrations over the years? The answer is twofold, covering both textual and contextual levels.

On the textual level, national identity formation is raised as an intrinsic aspect of all nationalisms. On the contextual level, the specific historical conditions of the Republic of Turkey have been discussed. What was called "iconification" describes the increasing abstraction, formalization, commodification, and icon-writing disengagement that are encountered as aspects of a single process of "superficialization" reflected in the fading of enthusiasm for celebrations. Iconification was also described through a process in which the meaning of national symbols became muddy. The same process is observed in the increased frequency of grand celebrations and inflated rhetoric.

In terms of the mood of celebrations, the early years of the republic distinguishes itself from the years to come in many respects. It is certain that additional research is required to illuminate the way in which transformation in the mood of celebrations has gradually taken on a different attitude. When examining the landmark events, however, such a transformation displays itself in sharper terms. My purpose has been to highlight, in effect, what has changed rather than how this change has taken place. Overall, the most significant change is found in the regime of representation. Even a superficial research conducted on the iconography and discourse of celebrations demonstrates that celebrations of Republic Day in Turkey has been absorbed by an intensifying desire to "represent more," which may have been doomed to ultimate frustration from the very beginning. As the desire to represent got more and more ambitious, symbols of (national) identity have been increasingly turned into objects of uncritical devotion.

Benjamin's "Theses on the Philosophy of History" (1992) talks about the notion of present time in which time is frozen. By definition, national holidays epitomize the concept of "frozen time" by their constant referral to the past in the form of anniversaries. "[I]t is the same day that keeps recurring in the guise of holidays, which are days of remembrance," writes Benjamin (253); for him, anniversaries are days that always remain the same, acting as moments to refresh collective memory in a flash—they serve as "a historical time-lapse camera" (254). The commonplace allegory of phantasmal sight of one's entire life in fast motion at the moment of death might illuminate this point, where the phantasmagoria is not the question whether one actually sees it or not, but the idea that it takes place in the flash of a split second registered as the "moment of death." Following the same allegory, one can argue that it would be really troubling to experience the same phantasm as a haunting hallucination over an extended period of time instead of a moment. This has been, I contend, what happened in Turkey in celebrations of the 75th year, which was extended over an entire year. Society's collective perception was saturated by national icons that began to live a life of their own rather than being symbols referring to past achievements of the nation.

NOTES

1. For i ek (1993), 3–4), "this thesis that Lacan is essentially a philosopher seems nonetheless all too hazardous, since it blatantly contradicts Lacan's repeated statements which explicitly dismiss philosophy as a version of the 'discourse of the Master'" (3–4). Yet, asks i ek, what if Lacan's endeavor is just another "philosophy qua antiphilosophy," just like many other examples ranging from Marx and Heideggerian phenomenologists to postmoderns and deconstructionists?

2. The paradox of nationalism is formulated by Anderson (1991) in a series of seemingly contradictory observations: "(1) The objective modernity of nations to the historian's eye vs. their subjective antiquity in the eyes of nationalists; (2) The formal universality of nationality . . . vs. the irremediable particularity of its concrete manifestations. . . . [and] (3) The 'political' power of nationalisms vs. their philosophical poverty and even incoherence" (5).

4. In Lacan, the objet petit a refers to a simple object of desire such as one individual desiring another, in contrast with what he called the *grand Autre* (sometimes translated "the capital Other"), which he defined as the place of speech and therefore of desire operating within the symbolic.

4. For a table of comparison of other aspects, see Spillman (1997).

5. Ataturk, the founder, is considered to be the "father" of all Turks.

6. The military intervention that took place in 1980 is also known as the September 12 Military Coup. The military junta in this intervention claimed to restore democracy in Turkey, which was believed to be corrupted because of the antagonistic attitudes of the political leaders. This, in turn, was regarded by the junta as the main cause of street killings and overall anarchy in the country.

7. It would be a serious mistake, though, to say that such figures did not exist. Although relatively absent, it is known that during the early years there was a widespread practice of erecting Ataturk's statues, or adorning the streets with green leaves and Turkish flags. On the other hand, it seems that the presence of national flags, Ataturk's portraits, and so forth, have served only one purpose: to adorn. The ideological apparatus shaping the larger meanings relied on writing rather than images.

8. *Hakimiyet-i Milliye*, literally meaning "national sovereignty," is considered to be the official newspaper of the ruling party, CHF (*Cumhuriyet Halk Fırkası*; Republican's People's Party), and thus the state during the early years of the republic.

9. Ghazi, literally meaning "veteran," was the widely used title for Ataturk during his lifetime.

10. As a methodological point, it should be noted that reviewing publications of the time does not allow one to see whether this hegemonic articulation of nationalistic ideology had serious opponents. Still, from the discussions in the parliament and especially from a couple of unsuccessful attempts to form political parties other than CHF, it is known that ideas diverging from the official ideology were existent. One has to be extremely naïve to think otherwise. The analysis of blanket nationalistic discourse occupying every newspaper of the time would only allow "cracks" through which oppositional views might surface. The information to be found in these cracks naturally represents an unintended flow.

11. The caliph was the religious leader of the Ottoman Empire. In 1924, Ataturk abolished the institution of caliphate that is considered a significant step toward building a secular state apparatus.

12. The September 12, 1980, military intervention radically altered the existing system of higher education and made "Principles of Ataturk and History of Reforms" a compulsory course to be taught every semester in all standard four-year university programs. This program is still in effect in Turkey.

13. Kemalism is the political stance advocating the views and principles of founder Mustafa Kemal Ataturk.

14. In Istanbul, the "straight" homeowners who live on a street that is also inhabited by prostituting transvestites hang Turkish flags to indicate that they are not "one of them." It was also interesting to observe in the demonstrations organized by various Islamist groups carrying Turkish flags to indicate that they are not against the Turkish state. "Illegal home owners" (owners of houses built on the state's or someone else's property—rapid urbanization in big cities such as Ankara and Istanbul has resulted in huge slum areas inhabited by the majority of the city population) also take advantage of the quasi-sacred status of the Turkish flag and wave it against the municipal demolition teams and security forces.

15. It is common knowledge that some Islamic groups popularized the slogan "75th-Year of Oppression" among their supporters. One news item reported that unidentified person(s) burned a 75th-year logo flag in Istanbul (*Hurriyet*, November 22, 1998, 8).

16. Prestige ads can be defined as advertisements promoting the name of the company, without any direct sales concern. It should be noted that the Republic Day holiday is also utilized by many firms for direct commercial purposes. One ad, for example, read "November 29 Package, the most meaningful of all holidays," advertising a special holiday package for a hotel chain. The central figure of the ad was the 75th-year logo flag.

17. The Second Republic movement can be described as an intellectual current questioning the legitimacy of the principles of (the first) republic from the years of its very constitution, from 1923 on. Basically what is demanded is a transformation in the state structure from a "political state" to a "liberal state." According to proponents of the Second Republic, such a transformation would eliminate civil/military bureaucratic oligarchy, ruling the state apparatus and leading the country by a handful of professionals. The debate has been fierce, since questioning the foundations of the republic has traditionally been sanctioned both by law and by the dominant republican doctrine internalized by heart by many intellectuals and government officials alike.

REFERENCES

Anderson, B. R. O'G. (1991). *Imagined communities: Reflections on the origin and the spread of nationalism*. London: Verso.

Benjamin, W. (1992). Theses on the philosophy of history. *Illuminations*, 245–55. London: Fontana Press.

Bhabha, H. K. (1990) DissemiNation: Time, narrative, and the margins of the modern nation. In H. K. Bhabha (Ed.), *Nation and narration*, 291–322. London: Routledge.

Brennan, T. (1991). The national longing for form. In H. K. Bhabha (Ed.), *Nation and narration*, 44–70. London: Routledge.

Etingu, T. (1973, November 26). 50. Yıl ve Gerçek Dostlarımız. [50th year and our true friends]. *Cumhuriyet*, 4.

Kristof, N. D. (1999, July 15). A would-be anthem in search of meaning. *The New York Times*, 6.

McLuhan, M. (1964). *Understanding media*, New York: Methuen.

Öztürkmen, A. (1996). Cumhuriyet Bayramlari: Şekli ve Hatırası [Republic holidays: Their form and memory]. Toplumsal Tarih, *28*, 29–35.

Pamuk, O. (1997, May 18). Bayrak [The flag]. Radikal Iki, *32*, 16–17.

Selçuk, İ. (1973, October 26). Pencere [Window]. *Cumhuriyet*, 1.

Spillman, L. (1997). *Nation and commemoration: Creating identities in the United States and Australia*. Cambridge, UK: Cambridge University Press.

i e k, S. (1993). *Tarrying with the negative: Kant, Hegel, and the critique of ideology*. Durham, NC: Duke University Press.

UKRAINE

In Search of Holidays

The Case of Ukraine

Natalia Kostenko, Tatyana Androsenko, and Ludmila Males

CHANGES IN THE ORDER OF HOLIDAYS

Ukraine and its holidays are a relatively new theme in the social discourse, though the history of this land is rather long and has been related to the history of Russia since the 9th century, or since Kievan Rus times—the first state founded on the territory at present occupied by Ukraine. In the period 1922 to 1991, Ukraine was one of the Soviet republics. Since 1945, it has been a UN member. Then, after the collapse of the Union of Soviet Socialist Republics (USSR) in 1991, Ukraine became an independent state in eastern Europe with a population of 50 million. During independence, Ukraine, like other post-Soviet nations, has been effecting political and economic reforms directed at democratic transformations in society. The subject for discussion proposed in this chapter is the formation of civil and individual identity in citizens of the young and sovereign state via their adaptation to the new symbolic order, which also includes holidays and rituals. Expanding on this point is extremely important for understanding the modern Ukrainian community and the status of the Ukrainian culture among others.

In any ultimately formed community, holidays legitimately structure the cultural and social space, determining the temporal rhythm of social life. Their mythological grounds are primarily manifest by means of the fact that they "naturalize" the idea of order, providing it with naturalness and balance. At the same time, holidays are symbols of the order and its embodiment, which excludes fortuity and vagueness. In socially hazardous periods, they may remain nearly the last isles of order, the territory on which the community persistently confirms its identity.

The current Ukrainian situation is unique in that it is a kind of "arrangement" with obvious radical permutations from previous social structure and the formation of a new one. As a result of political and economic transformations of the 1990s, the current state of the Ukrainian community is characterized with complex social stratification, pluralism in values, and a variety of cultural paradigms. These are the conditions under which the confirmation of the national self-identification of Ukrainian citizens occurs, since Ukraine became independent in 1991. Therefore, the symbolic environment that spontaneously or deliberately encloses this process is full of contradictions. Permutations in the internal" order of society are embodied in the arrangement of the holiday space.

Another source of change in the symbolic universe is outside" influences that come from the global culture and multicultural interactions. They also specify the rituals and holidays, which are seemingly quite firmly rooted in the local environment and facilitate the dissemination of symbolic actions which are new to Ukrainians' lifestyles.

HOLIDAY NETWORKS

At present, the common holiday space with regard to holidays marked in Ukraine has expanded notably; further, its structure has changed. Analytically, a number of holiday networks can be identified:[1]

- *Former Soviet holidays*—Great October Revolution Anniversary, International Working People Solidarity Day or May Day, International Women's Day
- *New Ukrainian holidays*—Independence Day, Constitution Day, Ukrainian Police Forces Day
- *Religious holidays* (not previously officially celebrated in Ukraine)— Orthodox Christian Christmas, Easter, Trinity, Salvation, and other confessional holidays
- *Recently emergent holidays* (that come from the West)—St. Valentine's Day, Halloween

The most developed approaches to the study of rituals and holidays focus attention on their mythological grounds (Barthes 1989; Levi-Strauss 1994). Ukrainian researchers have also made a considerable contribution to work on contemporary myth and its ritual implementation ("The Myths" 1998). We have not set ourselves such a task in this chapter; instead, we will attempt to track down changes in the space of the Ukrainian holidays within the most obvious continua. There are at least three of them: *publicity—a private sphere, religious—secular*, and *citizenship—consumerism*. The continua cross, and the attitudes of

Ukrainian citizens toward participation in the holidays as the "embodied arrangement" of their lifeworld take shape in the area of these crossings.

Primarily, it is worthwhile to mention a different type of lingual legitimization of the definition of a holiday. At present, Ukraine's state language is Ukrainian, though in daily life only approximately half of the population speak Ukrainian, while the others speak Russian. In the Russian language and the Soviet mentality, the meaning of the word *holiday* (*prazdnik*) does not have a sacred sense, as it has in most European languages (Lane 1981, 15–16). Etymologically, the word *prazdnik* means "no work (more accurately, idleness)," or "celebration" Leontyev 1977). In the Ukrainian language, a holiday is a *svyato*, which corresponds to "holy" in the English "holiday." The language that strengthens the Ukrainian mentality thus in a way works in support of the claims of the "special days" on sanctification, if they are assigned this name. But this does not at all mean the imperative of sacredness in the organization of these days. In reality, the ideological (religious or secular) and entertaining dominants quite often overlap both at a public and an individual level, swapping over the priorities in each of the "holiday networks."

In Soviet times, celebrations of religious holidays were not commonly accepted; in other words, they were prohibited. Religious holidays had been retained only due to having gone deeply into privacy, being rooted in the structure of everyday life. Hence, the variegation of rituals, especially of a folklore origin, was considerably simplified, reduced to purely casual elements. Today, a reverse process is taking place as the religious holidays are being introduced back into the public sphere—and this does not eliminate their certain politicization because many Ukrainian political parties have armed themselves with Christian ideas.

Conversely, the basic Soviet holidays seem to have been forever withdrawn from Ukrainian public life as ideologically ineligible, though some of them quite firmly stick in citizens' minds. Being the political identity card of the former USSR, their 70-year-long existence marked a transformation into a finely tuned and severe ritual, leveling down the once relevant value pathos. Since the 1980s, yearly public marches and military parades on state holidays became exclusively institutional actions, where citizen involvement was controllable and did not require certain authentic participation. The informal celebration was continued at party meals among friends and relatives during officially established days off. This pattern of celebrating the former Soviet holidays has been kept today as part of the daily schedule. Some leftist-minded population groups do not forget their ideological color, either. Certain Soviet holidays have legitimately transformed into being "commonly human," as they have retained their publicity and twofold attitudes toward them, as in the case of Women's Day on March 8 and Men's Day (the former Soviet Army Day) that can leave one feeling confused regarding the reason for the celebrations. The new Ukrainian state holidays are still a privilege of the official public sphere, while the holidays taken up as a Western tradition are conversely a prerogative of the private and corporate, a young and more mobile cultural environment.

A certain test for how deeply a holiday is rooted in the symbolic universe, regardless of its public versus private or sacred versus casual orientation, is whether the holiday is given the status of a day off. Work leave, entertainment, and the consumption of varied symbolic benefits are integral functions of a "real" holiday. This is indicated by lexical associations for the words prazdnik and svyato, which imply official days off (May Day, New Year's Day), and *veselye*—fun, hilarity (30 and more associations for each) (Leontyev 1977). In the case of canceling the workday, the former Soviet holidays have almost completely vanished, remaining significant only for historians—as it was the case with the USSR Constitution Day, which was celebrated on October 7 after the third USSR Constitution was adopted in 1977. The basic religious holidays, as they have acquired the status of days off, have expanded the area of their influence over the rest of the public. The new official holidays were initially proclaimed days off; however, despite the state's efforts to display them as "top-standard celebration" rituals, mass consciousness is still fitting them into the "operative mode of the state construction." In turn, the popular Western holidays like Halloween and Valentine's Day are being forcefully confirmed via advertising, proclaiming compensation for the absence of a day off by providing other temptations of consumption.

Any symbolic benefits to which holidays may be referred have a twofold reality of meanings and objects of consumption. Their purely symbolical and market values "remain independent on each other" (Bourdieu 1993, 50). But these values may correlate differently. Holidays taken mostly as days off or as entertainment hold the least stable positions in the symbolic space, especially in cultures that do not regard enjoyment as a special cultural value, as is typical for the Russian and Ukrainian cultures and their spirituality-driven ideological versions. The situation may change, but at present the sociological studies of Ukrainian citizens' attitudes toward holidays have, so far, confirmed this thesis.

POPULARITY AND IMPORTANCE OF HOLIDAYS FOR UKRAINIAN CITIZENS

For studying Ukrainian citizens' attitudes toward holidays, the authors of this chapter in cooperation with GfK-USM conducted a sociological survey in October 1998.[2] This study was conducted within an all-Ukrainian monthly survey (GfK-USM Omnibus). The sample is representative for the Ukrainian population aged 15–59 (N = 1,000). The tools were developed and data analyzed by the authors of this chapter. The full research data is published with the company's authorization.

The study covers the following attitudes from the respondents to holidays:

- What holidays respondents celebrate and how they do it.
- Holidays' importance ranking—done by respondents (a) personally for oneself; (b) for other Ukrainian citizens; (c) for Ukraine as an independent state.
- A set of questions to find out respondents' overall attitudes to holidays.

According to this study, more concentration in the spiritually religious and world-important events is typical for citizens of Ukraine (see Figure 1).

The most popular Ukrainian holidays are New Year's Day (January 1), One's Birthday, Christmas (January 7) and Easter, Women's Day (March 8), and Victory Day (May 9). They belong to Soviet traditions, but today, they are more widely interpreted as existentially valued. As can be seen in Figure 1, these days are marked by almost all of the Ukrainian population, at 90 percent.

The least popular are holidays connected with political or state attributes both of the past and the present. It is notable that a certain balance is kept between the national and Soviet "cultic" holidays. Approximately half of all Ukrainians mark Ukraine's Independence Day (61 percent) and Constitution Day (41 percent), and just as many celebrate October Revolution Day (52 percent).

The popularity of holidays and their factual celebration is, to a great extent, determined by their symbolic meaning, based on their historic relevance, the degree of legitimization in the state, value background, and the popularity of rituals. As a result, the importance of each holiday is considered at three levels: personal, social, and state (public). The general picture of the importance of holidays for Ukrainian citizens is presented in Figure 2.

According to Figure 2, the most important in terms of all three constituents are the holidays that possess stable traditions of value and rituals: New Year's Day (4.4–4.7), Easter and Christmas (4.4–4.6 for each), Trinity and Baptism (January 19) (3.7–3.9 for each)—the religious holidays—and Victory Day (4.1–4.4) and Women's Day (3.9–4.2)—the secular holidays.

Christian traditions, despite their ideological taboos, have maintained their influence on Ukrainian citizens in Soviet times. With the development of democracy, Christianity became a legally permitted area of value and culture proposed by the state for the population instead of Marxism-Leninism, which was no longer relevant. Since late in the 1980s, the number of believers has increased considerably because the masses turned to religion as they had lost their previous ideals and were seeking spiritual support under the conditions of Ukraine's political and economic instability. Today, Christian holidays are marked en masse, which certainly should not be considered so much an indicator of the "genuine" religiousness of Ukrainians as an attempt to return them into the womb of the cultural tradition.

Women's Day may also be undoubtedly referred to as one of the phenomena that inevitably emerge in the period of a society's political and cultural transformation. This holiday, introduced in 1918—the first year of the Soviet power as a

Figure 1 Popularity of Holidays for Ukrainian Citizens
(Percent of Those Who Celebrate Holidays, N = 1,000)

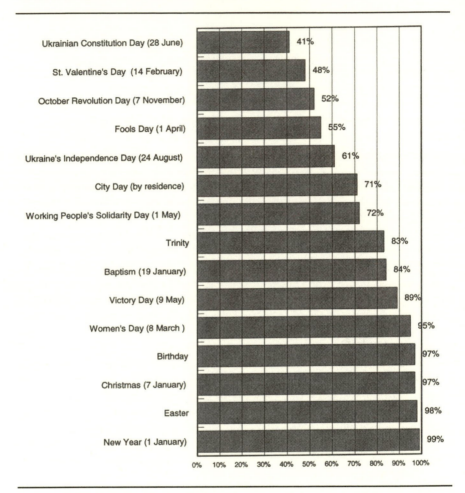

Source: GfK-USM Omnibus (October 1998).

symbol of women's emancipation and equality with men—is presently not loaded
with any hidden radical feminist meanings. Conversely, the majority associate it
with female imagery, and in the way of its celebration, it resembles the traditional
for many cultures' reverence for the Woman, the Mother. At the same time, contemporary Ukrainian women quite often state regret and disapproval with regard
to a certain compulsion concerning the public acknowledgement of their merits on
a specially assigned day once a year.

Figure 2 Symbolic Importance of Holidays for Ukrainian Citizens

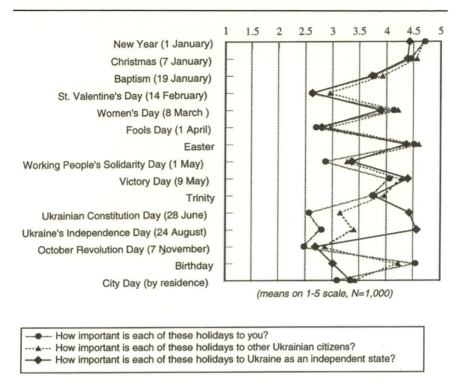

(means on 1-5 scale, N=1,000)

---···●--- How important is each of these holidays to you?
---▲--- How important is each of these holidays to other Ukrainian citizens?
—◆— How important is each of these holidays to Ukraine as an independent state?

Not important Very important

Source: GfK-USM Omnibus (October 1998). It was initially published in the GfK-USM newsletter (January 1999)—an informational leaflet published by GfK companies in all GfK countries.

Victory Day, the day of the victory over Nazism, which has been extremely important since the day of this epochal historical event (May 9, 1945), has always had a sacred sense for the Ukrainian people. Despite its official pompousness of celebration during the 1970s and 1980s and a general expansion in antimilitarist attitudes, this holiday has not lost its "sanctification," but in fact has been strengthened. It is backed by stable mythological grounds as the victory of Good over Evil. For most Ukrainians, Russians, Belorussians, and residents of all former USSR republics, this date is very important as a symbol of their own significance and national prestige in the eyes of the rest of the world and as the day of mourning for those who perished. It is a day of memory and for honoring the living veterans who are passing away one by one. With this holiday in the background, more crucial are questions on history lessons about the current unstable economic situation. Now it has made room for memories of another drama; and this day has been more than once marked by gatherings of western Ukrainian World War II veterans who fought for Germany. The authorities and the local population feel differently about this fact, ranging from frantic protests to showing tolerance, which had been absolutely impossible until recently.

All of these exclusively important holidays are firmly attached in the privacy of most citizens as traditional family holidays. New Year's Day, Easter, Christmas, and Women's Day are marked at home, with family and relatives, by over 70 percent of respondents (GfK-USM Omnibus, October 1998 [N=1,000]). Approximately one-half gather with their families for Baptism and Trinity (46–48 percent), and one-third celebrate Victory Day with their relatives (36 percent). At the same time, these holidays have high ritual efficacy, such that the observation of their typical rituals incorporates a large proportion of Ukrainian citizens. This primarily relates to religious ceremonies and rites. Over one-half of the adult Ukrainian population (55 percent) go to church on Easter and over one-quarter do so on other Christian holidays. As a secular holiday, Victory Day may thus be referred to, since 11 percent of Ukrainian adults take part in marches organized in its honor.

The most popular holidays are followed by City Day, the celebration of which was recently begun in Ukrainian cities, and May Day. Despite belonging to different periods of Ukrainian life, these holidays' symbolic natures are similar in many ways. Both are oriented to the public sphere and the formation of the feeling of civil unity. May Day, which is International Working People's Solidarity Day, is certainly a traditional holiday with a good experience of a truly Soviet festival. For various reasons, this holiday is not accompanied by strict political attributes, and it has acquired a more neutral meaning as the holiday of spring. For Ukrainian citizens, marking May Day and City Day means strolling about town and getting involved in mass entertainment (25 percent and 47 percent, respectively—GfK-USM Omnibus, October 1998 [N=1,000], though for one-quarter of Ukrainians, May Day also remains a family holiday (25 percent) and for many this is also an opportunity to go to the country to cultivate their dacha plots/agricultural areas. These days, their significance as holidays is much less considerable than that of the previous ones (3.1–3.4, 2.9–3.4, respectively, as seen in Figure 2).

Not so popular are the new national holidays—Independence Day and Constitution Day—mainly because they are perceived as directives, sanctioned by authorities who are not very trustworthy for the Ukrainian population who blame them for the economic crisis and worsening the financial situation for a large proportion of the population. These holidays have a great significance for the independent state (4.4 and 4.6, respectively), but as Figure 2 shows, they are still far beyond picking up citizens' personality sense (2.5 and 2.8). At the same time, assuming that these holidays' significance is large enough for other Ukrainian people, the majority of the respondents admit their potential in influencing private lives. Great October Revolution Anniversary, a former national holiday symbolizing the establishment of a socialist system, is gradually leaving the symbolic universe, as it is losing value at both the public and the personal levels.

All Fools' Day and St. Valentine's Day do not belong to official Ukrainian holidays and are not perceived in their traditional meaning as work leave; yet, they are popular with half of the Ukrainian population (55 percent and 48 percent, as seen in Figure 1), mostly with youth, and are marked among friends. The symbolic significance of these holidays is the smallest of the three levels (2.7–3, 2.6–3).

SYMBOLIC SPACE OF THE UKRAINIAN REGIONS

Symbolic space is considerably differentiated by region. These differences are originated deeply in Ukrainian history and its continuous geopolitical problems. Ukraine's geographical location on the border of three worlds and three religious and cultural systems (the Orthodox world, western European Catholicism, and the Muslim world) in different periods facilitated these systems' influence on the Ukrainian culture.

In terms of its cultural and symbolic priorities, the Ukrainian territory is broken down into three formations. The first comprises the capital of Ukraine—the city of Kiev—and its neighboring northern and central regions that because of their closeness to the official center, compared to other regions, display greater involvement of citizens in celebrating the new Ukrainian holidays (Independence Day and Constitution Day).

The eastern and southern regions form the second territorial unit that possesses specific cultural characteristics. In terms of their ethnic and cultural composition, these regions are oriented toward Russia, as they have long been subject to its influence; further, some territories, such as Crimea, were part of it for a long time and were quite recently annexed to Ukraine. As long as 10 years ago, the Russian cultural influence was taken as socialist; hence, the Soviet holiday traditions are strongly manifested in these regions. To a certain extent, resistance against the Ukrainian national ideology and symbols is apparent, which also relates to the national holidays.

The third ideological environment is represented by the western region of Ukraine, where lifestyles notably include western European cultural patterns. The western region is the center of the Ukrainian nationalism and opposition against the Communist ideology, since this territory's annexation to the Soviet Union late in the 1930s was regarded by a large proportion of its population as an act of violence. In this region, a predominant ideological influence is retained by the

Orthodox and Greek-Catholic churches, which in the Socialist period was also part of the cultural resistance. As a result, the general picture of the western region's holidays is characterized by the population's primary orientation toward religious rituals and the holidays celebrated in confirmation of the national idea, like Independence Day and Constitution Day. This is counterbalanced by minor involvement in the former Soviet holidays.

The vectors of shift in symbolic dominants thus form the following picture: in the east–west direction of Ukraine, the role of national and religious ideas grows, as the importance of Soviet traditions drops. South to north, national attributes also grow in importance and the Soviet ones subside; however, religious preferences are less vividly manifest in this direction, so, in its essence, it is purely secular.

TYPES OF ATTITUDES HELD BY UKRAINIANS TOWARD HOLIDAYS

Ukrainians' perception of and attitudes toward holidays are influenced by a number of value components, which were singled out and interpreted by the authors by means of the factor analysis of empirical data:

- *Festive romanticism*, which defines holidays as an opposition to everyday life and a way out of routine casualness.
- *Religious romanticism*, which reflects a growth in the reputation of Christianity as a system of sacral values, official ideology, and a common vision of the world.
- *Extremism* as two opposite poles—for and against Soviet holidays.
- *Pessimism* as disapproval of a "feast during the plague," meaning a worsening in citizens' financial situations.
- *Consumerism* as an orientation toward an expansion in the state holidays network and budgetary allocations for its implementation.

Combinations of these factors of value are compiled into special types of people's attitudes toward holidays. Cluster analysis presents such a typology, conditionally singling out the "tolerant," "nationalists," "pessimists," "romantics," and "atheists."

Just over more than one-quarter of the population (26 percent) is characterized by *tolerant* attitudes toward any holidays celebrated in Ukraine. The people included in this group accept the idea of an independent Ukrainian state in which religious and national ideals will be predominant. They consider themselves religious, abiding by religious rituals; however, at the same time, they pay a tribute of respect to the Soviet holiday traditions. For this population group, holidays reflect the Ukrainian history in the context of their own biography, and such an attitude toward them is based on a wish to preserve habitual cultural patterns, not breaking the natural course of historic events. Therefore, this group includes almost two-thirds of women (63 percent women versus 37 percent men), who are more tolerant toward cultural traditions. In terms of age composition, this is an older and middle-aged population group with over one-half of the group consisting of people over age 40 (53 percent), one-quarter in the 30–39 range (26 percent).

Approximately one-fifth of the adult population are regarded as *nationalists*. They are distinctive for hostility toward Soviet holidays, because for this group the formation of the Ukrainian national values is unthinkable without a crucial act of breaking with the Soviet past. According to them, the only official ideology of Ukraine should be Christianity and national ideals. Such a point of view is typical for the most mobile population group, aged 20–39 (54 percent), in addition, the nationalists are mostly residents of the western region (48 percent), who account for about one-half of this group.

The third largest group (19 percent) is made up of *pessimists*. Grand public celebrations with an economic crisis in the background often inflict active rejection and alienation from citizens, since they are associated with the government's inefficiency and social injustice. Most pessimists have income below the average (73 percent); therefore, it is quite clear that they are too burdened with their own material problems to really enjoy festive days. There are more men in this group (59 percent) and people over age 40, who have difficulty adapting to the current economic situation in Ukraine.

The fourth group, *festive romantics*, gladly mark holidays without thinking of their symbolic meaning. They attach importance to the fact of a holiday itself as important, as a day with an atmosphere of "festivity" and "idleness," as opposed to casual life. It is typical for them to express consumer attitudes to these benefits, which are expressed in wishing more vividness for the current holidays and the introduction of new holidays in the culturally symbolical usage of Ukraine. Such views are mainly shared by youth and teenagers, as people under age 30 account for 54 percent of this group.

As to the smallest group, *atheists* (16 percent), its main difference from the others is manifest by skeptical attitudes toward religion and religious and national holidays. The proportion of men among them is 58 percent of youth and people under age 40 (72 percent).

Thus, Ukrainians' attitudes toward holidays are quite varied, and the different types to a certain extent counterbalance each other.

INDEPENDENCE DAY

Independence Day was introduced in accordance with a decree from the first president of the independent Ukraine and the relevant Enactment from the Parliament of Ukraine in 1992—a year after declaring Ukraine's independence. It is marked annually on August 24. Independence Day is the holiday that today is quite able to claim itself as being the national day in Ukraine. As with most contemporary holidays, it is politically differentiating, so different political forces present and interpret it in opposite ways:

- For the *leftist wing*, this is an excuse to emphasize flaws of the Ukrainian reality, such as the economic crisis, pickets of Chernobyl fighters and miners, and poverty—linking their reasons to the withdrawal from the USSR, declaring independence, and appealing to socialist values.
- *Centrist parties*, which are most closely connected with authorities, focus attention on the process of celebrating a regular anniversary. They, more than others, point to the symbols of the historical event, such as installing a clock that showed how close the millennium was, awarding state prize nominees, choosing a project for the Independence Memorial, and the like.
- The *rightist radicals* are full of nostalgic memories about the first years of independence, when they took the lead in the nationwide upsurge and struggle against the Soviet Empire. Because, according to them, the authorities did not use this opportunity, they take the present as a recession in the efforts of building the Ukrainian state.

In fact, if in the period of asserting statehood, which began in 1991, certain enthusiasm from patriotically minded citizens was observed in expectation of social changes, today's wave of disappointment more likely results in alienation provided by most associations with the state and authorities. A great number of Ukrainian sociological surveys in 1993–98 show that the level of identification of citizens of the eastern and southern regions with Ukraine as a state is still quite minor, and the identity of the state itself or the choice of its development pattern to a great extent remains unclear. The evolution of Independence Day is recently based on an attempt to transform this holiday into an act of sole nationwide reverence for statehood. However, what is used for this is the experience-tested old "jubilee pattern," which combines a wide span of "daily celebration," ideological pathos in honoring celebrities and achievements and handing out governmental awards.

The mass media, mainly television and print, play a very important role in the celebration of Independence Day. They not only make the observation of events, but they have to instill into citizens' minds the elements of solemnity and devotion before and during the celebration.

Table 1 is an analysis of the presentation of Great October Revolution Day (November 7) and Independence Day (August 24) in the press over the period 1987–98, taking an example of one of the popular Ukrainian newspapers highlighting the country's cultural and political events: weekly *Literaturnaya Ukraina* [Literary Ukraine].[4] Two trends are apparent. In the first case, a reduction in the

Table 1 State Holidays' Presentation in the Ukrainian Press: 1987–98

	Great October Revolution Day	
Date	General Themes of Reports	Percent of All Materials
November 11, 1987	Solemn sessions in Kremlin,presentations of a secretary of the CPSU Central Committee.	90%
November 12, 1987	Report on the military parade. Enactment on awarding prizes.	30%
November 3, 1988	Lenin's portrait and slogans, a TASS report.	10%
November 10, 1988	Brief report on the solemn session, a presentation of a secretary of the Central Committee of Communists of the Writers' Union.	20%
November 2, 1989	Festive slogan, thematic picture reproduction.	4%
November 12, 1989	A note from a special correspondent on a literary party in honor of the holiday in the Writers' Union.	2%
November 8, 1990	"Scary October." Events' chronicle "on the spot." Canceling the day off, parting the marching paths of different political forces.	5%

	Independence Day	
Date	General Themes of Reports	Percent of All Materials
August 29, 1991	The act of declaring Ukrainian independence. Events chronicle. Banning CPSU, establishing new state attributes.	65%

(*continued*)

Table 1 State Holidays' Presentation in the Ukrainian Press: 1987–98
(*continued*)

	Independence Day (*continued*)	
Date	General Themes of Reports	Percent of All Materials
August 20, 1992	Festive slogan. Analysis of achievements and difficulties.	10%
August 27, 1992	Report at a congress of Ukrainians. Photographs of the solemn events.	25%
August 29, 1993	Summarizing: hopes and losses. Projects of finding a way out of the crisis.	20%
August 26, 1993	An appeal of alert to the president asking not to lose independence by creating CIS.	10%
August 25, 1994	Message of the third anniversary of independence.	<1%
August 24, 1995	Storyboard of photographs.	5%
August 22, 1996	Storyboard of photographs, poems, a presentation of the head of the Writers' Union.	25%
August 28, 1997	A special correspondent's notes. A presentation of the president at the second forum of Ukrainians for the anniversary independence.	75%

scale of celebrating; in the other, returning to the initial pattern. This means a U-turn in the celebration of Independence Day, from a critical analysis of the yearlong stage of work on building a state toward launching a planned action on the public authority presentation. In this direction, a wide range of advertising mechanisms is used: roundtables and other public discussions (surely accompanied by a television show), solemn sessions of authority representatives and celebrities, theatrical performances and pop shows, colorful outdoor billboards, and the renovation of Kreshatik, the main street of the Ukrainian capital. The participation of citizens in the advertising strengthens the dominance of festivity, putting the primary notions of value second.

The solemn military parade of 1988 is perceived in a special manner, as its photographs were placed on the covers of party newspapers of all political directions—the leftist newspapers *Kommunist* and *Tovarisch* (Comrade); centrist *Den/Day*, *Vseukrainskiye Vedomosti* (All-Ukrainian News); *Nezavisimost* (Independence); rightist *Chas-time* and *Shlakh Peremogi* (The Way of Victory). In line with the demonstration of weapons and force, governmental awards are honored. The new Ukrainian awards are named after ancient prominent public figures, for example, Yaroslav the Wise and Princess Olga, which again symbolically legitimates the existence of the independent Ukrainian state and its authorities.

Another interesting aspect of celebrating Independence Day is its spatial presentation. The pattern of its deployment downward, from the center to periphery, has been borrowed since the so-called command-administrative system times (1960–80). But if authorities successfully executed any inceptions from top to bottom to the lowest link in the chain, today without a repressive apparatus it fails to successfully attain this objective. Therefore, the symbols of Ukraine's statehood and independence are concentrated in the center and die down in the periphery. In the physical space at a "megalevel," it is concentrated in the capital of Kiev; at a "mesolevel" in the administrative centers of the country; at a "microlevel" on the main stage of a solemn concert; and in the space of signs on the leading articles of the central newspapers and in the main newscasts of the central television. This pattern is also true for social groups, as the starring part of the holiday is played by supreme authorities in line with the passiveness of ordinary citizens.

Undoubtedly, to develop one's own traditions for the national day is a difficult and long way. Today, its celebration in Ukraine repeats the features of the Soviet holidays overlapped with the borrowed Western patterns. On the other hand, resuming the parade, theatrical shows, and mass promenades facilitates the fact that the center regains its in-depth designation not only as a public place for marches and shows, but also as a symbol of unification. One thing is clear: the search for a real holiday will be a success only when its sense of value indisputably encourages the largest proportion of Ukrainian citizens.

Today, it is Independence Day that has the greatest opportunity compared to all the other Ukrainian holidays to become the true national day in the future. Despite the difficulties the Ukrainian democracy has gone through during its formation, the celebration of Independence Day—the date of the emerging of the new democratic state—finds favor with most Ukrainian citizens, especially youth, which in fact are carriers of the new national and democratic culture.[5]

NOTES

1. Ukrainian holiday networks at present are:

- *Former Soviet most important* holidays that since their official establishment in the USSR and up to the present day are days off in Ukraine: International Women's Day, International Working People Solidarity Day, Victory Day, Great October Revolution Anniversary. In addition, sufficiently popular in Ukraine is Soviet Army Day, also introduced in Soviet times, but not considered a day off.

International Women's Day (yearly; March 8)—A holiday of women's solidarity in their struggle for equal rights was decided on by the European Social Democrats in 1910 as it had been proposed by German and international Communist public figure Klara Zetkin; and after the October Revolution in 1917, it was officially confirmed in Russia and later in the former USSR and a number of Socialist countries (Bulgaria, Hungary, Poland, Romania, the German Democratic Republic, and Czechoslovakia).

International Working People Solidarity Day (or May Day) (annually; May 1–2)—Was adopted in 1889 by the International Association of Socialist Parties in memory of Chicago workers' manifestation and struggle against the police in May 1886. In Russia, it was marked by the Social Democrats since 1890, and after the October Revolution, it became an official holiday of the Russian Federation and then the former USSR and a number of Socialist countries.

Victory Day (annually; May 9)—A holiday of the victory over Nazism in World War II, adopted in 1945.

Great October Revolution Anniversary (annually; November 7)—The day when the Communist Party headed by Lenin overthrew Russia's bourgeois-democratic social formation and established a new Socialist state with the officially ruling Proletariat Dictatorship. As an official holiday, it was adopted by Russian Federation's Supreme Body–Soviets in January 1918.

Soviet Army and Navy Day (annually; February 23)—The day of celebrating the first large victories of the Red Army in 1918, which defended the young Soviet Republic in the period of World War I and the Civil War in 1918–22. Now it is marked as "Men's Day."

- *New Ukrainian Holidays*—Major holidays adopted in the independent Ukraine and considered days off: Independence Day and Constitution Day.

Independence Day (annually; August 24)—Was introduced in accordance with a decree from the first president of the independent Ukraine and the relevant Enactment from the Parliament of Ukraine in 1992—a year after declaring Ukraine's independence.

Constitution Day (annually; June 28)—Introduced in accordance with a decision of the Ukrainian Parliament in 1996—the year of adopting the Ukrainian Constitution.

- *Religious holidays* are mainly Orthodox, since the majority of Ukraine's population confess Orthodoxy. Major Orthodox holidays: Christmas (January 7), Baptism (January 19), Easter and Trinity.

- *Recently emergent holidays that come from the West*: St. Valentine's Day, Halloween

St. Valentine's Day (annually; February 14)—Sweethearts' day which is not official in Ukraine, but is widely celebrated by the youth.

Halloween (annually; October 31). All Saints' Day, which is not an official Ukrainian holiday, but is especially popular with students.

2. GfK-USM (Ukrainian Surveys and Market Research) is a company doing market-ing and social research in Ukraine. USM was founded in 1995 as an independent research agency. Since October 1998, it has been part of the worldwide GfK (Gesellschaft für Kon-sum) network.

3. These figures are the average scores for a holiday's significance at two of the three significance levels (personal, social, and state [public]). The first figure is the mean (average) with the lowest value compared to the others for a given holiday. The second figure is the mean with the highest value.

4. The authors conducted a study of *Literaturna Ukraina* publications issued during the period 1987–98 (1987–98: 45–46; 1989–98: 28–34), that is, during the period before and after gaining the independence of Ukraine (1991).

5. This summary may be confirmed by the results of a sociological survey of the Ukrainian population conducted by GfK-USM in August 1999 (GfK-USM Omnibus, Au-gust 1999) by the nationally representative sample (N = 1,000). The answer to the question "Do you see Ukraine's Independence Day as a holiday?" was yes by 63.2 percent of the re-spondents: 77.7 percent of respondents aged 15–19 and 72.5 percent of respondents aged 20–29 answered in the affirmative.

REFERENCES

Barthes R. (1989). *Mythologies*. In *Selected work: Semiotics—Poetics*, 72–131. Moscow: Progress.

Bourdieu P. (1993). The market of symbolic products. *Issues of Sociology, 1/2*, 49–62.

Lane, C. (1981). *The rites of rulers/ritual in industrial society—The Soviet case*. Cambridge, UK: Cambridge University Press

Leontyev A. A. (Chief Ed.). (1977). Holiday. In *Dictionary of associative norms of the Russian languages*. Moscow: Moscow University Publishers.

Levi-Strauss C. (1994). *Stone-age thinking*. Moscow: Respublika.

The myths of the contemporary Ukraine. (1998). *Spirit and Letter, 3–4*.

UNITED STATES

Martin Luther King Day

A Celebration of the American Architect of the Beloved Community

Teixeira Nash and Irelene P. Ricks

> The call for a worldwide fellowship that lifts neighborly concern beyond one's tribe, race, class, and nation, is, in reality, a call for an all-embracing and uncon-ditional love for all men. This often misunderstood and misinterpreted concept has now become an absolute necessity for the survival of man. When I speak of love, I am speaking of that force which all the great religions have seen as the supreme unifying principle of life. Love is the key that unlocks the door, which leads to ultimate reality.
>
> —Martin Luther King Jr., *Where Do We Go from Here?*

On January 15, 2000, for the first time in American history, the Reverend Doc-tor Martin Luther King Jr.'s birthday was observed in some form by all 50 of the United States, an event that had taken 15 years for the holiday celebration to be shared nationwide. Several states were reluctant to honor the memory of just Dr. King, piggybacking other local heroes onto the day, while others continued to ques-tion the legitimacy of the holiday. This congressionally legislated holiday was a bittersweet pill for former segregationists to swallow in both the South and the North. The simple, profound message of this man of the cloth may take yet another century to fully comprehend and accept.

Martin Luther King Jr. (1929–68) is a full-fledged, genuine American hero. In-disputably, he is the first American private citizen for whom a national holiday is dedicated. Admittedly, the holiday honoring King's birth has not been welcomed or celebrated by all Americans since its formal adoption by the U.S. Congress in 1983, but there are promising signs that all Americans, along with people around the world, will one day celebrate the Martin Luther King Jr. Day as a symbol of peace, justice, and equality.

King's challenging 1967 call for the "beloved community," resonates today as it did during the years of the civil rights movement. This preacher from Atlanta, Georgia, like many prophets before him, was a man who had climbed the mountain, and had walked the road to enlightenment, a path replete with danger and doubt. Since his assassination in 1968 at the age of 39, Martin Luther King Jr.'s appeal as an American hero has been sustained for over three decades. To invoke King's name is to conjure up the image of a man willing to take on the burden of social reformation with the ultimate sacrifice—his life. An application in January 2001 to the Vatican by members of a committee of Catholic bishops to honor King as a contemporary martyr enhances our global understanding of a man whose passion for universal love and brotherhood was soundly reinforced by his quest for secular justice and equal treatment for all mankind.

Although specific in his intent to dismantle racial segregation, King's approach to justice and freedom were not limited to the American civil rights struggle. He sought to establish and embrace a larger beloved community beyond the continental borders of the United States. At once politically and socially astute, King was able to negotiate the terms of his existence as a Black[1] freedom fighter within the American power structure by challenging discrimination and bigotry within the context of an ecumenical strategy. Moreover, King's abiding belief in the eventual reward of nonviolent direct action led him to adopt the nonviolent approach as a blunt weapon to strike at America's violent resistance to racial integration. By borrowing from international political leaders, such as Gandhi, Tillich, and Niebuhr, King successfully promoted his own American brand of social revolution. At the heart of King's social agenda was the belief that *all* people must learn to live in peace with each other in an environment that supports the full political and economic development of individuals regardless of race, religion, class, or other characteristics. In this manner, the model of King's beloved community expresses an ideal society in which peace, cooperation, and harmony replace conflict, selfishness, and chaos for the betterment of the whole community.

It is within the framework of the beloved community that we attempt to portray Martin Luther King Jr., an approach that explores both his humanity and his heroism. By providing this perspective, we hope to engender hope and deliberate action for the creative expression of a 21st-century model of King's beloved community.

THE LONG WALK:
THE POLITICAL TRANSFORMATION OF AMERICA

In one sense the civil rights movement in the United States is a special American phenomenon which must be understood in the light of American history and dealt with in terms of the American situation.
                                        —Martin Luther King Jr., *Where Do We Go from Here?*

To dissect the anatomy of any revolution is to strip it of its most potent limbs—heart, lungs, and muscle that are the foundation of its origin. The American civil rights struggle of the 20th century wore its heart on the sleeves of young men and women protesters who were barred from the ordinary civilities of American life such as access to public toilets, restaurants, hotels, and other places within the public domain. The movement exhaled its lungs in the eloquent oratory of leaders, such as King, Medgar Evers, and Malcolm X, and flexed its muscle on a powerful U.S. Supreme Court that was forced finally to concede to its own moral authority. Historians will note that much of the social progress made during the 1950s and the 1960s is owed to the courage and inspiration of young American men, women, and children who were determined to gain equality and freedom. Many, like King, were forced to make the ultimate sacrifice.

There is more to the story of Martin Luther King Jr. as a national leader than his pursuit of justice—more than his dream to integrate the South and unify a racially polarized Middle America. King's complexity lay in his articulation of a long-term vision for universal brotherhood on a scale found only in romantic political philosophies once espoused by renaissance idealists, utopians, and humanists.

What is the beloved community and how is it to be structured in a postmodern world? Before the theory is clearly understood, we need to understand its author. First, we must ask, "Who was this man called Martin Luther King Jr.? Who was this young preacher who gained such world renown?" If one gains insight and understanding about the man and his ideals, one can better understand those ideals, and, hopefully, enter the beloved community that was once his, but could be claimed by all of us who are committed to supporting its humane tenets.

SOWING THE SEED: THE FRAMEWORK FOR CIVIL DISOBEDIENCE AT THE TURN OF THE 20TH CENTURY

Social conditions in the South in the late 1800s and early 1900s were drastically altered by America's Civil War, a war that pitted neighbor against neighbor and father against son. In its aftermath, the entire country suffered from posttraumatic stress and the palliatives offered by either the public or the private sectors were few and of little effect. Although the war had ended decades before, the issue and incidence of slavery were still present, particularly in the southern states, who relied on slave labor for their entire economy. Furious over their defeat and loss of free labor, southern states were virulently opposed to reconciliation proposals designed to include former slaves as citizens in the political and social fabric of mainstream southern society.

As King (1967) stated in his last book, "The liberation from slavery in 1863, which should have initiated the birth of a stable Negro family life, meant a formal legal freedom." With Appomattox, 4 million Black people in the South owned their skins and nothing more. Newly freed slaves were thrown off plantations, penniless, homeless, still largely in the territory of their enemies and in the grip of fear, bewilderment, and aimlessness. Hundreds of thousands of men, women, and children became wanderers. Deprived of basic human rights, former slaves were forced to survive in a world that was still hostile, prejudiced, and often violent. Even some of America's most libertarian Founding Fathers, such as Thomas Jefferson, had declared the African an inferior human being; thus, emancipated and freed, African American men and women were obliged to make their own way without any humane entitlement. The "forty acres and a mule" that had been pledged was merely political rhetoric. From these broken promises, Martin Luther King Jr.'s determined and courageous forebears rose up to challenge this morass of injustice.

The Black church movement took place against the backdrop of Reconstruction, the period of U.S. history between 1865 and 1877, when southern states, having seceded from the Union during the Civil War, were reorganized and "reconstructed" under federal law back into the Union. This was not a restful political period and, in fact, was deeply resented by White southerners. After a decade of swallowing defeat and seeing former slaves actually elected to serve in the U.S. Congress, racist tempers started to rise. Riots erupted in Atlanta in 1906 and two years later in former president Abraham Lincoln's own hometown of Springfield, Illinois, which signaled the end of a peaceful reconstruction. Deadly racism took its place.

W. E. B. Du Bois, a prestigious professor from the North who taught at Atlanta University, joined with northern White philanthropists in the Niagara movement, creating the National Association for the Advancement of Colored People (NAACP) in 1909. The new association pledged to actively address the country's rampant racism against people of color, and legally respond to the increasing acts of harassment and violence. The young Rev. A. D. Williams, King's maternal grandfather, became one of its founders.

THE BEGINNING OF A LEGACY

Now of course I was religious. I'm the son of a preacher; I'm the grandson of a preacher, and the great grandson of a preacher.
—Martin Luther King Jr., "Why Jesus Called a Man a Fool,"
Mount Pisgah Missionary Baptist Church, August 1967

Martin Luther King Jr. was the son, grandson, and great-grandson of preachers on both sides of his family tree. His maternal great-grandfather, Willis Williams, began preaching in antebellum Georgia and witnessed the emergence of independent Black Baptist congregations after the Civil War. King's maternal grandfather, A. D. Williams, went to Atlanta from rural Georgia in 1894, and like his own father, became a preacher. Soon, he was asked to take on Ebenezer Baptist

Church, a small church with a membership of only 13. Although Williams had no formal education, he held a series of revivals and fundraisers that succeeded in raising a substantial amount of money, and increased the church membership to over 100. By 1900, the church had to move to larger quarters. Rev. A. D. Williams became a valued member of the Baptist Church circuit.

Realizing that he lacked school learning and anxious to be part of the growing Negro elite, Rev. Williams started attending Morehouse College part time and became one of its first three graduates in 1897. Now a "Morehouse Man" and an increasingly recognized preacher, Rev. Williams married Spelman woman, Jennie Parks, in 1899. The church grew along with Williams, who played a prominent role in the National Baptist Convention. He was loved and respected, a status shared by his only child, Alberta, who was a solid pillar of Ebenezer, serving as organist until her death. Alberta Williams was to become Martin Luther King Jr.'s mother.

THE KING LINE

So many of our forebears used to sing about freedom. And they dreamed of the day that they would be able to get out of the bosom of slavery, the long night of injustice.
—Martin Luther King Jr., "Unfulfilled Dreams," Sermon given at Ebenezer Baptist Church, March 1968

Michael King Sr., later known as "Daddy King," was the second of 10 children born to a sharecropper in Stockbridge, Georgia. His childhood was spent in the fields, tending to mules and crops, with little chance to attend even the meager schools that were available to Black children. One day, his mother gathered what little money she could pool together, bought her 14-year-old son an old Model T Ford, and sent him on his way to what she hoped would be a better life in Atlanta, a burgeoning city. Like his father, he assumed the mantle of preacher, and soon found himself with a growing flock of church constituents.

The one serious thing Mike King lacked was the ability to speak as articulately as those preachers who had been able to attend school or college. As fate would have it, King's older sister was a boarder at Rev. Williams's house, and after several visits, he saw Miss Alberta Williams. He immediately decided that she would be his bride one day, lofty dreams for a preacher not far removed from mules, but King did not suffer from lack of ambition or faith. King made up his mind to become truly educated, and courageously entered grammar school at the age of 20, while also working and preaching. He was also determined to attend college to gain the intellectual respect he so craved, not only to impress Miss Alberta, but also to be accepted in the elitist circles in Atlanta. After completing his requirements, Mike King literally "talked" his way into Morehouse College. After receiving permission from Rev. Williams to court his daughter, Michael

King and Alberta Williams were married in 1926, and moved into the Williams home on Auburn Avenue.

Michael Luther King Jr. was delivered in his parent's bedroom on January 15, 1929. His sister, Christine, had arrived 16 months earlier, and his brother, A.D., 17 months later. Everyone called him Mike Jr. throughout his childhood. Life was full of love and church in the Williams' household, held firmly together by the powerful Rev. Williams, pastor of Atlanta's jewel, Ebenezer Baptist Church.

In 1934, Rev. King attended an international convention in Germany and also traveled to the Mediterranean. Awestruck by the enlightening experience, he changed his name to Martin Luther in honor of the 15th-century church reformer. He also changed his young son's name in 1934, although hometown people would continue to call young King Mike and "M.L." throughout his childhood. Young King eagerly immersed himself in Ebenezer activities, and like most church offspring, he was able to observe and recite litany and verse as it was being created. King Sr. was elected a trustee of Morehouse College, and made a point of taking his children to concerts and educational programs. Determined that his children would be exposed to the best that Atlanta had to offer, he enrolled young King in the Atlanta University Laboratory School as a seventh grader. M.L. rode a segregated bus to the school, located on the more elite west side of town.

The protected church environment of the King family was relatively undisturbed by World War II, in fact, things were pretty much normal to the King children. The Laboratory School was an experiment to prove that Negroes could learn as well as Whites, if taught by qualified teachers. Young King was a healthy testament to this theorem and excelled at his new academic challenge. With the expansion of World War II, many of the Laboratory School's teachers were called to the draft, eventually causing the school to close its doors. Because M.L. had been an extraordinary student, he was sent to the city's only Negro high school, Booker T. Washington, in 1942, as a 13-year-old 10th grader. He again rode a segregated city bus through downtown Atlanta to attend classes.

Negro colleges were facing hard times during the war because of the drafting of young male students and teachers. To keep money coming in, Morehouse president Benjamin Mays welcomed younger students to fill the classrooms. Martin Luther King Jr. was recruited at the age of 15, and like his father and grandfather before him, he became a Morehouse Man. He later remarked that he had felt out of his depth at first, since he could read only at the eighth grade level. Needless to say, young King buckled down and quickly caught up to his more mature classmates. He made friends easily and soon became known for his natty dressing and glib tongue. Many of King's peers looked to the church as the most lucrative career to pursue. On entering college, Martin had thought he would study medicine, but science and mathematics were not his forte. He then toyed with the idea of the law. One of his classmates wisely noted, "idealists must look to the Law; breadwinners to the Church," an observation not lost on King.

A SHORT JOURNEY TO MANHOOD

How do you go about loving your enemies? I think the first thing is this: In order
to love your enemies, you must begin by analyzing yourself.
                              —Martin Luther King Jr., Sermon given at Dexter Avenue
                                                   Baptist Church, November 1957

King had a rich liturgical background upon which to draw. During this period
of his life, however, the pain and trauma of his grandmother's death and a growing
disaffection with the fundamentalist practices of his father's church profoundly influenced him, and he began to embrace a version of agnosticism. His closest friend
was a war veteran named Walter "Mac" McCall, who was viewed as a radical. King,
protected all of his life, was intrigued with McCall's rebelliousness and questioning. When they attended church, they would position themselves in the remote
balcony, surveying the services below as detached anthropologists.

Soon, King was confronted directly with the challenge of overt racism and fear.
When he approached his father with the problem of the White man's inhumanity,
Daddy King would reduce the issue to its most simple form: "He was right; segregation was wrong, and the hatefulness of White people was a mystery best left to
God." This posture did not mean that King Sr. was oblivious to segregation or that
he was content to let sleeping dogs lie. He had been active in the NAACP, and
through the church, he had come to the aid of fellow Negroes who had suffered all
manner of injustice. His "mystery answer" to his son had more to do with the inner
souls and morals of Whites, a complex metaphysical task he would just as soon
leave to God. During this period of growing segregation and Jim Crow, Negroes
lived in real fear of their lives, should they step too far afield. Just as in the brutal
days of slavery, the law enforced oppression, and guns were in the hands of the en-
forcers. King, like some of his classmates, felt they could and should solve this moral
"mystery" themselves through social activism. He learned in his sociology studies
that racism was a by-product of an economic system that was put in place to benefit Whites. King reasoned that this thesis was inhumane and un-American.

Morehouse introduced him to liberal "free-thinking," opposite from the rigid
fundamentalism of his father's church. Mac, his new friend and classmate, provided
an instant worldview to the 15-year-old-King. At Morehouse, they were both
viewed as the movers and shakers. Always immaculately dressed, a carryover from
King's high school days, he continued to be viewed as a dandy, mindful not only
of his clothes, but of his presentation and speech. He knew that he was expected
to excel. In spite of feeling deep down that his sister, Christine, was smarter, he always made a favorable impression on his peers, his professors, and his father's
Ebenezer congregation. During this period, he was in the midst of a growing civil
rights struggle. While the elder King had been an officer of the NAACP, he was not
an advocate of direct confrontation against the White establishment; God would
take care of the attitude and the behavior of Whites.

At Morehouse, there was a new attitude: fear of Whites and the growing injustices to Coloreds were discussed openly and freely. King accepted racism as a social phenomenon, and decided to major in sociology with the hope such study would prepare him for his life's work.

A JOURNEY WITHIN—
EARLY REFLECTIONS OF "THE DREAMER"

"In the quiet recesses of my heart," King once remarked, "I am fundamentally a clergyman, a Baptist preacher.
           —Martin Luther King Jr., *Autobiography of Religious Development*

In spite of King's immersion into the world of free thought, he eventually decided to pursue the ministry along with his friend McCall. By his senior year at Morehouse, he had distinguished himself as a progressive thinker and impressive orator, and so he made the decision to go north to attend Crozer Theological Seminary in Chester, Pennsylvania, just outside of Philadelphia. The year was 1948 and King was 19. At Crozer, he was exposed to a form of liberalism rarely, if ever, experienced in the South or the North. Expecting to see only a handful of other Negro students, King found almost one-third of his class to be non-White. This voluntary demonstration of racial diversity was unheard of, even in the North, but Crozer's liberal experiment was brief, starting and ending with King's class. It was, indeed, providential that King found himself in such a unique setting.

While Crozer Seminary was perhaps the only one of a very few liberal ports in the storm, religious fundamentalism was, at the same time, experiencing an explosive new birth in the South. In response to this frightening southern movement, Crozer's board and administrators gradually returned the school to its more conservative mode. King, however, landed at Crozer at an ideal time to spur his own intellectual growth. His class, the freshman class of 1948, was Crozer's first and last class that was purposely recruited to reflect the "real" America, the burgeoning melting pot of diverse racial and ethnic bodies. The effort was not lost on King. He took full advantage of the opportunity to begin to synthesize his own unique background—a love-filled childhood, exposure to the Negro "giants" of the day, a carefully tutored bible education and heritage, and, finally, his recent baptism in liberalism at Crozer. He began to consciously reason and analyze profound religious, social, and political concepts, a remarkable feat for one so young. No one realized, least of all the young, ebullient King himself, that he would have so little time.

For the first time, King became aware of the "two-ness" described by Du Bois—the schizophrenic existence of the Negro American in a White culture. In later writings, King said that he consciously became more like his idea of White people and less like White people's idea of him as a Negro. This was a natural reactive behavior for a young man of the South—a South that had segregated him because of a belief in his genetic inferiority. His conclusion was not unreasonable—this was his first experience to "meet" Whites on equal ground. Determined to excel, he read voraciously, digesting and analyzing concepts as if they were food. King's reputation for scholarship and oratory was beginning to receive wide attention. At the young age of 22, he was invited to preach at Concord Baptist Church in Brooklyn, New York. King was named class valedictorian. His appetite for knowledge and moral consciousness was barely whetted. Further, Martin Luther King Jr. began to know that he *did not know*.

DISCOVERY OF THE BELOVED COMMUNITY

It is quite easy for me to think of a God of love mainly because I grew up in a family where love was central and where lovely relationships were ever present.
—Martin Luther King Jr., *Autobiography of Religious Development*

In his studies at Crozer Seminary, King was introduced to the German theologian Walter Raushenbusch, who spoke of Christianity as "a spirit of brotherhood epitomized in social responsibility—leading to love perfection among all the earth's people." This "social gospel" theory was completely appealing to King, who felt that love and reason could bring out in all people a basic goodness that was deeper than racial hatred or personal animosities. Even at this early age, King dreamed of his beloved community. King's love affair with Raushenbusch's Social Gospelism came to an abrupt turn in the road when he met up with Reinhold Niebuhr's philosophical theories in his senior year at Crozer. Having accepted the comforting optimism of the Social Gospel, King was unprepared for the nihilism of Niebuhr who in his *Moral Man and Immoral Society* (1930) spelled out the basic corruption and evil in the universe. War, cruelty, and injustice take place because man is basically sinful. Further, society, which is the collective mind, only responds to power. Niebuhr noted that human beings can respond to reason, to the call for justice, even to love perfection, but they are always prey to the collective drive of evil. Religion can appeal to human beings to resist evil. King was particularly touched by Niebuhr's statement that Whites would only extend equal rights to Negroes through force, as history has demonstrated.

During this period, revolutionary events were taking place across the Atlantic in South Africa, precipitated by the "peculiar efforts" of a frail Indian named Mahatma Gandhi, who used persistent pacifism and annoying nonviolence to pressure the Whites of South Africa to extend equal rights to non-Whites. Gandhi had been influenced by Tolstoy's "resist-not-evil" interpretation of the Sermon on the Mount. Gandhi had interpreted Tolstoy's charge—resist not evil—to mean that upon confronting the evil of the world, such as the racial brutalities of South Africa, one should not respond with violence. Rather, one should organize nonviolent responses to injustice as a means of calling attention to the injustice, thereby appealing to the moral or good side of man.

Niebuhr launched a particularly harsh criticism of Gandhi's so-called non-violent tactics. In his mind, Gandhi's nonviolent activities totally belied the meaning of resist not evil, in fact, they created another form of coercion and societal pressure. At this critical juncture in King's growth, these conflicting views acted as a stimulus to his own efforts to crystallize and resolve these moral-political issues. As a blossoming activist for his people, King started to assume responsibility even in his twenties. He also became concerned with the ideal versus the more practical notions of justice. He was fascinated and challenged by the juxtaposition of the agape (love) expressed in traditional philosophy and religion as it related to the more normative expressions of love and behavior in contemporary society.

A few years later, King wrote a paper in which he said, "Justice is never discontinuously related to love. Justice is a check upon ambitions of individuals seeking to overcome their own insecurity at the expense of others. Justice is love's message for the collective mind."[2] True justice is the tool with which man ensures the health of the beloved community. King reveled in philosophical arguments, never tiring of seeking answers to ethical questions and the mystery of God. He became a veritable sermon master at Crozer and soon found himself preaching at churches up and down the East Coast. His keen mind and presence impressed far older professors, philosophers, and preachers. He did not hesitate to share his views with intellectuals near and far. Crozer students would crowd into his practice sermon classes, which he fine-tuned as prodigiously as a stage actor.

King blossomed in this rarefied scholastic atmosphere, and he yearned to continue his studies. His plan was to attend Yale University's Divinity School; to be safe, however, he also applied to Boston University and to the Divinity School of Edinburgh University in Scotland. Yale turned him down, in spite of his outstanding record. Upon graduation at the top his class, King decided to attend Boston University, concentrating on the philosophy of religion. He wanted to eventually teach at a university, an idea diametrically opposed to Daddy King's fervent wish for his son to join him in the ministry. King was determined to continue his studies.

There were still some unanswered questions in his mind, not only about religion and morality, but also about his own role in society. Although he was intellectually ambitious, he did not concentrate on materialistic goals; in fact, he was embarrassed by his father's constant push for money for the church and for his own personal consumption. Above all, he knew that he lacked the scientific arguments he would need as weapons in an immoral world. If he was to become a leader—and he was confident he would—he was convinced that he had to find persuasive answers to those questions for himself and for the Negro community he wanted to serve.

King was anxious to go to Boston for another reason: he had become intrigued with the ideas of Prof. Edgar S. Brightman, a proponent of "Personalism," a system of belief based on one's own experience of God," with the idea that "belief is something upon which human life is most dependent—that something of supreme value which constitutes the most important condition."

GETTING READY FOR THE OUTSIDE WORLD

So many of us in life start out building temples: temples of character, temples of justice, temples of peace. And so often we don't finish them. Because life is Schubert's "Unfinished Symphony." At so many points we start, we try, we set out to build our various temples. And I guess one of the great agonies of life is that we are constantly trying to finish that which is unfinishable.
—Martin Luther King Jr., "Unfulfilled Dreams," Sermon given at Ebenezer Baptist Church, February 1968

By 1952, King had settled in quite nicely in Boston. There was a certain comfort in the North, although prejudice and discrimination were still present. His world continued to enjoy a certain academic protection from the outside world. There were some Black colleagues who criticized King and his Dialectical Society brethren for being too aloof from the cold realities of racism, McCarthyism, and the rising fallout from the cold war. Always concerned about the public's perception of him and its impact on his career, King never wrote or directly addressed the race issue while in college.

Under the leadership of President Harry S. Truman, the country had entered the Korean "conflict," and many young Americans of every color and creed were sent to Southeast Asia to fight a war they did not understand. King was to be become deeply involved in America's role in Southeast Asia in 10 years, but the Korean conflict did not engage his interest. Martin Luther King Jr. had a mission, and that mission was to prepare himself intellectually and spiritually for the outside world. He also knew that he would need a good woman to join him and make him respectable, a notion he announced to his closest friends. He and his colleagues did not suffer from lack of female company, but King knew that a man would be more respected if he had the stability of a family.

In early 1952, purely on a gambit, King called a young music student at the New England Conservatory named Coretta Scott. The daughter of Obidiyah Scott, an Alabama farmer, he soon found out that this young woman was no shrinking violet. Through sheer hard work and perseverance, Coretta Scott and her sister had managed to attend and graduate from Alabama schools, and then eventually from Antioch College in Ohio. She wanted to become an opera singer and had won a scholarship to the prestigious New England Conservatory to study. Although she was two years older than King, she immediately felt drawn to him. As he told her shortly after their meeting, "The four things I look for in a wife are character, intelligence, personality, and beauty, and you have them all."

Thus, their courtship began. Martin and Coretta Scott were married on June 18, 1953, and moved into the King home for the summer, before returning to Martin's apartment in Boston in order for him to complete his course work and begin his dissertation.

ANSWERING THE MONTGOMERY CALL TO PREACH

But one day after finishing school, I was called to a little church down in Montgomery, Alabama, and I started preaching there. Things were going well in the church; it was a marvelous experience.
>   —Martin Luther King Jr., "Why Jesus Called a Man a Fool," Sermon
>   given at Mount Pisgah Missionary Baptist Church, August 1967

Martin Luther King Jr. took over the leadership of Dexter Avenue Baptist Church in September 1954 at the age of 25, and like his father and grandfather before him, immediately set down the principles of rule and finance under which his pastorate would function. He called for the establishment of 12 church clubs who would work to organize events and collect funds for the church. Finance would be centrally controlled under his direction. Although the congregation and church leaders initially balked at King's bold plan, they soon fell into line with their new young minister.

Within months, Dexter Avenue Baptist Church began to prosper, and Martin Luther King Jr. became the talk of Montgomery, Alabama. As any good preacher, King sought out the Black community, particularly those who would enhance his efforts for his church and his young family. He would travel to Boston to meet with advisers and received his doctorate in systemic theology from Boston University in 1955. King was at home in Montgomery and quickly became known and admired by a wide range of people. A beautiful baby girl, the first of his four children, was born in November 1955. The young minister and his family had settled in.

ANSWERING THE CALL TO LEADERSHIP

We are here this evening for serious business. We are here in a general sense, because first and foremost—we are American citizens—and we are determined to apply our citizenship—to the fullness of its means. But we are here in a specific sense—because of the bus situation in Montgomery.
>   —Martin Luther King Jr., Speech at the Montgomery
>   Improvement Association, December 1955

In the mid-1950s, race relations were continuing to escalate, and the city's Blacks were becoming more and more frustrated with Jim Crow and segregation. Nowhere was this situation more explosive than on Montgomery's public buses. Strictly regulated by city ordinance, buses were divided into two clear seating sections: the front section for White riders, the back for Negroes. Either group generally could access a center neutral section should seating reach overflow status, but White riders were always given preference for seating. Most of Montgomery's domestic and unskilled workers rode the buses, oftentimes jammed into the rear even when there was seating in a front section. If a Black rider were to cross the color line, bus drivers were deputized by the police to arrest accused perpetrators. This had happened on several occasions and many in the Black community were anxious to take some type of action.

E. D. Nixon, one of Montgomery's Black leaders, knew that the situation was close to exploding. He was highly respected, not only for his size, but also for his long history of successful negotiation with the White establishment through membership in A. Phillip Randolph's Union of Sleeping Car Porters, the only recognized Black union in the country. Nixon was not alone in his interest in active protest.

The Women's Political Council of the Dexter Avenue Baptist Church, under the leadership of Jo Ann Robinson, was also anxious to weigh into active protest, and had been looking for an opportune moment to lead a boycott of the buses. There had been several protest incidences, but in each case, the persons attempting to challenge the buses could not stand up to close public scrutiny.

This stalemate was unexpectedly broken one day when Rosa Parks, a dignified Montgomery seamstress and secretary of the local NAACP, decided that she would keep her seat in the neutral section of the bus. When asked by the driver to give up her seat for a White male rider, Mrs. Parks politely but firmly refused to move to the back. The driver went for the police to arrest her. After several calls, E. D. Nixon along with Clifford Durr, a White lawyer and friend of the movement, went and posted bond for Mrs. Parks's release. This was, indeed, the moment for which the fledgling civil rights groups were waiting. Ms. Robinson immediately went into action with her Women's Political Council, distributing thousands of flyers to Montgomery's Black citizens urging them to join a one-day boycott of the buses. E. D. Nixon gathered together the city's Black leaders such as Rev. Ralph Abernathy and the new young Dexter Avenue minister Martin Luther King Jr.

Within 24 hours, the group held their strategy meeting at Dexter, outlining their citywide boycott. This was an incredible undertaking, given that this occurred before the computer and electronic communication. Taxi drivers and private citizens were mobilized to serve as temporary public transportation. During subsequent planning meetings, the growing group of citizens decided to form a new organization, the Montgomery Improvement Association. King was elected its new president, a tremendous challenge for one so young and inexperienced. But the other leaders and citizens sensed that this particular young preacher would be exactly the right person for the job. Never one to back away from a challenge, King accepted the post with a measure of fear and excitement, perhaps even a sense of inevitability.

He addressed the group that evening after he had informed Coretta of his new task. Although King had preached in churches all over the country by this time, the address he gave to the Montgomery Improvement Association at Dexter Avenue

Baptist Church placed him at the most important crossroad of his life. He rose to the occasion as a preacher and as a people's torchbearer. He had stepped forward, fully understanding the danger in which he placed his family and his people, telling the assembled members that there was an urgent need for courage and unity in their pursuit for an end to segregation on the buses. There had been a precedent of protest set by the labor movements of America. The people of Montgomery had the right to seek justice.

Above all, King spoke of the power of love: "And I want to tell you this evening that it is not enough for us to talk about love. Love is one of the pinnacle parts of the Christian faith. There is another side called justice. And justice is really love in calculation. Justice is love correcting that which would work against love." His address that evening solidified his role as leader of the Montgomery Bus Boycott effort. His clear and persistent focus on nonviolent protest and love would set him apart from traditional leaders and propel him onto the political stage he was to occupy for the rest of his life. Still in his twenties, he quickly became known as the foremost leader of the civil rights movement and a powerful force who would fight for the downtrodden and disenfranchised.

Acknowledging, but not totally following the nonviolent model of Mahatma Ghandi, King refined the Black civil rights movement, making it his unique model of protest for the world. In explaining the main characteristics of his nonviolent approach, King, like Ghandi, stressed that the resistance was against the forces of evil, not against the perpetrators of that evil—that is, between justice and the injustice of segregation. King was convinced that Whites were as much victims of this unjust system as were Blacks. The boycott was not undertaken to put the bus company out of business; rather, it wanted to rid the company of unfair practices so that all of Montgomery's citizens could freely ride.

King traveled all over the United States, most often at the invitation of Roy Wilkins, the NAACP's executive director, who gave unstinting support to the Montgomery Boycott. As in *Brown vs. the Board of Education* (1954), the NAACP was to continue to be the primary legal vehicle through which the boycott and other civil rights efforts would reach resolution. Like any pioneer, Martin Luther King Jr. was not wholeheartedly welcomed by the majority establishment. He posed a threat to business as usual which had been brutally discriminatory in America for centuries. Southern White leaders in both the public and the private sectors were anxious to silence him and other civil rights leaders. Many of these attempts to stem the flow of protest were violent and lawless, many times carried out by the law enforcement hierarchy. During 1956, King's home was bombed and many of Montgomery's Black and sympathetic White citizens were subjected to vicious attacks.

In February 1956, the NAACP filed a lawsuit in Alabama's federal court on behalf of the Montgomery Improvement Association. The injunction sought to end Montgomery's segregated bus seating on constitutional grounds. Unexpectedly, the court ruled in favor of the association, causing the city to seek redress from the Supreme Court. That November, the Court upheld the lower court's decision, thus ending the practice. The one-year, nonviolent boycott had been completely vindicated. News outlets around the world heralded the accomplishment of King's leadership and the common people he had lead.

KING SEEKS A NEW SOCIAL PARADIGM FOR AN AMERICAN BELOVED COMMUNITY

In one sense the civil rights movement in the United States is a special American phenomenon which must be understood in the light of American history and dealt with in terms of the American situation. But on another and more important level, what is happening in the United States today is a significant part of a world development.

—Martin Luther King Jr., *Where Do We Go from Here?*

After the euphoria of the boycott victory, Southern leaders searched for a new mechanism to attack the gross inequities of the Jim Crow South, which continued its lynchings, segregated schools, and all manner of intimidation. Although the boycott had been nonviolent, the bloody backlash was marked by an escalating wrath of bombings and murders. King realized that there needed to be another broader-based organization to address the systemic issues of racism and segregation. Initially calling together a group of ministers in early 1957, King appealed for unity and a more organized campaign to thwart the evils now ravaging the South. The group would name itself the Southern Christian Leadership Conference (SCLC). King's circle of colleagues and advisers soon extended far beyond the clergy and included a wide range of people such as Bayard Rustin, James Lawson, Clarence Mitchell, Stanley Levison, Harris Wofford, Harry Belafonte, Ella Baker, and Adam Clayton Powell, each of whom played a significant role with King and the civil rights movement.

The late 1950s saw America's first serious attempts to legislatively address systematic racism. King was eventually to meet first with Vice President Richard M. Nixon, then with President Dwight D. Eisenhower to personally appeal to them for the administration's action on behalf of the nation's Black citizens. Although the president seemed willing to concede, then Senate majority leader Lyndon B. Johnson is given the credit for masterminding civil rights legislation.

Although he had been harassed and bullied by racist police and other Jim Crow citizens and officials, King experienced his first serious brush with death in 1958, at the hands of a deranged Black woman in a department store in New York City. King had traveled to New York to attend a book signing for his first book, *Stride towards Freedom* (1958), a thoughtful account of the bus boycott experience. While signing the book, he was stabbed in the chest. King was literally fractions of an inch away from death, causing him to take serious stock of his life and career.

Soon after this attempt on his life, King made a pilgrimage with Coretta to India to learn more about Gandhi—his self-discipline and his humility. He wanted to better understand Gandhi's dynamics of redemption and suffering. But King was also able to observe the breadth of poverty and ignorance that continued to afflict the Indian people. Like Ghandi, King emphasized that the nonviolent resistance in the Montgomery boycott was directed against the forces of evil rather than against the people who happened to be doing the evil. King stressed that the struggle was not between Whites and Blacks, but between justice and injustice of segregation. He said, "This is not a war between the white and the Negro, but a conflict between justice and injustice" (*New York Times*, February 24, 1956).

King felt that people must act in such a way as to make possible the coming together of people of all colors on the basis of a harmony of interests and understanding. Ghandi had called for "an overflowing love for all" and was convinced that this "love" could convert the opponent and achieve reconciliation. King shared Ghandi's conviction that no human being was so bad as to be beyond redemption. This theme of reconciliation was followed 40 years later in the reconciliation of the people of South Africa through the leadership of Nelson Mandela and Bishop Desmond Tutu.

On his return from India, King and the SCLC began to give support to youth involved in sit-ins throughout the South. Begun in 1960 in Greensboro, North Carolina, when four students from North Carolina A&T College set out to integrate a Woolworth's Five & Dime lunch counter, the movement quickly spread to 31 cities and nine states within three months. Coming together in April of that year, student leaders from 60 colleges met at Shaw University in Raleigh, North Carolina, and formed the beginning structure of the Student Nonviolent Coordinating Committee (SNCC) with Marion Barry as its first chair. SNCC's young members were focused on two primary areas: voter registration and public accommodations. Through sit-ins and "freedom rides," legislation eventually was passed in both areas. These victories came, in some instances, at the highest price, because die-hard segregationists were loath to relinquish their exclusive autonomy over these basic civil rights.

SCLC achieved a new level of civil rights effectiveness in 1962–63 when it organized civil rights campaigns and demonstrations in Alabama, Florida, and Virginia. By this period, the organization had 85 chapters and a staff of 50. SCLC did not confine its activities just to the South, expanding its program to include African American communities in the North. It should be noted that there was continued violence inflicted on civil rights activists in the form of bombings, lynchings, and physical harassment by citizens and officials alike. The bombing of churches was particularly heinous, climaxing in 1963 with the killing of four young girls attending church.

"LETTER FROM A BIRMINGHAM JAIL"

In any non-violent campaign there are four basic steps: collection of the facts to determine whether injustices exist; negotiation; self-purification; and direct action. We have gone through all these steps in Birmingham. There can be no gainsaying the fact that racial injustice engulfs this community. Birmingham is probably the most thoroughly segregated city in the United States. . . .

—Martin Luther King Jr., "Letter from a
Birmingham Jail"

In the civil rights struggle, 1963 was a landmark year. Over 1,000 cities were engulfed in civil turmoil, violence bubbling just below the surface. The American Negro had waited patiently for America to right the wrong so long inflicted on him. The much-admired President John F. Kennedy had been slow to address the urgent legislation and action to carry out the intent of new civil rights laws. In Birmingham, Alabama, the nation's most segregated city, King assembled a group of 11 of his most trusted colleagues to strategize a "Birmingham Campaign" to more systematically demonstrate, sit-in, protest, and nonviolently demand an end to this cruel stalemate.

King (1998) knew in his mind and heart that "freedom is never voluntarily given by the oppressor; it must be demanded by the oppressed" (191). He contended, however, that within human nature there is an amazing potential for goodness and nonviolent behavior that can so arouse the conscience of the opponent that it can actualize this potential for goodness. The campaign in Birmingham organized followers into groups that were detailed to different tasks that were primarily focused on the business community. Volunteers had to sign a commitment card that listed specific requirements of nonviolent protest, important because there would be incidents when protesters were beaten and jailed.

After several days, King was arrested and put in solitary confinement. After reading a published statement by eight fellow clergymen from Alabama, King composed his famous "Letter from a Birmingham Jail" response scratched out on the margins of newspapers and scraps of notepaper smuggled into him by a friendly Negro trustee. Published in papers throughout the country, President Kennedy and others professing human rights could no longer ignore demands for equal justice now, not in some distant future.

More so than at any other time during the civil rights struggle, young children took active roles in the nonviolent protests. King welcomed their innocent courage and enthusiasm. Newspapers and television stations began to broadcast the ugly images of peaceful men, women, and children being whipped and hosed down—charged and bitten by trained attack dogs. The shame of the South became a national embarrassment for all decent people. Eventually, President Kennedy, coached by his brother, Attorney General Robert F. Kennedy, determined that his administration had to be on the right moral side of the issue, putting all of his resources behind the "Birmingham agreement," signaling to the nation that business would not be as usual. Civil and human rights would finally be on the table and people of color would have the right to vote and fully participate in America's opportunities.

"I HAVE A DREAM" DEEPLY ROOTED IN THE AMERICAN DREAM

I have a dream that one day this nation will rise up and live out the true meaning of its creed: "We hold these truths to be self-evident; that all men are created equal." I have a dream that one day on the red hills of Georgia the sons of former slaves and the sons of former slaveowners will be able to sit down together at the table of brotherhood; I have a dream...
—Martin Luther King Jr., "I Have a Dream," August 1963

More was to come in the indelible year of 1963. This was the year of the "March on Washington," a freedom march that was expertly orchestrated and choreographed by the nation's leaders in civil rights, union workers, and clergy. Chaired by A. Phillip Randolph, the Black, patrician head of America's first organized Union of Black Sleeping Car Porters, the march took place in August 1963. The March on Washington was conceived to draw attention to the inequities facing the Negro in America. This was, without a doubt, the nation's most impressive march on behalf of human rights down the center of the Capitol's mall. There were over 250,000 people, although most marchers will claim that they were over a half million strong. People came from every town, city, and hamlet of the United States, and there were people of all colors, ages, and religions. This was a march for freedom and it served as a climax of years of struggle. Although Martin Luther King Jr. was not the chairman of the march, he was its most eloquent spokesman. His words ring out today as clear as they did on that warm day in August.

King's stature as a leader was made concrete that day in August. Meeting with President Kennedy later that afternoon solidified a political partnership between the civil rights leadership and the political movers and shakers. The relationship was short-lived because Kennedy was assassinated three months later. Although 1963 had been a year of triumphs for the movement, it had been a year of sorrow with the death of Medgar Evers, a young southern Negro leader; four little girls in a church; and, now, the president.

CIVIL RIGHTS— A CONTINUUM FOR EQUAL OPPORTUNITY

After gaining some measure of political breakthrough, King began to focus on the realities of poverty in this country, understanding that poverty struck Native Americans, Appalachian Whites, and Chicanos as much as his Southern Black constituents. He started to organize his thoughts and actions around the plight of the poor and the disenfranchised. King challenged political leaders and colleagues to broaden their lenses, to join with him in a march toward a new freedom from not only slavery, but freedom from economic exploitation and domination. He challenged followers to create a new society with a power to break beyond self-centered goals. In recognition of King's work, he was awarded the prestigious Nobel Prize for Peace in 1964.

Many in the country felt that King was going too far; he was entering international affairs that were outside his comprehension and experience. King became even more focused on the nation's economic inequities, pointing out that the poor bore the brunt of the country's labor and military activities. He became the champion of the downtrodden, not isolating any ethnic or racial group; leading poverty marches in cities all over the country. In his last book, King (1967) states, "We still have a choice today: nonviolent coexistence or violent coannihilation. This may well be mankind's last chance to choose between chaos and community."

Martin Luther King Jr. was assassinated in Memphis, Tennessee, after leading and addressing striking Black sanitation workers.

ENSHRINING THE LEGACY

Passage of the National Martin Luther King Jr. Holiday

The old maxim that "all politics are local" held true as was revealed in the repeated and unsuccessful attempts to commemorate Martin Luther King Jr.'s sacrifices to his country in the form of a national holiday. Groups and prominent individuals from around the country lobbied Capitol Hill and the White House to honor King, some only days after his death. The earliest demand made was by Representative John Conyers (D-MI) four days after King's assassination. Conyers submitted the first legislation proposing King's birthday as a holiday on April 8, 1968.

Nine months later, on what would have been King's 40th birthday, about 1,200 automotive plant workers in North Tarrytown, New York, stayed home from work on January 15, 1969, in observance of King's birthday. Management's response was to suspend 60 and threaten the others with disciplinary action. Undaunted by an apathetic response to his first legislative effort, Representative Conyers teamed up with the dynamic and outspoken Representative Shirley Chisolm (D-NY) who announced hearings to study the holiday issue after 6 million signatures were submitted to Congress on March 25, 1970. Not waiting for U.S. congressional action, the state of California passed the first-ever state legislation on April 10, 1970, making King's birthday a school holiday.

In that same year, Seattle, Washington's, school board designated King's birthday as a school holiday commencing in 1971. To affirm his commitment, State Representative George Fleming began hearings to make the date a state holiday despite resistance from local organizations, such as Seattle's own Todd Shipyards, which fired six workers who had been discovered distributing leaflets to support a King holiday.

It was not until 1983, nearly 20 years after his death, that the U.S. House of Representatives had sufficient votes to approve legislation (338-90) to make the birthday a legal holiday on the third Monday in January beginning in 1986. Powerful southern senators, such as Jesse Helms (R-NC), tried hard to derail the Senate's passage, but were unsuccessful. The U.S. Senate approved the holiday by a vote of 78–22.

On November 2, 1983, Republican president Ronald Reagan signed the bill that would make the third Monday of January a national day of remembrance of Martin Luther King Jr. With a stroke of his pen, President Reagan honored the earlier commitment of his own state, California, where he had once served as governor, in an act that many regard as more an example of reluctant verisimilitude than genuine appreciation.

It would take three more years before the third Monday of January became an official national holiday. At last, after nearly 20 years of political haranguing and moral battles fought by those in the trenches, January 20, 1986, became the first national observance of Martin Luther King Jr.'s birthday as a legal holiday.

Conscripted Peace:
America's Compromise on Civil and Human Rights

In 2001, the United States shares the memory and legacies of the Reverend Doctor Martin Luther King with the world. No longer a legal battle of wills between the Left and Right over whether the holiday is legitimate, the new challenge for Americans is to go beyond the conventional ways of celebration in department store sales and backyard barbecues to find new opportunities to question how we can best effect the purposes of King's life. We must determine how we, as a nation of immigrants and indigenous peoples, can best answer King's lifelong call for a worldwide fellowship that lifts neighborly concern beyond one's tribe, race, class, and nation—a call for an all-embracing and unconditional love for all—a call for the beloved community.

NOTES

1. The authors use capitalization when referring to any racial group. Many publications do not yet follow this grammatical usage; it took 50 years before the *New York Times* capitalized the word *Negro*. The authors feel that this "lowercase" practice is but another instance of subtle discrimination, which they choose not to perpetuate.

2. Written by King at Boston University in 1952.

REFERENCES

Ansbro, J. J. (1982). *Martin Luther King, Jr.: The making of a mind*. Maryknoll, NY: Orbis Books.
Bennett, L. Jr. (1964). *What manner of man*. New York: Johnson.
Branch, T. (1989). *Parting the waters*. New York: Simon and Shuster.
Carson, C., and Holloran, P. (Eds.). (2000). *A knock at midnight*. New York: Warner Books.

Dyson, M. E. (1999). *I may not get there with you*. New York: Free Press.

Harding, V. (1983, September 1). Reflections on the movement. *The National Leader, 12.*

King, C. S. (1969). *My life with Martin Luther King, Jr.* New York: Holt, Rinehart and Winston.

King, M. L. Jr. (1964). *Why we can't wait*. New York: Mentor Books.

King, M. L. Jr. (1967). *Where do we go from here: Chaos or community?* Boston: Beacon Press.

King, M. L. Jr. (1992). *Autobiography of religious development*. In *The papers of Martin Luther King Jr.*, vol. 1. Berkeley: University of California Press. (Originally published in 1951)

King, M. L. Jr. (1998). The Autobiography of Martin Luther King. C. Carson (Ed.). New York: Warner Books.

Lewis, J. (with D'Orso, M.) (2000). *Walking with the wind: A memoir of the movement.*

Martin Luther King, Jr. (1999). Encarta©Africana, Microsoft, Corporation. Africana.com.

Salley, C. (1993). *A ranking of the most influential African-Americans, past and present*. New York: Citadel Press.

Thernstrom, S., and Thernstrom, A. (1997). *America in black and white: One nation indivisible, race in modern America*. New York: Simon and Schuster.

Young, A. (1994). *A way out of no way*. Nashville, TN: Nelson.

APPENDIX A

National Holiday Celebrations

Afghanistan—August 19

Albania—November 28

Algeria—June 5 (Independence Day),
    November 1

Andorra—September 8

Angola—November 11

Antigua—November 1

Argentina—May 25, July 9 (Independence
    Day)

Armenia—September 21

Australia—January 26, October 26

Azerbaijan—May 28

Bahamas—July 10

Bahrain—December 16

Bangladesh—March 26

Barbados—November 30

Barbuda—November 1

Belarus—July 27

Belgium—July 21

Belize—September 21

Benin—August 1

Bhutan—December 17

Bolivia—August 6

Botswana—September 30

Brazil—September 7

Brunei Darussalam—February 23

Bulgaria—March 3

Burkina Faso—August 4

Burundi—July 1

Cambodia—November 9

Cameroon—May 20

Canada—July 1

Cape Verde—July 5

Central African Republic—December 1

Chad—August 11

Chile—September 18

China—October 1 (Independence Day)

Colombia—July 20

Comoros—July 6

Congo—August 15

Costa Rica—September 15

Côte d'Ivoire—December 7

Croatia—May 30

Cuba—January 1

Cyprus—October 1 (Independence Day)

Czech Republic—October 28

Democratic People's Republic of Korea—
    September 9

Denmark—April 16 (Queen Magrethe
    Day)

Djibouti—June 27

Dominica—November 3

Dominican Republic—February 27

Ecuador—August 10

Egypt—June 18 (Independence Day), July
    23

El Salvador—September 15
Equatorial Guinea—October 12
Eritrea—May 24
Estonia—February 24
Fiji—October 10
Finland—December 6
France—July 14 (Bastille Day)
Gabon—August 17
Gambia—February 18
Georgia—May 26
Germany—October 3
Ghana—March 6
Greece—March 25 (Independence Day),
    October 28
Grenada—February 7
Guatemala—September 15
Guinea—October 2
Guinea-Bissau—September 24
Guyana—February 23
Haiti—January 1 (Independence Day),
    March 7 (all week)
Honduras—September 15
Hungary—March 15, August 20, October 23
Iceland—June 17
India—January 26, August 15
    (Independence Day)
Indonesia—August 17
Iraq—July 17
Ireland—March 17
Islamic Republic of Iran—February 11
Israel—April 21 (Independence Day), May
    2 (Holocaust Memorial Day), May
    10 (Independence Day)
Italy—June 2
Jamaica—August 2, August 6
Japan—May 4, December 23 (Emperor's
    Birthday)
Jordan—May 25
Kazakhstan—October 25
Kenya—December 12 (Independence Day)
Kiribati—January 5
Kuwait—February 25
Kyrgyzstan—August 31
Lao People's Democratic Republic—
    December 2
Latvia—November 18
Lebanon—September 22 (Independence
    Day), November 22

Lesotho—October 4
Liberia—July 26
Libyan Arab Jamahiriya—September 1
Liechtenstein—August 15
Lithuania—February 16, March 11, July 6
Luxembourg—June 23
Macedonia—August 2
Madagascar—June 26
Malawi—July 6
Malaysia—August 31
Maldives—July 26
Mali—September 22
Malta—September 21
Marshall Islands—May 1
Mauritania—November 28
Mauritius—March 12
Mexico—September 16
Micronesia—November 3
Monaco—November 19
Mongolia—July 11
Morocco—March 3, November 18
    (Independence Day)
Mozambique—June 25
Myanmar—January 4
Namibia—March 21
Nepal—December 28
Netherlands—April 30
Nevis—September 19
New Zealand—February 6 (Waitangi Day)
Nicaragua—September 15
Niger—December 18
Nigeria—May 27, October 1
    (Independence Day)
Norway—May 17
Oman—November 18
Pakistan—March 23, August 14
    (Independence Day)
Panama—November 3
Papua New Guinea—September 16
Paraguay—May 15
Peru—July 28
Philippines—June 11, June 12
    (Independence Day)
Poland—May 3
Portugal—June 10, December 1
    (Independence Day)
Puerto Rico—July 25 (Commonwealth
    Day)

Qatar—September 3
Quebec—June 24
Republic of Korea—August 15
    (Independence Day)
Republic of Moldova—August 27
Romania—December 1
Russia—June 12 (Independence Day)
Rwanda—July 1
Saint Kitts—September 19
Saint Lucia—February 22
Saint Vincent and the Grenadines—
    October 27
Samoa—June 1
San Marino—September 3
São Tomé and Principe—July 12
Saudi Arabia—September 23
Senegal—April 4
Seychelles—June 18
Sierra Leone—April 27
Singapore—August 9 (National Day)
Slovak Republic—January 1 (established),
    September 1 (Constitution Day)
Slovenia—June 25, December 26
    (Independence Day)
Solomon Islands—July 7
Somalia—October 21
South Africa—April 27
Spain—October 12, December 6
    (Constitution Day)
Sri Lanka—February 4
Sudan—January 1

Suriname—November 25
Syrian Arab Republic—April 17
Swaziland—April 25 (National Flag Day),
    September 6
Sweden—June 6
Switzerland—August 1
Syrian Arab Republic—April 17
Tajikistan—September 9
Thailand—December 5
Togo—January 13, April 27
Trinidad and Tobago—August 31
Tunisia—March 20, June 25 (Republic
    Day), October 15 (Liberation Day)
Turkey—August 30 (Victory Day),
    October 29
Turkmenistan—October 27
Uganda—October 9
Ukraine—August 24
United Arab Emirates—December 2
United Republic of Tanzania—April 26
United States—July 4 (Independence Day)
Uruguay—August 25
Uzbekistan—September 1
Vanuatu—July 30 (Children's Day)
Venezuela—July 5
Vietnam—September 2
Yemen—May 22, November 30
    (Independence Day)
Zaire—June 30
Zambia—October 24
Zimbabwe—April 18

APPENDIX B

International Calendar of Celebrations

Note: The days of celebration listed here are in some instances approximate, as some countries observe their national holidays in terms of independence or other reasons for celebration.

JANUARY

1   Confraternization Day—Brazil
    Festividad de Santa María y San
      Manuel—Spain
    Independence Day—Haiti
    National holiday: Cuba, Sudan
    New Year's Day
    Paradura del Niño—Venezuela
    Slovak Republic established

2   Public holiday: New Zealand

4   National holiday: Myanmar
    Public holiday: New Zealand

5   National holiday: Kiribati
    Twelfth Night—Christian

6   Epiphany—Catholic (traditional),
      Greek Orthodox, Protestant
    Theophany (Christmas)—Armenian

7   Christmas—Ethiopian ("Ganna," date
      approximate), Russian Orthodox

8   Hari Raya Pusa—Singapore
    Idul Fitri Festival Day—Indonesia

10 Seijn-No-Hi (Adults' Day)—Japan

11 Children's Day—Thailand
    Hostos's Birthday—Puerto Rico
    National Day—Nepal

13 National holiday: Togo
    Silverterklause—Switzerland
    St. Knut's Day—Sweden

14 Fiesta do Bonfim—Brazil
    New Year—Russian Orthodox

15 Arbor Day—Jordan
    Dia del Maestro—Venezuela
    Martin Luther King Jr. Birthday—
      United States (observed on the
      third Monday)

20 Babin Den—Bulgaria

25 Robert Burns Night—Scotland

26 National holiday: Australia, India

27   St. Devote—Monaco

30   Three Hierarchs' Day—Greece

FEBRUARY

1   St. Brigid's Day—Ireland

2   Groundhog Day—United States

3   Setsubun (Bean-Throwing Night)—
      Japan

4   National day: Sri Lanka

5   Constitution Day—Mexico
      Teacher's Day—Ghana

6   Sapporo Snow Festival—Japan
      Waitangi Day—New Zealand
      (national holiday)

7   National holiday: Grenada

8   Hari-kuyo (Needle Mass)—Japan
      Kitchen God Celebration—China
      Slovene Cultural Day—Slovenia

9   Argungu Fishing Fesitval—Nigeria
      Education Day—Nepal
      Mar Maron—Lebanon

11   Indian Children's Day—Ecuador
      National Foundation Day—Japan
      National holiday: Islamic Republic
      of Iran
      St. Vartanatz—Armenia
      Youth Day—Cameroon

12   Lincoln's Birthday—United States
      Union Day—Myanmar
      Youth Day—Venezuela

14   Eve of Great Lent—Armenia
      Literacy Day—Liberia
      Valentine's Day: Canada, Europe,
      United States

15   Bun Day—Iceland
      Fastelavn—Denmark
      Presidents' Day—United States
      (observed on the third Monday)

16   Losar—Tibet
      Lunar New Year: China, Korea
      National holiday: Lithuania
      Tet—Vietnam

18   National holiday: Gambia

19   National Democracy Day—Nepal

22   National holiday: Saint Lucia
      Unity Day—Egypt
      Washington's Birthday—United
      States

23   National holiday: Brunei, Dar es
      Salaam, Guyana

24   National holiday: Estonia

25   National holiday: Kuwait

26   Kuomboka—Zambia (date
      approximate)
      Saint-Devote, Patron Saint of the
      Principality—Monaco

27   National holiday: Dominican
      Republic

28   Kavala Day—Finland
      National holiday: Andorra

MARCH

1   Chalanda Marz—Switzerland
      Makha Bucha—Buddhist
      March festival—Bulgaria
      Sam-11 Chul—Korea (national
      holiday)
      St. David's Day—Wales
      Whuppity Scoorie—Scotland

2   Lantern Festival—China

3   Fasnacht—Switzerland
      Hina-matsuri (Doll's Festival)—
      Japan
      National holiday: Bulgaria, Morocco

4   Children's Day—Belize

6   Magellan Day—Guam
      National holiday: Ghana

7   National holiday (all week): Haiti

    Vasaloppet—Sweden

8   Commonwealth Day—United
    Kingdom

11 National holiday: Lithuania

12 National holiday: Mauritius

14 Bretzelsonndeg—Luxembourg

15 Adam's Peak Pilgrimage—Sri Lanka
    National holiday: Hungary
    Youth Day—Zambia

17 National holiday: Ireland (St.
    Patrick's Day)

18 Youth Day—Portugal

20 Marzenna Day—Poland
    National holiday: Tunisia

21 Benito Juárez's Birthday—Mexico
    National holiday: Namibia
    Nowruz (New Year): Afghanistan,
    Baha'i, Iran, Kurdish, Parsi
    World Day of Poetry and
    Childhood
    Youth Day—Tunisia

22 Children's Day—Lebanon
    New Year (Civil)—India

23 National holiday: Pakistan

25 Lady Day—Sweden
    Independence Day—Greece

26 National holiday: Bangladesh

27 Armed Forces Day—Myanmar

APRIL

1   April Fool's Day—Canada, United
    States
    Islamic Republic Day—Iran

3   Sizdar Bedah—Islamic Republic of
    Iran

4   National holiday: Senegal

5   Arbor Day—Korea
    Ch'ing Ming Festival—China

6   Chakri Day—Thailand

7   International Children's Book Day
    Viernes Santo—Ecuador
    Women's Day—Mozambique
    World Health Day

8   Festival of the Sardine—Spain

9   Araw ng Kagitingan (Heroes'
    Day)—Philippines
    Martyrs' Day—Tunisia

12 Children's Day—Bolivia
    Sham el Nessem—Egypt, Sudan

13 Baisaikhi—Bangladesh, Hindu, Sikh

14 Family Day—Thailand
    Pan American Day
    Youth Day—British Virgin Islands

16 Queen Margrethe Day—Denmark
    (national holiday)

17 National holiday: Syrian Arab
    Republic

18 National holiday: Zimbabwe

19 King's Birthday—Swaziland

21 Independence Day—Israel
    Kartini Day—Indonesia
    Tiradentes (national hero)—Brazil
    Women's Day—Ghana

23 Children's Day—Turkey

25 Anzac Day—Australia, New
    Zealand
    Liberation Day—Italy, Portugal
    National Flag Day—Swaziland
    World Children's Day

26 Arbor Day—United States
    National holiday: United Republic
    of Tanzania

27 National holiday: Sierra Leone,
    South Africa, Togo

29 Greenery Day—Japan

30   Children's Day—Mexico
      National holiday: Netherlands
      Walpurgis Night—Northern Europe

MAY

1   Hidrellez—Turkey
     International Labor Day
     Lei Day—Hawaii
     May Day
     National holiday: Marshall Islands
     Teacher's Day—Iran
     Women's Day—Portugal

2   Education Day—Indonesia
     Holocaust Memorial Day—Israel

3   Constitution Memorial Day—Japan
     National holiday: Poland

4   Dodenherdenking (Memorial
       Day)—Netherlands
     National holiday: Japan
     Youth Day—China

5   Bevrijdingsdag—Netherlands
     Children's Day—Japan, Korea
     Cinco de Mayo—Mexico
     Coronation Day—Thailand
     Liberation Day: Denmark,
       Netherlands

6   Martyrs' Day—Syrian Arab Republic

7   Rabindranath Tagore Birthday—
       Bangladesh, India

8   Day of Defeating Fascism—Slovak
       Republic
     Den osvobozeni (Liberation-Nation
       Day)—Czech Republic
     Octave—Luxembourg
     Parent's Day—Korea
     World Red Cross Day

9   Cat Festival—Belgium
     Zahal Memorial Day—Israel

10   Independence Day—Israel

11   Joan of Arc Day—France

13   Cricket Festival—Italy

15   Armed Forces Day—United States
     National holiday: Paraguay
     Teacher's Day—Korea

17   National holiday: Norway
     World Day of Communications

18   Batalia de las Piedras—Uruguay
     Vesak Day—Singapore

19   Youth and Sports Day—Turkey

20   National holiday: Cameroon

21   Combate Naval de Iquique—Chile

22   Buddha's Birthday—China, Korea
     Luilak—Netherlands
     National holiday: Yemen

23   National Day—Morocco

24   Bermuda Day
     National holiday: Eritrea
     Slavic Script and Bulgarian Culture
       Day
     Victoria Day—Canada

25   Africa Freedom Day
     Children's Day—Italy
     National holiday: Argentina, Jordan

26   National holiday: Georgia

27   Children's Day—Nigeria

28   National holiday: Azerbaijan

30   Cavalcata Sarda—Italy
     National holiday: Croatia

31   Cataclysmos—Cyprus

JUNE

1   Gawai Dayak—Malaysia (Sarawak)
     Madaraka Day—Kenya
     National holiday: Samoa

2   Children's Day—Ecuador
     National holiday: Italy
     Youth Day—Tunisia

3   Children's Day—Yemen
     Day of the Arab Child
     Fronleichnam—Austria, Germany

5   Constitution Day—Denmark
     Independence Day—Algeria
     World Environment Day

6   Memorial Day—Korea
     National holiday: Sweden

7   Public holiday: Ireland

10   Army Day—Jordan
     National holiday: Portugal

11   National holiday: Philippines

12   Independence Day: Philippines,
     Russia
     Trooping the Colour—England

14   Flag Day—United States

15   Valdemar's Day—Denmark

16   Day of the African Child
     Day of the Reconciliation—
     Hungary

17   Children's Day—Indonesia
     National holiday: Iceland

18   Dragon Boat Festival—China
     Independence Day—Egypt
     National holiday: Seychelles
     Tan-O (Day of Swings)—Korea

20   Dia de la Bandera—Argentina
     National O.R.T. Day—Madagascar

23   National holiday: Luxembourg
     Victory Day—Estonia

24   Dia del Campesino—Peru
     National holiday: Andorra, Quebec

25   Midsommarafton—Sweden
     National holiday: Mozambique,
     Slovenia
     Prophet Mohammad's Birthday—
     Islamic
     Republic Day—Tunisia

26   National holiday: Madagascar

27   Festa del Giglio—Italy
     National holiday: Djibouti

28   Mnarja—Malta

30   National holiday: Zaire

JULY

1   National holiday: Burundi, Canada,
     Rwanda
     Republic Day—Ghana

2   Family Day—Lesotho

4   Day of the Child—Argentina
     Independence Day—United States

5   National holiday: Cape Verde,
     Venezuela

6   National holiday: Comoros,
     Lithuania, Malawi

7   Farmer's Day—United Republic of
     Tanzania
     National holiday: Solomon Islands

8   Festa dos Tabuleiros—Portugal
     Ommegang Pageant—Belgium

9   Aborigine's Day—Australia
     Independence Day—Argentina

10   National holiday: Bahamas

11   National holiday: Mongolia
     World Population Day

12   National holiday: São Tomé and
     Principe

14   Bastille Day—France

15   O-bon—Japan
     St. Swithin's Day—England

17   Constitution Day—Republic of Korea
     Gion Matsuri—Japan
     Kinderzeche—Germany
     National holiday: Iraq

18   Festa del Redentore—Italy
     Jura de la Constitución—Uruguay

19   President's Day—Botswana

20   Children's Day—Indonesia
      National holiday: Colombia

21   National holiday: Belgium

23   National holiday: Egypt

25   Commonwealth Day—Puerto Rico
      Procession of the Penitents—Belgium
      Santiago Apostol—Spain

26   National holiday: Liberia, Maldives

27   National holiday: Belarus

28   National holiday: Peru

29   Olsok Eve (St. Olaf's Day)—Norway

30   Children's Day: Vanuatu (national
      holiday)

AUGUST

1   National holiday: Benin, Switzerland

2   Emancipation Day—Bahamas
      National holiday: Jamaica,
      Macedonia

4   National holiday: Burkina Faso

6   National holiday: Bolivia, Jamaica
      Somers' Day—Bermuda

7   Battle of Boyaca—Colombia

8   Victory Day—Iraq

9   National Day—Singapore

10   National holiday: Ecuador

11   National holiday: Chad
      Navasard—Armenia

12   Mother's Day/Queen's Birthday—
      Thailand

13   Women's Day—Tunisia

14   Fete des Cuisinieres (Festival of the
      Women Cooks)—Guadeloupe
      Independence Day—Pakistan

15   Independence Day—India, Republic
      of Korea
      National holiday: Congo,
      Liechtenstein

16   Day of the Child—Paraguay

17   Chil-Sok—Korea
      Dia de San Martín—Argentina
      Festival of the Seven Sisters—China
      National holiday: Gabon, Indonesia

19   National holiday: Afghanistan

20   Children's Day/Queen Mother's
      Birthday—Nepal
      National holiday: Hungary

24   National holiday: Ukraine

25   Chung Yuan—China
      National holiday: Uruguay

27   National holiday: Republic of
      Moldova

30   Victory Day—Turkey

31   Children's Day—Ghana
      National holiday: Kyrgyzstan,
      Malaysia, Trinidad and Tobago

SEPTEMBER

1   Constitution Day—Slovak Republic
      National holiday: Libyan Arab
      Jamahiriya, Uzbekistan

2   National holiday: Vietnam

3   National holiday: Qatar, San Marino

6   National holiday: Swaziland

7   National holiday: Brazil

8   National holiday: Andorra
      World Literacy Day

9   Children's Day—Costa Rica, Guyana
      National holiday: Democratic
      Peoples Republic of Korea, Tajikistan

11   Dia del Maestro—Argentina

13   Aniversario y muerte de los Niños
      Heroes—Mexico

15   National holiday: Costa Rica, El
      Salvador, Guatemala, Honduras,
      Nicaragua
      Respect for the Aged Day—Japan

16   National holiday: Mexico, Papua
      New Guinea

18   National holiday: Chile

19   National holiday: Nevis, Saint Kitts

21   Day of the Students—Argentina
      International Day of Peace
      National holiday: Armenia, Belize,
      Malta
      World Gratitude Day
      Youth Day—Bolivia

22   Independence Day—Lebanon
      National holiday: Mali

23   National holiday: Saudi Arabia

24   National holiday: Guinea-Bissau

25   World Maritime Day

26   Youth Day—Turks and Caicos

28   Confucius's Birthday—China

30   National holiday: Botswana

OCTOBER

1   Armed Forces Day—Korea
      Independence Day—China, Cyprus,
      Nigeria
      International Day for the Elderly

2   Gandhi's Birthday—India
      National holiday: Guinea

3   Foundation Day—Republic of Korea
      Leiden Day—Netherlands
      National holiday: Germany
      White Sunday—Samoa
      World Habitat Day

4   Dierendag—Netherlands

      National holiday: Lesotho
      Universal Children's Day

5   Implantacao da Republica—Portugal

6   International Children's Day—
      Sweden

9   Han-Kul-Nal (Alphabet Day)—Korea
      National holiday: Uganda
      World Post Day

10   Kathen Festival—Thailand
      National holiday: Fiji

12   Children's Day—Brazil, Iraq
      Dia de la Raza—Latin America
      National holiday: Equatorial
      Guinea, Spain
      Nuestra Señora del Pilar—Spain

15   Liberation Day—Tunisia

16   World Food Day

17   Chung Yang—China

19   Constitution Day—Niue

20   Birthday of the Bab—Baha'i

21   National holiday: Somalia

22   National holiday: Holy See

23   Chulalongkorn Day—Thailand
      National holiday: Hungary

24   National holiday: Zambia
      United Nations Day

25   National holiday: Kazakhstan
      St. Crispin's Day—England, France

26   National holiday: Australia

27   National holiday: Saint Vincent and
      the Grenadines, Turkmenistan

28   National holiday: Czech Republic,
      Greece

29   National holiday: Turkey

30   Los Angelitos—Mexico

31   Exaltation of the Shellfish—Spain
      Halloween

NOVEMBER

1   National holiday: Algeria, Antigua,
      Barbuda
      Peace Day—Puerto Rico

3   Culture Day—Japan
      National holiday: Dominica,
      Micronesia, Panama

4   Mischief Night—England

5   Dia del Puno—Peru
      Guy Fawkes Day—England

7   Rebenlichter—Switzerland

8   La Quintaine—France

9   National holiday: Cambodia
      Tree Festival—Tunisia

11   Armistice Day—Australia, Europe,
      New Zealand
      National holiday: Angola
      Remembrance Day—Canada
      Veterans Day—United States

12   National Health Day—Indonesia

14   Children's Day (Nehru's Birthday)—
      India
      King Hussein's Birthday—Jordan
      Remembrance Sunday—United
      Kingdom

15   Shichi-go-san—Japan

18   Independence Day—Morocco
      National holiday: Latvia, Oman

19   Discovery Day—Puerto Rico
      National holiday: Monaco

20   Africa Industrialization Day

22   National holiday: Lebanon

23   Labour Appreciation Day—Japan

25   Children's Day—Ethiopia
      National holiday: Suriname
      St. Catherine's Day—France, French
      Canadian

28   National holiday: Albania,
      Mauritania

30   Bonifacio Day—Philippines
      Independence Day—Yemen
      National holiday: Barbados

DECEMBER

1   Independence Day—Portugal
      National holiday: Central African
      Republic, Romania
      World AIDS Day

2   National holiday: Lao People's
      Democratic Republic, United Arab
      Emirates

5   Children's Day—Suriname
      International Volunteer Day
      National holiday: Thailand

6   Constitution Day—Spain
      National holiday: Finland

7   National holiday: Côte d'Ivoire
      Student's Day—Iran

10   Human Rights Day
      Nobeldagen—Sweden

11   Children's Day—Greece, Sierra Leone

12   Jamhrui (Independence Day)—
      Kenya

14   Day of the Girl Child—Mauritania

15   Constitution Day—Nepal

16   National holiday: Bahrain

17   National holiday: Bhutan

18   National holiday: Niger

19   National Social Solidarity Day—
      Indonesia

21   St. Thomas' Day—Guatemala

23   Joseph Smith's Birthday—Mormon
      Emperor's Birthday: Japan
      (national holiday)

Night of the Radishes—Mexico
Victory Day—Egypt

24   Development Day—Senegal

25   Christmas—Christian

26   Independence Day—Slovenia
St. Stephen's Day—Europe
Wren Day—Ireland

28   National holiday: Nepal

30   Rizal Day—Philippines

31   Hogmanay—Scotland
La Quema del Ano Viejo—Ecuador
New Year's Eve
Omisoka (Veille du jour de l'an)—
Japan

Index

About the Contributors

MAHER N. AL-HAJJI (Ph.D., Indiana University) is an assistant professor in the Department of Mass Communication at Kuwait University. During seven years in television and film production at Kuwait Television, he was live-action director for the Arabic version of *Sesame Street*, animation and special effects training, and director of cinematography. Associate producer and costar in *Behind the Lines* (1992) and coauthor of "American Students' Perceptions of Arabs in Political Cartoons" in *The U.S. Media and the Middle East* (1995), he has contributed to a number of international conferences.

SUSANA N. VITTADINI ANDRÉS (Ph.D., University of Buenos Aires) is an associate professor at the University of Tamkang, Tamshui, Taipei, Taiwan, and has also been teaching constitutional law at the College of Law, University of Buenos Aires, and at Belgrano University, Argentina. Her publications include *An Issue of U.S. Foreign Policy: The Judicial Branch and Transnational Abductions* (2004) and *El Juicio Politico y la Constitución Nacional* (2003), and she coauthored volumes 1 and 2 of *Lecciones de Derecho Constitutional, Temas de Derecho Constitucional, Dogmática Constitucional, Derechos Constitucionales Fundamentales* (1997, 1998).

TATYANA ANDROSENKO is a GfK-USM researcher who earned an M.A. in sociology from The National University Kyiv Mohyla Academy, Ukraine. She works in the area of the sociology of culture.

KWASI ANSU-KYEREMEH (Ph.D., La Trobe University, Melbourne, Australia) is an associate professor at the School of Communication Studies, University of Ghana–Legon, where he lectures in communication research methodology and development communication as well as serving as its director. He has taught at the University of Windsor, Ontario, Canada, and is the author of *Communication, Education and Development* (1997), and numerous book chapters and journal articles as well as the editor of the two-volume *Perspectives on Indigenous Communication in Africa* (1998).

NIBAL K. BOURISLY (Ph.D., Indiana University) is an assistant professor in the Department of Mass Communication at Kuwait University. Her doctoral dissertation was *Opening up the Globalization Process: The Case of Advertising Agencies in Kuwait* (2000), and she has been responsible for a number of conference presentations.

DEREK FOSTER is a Ph.D. candidate at Carleton University's School of Journalism and Communication in the Faculty of Public Affairs and Policy Management in Ottawa, Ontario. His dissertation examines squeegee kids and how they were constructed as a political enemy in Canadian public discourse. He has published articles on topics such as Internet culture, Marshall McLuhan and William Gibson, professional wrestling, Canadian television, political mythmaking, and audience responses to reality television.

LINDA K. FULLER (Ph.D., University of Massachusetts), a professor with the Communications Department of Worcester State College, is responsible for more than 250 professional publications and conference reports and is the author/(co-) editor of more than 20 books—including the following for Greenwood Press: *The Cosby Show: Audiences, Impact, Implications* (1992), *Community Television in the United States: A Sourcebook on Public, Educational, and Governmental Access* (1994), and *Dictionary of Quotations in Communications* (with Lilless McPherson Shilling, 1997). Her next books are on the subjects of international community media, film aesthetics, telecommunications in popular culture, and sportscasting. A resident of Wilbraham, Massachusetts, Linda was a Fulbright Senior Fellow at Nanyang Technological University in Singapore for 1996 and was awarded another Fulbright to do AIDS-related research in sub-Saharan Africa (Senegal) in 2002. She has been a visiting scholar at Northeastern University for the 2003–05 academic years.

NATALIA KOSTENKO is a professor in the Sociology Faculty of the Kyiv Shevchenko University, and a senior fellow in the Sociology Institute of the Academy of Sciences of Ukraine. Holding both a Ph.D. in philosophy from the Philosophy Institute of Ukraine and a Ph.D. in sociology from the Sociology Institute, she is the author of many works in the sociology of culture and mass communication, including *Values and Symbols in Mass Communication* (1993).

LUDMILA MALES is a postgraduate student at the Kyiv Shevchenko University, holding an M.A. in sociology from there. She works in the area of theory and history of sociology.

JORGE MARTÍNEZ BÁRCENA (Ph.D., Complutense University of Madrid) has done extensive research on 19th-century public monuments as political symbols of nationalism. From 1998 to 2002, he held a research scholarship funded by the Regional Government of Madrid. In addition to this, he has been awarded with a grant by the Spanish Ministry of Education and a research scholarship by the Spanish Parliament. He has also been an Erasmus visitor at the University of North London and a visiting researcher at Harvard University.

SORIN MATEI (B.A., Bucharest University; M.A., Fletcher School of Law and Diplomacy, Tufts University; Ph.D., Annenberg School for Communication, University of Southern California) is an assistant professor in the Department of Communication, Purdue University, and has done extensive research on culture and communication systems, globalization, and the social impact of new communications media. The author of a largely debated article on Romanian intellectuals (see http://matei.org/secret), he has presented papers numerous conferences and his work is published in the *Electronic Journal of Communication*, *Communication Research*, and *American Behavioral Scientist*. He is a former member of the International Communication Association board of directors.

IGNACIO MOLINA A. DE CIENFUEGOS (Ph.D., Autonomous University of Madrid) has been lecturer in politics at that university since 2000. He has previously been a visiting fellow, as a Fulbright grantee, at Harvard University (1998–2000), junior visitor at Nuffield College/Oxford (1997–98), and a researcher at the Juan March Institute, Madrid (1993–97). He is the author of the dictionary *Conceptos Fundamentales de Ciencia Política*, has published in several international journals, and has been involved in a number of research projects on aspects such as European integration, Spanish policy making, and the processes of regional decentralization in Spain.

MOHAMMED MUSA (Ph.D., University of Leicester, England) currently lectures in the Department of Mass Communication and Journalism at the University of Canterbury, New Zealand. He has published and has research interest in news flow, news agencies, international communication, new communication technologies, and media ownership and control.

KNUT MYKLAND, author of the history of Norway's national day, is a professor at the Institute of History at the University of Bergen.

HALIL NALÇAOGLU (B.S., Middle East Technical University; M.A., Ankara University; Ph.D., University of Massachusetts) is associate professor in the Department of Journalism, Faculty of Communication, at Ankara University, Turkey.

TEIXEIRA NASH (B.A., M.F.A., Howard University) is a Massachusetts native and internationally recognized artist and writer who has spent a good deal of her life in African affairs and community development. Former chair of the District of Columbia Commission on the Arts and Humanities, she is the owner of Forever Raven, a small company specializing in the production of original works of art.

AYO OYELEYE (Ph.D., University of Leicester, UK) is programme director for matters in media and communication of the Media Department at the University of Central England in Birmingham. His research and teaching interests are development and international communication, technology and social change, political communication, and consumer culture.

PAREHAU RICHARDS was, until recently, a lecturer in Maori management and tourism at the University of Waikato, New Zealand. Of Te Whanau-a-Apanui and Tanui descent, she has worked on issues relating to Maori welfare, with specific reference to health services. Deciding on a career change to teach secondary school children, she is an experienced performer in kapa haka groups through which Maori present traditional and contemporary perspectives of their culture through song and dance.

IRELENE P. RICKS (B.A., Georgetown University; Ph.D., Howard University) is a native Washingtonian who has served as a public policy analyst for members of Congress, White House staff, and private research. Her academic and research interests are international economic policy and issues affecting women and minorities in higher education. Dr. Ricks served as grants administrator for the Graduate School at Howard University (1997–2001) and is currently director of minorities affairs for the American Society for Cell Biology in Bethesda, Maryland.

CHRIS RYAN, professor of tourism at the University of Waikato, New Zealand, is an editor of *Tourism Management* who has researched issues of heritage, tourism and culture with specific reference to issues pertaining to Australia and New Zealand. A member of the International Academy for the Study of Tourism, he has published over 100 papers and written seven books, his latest being *Sex Tourism—Liminalities and Marginal People* (2001).

STEPHEN M. RYAN, originally from England, has lived in Japan since 1984 and has taught in high schools and universities there—currently at Eichi (Sapientia) University. He is the author of a number of studies in the areas of intercultural communication and language teaching.

SCOTT M. SCHÖNFELDT-AULTMAN (M.A., Speech and Communication Studies, San Francisco State University; Ph.D., Cultural Studies, University of California at Davis) is assistant professor of communication at Saint Mary's College of California. His research, while broadly concerned with culture and communication, focuses on rhetoric, whiteness, and diasporic identity. His dissertation, *White*

Rhetoric: South African Expatriate Discourse in the United States (2004), evidences these theoretical interests.

LEANNE WHITE is a lecturer in marketing at Victoria University, Australia. She is currently completing her doctoral thesis: "Marketing Brand Australia: National Images and Icons at the Millennium Games." Her M.A. thesis, *Commercial Nationalism: Images of Australia in Television Advertising* (1994), examined the country's images on television, particularly during Australia's bicentennial year of 1988. Leanne's key research interests are national identity, commercial nationalism, Australian popular culture, advertising, and public relations.

TSEGAY WOLDE-GEORGIS (Ph.D., University of Denver) was former head press officer at the Embassy of Ethiopia, and was also an Advanced Study Program (ASP) Post Doctoral Fellow at the National Center for Atmospheric Research in Boulder, Colorado, and taught third world politics, philosophy, and rural development at the Universities of Natal (Durban, South Africa) and Asmara (Eritrea). Dr. Wolde-Georgis has published on land tenure issues and the use of climate information for food security in Ethiopia. Currently, he is a senior staff associate and coordinator of the Africa Program at the International Research Institute for Climate Prediction (IRI) of the Earth Institute of Columbia University.

XU XIAOGE (Ph.D., Nanyang Technological University, Singapore) is an assistant professor at the School of Communication and Information, Nanyang Technological University, Singapore. He has published in *Mass Communication Review, Asian Journal of Communication, American Communication Journal, Journalism and Mass Communication Educator, Journalism and Communication, Modern Communication*, and *Media Asia*. He also has published two book chapters and one book. His major academic interests include values and media, image and media, press models, online journalism, international journalism, and media literacy.

CHEN YANRU (Ph.D., Nanyang Technological University, Singapore) has been educated in China, the United States, and Singapore. She is now a professor in the Department of Journalism and Communication at Xiamen University in the People's Republic of China. Her main research interest is in the role of communication in national development. In addition to two books (in English) and several book chapters, she has published in a number of communication journals. Her book *Reviving the National Soul: Communication Campaigns and National Integration in China's Market Economy Era* (2002) won the only First-Class Award for Outstanding Research in Social Sciences in 2003.

GUST A. YEP (Ph.D., University of Southern California) is professor of speech and communication studies and the human sexuality program at San Francisco State University. His research focuses on communication at the intersections between culture, gender, sexuality, and health, and his work has appeared in numerous books and scholarly journals such as *AIDS Education and Prevention, Communication Quarterly, Hispanic Journal of Behavioral Sciences, International Quarterly of Community Health, Journal of Health Communication, Journal of Homosexuality, Journal of Social Behavior and Personality*, and *Journal of Gay, Lesbian, and Bisexual Identity*. Recipient of more than a dozen research grants and several teaching and community service awards, Dr. Yep is also a member of several editorial boards, including the *Journal of Homosexuality*.